SOUTH
FROM THE
SPANISH MAIN

THE GREAT EXPLORERS SERIES

CONCEIVED BY
Vilhjalmur Stefansson

GENERAL EDITOR
Evelyn Stefansson Nef

BOOKS ALREADY PUBLISHED

BEYOND THE PILLARS OF HERACLES
The Classical World *by Rhys Carpenter*

SOUTH FROM THE SPANISH MAIN
South America, *edited by Earl Parker Hanson*

SUBJECTS IN PREPARATION

Asia, *edited by Owen Lattimore*
The Pacific World, *edited by Alexander Laing*

OTHER AREAS TO BE COVERED

North America—*Sea* · North America—*Land*
Africa · The Arctic · The Antarctic

SOUTH AMERICA SEEN THROUGH
THE EYES OF ITS DISCOVERERS

South
from the
Spanish Main

Edited, annotated and introduced by

EARL PARKER HANSON

DELACORTE PRESS

FOR MY TWO FINE DAUGHTERS-IN-LAW

Here listed in the order of their marriages
to my two fine sons:

Barbara—Mrs. David, née Rullan—Hanson;
and Julia—Mrs. John, née Lubris—Hanson.

Acknowledgment is made to the following publishers, authors and agents for permission to reprint selections from their works:

AMERICAN GEOGRAPHICAL SOCIETY for Special Publication No. 17, "The Discovery of the Amazon, According to the Account of Friar Gaspar de Carvajal, and Other Documents" with an Introduction by José Toribio Medina, translated from the Spanish by Bertram T. Lee, edited by H. C. Heaton; and Special Publication No. 5, "Desert Trails of Atacama" by Isaiah Bowman.

CAMBRIDGE UNIVERSITY PRESS, publishers for The Hakluyt Society, for excerpts from "Select Letters of Christopher Columbus," "The Letters of Amerigo Vespucci," "The First Voyage Around the World" by Magellan, "Narrative of the Proceedings of Pedrarias Davila," "The Expedition of Ursúa and Aguirre" by Pedro de Ursúa, "The Conquest of the River Plate" and "Journey of the Travels and Labours of Father Samuel Fritz" by Father Samuel Fritz.

DOUBLEDAY & COMPANY, INC. for the excerpt from the Introduction by Leonard Engle to *The Voyage of the Beagle* by Charles Darwin. Introduction copyright © 1962 by Doubleday & Company, Inc.; reprinted by permission of the publishers.

E. P. DUTTON & CO., INC. for *Latin America: A Descriptive Survey* by William L. Schurz.

FUNK & WAGNALLS, a Division of Reader's Digest Books, Inc., and the Hutchinson Publishing Group Ltd., for *Lost Trails, Lost Cities* by Colonel P. H. Fawcett, selected and arranged by Brian Fawcett.

GORDIAN PRESS, INC. for *Ancient Civilizations of the Andes* by Philip Ainsworth Means. Copyright 1959 by Louise Munroe Means; and *Fall of the Inca Empire* by Philip Ainsworth Means.

MARGRETTA HARLOW for *The Discoverie of the Large and Bewtiful Empire of Guiana* by Sir Walter Raleigh. Introduction by V. T. Firlow. The Argonaut Press, 1928.

HARPER & ROW, PUBLISHERS, for *Pedro de Valdivia* by R. B. Cunninghame Graham. Reprinted by permission of Harper & Row, Publishers.

MEREDITH PRESS for excerpt from *Lost City of the Incas* by Hiram Bingham. Copyright © 1948 by Hiram Bingham. Reprinted by permission of Meredith Press.

THE ODYSSEY PRESS INC. for *Latin America* by Preston E. James.

Peruvian Times and Gene Savoy for excerpts appearing in Chapter 23.

UNIVERSITY OF CALIFORNIA PRESS for *The Naturalist on the River Amazons* by Henry Walter Bates.

VANDERBILT UNIVERSITY PRESS for *The Araucaniad*, translated by C. Maxwell Lancaster and Paul T. Manchester.

CONTENTS

PREFACE

THE concept of man fencing against an all-powerful nature and sometimes winning has an appeal not only for adolescent boys, but also, in our age of anxiety, for grown men, afflicted with self-doubts that accompany times of too rapid change such as we have lived through in the last quarter century. There is psychological comfort for us all in the knowledge that man, even now, has an opportunity to pit his wit and strength against a strong enemy, nature, and win.

South America from the beginning of its history has presented such a picture to the men who discovered and settled her lands. For geographically we are dealing with a continent of superlatives and contrasts. It extends from the tropical to the polar worlds. Southernmost South America, Tierra del Fuego, surely one of the most romantic names in geography, has glacier-covered mountains and a sub-Antarctic climate. This continent has the driest desert in the world, the Atacama, one of the rainiest inhabited spots in the world, Buenaventura in Colombia, and the largest river in the world, the Amazon. It has steaming jungles, insect-infested swamps, rain forests, energy-robbing high mountains; but it is rich, rich in minerals, rich in fertile soils, rich in peoples. Rich is a key word when dealing with the history of South America; it is a clue to her glory and her shame. In the beginning it was gold, silver, and slaves, free for the taking, that irresistibly attracted the Spaniards to the land. They were greedy, ambitious, cruel and hungry men. Hungry for gold and silver and all that they symbolized—power, that is—for if you had those, the other came naturally. This hunger was so strong that men were willing to starve for it, kill for it, intrigue for it, enslave for it, blackmail and torture humans for it—in fact to do all the things that make the tapestry of Latin American history so blood-streaked and horrible that we may as well post a sign here: those with delicate sensibilities and stomachs should go no farther.

The Spanish conquest of South America is one of the cruelest known to history. Men always try to justify their misdeeds, so the conquest of Latin America was undertaken in the names of King and God. Whatever name rightly or wrongly was invoked, the real motive behind the ghastly mass enslavement becomes visible. However elegantly embroidered some of the narratives may be, it is revealed again and again as the obscene lust for gain, which was to be wrung from a virgin country and an innocent people by *any* method so long as it was successful. If one could obtain the loot, then, as now, few asked for the details of *how* it was gotten; they asked only for their cut.

In reading the accounts of Spanish behavior in Latin America one is almost overpowered by the evil of the white men and their success. It comes as a distinct relief when occasionally the Indians manage to turn the tables, usually by abandoning their settlements and, like the Russians in Napoleon's time and in World War II, adopting a scorched-earth policy, so that the Spaniards arrived and found nothing but ashes to pay for their hard journeys, and they often starved. When Indians did not give the questioning Spaniards the answers they wanted to hear, they would be "put to the torture," as the contemporary phrase had it. They learned quickly what answers were wanted and to give them. Many a wild-goose chase ensued, for the informers would paint a vivid picture of a golden land that was, not unnaturally, a goodly distance away from the informer's own settlement. They hoped thus to divert the Spanish, and they often did.

The Indians also suffered from a form of politeness that afflicts many so-called uncivilized persons who believe "it is more blessed to please than to inform." They would carefully listen to the tone of voice of the questioner as he asked leading questions, and then tell him the answer they thought he wanted to hear. This game of "fool the white man" is old among both North and South American Indians. Many an anthropologist's informant has made merry the night before with his family and friends thinking up wild tales that would be told with perfect seriousness the next day to an anthropologist who carefully took it all down. Many a learned paper has been written based on such Indian invention. It has happened often that an explorer has noted the intellectual brightness and quickness of the Indians, especially where new language and music were concerned, and another explorer will describe the same Indians as stupid, lazy, and incapable of thinking interesting or complicated thoughts.

Vilhjalmur Stefansson, who first thought of the Great Explorer series, was twice president of the New York Explorers Club. Our house on St. Luke's Place in Greenwich Village was a kind of Club annex, with Arctic explorers stopping in, next door to where we lived, at the Stefansson Library to borrow material on their way north or to bring it back and report on their return. One of the then young men who was making a name for himself and who was equally at home in Iceland or the Amazon was Earl Parker Hanson. Although his major field experience was tropical, like other non-Arctic explorers he adopted the general thesis of Stefansson's northern exploration theories and adapted them to his needs. One of these tenets was: Don't be afraid of learning from a so-called primitive person. He has been surviving for a long time in the climate where you find him. Learn all you can about his way and then improve on it if you can.

Earl Hanson, who is to be your guide in *South from the Spanish Main*, is one of the lucky men who has a good ear and a facility for languages. In whatever country he happens to find himself he learns the language, the folk songs, and talks to *everybody*, discovering things which often elude his colleagues. While primarily an explorer and geographer, he has been a journalist, the Chairman of the Department of Geography and Geology at the University of Delaware, a special consultant to various U.S. government agencies, and has written sixteen books. Today he lives in Puerto Rico, where he is consultant to the Department of State of the Commonwealth.

Lest you think the entire picture of South America is a dark one, let me hasten to assure you that you will be introduced herein to good men as well as bad, to great scientists like the young Charles Darwin and the famous Alexander Humboldt, to a delicately made French lady, Madame Godin, who survived the long and terrible journey which killed her male companions, to be reunited with her husband after twenty years of separation. You will meet many others. The canvas stretches from Columbus's day to the new ferment of activity taking place at this very moment on a huge scale in the Amazon River basin in which six countries are participating. This basin area, about the size of the United States minus Hawaii and Alaska, was virtually abandoned during the depression years in the 1930s but may soon resemble our own West in its frontier days. Highways and schools are being built, people and machinery are moving in, a planned, integrated development is taking place. It is an exciting drama to watch. Here is how it all began.

EVELYN STEFANSSON NEF

January 25, 1967
Washington, D. C.

INTRODUCTION

BEGINNING with Columbus' first South American land-fall in 1498, this volume tells the general story of the exploration of South America by Europeans, through the written accounts left by the explorers themselves. Necessarily it can only indicate trends by covering the high spots. Many of the explorers whose work opened the continent to today's "knowledge" wrote no popular accounts which would fit into a volume of this kind. Moreover, the complete, detailed account of South American exploration would require a lifetime of research and fill more volumes than does our largest encyclopedia.

Avoiding the knotty question, never answered in a satisfactory manner, of what constitutes exploration, the editor has for convenience' sake divided South American exploration into several general parts, namely:

1. In the beginning, for reasons brought out in Chapter I, men from Spain and Portugal tore the continent to pieces in search of *Lebensraum* for their feudal culture, wealth for themselves and their king, and souls for the Christian heaven. Those, like Pizarro, who found what they were after, were lucky. But for every *conquistador* who hit the jackpot, dozens of others ranged heroically through the continent's least accessible parts, seeking similar bonanzas, usually without success. Orellana, descending the Amazon, and Berrio, determinedly seeking El Dorado, were in that category. Though not stemming from the Iberian Peninsula, England's tragic Sir Walter Raleigh belonged with the *conquistadores*, being interested far less in widening the world's knowledge of South America than in taking new

lands and vast riches away from Spain and giving them to the English crown.

The search for lands and wealth inevitably led to bitter rivalries between Spain and Portugal, which, in turn, resulted in much conquest and exploration. Chapter XV, on Father Samuel Fritz, who traversed no regions not previously seen by Europeans, though he did add to the world's geographic knowledge by compiling a remarkably accurate (for those days) map of the Amazon, illustrates the valiant and often tragic role played by the Jesuit missionaries in that international struggle.

2. Early in the eighteenth century, the exclusivism of Spain and Portugal in South America began to abate with the arrival of explorers from northwestern Europe. These were the scientists, seekers after knowledge for its own sake, spurred by the scientific awakening under which northwestern Europe became, on the one hand, quite satisfied that it knew a great deal, and, on the other, aware that there was a great deal more that it did *not* know. Such men came to be welcomed by the Spanish and Portuguese authorities in South America because, while they made many scientific and factual discoveries, they could be trusted—unlike Raleigh—not to interfere in politics and questions of local sovereignty. As late as 1931, the present editor, waiting for official Venezuelan permission to ascend the Orinoco River to the country's farthest southern boundaries, explained to a chance friend that he was merely planning to make a survey of the earth's magnetic behavior for the Carnegie Institution of Washington. "Ah," came the answer. "*Bienvenido*. We Venezuelans love scientists. They enrich our knowledge of our land but never meddle in revolutions and other political matters which are our own business."

The literature left by the scientific explorers is rich, voluminous, and fascinating. For reasons of space, the four selected here—Condamine, Humboldt, Darwin, and Bates—will have to suffice as being representative of a large class of explorers, whose fieldmen are still active to this day. Let it be understood and accepted that these scientists did not, and do not, work in lands never before seen by Europeans. In almost all cases they worked in regions which were already fairly well "known," though not to the cultures which the scientists represented and not from the point of view of their particular disciplines. They were and are no less explorers for working in lands already settled by Europeans and for generally having to obtain permission from local government officials for carrying on their work.

3. My long Chapter XX, on the voyages of Herndon and Gibbon, can hardly be said to deal with "scientific" exploration. The work of those two, however, was important and belongs in the category of exploration because it was an early manifestation of the United States' gathering awakening to the fact that it belongs to the world and could not, and cannot, exist in proud isolation. Even before the Civil War, the young United States had developed problems which might be solved through economic expansion, as well as territorial where possible. The classic Lewis and Clark expedition through disputed and often "unknown" territory was one manifestation of that growing realization; that of Herndon and Gibbon, which was in no way aimed at territorial expansion but at cultural and commercial expansion, was another. It made no difference that virtually all the lands traversed by Herndon and Gibbon were already well known and even settled and ruled, first by Spain and Portugal and later by their local independent successors; they were *not* well known in the United States, which made true exploration out of their voyage. Representative of the idea that the United States must seek its well-being in all parts of the world, and even the universe, Herndon and Gibbon can be said to have been precursors of the many Americans who today carry out an almighty program of research and exploration in the polar regions and other relatively inaccessible parts of the world, to say nothing of the moon and outer space.

4. The early territorial rivalries between Spain and Portugal lingered many years after boundaries had been set by agreements and treaties. Those boundaries, in the continent's interior, long remained poorly defined and were the subject of many disputes. As late as 1932, this editor witnessed preparations for a Peruvian raid down the Amazon, to wrest the hamlet of Leticia away from Colombia. The boundary between the two countries had been officially "settled" some years earlier, but had not been acceptable to the people of eastern Peru, in the City of Iquitos, who set out to win their "rights" by embroiling the two countries in one of the modern boundary wars.

The vagueness of interior boundaries has, during the past

century or less, led to a tremendous amount of exploration and interior survey work aimed at settling once and for all the local sovereignty problems for all parties concerned. Most of the men engaged in that work have left no written records of their activities and experiences, as opposed to maps and technical measurements, prepared for use at the diplomatic conference tables. For the present volume the accounts left by Schomburgk and Fawcett were selected as being representative of that type of exploration.

As I write this, it occurs to me that all the voyages included in the first part of this volume, with the one exception of Raleigh, were made either by Spaniards or by men of other nationalities serving Spain. That Columbus is reported to have been a Genoese, Magellan a Portuguese, and Father Samuel Fritz a Bohemian did not mean that those men did not represent Spain in the sense of serving that nation's interests. Portugal's rich literature of the day, covering its epic voyages and explorations, is primarily devoted to the eastern half of the world. Portugal was interested in India and its environs; America was almost an afterthought and its opening was not well documented. The Portuguese efforts of exploring and opening today's Brazil is not represented in this volume, in part because firsthand accounts of that work are hard to find, in part because few seem to have been written. The bold and fierce *bandeirantes,* who tore much of Brazil's interior apart and opened it for settlement, do not seem to have produced firsthand accounts of their work, in part, perhaps, because many of them were illiterate, in part because some may have been *too* literate. They must have been aware that they were operating in lands granted to Spain by the Pope, under his novel scheme of a line of demarcation, discussed in Chapter I.

For reasons set forth in the Epilogue, the present account ends with Hiram Bingham and does not enter into the modern day. Literally hundreds of expeditions, including my own of 1931–33, have worked in the South American interior, especially the Amazon basin, since the turn of the century. At times, as during World War II, that activity was greatly accelerated for understandable reasons related to national security. At other times it was taken over in great measure by men who yearned merely to be "explorers," have adventures, enjoy publicity, write books, lecture to women's clubs, and join New York's famous Explorers Club. Taken in its entirety, the twentieth-century exploration of South America is itself a fascinating and valuable story which, for reasons of space, cannot be told in a volume of this kind. It merits its own future book.

I cannot close this preface without giving thanks to several people who have helped me in the preparation of this work. Outstanding among them is Mrs. John Nef, formerly Mrs. Vilhjalmur Stefansson, who wrote under the name Evelyn Stefansson, and who, together with her late husband, conceived of the series of which this work is a part. She has been most kind and patient with me through the long delays involved in completing it. The book was written in Puerto Rico, where the required materials are in many cases sorely lacking. My thanks go to Srta. Carola Rosas of the Library of the University of Puerto Rico, who has been most helpful in obtaining books for me on interlibrary loans; by the same token they go to the Library of the University of Florida, and others, who have cooperated splendidly by sending such books to Puerto Rico. Sra. Carmen Inés Peña de Pagán, formerly Librarian of the Department of State, Commonwealth of Puerto Rico, has also been helpful throughout. Finally, my thanks to Sra. Ana Luisa Delfaus, and several other friends in the Puerto Rican Department of State, for the fine help they gave in typing an almost endless number of manuscript pages.

EARL PARKER HANSON

San Juan, Puerto Rico

I

HISTORIC
BACKGROUND

THE final—and at long last effective—discovery and exploration of the Americas by European men and societies resulted from the condition known as "overpopulation." Western
Europe was too crowded, had for centuries been too crowded,
as for centuries it had also been too continuously beset by
enemies, external and internal. The external enemies were the
Slavs of Poland and Russia who wanted no land-grabbing inva-
sions from their western neighbors, and the Mohammedans
farther south, who were similarly minded. The internal enemies
were Europe's prevailing concepts of the world's nature, inherited from the ancient Greeks and hardened during the
Dark and Middle Ages—which failed to inherit the spirit
of free inquiry from the ancient Greeks—into accepted
dogma.

The geographic concepts of the Middle Ages were riddled
with awesome monsters and marvels which constituted at one
and the same time a great challenge and a great peril. But by
far the most important—in the sense of being the most inhibit-
ing—medieval notion of the world's nature was the twin concept
of the burning tropics and the frozen north. South of Europe lay
the tropical zone, where the sun made things so hot that no life—
at least no European life—could exist there. The north was so
cold that man could not penetrate the Arctic and live. The only
part of the world habitable by man was therefore the ring now
called the North Temperate Zone. The ancient Greeks had

thought that the South Temperate Zone was possibly also habitable and perhaps even inhabited by human beings, but that idea had come to be effectively dispelled by Christian theology. Not only were all human beings descended from Adam and Eve, who could not possibly have lived simultaneously in both the North and the South Temperate Zones, but all men and women were creatures of God and were promised salvation through the Pope as God's representative on earth. Since even the Pope could not possibly reach the South Temperate Zone, it followed that people could never have existed there.

Hemmed in by the Mohammedans in the east, by the burning tropics in the south and the frozen arctic in the north, by monsters and marvels in the west (few medieval Europeans believed that the earth was flat), plagued by a teeming and growing lower class whose members—as usually happens in such situations— fervently practiced the arts of love with catastrophic results, dreaming of Asia's vast riches as reported by such ancients as Alexander the Great and later confirmed by Marco Polo, Europe suffered from dreadful internal pressures. Eventually, inevitably, those pressures resulted in the explosion which blew Columbus all the way across the Atlantic Ocean and came soon to billow into the inspiring but also terrifying movement known as the Renaissance, when all knowledge, once held sacred, had to be reexamined.

Today it is again fashionable to talk about the perils of overpopulation. Actually, the term is meaningless in the sense of being mathematically unmeasurable. Even the gloomiest of our prophets of imminent doom-through-proliferation have failed dismally to define the term "overcrowding." A land with a thousand people per square mile is not overpopulated if its inhabitants enjoy a reasonably good life with sufficient food, health, and general well-being for all; a land with fifty per square mile *is* overpopulated if its people suffer illness, hunger, and other privations. Hanson's Law reads: *It is never a land that is overpopulated in terms of inhabitants per square mile; it is always an economy, in terms of square meals per inhabitant.* It is therefore idle—if also convenient—to talk of medieval Europe having been overcrowded. What *was* overcrowded was the institution of feudalism, stubbornly maintained by the nobles in cahoots with the Church.

When Columbus aimed at Asia in 1492 but was fortunately blocked by America, he inadvertently saved the institution of feudalism—at least for Spain and Portugal—for another four and a half centuries. Of all the things which the Iberians were to import into the New World—among them horses, firearms, fierce dogs, European domestic crops and animals, and a European way of life for the migrant Europeans—by far the most important were feudalism and medieval Catholicism, each supporting the other. The main difference between European feudalism and the brand which is only now breaking down in the Americas was that in Europe the people had to be the serfs, while in America God had provided and set apart a whole racial group to fill that role.

While Spain and Portugal were saving feudalism as such by exporting it to vast new lands, the rest of western Europe—England, Germany, the Netherlands, and even France—perforce abolished the institution itself and substituted for it the capitalism, with its own sustaining, newly invented religions, which could support more people than could its predecessor. The main reason for the marked cultural differences between today's Anglo-America and Latin America is that North America came to be settled more than a century after the Spaniards and Portuguese had started the job in their parts of the hemisphere, and that, during that century, the people of northwestern Europe had come to develop an entirely new set of ideas by which to live.

While South America is changing rapidly today, many aspects of the feudal system inaugurated under Charlemagne around the year 800 can still be found there. The land, divided into great estates, was the property of members of the upper class, who also had a monopoly on something resembling gracious living. The toiling serfs belonged to the land, comprising the most important segment of its natural fauna; without them, the soil would have been as infertile as though it were located in the Sahara. The serfs owed their labor to their masters, who in turn owed protection to their subjects. The clergy were there to keep the balance between them and to see that God's Church received its just deserts.

As was to be the case in South America for centuries after Columbus' four voyages, efforts were made in medieval Europe to keep every landed estate as self-sufficient as possible, producing its own food, clothing, shoes, ironware, masonry, and pottery. Trade was looked on askance, virtually as a sin. It was carried on primarily by Jews, and—during the early Middle Ages —consisted mainly of bringing in luxury items for the rich. Most of the imports came from Asia and constituted a business in which the Mohammedans insisted on acting as both suppliers and middlemen. However, as Europe's pressures built up with the passage of time, the need for trade and ever more trade became increasingly great; hence—again—the need for a great age of voyaging, exploration, and conquest.

Charlemagne's feudalism didn't work out too badly as long as a proper numerical balance prevailed among the serfs, the nobles, and the lands supporting them all. But even the great Emperor, the founder of the Middle Ages, felt the need for geographic expansion, which he met by pushing eastward among the Saxons with the sword in one hand and the Bible in the other—a general procedure which was to be followed quite successfully centuries later by the *conquistadores* of South America's Indians. Like North American slavery, which was to lead to the Civil War, feudalism had to expand geographically at all times, to keep from being destroyed by man's propensity for proliferation on the one hand and the destruction of his soils on the other. A noble whose lands were comfortably worked by, say, 500 serfs was in a dilemma when he woke up one morning to discover that the latter had multiplied to 700. What was he to do with those who were surplus to his lands and his system for working them? Push them off on his neighbor's estate? His neighbor had too many himself. More room was called for, ever more room, if feudalism itself was to survive.

So came the Crusades as mighty eastward probes, early manifestations of the same *Drang nach Osten* in search of *Lebensraum* which was centuries later to lead to Hitler's ill-fated adventure in the Soviet Union. Actually armed quests for new lands on which to settle Europe's suffering millions, and new trade outlets in Asia, the Crusades were disguised as great religious movements by the Church, which was determined to keep control, not liking the idea of great masses of people getting out from under its jurisdiction. Similarly, the *conquistadores* of the sixteenth century were crusaders in America, carefully watched by the Church, whose banner they carried to reconcile atrocities with conscience.

The failure of the Crusades to find new lands for Europe's people and new outlets for its trade increased the sufferings at home. Europe's roads came to be crowded with a dangerous, hungry, rebellious, criminal *Lumpenproletariat,* its horrible cities were pestholes, worse, by far, than are the slums of today's Rio de Janeiro and Lima. The Hundred Years' War, the famine of 1315–17, the Black Death of 1347–50 were among the prices paid for failure to expand the economy to keep pace with population growth. Eventually things grew so bad that something *had* to be done if feudalism was to be saved. Since the Mohammedans stubbornly refused to make way in the east, they must be outflanked. If Europe could not go through them, it must go around them to the fleshpots of Asia.

Early in the fifteenth century the Portuguese, under Prince Henry the Navigator, inaugurated a systematic program of education, training, speculation on the earth's nature, shipbuilding, and voyaging. Cautiously, expedition after expedition was sent forth, groping down Africa's coast, looting that continent of gold, ivory, and Africans, but also testing the ancient notion of the burning tropics where no life could exist. Each voyage probed farther south than its predecessor, until, in 1488, Bartolomeu Díaz de Novaes triumphantly rounded the Cape of Good Hope and so pointed the way to India which Vasco da Gama was to sail some ten years later.

The Portuguese believed that their efforts had earned them a monopoly in exploration and conquest throughout the non-Christian world, and in 1484 Pope Innocentius VII generously granted it to them. The Portuguese were therefore incensed in 1492, when Spain's Ferdinand and Isabella hired an Italian to sail westward to the Indies. The fact that Columbus had first offered to make the voyage for Portugal, just as the Portuguese Magellan was a little later to offer to sail around the world for Portugal and hired himself out to Spain only after being turned down by his own country, did not diminish the indignation. The Portuguese complained to the Pope about the behavior of the Spanish monarchs.

That Pope was a Spaniard, Alexander VI, a practical politician and the most worldly of all pontiffs. He said that the non-

Christian world was large, with plenty of room for both of the ardently Catholic Iberian nations. He drew a line north and south on the Atlantic, 100 leagues west of the Azores, and decreed that half of the pagan world, a hundred and eighty degrees east of the line, was to belong to Portugal, with exclusive rights to discover, explore, settle, and rule there, while the other half would accrue to Spain. As for the rest of Europe, he took care of that matter quite clearly in two bulls which he issued on successive days in May, 1493. In the first document he gave to the Catholic kings of Spain and their heirs and successors the countries and islands discovered by their envoys and to be discovered thereafter "together with all their dominions, cities, camps, places and villages, and all rights, jurisdictions and appurtenances of the same." Addressing himself to the Spanish monarch, he strictly forbade "all persons of no matter what rank, estate, degree, order, or condition to dare without your special permit . . . to go for the sake of trade or any reason whatever, to the said islands and countries after they have been discovered and found by your envoys or persons sent out for the purpose." The line of demarcation, keeping other Europeans from even discovering lands not yet seen by Spaniards or Portuguese, appeared in the following day's bull.

That somewhat high-handed geopolitical decision, amended 13 years later, was to prove one of the most troublemaking ever handed down. Almost immediately a howl arose in northwestern Europe and especially in England, whose problems of overpopulation—meaning underemployment, hunger, illness, and crime—were at least as pressing as were those of Spain and Portugal. In 1527, one Robert Thorne, an English merchant living in Spain where he observed and sensed the excitement arising from the various voyages of exploration, wrote an impassioned letter to King Henry VIII, urging the latter to lead England into a program of voyaging, conquest, and settlement. He was the first publicly to advance the idea of sailing to the east by way of the north, arguing that Englishmen who sailed to the Spice Islands, India, and China via the Polar Sea, would not only have far shorter distances to travel than did the Iberians with their two southern passages, but would also avoid conflict with the Spaniards and the Portuguese, who thought that they owned not only the lands so sweepingly granted to them by the Pope, but also the sea routes leading thereto. In his letter he refuted the idea of the burning tropics and the frozen north with the famous Renaissance statement: "I assert that there is no land uninhabitable nor sea unnavigable." As for historical developments and the actions of several popes, he wrote, picturesquely but somewhat inaccurately: [1]

> Now, in 1484 the King of Portugal wanted to arm certain caravels and discover the Spice Islands. But he was afraid that he might merely have the expense and danger of discovering them, only to find all the other Europeans sailing there and cashing in on his work. So he first advised all the other Christian princes of what he was going to do. He said he was going to sail among the infidels to take new lands away from them; he said he would need an army for the job, and told them he would cut them in on the profits if they would share expenses.
>
> But they say that all the princes in Christendom sent word that they would have nothing to do with the scheme. So the King of Portugal sent word to the Pope of what he wanted to do, and that nobody would help him. In view of that, he told the Pope, he thought that anything he might discover should belong to him, and nobody should meddle with it.
>
> Now, the Pope didn't say like Christ: 'Quis me constituit judicem inter vos?' [Who appointed me a judge between you?] He not only guaranteed that everything discovered, from Occident to Orient, should belong to the King of Portugal, but also that no other prince should do any discovering under penalty of severe censure; and if any of them should set out to discover things after all, everything they found should belong to the King of Portugal.
>
> So the King armed a fleet and discovered Calcutta in 1487. Then the King of Spain, who was perfectly willing to discover islands in the West without permission from the King of Portugal, armed certain caravels and discovered the West Indies, especially Ladominica [Hispaniola, island of Haiti and Dominican Republic] and Cuba, where he obtained much gold.
>
> When the King of Portugal heard of that, he sent word to Spain and demanded the islands, since the Pope had specifically said that everything that was discovered should belong to him, and that nobody should do any discovering without permission from him.

[1] Rewritten in modern English by the editor. A longer portion of the letter, in modern English, was published in *New Worlds Emerging*, by Earl Parker Hanson (New York: Duell, Sloan and Pearce, 1949).

Now it seems that about that same time a lot of Jewish refugees had gone from Castile to Portugal for fear of being burned at the stake if they stayed—they being persecuted because they didn't want to turn Christian. They took a lot of gold and silver out of Spain with them. So the King of Spain answered that what the King of Portugal demanded was perfectly reasonable, and that he, being always obedient to the Pope, would gladly give him the newly discovered islands in the West Indies. However, he reminded him that it was also decreed that no king should receive the other's fugitives or their goods, and what about those Jews? He said that if the King of Portugal would pay him the million or more in gold which the Jews had carried out of Spain to Portugal, he, the King of Spain, would be glad to give him the West Indies and desist from any more discovering. But if the King of Portugal refused to give him the money, he would not only not give him the West Indies but would go out and discover things whenever he wanted to.

But the King of Portugal either wouldn't or couldn't pay all that money. So he couldn't keep the King of Spain from discovering things. He therefore made the best of it and made a deal whereby they should both go ahead and discover, and should divide the world between them.

In 1528, a year after receiving that letter, King Henry VIII took England's Catholic Church away from the Pope and placed it under his own jurisdiction. The papal line of demarcation may well have been at least as influential in causing that action as was the knotty problem of divorce.

The papal line also created serious dissensions between Portugal and Spain. Portugal objected to it on the ground that it gave too much territory to Spain. A new line was therefore drawn in 1506 by Pope Julius II, running from pole to pole, 370 leagues west of the Cape Verde Islands. Having agreed to the decision in principle, the two Iberian nations began immediately to argue over the question of where, precisely, Pope Julius' line cut across South America. The argument was complicated by the fact that the mariners of those days, while able to measure latitudes with reasonable accuracy, could only guess at longitudes, or distances east and west. Moreover, the Cape Verde Islands are scattered over a rather large area, spanning about 175 miles from east to west. In locating his line, had the Holy Father referred to the geographical center of that area, its eastern edge, or its western? The question was worth arguing. Shifting the papal baseline back and forth 175 miles at the Cape Verde Islands brought into dispute more than a million square miles of the earth's surface, somewhere in or near the Americas.

Approximately halfway around the world from the papal line which nobody could locate with any degree of certainty, 180 degrees away, were the Moluccas, whence came the spices so avidly sought by Europe. Did they belong to Spain or to Portugal? The latter nation claimed them, having been the first to reach them via the southeast passage around Africa. The Spaniards believed that the Moluccas probably belonged to them but did nothing about the matter until 1518, when they hired Magellan, who was angry at his own monarch for having turned down his proposal, to sail to the islands via the southwest passage—if he discovered one—around South America. Undoubtedly, Magellan was hired in part to settle the question of sovereignty over the Spice Islands in Spain's favor, a fact which caused the Portuguese to call him a traitor. Five years after the return to Spain of the only remaining vessel of the Magellan expedition's original five ships, Robert Thorne wrote to his king in his famous letter:

> The trouble is that we have no sure way of determining longitudes, so that distances east and west have to depend on the judgment of the mariners. There are therefore many islands which Spain and Portugal both claim, though it does seem that the Portuguese have issued a lot of faked maps and that the Spice Islands really do belong to Spain.

In writing the letter, Thorne had the benefit of a certain amount of information from spies. He reported: "Recently I invested money in an expedition of three ships and a caravel, principally so that two English friends of mine could go along and find out about the Spice Islands and about what those people knew about the sea routes to them." However, what information his informers brought back from their voyage was hearsay so far as the Spice Islands were concerned. The expedition was that of Sebastian Cabot, who had been sent out in 1526 to check up on, and perhaps improve upon, Magellan's findings. But he never reached the Strait of Magellan, let alone the Moluccas. He reached and named the Río de la Plata, sailed up that estuary some 500 miles, decided that it was not a sea route to the Pacific, and sailed back to Spain.

Naturally, arguments about the papal line of demarcation and its precise location also played an important role in the exploration of South America. There was no question that the line ran somewhere inland from the Brazilian bulge, which therefore belonged to Portugal. But how far inland? Obviously, since they were the first to explore and conquer it, the Spaniards were convinced that the Río de la Plata territory belonged to them through the Pontiff's generosity. Farther north, however, it did not take the Portuguese long to expand their claimed territories ever farther westward, far beyond the westernmost longitudes of Río de la Plata and today's Paraguay.

The papal line of demarcation came eventually to be scrapped as a means for defining boundaries, not only because nobody could tell precisely where it cut across the continent, but also because of the extreme difficulties involved in policing the huge territories to keep out alien invaders. Hence the two powers settled down in South America to a *modus vivendi* around approximately the international boundaries one sees on modern maps. Similarly, the principle of specific sea routes being owned by specific nations had eventually to give way—precisely because of the difficulties involved in policing the routes to exclude foreigners—to the principle of the freedom of the seas.

So, gradually, through struggle and turmoil, heroic exploration and barbarous enslavement, emerged the beginnings of today's South America, where history is repeating itself in that the ancient feudalism is breaking down under the pressure of growing populations, and where, at least in the Amazon basin, a new era of exploration, scientific examination, settlement, and economic development has set in.

II

THE LAND

THE early European explorers and conquerors of South America were men whose valor was often matched by their brutality. They tore the continent apart in a frenetic search for gold, fertile lands, Indian slaves, fame for themselves, and new souls for their Christian heaven. They have left us a literature which is rich in accounts of heroic—and at times despicable— deeds, but lamentably poor in descriptions of the lands in which those deeds were performed. Sancho's account of the conquest of Peru (Chapter VIII) and Carvajal's of the first European descent of the Amazon (Chapter X) are sagas of daring achievement but mighty poor as descriptive geography. One searches them in vain for a clear picture of Peru's physical nature or the nature of the Amazon River and the lands through which it flows. The best sources of such materials are the modern travelers and geographers from whose writings much of the present chapter was taken.

The Continent

The drama of South America's conquest and exploration, rising at times to strident, climactic crises, and then subsiding again to the naturalists' quiet, dedicated study of plants and animals, is staged on a continent nearly seven million square miles in area, comprising one eighth of the globe's land surface. North and south, from the topmost point of the continent's Caribbean coast to the southernmost islands off Cape Horn,

South America extends some 4,700 miles through 68 degrees of latitude, from about 12° N, down past the equator, to some 56° S. At its widest, about 5° south of the equator, it encompasses more than 3,000 miles from east to west; from there it tapers down steadily until coming virtually to a point in subantarctic regions.

Two "highland" regions, one enormous system of mountains, and five river systems with their plains, shape the general topographic pattern of South America. The continent's oldest lands are the Guiana Highlands, lying north of the equator and the Amazon River valley, and the Brazilian Highlands, lying south of both. Before the Cretaceous period of the Mesozoic era, from sixty million to a hundred and thirty million years ago, they *were* South America. Between them was an ocean strait where now flows the Amazon, and there was no Isthmus of Panama in the north to block the venturesome journey of some Columbus toward an India, which in those days didn't exist either. Today's remnants of those highlands—so implacable are the erosive actions of wind, sand, water, frost, heat, and earth tremors—are considerably lower and smaller than were their primeval predecessors.

It was during the Cretaceous period that the Andes, the Isthmus of Panama, and the Rocky Mountains heaved themselves up from the ocean to form the earth's longest mountain system, running 9,000 miles north and south and covering three quarters of the distance from pole to pole. In the Andes that system's origin and relative youth are attested by the fact that fossils of marine life are found at elevations of ten and more thousands of feet above the sea from which they had once been lifted. The system's many active volcanoes, plus the innumerable, devastating earthquakes which still bedevil it all the way from Alaska to southern Chile, also attest to its youth and resulting instability.

While one branch of the Andean system flows into South America from Panama, another runs parallel to Venezuela's Caribbean coast, swings southwestward into Colombia, and there joins the main ranges. Between that Venezuelan chain and the Guiana Highlands is the Orinoco River, with its many tributaries, and the great plains, which were for centuries the locale of Venezuela's important cattle industry. The Orinoco flows for some 1,500 miles along the west and north edges of the Guiana

Highlands, and it was from that river that so many early explorers tried in vain to enter the relatively inaccessible mountains in their search for El Dorado (Chapters XIII and XIV).

In Colombia, between Andean ranges, the Magdalena and Cauca rivers flow northward, eventually to unite and flow into the Caribbean Sea. Both are important but it is especially the latter, with its fertile valley, which contributes to the country's agricultural life.

From the eastern slopes of the Andes, between about 3° N latitude and some 18° S, along a mighty sweep of more than a thousand miles, spring hundreds upon hundreds of eastward-flowing creeks and rivers whose waters sooner or later flow into the Amazon. Other rivers flow southward into the mainstream from the Guiana Highlands, and northward from those of Brazil, forming the Amazon system's gigantic dendritic pattern on the world's largest alluvial plain.

Another system of rivers drains the Brazilian Highlands toward the south, and the southern Andes toward the east. Those streams form the Paraná and Paraguay rivers which, together with the Uruguay, flow into the Atlantic via the mighty estuary known as the Río de la Plata, the Silver River, which was first explored as a possible route to India.

Finally, there is Brazil's São Francisco River, which flows northward from the Brazilian Highland as though—for a time— to join the Amazon. However, at about 10° S latitude, it is deflected to sweep to the Atlantic in a great arc, the falls and rapids of which, where the river finally leaves the uplands, are today being harnessed for important hydroelectric projects.

The Andean Regions

Between 40 and 60° S latitude, the waters of the southern oceans are moved, by the prevailing west winds, to flow in a general west to east direction. When the South Pacific's "West Wind Drift" reaches South America, a part of it passes Cape Horn and then swings northward along the continent's lower east coast; most of it, however, is deflected northward by the west coast, flowing toward the equator, where it turns toward the west again in the South Pacific's endless counterclockwise movement. Having come up from subantarctic regions, it is a "cold" current where it courses along the west coast, meaning that it is colder than the land on its right and the waters on its left. Naturally, however, it warms up as it approaches the equator. By the time it swings westward it has been transformed into the warm "South Equatorial Current" on which, in 1947, Thor Heyerdahl and his companions drifted to Polynesia in a picturesque effort to show that the early Polynesians *might* have come from Peru, though the general consensus is that the prehistoric human flow ran largely the other way.

The part of the ocean stream which flows along the coast of northern Chile and all of Peru used to be called the "Humboldt Current," after its discoverer, though today geographers seem to prefer to call it the "Peru Current." It is responsible for the fact that the Atacama region of northern Chile is the driest desert on earth, while Peru's coastal region is also desert except where it is cut by rivers with their green valleys. Moisture-laden winds blowing toward South America from the Pacific are cooled as they pass over the current; the cooling condenses the water out of them to rain on the sea, leaving little or nothing to be dropped on the coastal regions where, of course, the winds are warmed again by the sun-drenched earth.

The first Europeans to strike southward from Panama (Chapters VII and VIII) encountered dense tropical vegetation on the coasts of today's Colombia and Ecuador. With a precipitation of more than 300 inches per year, the city of Buenaventura on Colombia's Pacific coast is one of the rainiest inhabited spots on earth. Ecuador's coast is hot and humid, and not until passing south into Peru does one find the climate changing to warm and dry.

The Andes are composed of many ranges which separate again and again to make room for upland plateaus, and then come together once more in their several "knots." Since they are the world's second highest mountains, reaching their peak of 23,081 feet above the sea in Mount Aconcagua on the Argentine-Chilean border, their interior, inhabited plateaus are considerably elevated. Bolivia's *altiplano,* the desolate tableland which is the center of the nation's life—about 450 miles long and some 75 miles wide—lies at an average altitude of some 12,500 feet, so ranking with the Tibetan plateau as the highest inhabited region on earth. Lake Titicaca, between Peru and Bolivia, the world's highest body of navigable water and the place of origin of the Incas, is approximately at the same altitude or higher than the peak of Oregon's Mount Hood.

Geographers divide the Andean regions into three parallel zones, each of which contains many natural subdivisions, namely: (1) the coastal region, called *los Llanos* (the plains) by early Spanish writers; (2) the highlands, or *Sierra*, including the main ranges of the Andes and the lofty tablelands between them; and (3) the eastern slopes, known as *Oriente* in Ecuador, *Montaña* in Peru, and *Yungas* in Bolivia. It was in the arid regions of the Andes, between northern Ecuador, where the interior is considerably drier than on the coast, and the southern edge of Chile's Atacama Desert, that South America's aboriginal inhabitants built up a succession of admirable societies, of kingdoms and empires, culminating in that created by the Incas which came finally to be destroyed by the Spanish invaders.

Philip Ainsworth Means, the archeologist, historian, and writer, has pointed out that there are some 60 river valleys along the coast between northern Ecuador and central Chile, separated from one another by wastes of desert. Some of the rivers are seasonal, flowing only during the highland rainy season (October to May), while others are perennial, though with marked differences between their high-water and low-water flows. Of the valleys at the rivers' mouths, he writes:

> In this favored territory . . . the soil is very rich because of the silt laid down upon it annually by the river when at flood and, moreover, the arable land was for centuries extended by skilfully planned works of irrigation, many of which fell into disuse after the Spaniards came. . . . Thus, at an early date, the coast valleys became the seat of an intensive and abundantly productive husbandry which cultivated potatoes, maize, squash, beans, sweet potatoes, peppers, all of which, supplemented by many fruits, nuts, and spices, gave the happy people of the coast one of the best vegetable diets the world has ever seen, and to comestibles of that kind they could add a vast variety of sea-food, and likewise game-birds, venison, and other meats from the higher parts of their valleys. . . .

Such are the chief characteristics of those coastal valleys whose streams are of the perennial type. Of the forty-four valleys on the Peruvian coast alone thirty-one have sources high enough in the western slopes of the Andes to ensure a flow, albeit a greatly fluctuating flow, throughout the year. . . .

In sharp contrast to the valleys, where the most intensive agriculture has been practiced for centuries, the remainder of the coast is now altogether uncultivated and all but uninhabited.[1]

Going on to the inland valleys, Means begins with Ecuador:

It may be said that the average width of the Ecuadorean highlands is about 100 miles and its length about 350, giving an area of some 35,000 square miles from which something—perhaps 10,000 square miles—should be deducted to allow for lands too lofty and too bleak for sedentary occupation by mankind. In other words, an area of some 25,000 square miles, roughly equivalent to New Hampshire, Massachusetts, Connecticut, and Rhode Island added together, was available to societies of the pastoral and agricultural type, the elevation of the area in question varying between about 14,000 feet and about 7,000 feet.

After describing several elevated drainage basins in northern Peru, Means says:

From the historical point of view the Urubamba Valley and its tributaries form one of the two most important *hoyas* [drainage basins] of the Andean highland zone, the other being the Titicaca basin, of which more will be said presently.

What is there in the environmental complex of this *hoya* of the Urubamba that made it inevitable that it should become the birthplace, the cradle, the home, and the tomb of one of the most remarkable civilizations that mankind has ever constructed? Lying on an average of about 11,000 feet above sea-level, that portion of it which is known as the Cuzco Valley, wherein took place the epochal developments referred to, is a temperate region capable of sustaining intensive agriculture, and, moreover, is productive of the raw materials for pottery, for textiles, for metal-working, and for architecture in stone. The mere physical presence of these advantageous circumstances is not enough, however, to explain the flowering of advanced culture in that region. In order to be made use of these elements must be able to draw upon a definite amount of

[1] Philip Ainsworth Means, *Ancient Civilizations of the Andes* (N.Y.: Charles Scribner's Sons, 1936).

human energy, ingenuity, and application. In such a climate as that of the Cuzco Valley man can supply these factors, thereby engendering culture by combining them with those other factors which are so bountifully supplied by nature. In a climate more enervating man's energies would have been sapped by lassitude; in a colder, they would have been exhausted by the unremitting struggle to keep his body above the freezing-point and by anxiously hunting about for edible matter. Here there was a felicitous balance of factors, and, as a result, a great civilization was born.

About 200 miles roughly southeast of Cuzco, on today's border between Peru and Bolivia and south of one of the several *nudos,* or knots, in which the Andean ranges occasionally come together, we come to the important Lake Titicaca region, of which Means writes:

> Crossing that Pass one enters the basin of Lake Titicaca, bounded by the Knot of Vilcañoa on the north, the Maritime Cordillera on the west, and the Eastern Cordillera—in these parts known as the Cordillera Real or Royal Cordillera—on the east. It is a territory which is some 120 miles wide and some 500 miles long, having towards its northern end the famous Lake of Titicaca . . . which is about 40 miles wide and about 120 miles long, lying at an altitude of slightly over 12,500 feet above sea-level. Towards the south this immense area, roughly equal to Maine, New Hampshire, Vermont, and Massachusetts added together, is less definitely outlined than in the north for, instead of being enclosed by ranges, it falls away gradually beyond Lake Poopó to the great *salares* or salt-beds of Coipasa and Uyuni, which are, presumably, the vestiges of ancient lakes.
>
> It is the country immediately adjacent to Lake Titicaca that particularly demands the attention of the historian. Here, as when contemplating the Cuzco Valley, he must ask himself just how and why this region produced a great civilization. Although it is more than 1,000 feet higher than the Cuzco Valley, the country beyond Lake Titicaca is, for some distance back from the shore, well below 14,000 feet, which is the upward limit of potato-cultivation. Agriculture was, therefore, possible —but under more difficult circumstances—and the other raw materials for culture were also present, as were likewise human energy, enterprise, and perseverance. Therefore, this is another region in which we need not be surprised to find that important

cultural progress was inaugurated and carried forward to note-worthy culminations.

Moving southwest from Lake Titicaca, Means arrives at Chile's desert, the Puna de Atacama, which was sparsely settled before the Spanish conquest, in part because water resources are there few and far between, in part because its native peoples had been latecomers, immigrants who moved into the land only after adjacent, more favorable regions had been fully developed. It was that desert which gave Valdivia so much trouble on his southward march into Chile (Chapter IX).

The great authority on Atacama was Dr. Isaiah Bowman, at one time Director of New York's American Geographical Society, and later President of Johns Hopkins University. Bowman, who died in 1950, was one of the outstanding American geographers, a world leader of geographic thought, who carried out a large amount of scientific geographic exploration in South America. Between 1907 and 1913 he made three detailed scientific surveys of various parts of the Atacama Desert regions, the results of which were published in 1924. Of the desert's Pacific coast, he wrote as follows:

If the high and bold coast of northern Chile excites the imagination in these times, what must it have seemed to the sea-voyagers of the sixteenth century, the hulls of whose tiny caravels would find ample room in a single smoke-stack of either the *Leviathan* or the *Majestic*. The so-called ports of northern Chile are either open roadsteads or occupy mere shallow bights in this forbidding coast; and the towns stand upon narrow marine terraces cut in a past age and now up-lifted from a narrow shelf that furnishes barely room enough for a settlement. In places two or three thousand feet of steep scarp, as barren apparently as if no rain ever fell, shut off all view of the distant mountains. There are no openings here and there where green valleys lie floored with cultivated fields as on the coast of Peru. It is a simpler coast than that further north and far more desertic in aspect. The streams disappear for the most part in inland basins, and the coast is almost entirely without a touch of green. Except for one river, the Loa, there is not a single stream that reaches the sea in 1,600 miles of territory from Arica to the mouth of the Copiapó River. There are dry *arroyos* that nick the great western scarp of the coastal desert, but they carry water only in times of highly exceptional rain separated by ten or fifteen, and in some cases fifty, years of drought.[2]

After some pages of description, he writes: "In northern Chile there is no hint of water until one reaches the foothills of the Andes far beyond the Coast Range and across the intervening desert."

On my first pack-train journey into northern Chile . . . I was delighted to find all my expectations of desert scenery realized. For the first fifty miles there was but a single spot where a natural growth of green could be seen from the trail and but one other where there was any green growth at all, and that beside a desert well about which were clustered a few low huts. All the rest was naked rock and sand, brown and yellow in color yet appearing stark and colorless in tone in the midday sun when the whole landscape is overlighted; glowing with color as the sun declines and the shadows of the ravines come out.

He writes as follows about the higher Andean ranges east of the desert:

The snows of the higher cordilleras give the summit peaks a clearer outline against the dark blue and purple of the sunset sky in the east. From the mountains the desert plain appears to extend indefinitely westward and to have a much wider range of color and form. . . .

The deserts of the world are not lifeless places, although lifeless tracts of more or less limited extent can be found in almost all deserts. In northern Chile where is the driest climate in the world there are villages, because even there the desert is not absolutely rainless, and where there is rain there are streams and settlements beside them. It is the rarest occurrence to find a watered spot in the desert that has not been settled by man.

That, in general terms, is the Atacama Desert through hundreds of miles of which Valdivia made his way in 1540, the world's driest wasteland, hundreds of square miles of its surface covered by salt beds or the nitrates which were centuries later to achieve supreme economic importance, with Indians living only

[2] Isaiah Bowman, *Desert Trails of Atacama* (Special Publication No. 5; N.Y.: American Georgraphical Society, 1924).

in the sporadic places where water was to be found. Chiu Chiu, a small village on the Río Loa near an ancient Indian ruin (Atacama Chica) where Valdivia made camp for a while, is dismissed by Bowman with a few brief mentions. San Pedro de Atacama (Atacama Grande), on the other hand, is described in detail by him since it is today virtually as important economically as it was to the Indians of Inca times.

> Upon the western side of the Puna de Atacama, where the main chain of the cordillera surmounts it, is a line of settlements of which the first—from the north—is San Pedro de Atacama. With elevation of 8,000 feet it is neither a high plateau town . . . nor a desert valley town. . . . Its site is so elevated that snow has been known to fall; yet the daytime temperatures are those of the high desert type. It lies in a desert basin midway between the cold puna and the desert pampa.

Like the pre-Spanish Indians before them, today's inhabitants of San Pedro de Atacama earn their living by agriculture, practiced through a carefully regulated system of irrigation.

At about 27° S latitude, the desert gives way to the green valley of the Coquimbo River, beyond which lies Chile's famous Central Valley, where Valdivia established his first settlement, today's capital city of Santiago. In 1941 I wrote:

> . . . the country's breadbasket, a strip five hundred miles long and nowhere more than a hundred and fifty miles wide, that contains some of the world's most fertile agricultural lands.
>
> But not by any means is all of this area—about as large as the state of Nebraska—fit for cultivation. In the east, the western slopes of the Andes cover an uninhabited strip some fifty miles wide; in the west the barren range of coastal hills takes another twenty miles or so out of cultivation. In between, broken by spurs that extend from both ranges and that sometimes almost meet, is a deep trough which the rushing rivers have in the course of ages filled with rich alluvial material and built up into a continuous, nearly level plain from Santiago to Puerto Montt. But if the tillable lands in central Chile comprise only from eight to eleven percent of its total area, they make up for that fact by their almost inexhaustible fertility. . . . It was here that the early settlers found they had no trouble whatever in growing the fruits and grains for which they had brought seeds from Spain. They had no trouble in part because the

region's climate is remarkably like the Mediterranean climate that thousands on thousands of travelers from England and the United States have sought for hundreds of years for rest and recuperation.[3]

Beyond the southern edge of Chile's agricultural heartland, across the Bío-Bío River at about 38° S latitude, Valdivia encountered forested country and the fierce Araucano Indians who gave him so much trouble and eventually killed him. I described it thus:

> South of the Central Valley, beyond the Bío-Bío River, lies first the far-famed lake region, "The Switzerland of South America," and then a truly bewildering maze of thousands of islands and fjords, vast bogs, and dense forests. . . . And in the far south this almost uninhabited labyrinth opens onto the Strait of Magellan and the vast sheep plains of Tierra del Fuego.

The Amazon Basin

Moisture-laden winds, blowing from the Atlantic Ocean across South America, are forced to rise when they reach the Andes mountains. In rising they are cooled adiabatically, and so lose their moisture through condensation, to roll down the Andean east slopes and form the Amazon river system.

A large number of explorers and special investigators has left us detailed descriptions of the Amazon basin—or at least parts of it. Dr. William Lytle Schurz, one of the outstanding modern North American authorities on Latin America, a man with many years of service in those regions (including the command, in 1923–24, of an expedition sent to the Amazon by the U.S. Department of Commerce for the purpose of making a survey of crude-rubber possibilities), gives a graphic description of the basin in his book on Latin America.

> The Amazon valley is the largest lowland in Latin America. It includes most of Brazil above the 15th parallel, that is, the greater part of that gigantic country, and parts of Venezuela, Colombia, Ecuador, Peru, and Bolivia. The basin of the Ama-

[3] Earl Parker Hanson, *Chile, Land of Progress* (N.Y.: Reynal and Hitchcock, 1941).

zon and that of the Orinoco merge imperceptibly into one
another where the Río Negro and the Atabapo approach within
a short distance of each other, and the two river systems are
actually connected by the natural canal of the Cassiquiare. . . .
The vast forested plain of Amazonia, as it spreads out westward
. . . continues with very little rise until it reaches the last out-
work of the Andes. Where the Marañón-Amazon suddenly
breaks out through the narrow canyon of the Pongo de Manseriche into the Amazonian plain, the lowlands approach to less
than 300 miles of the Pacific. . . .

Contrary to a common impression, the Amazon valley is not
an immense swamp. At its worst, few areas of the earth are
less suited to human habitation than the tidal forests of the
Amazon delta. Yet, people live in this periodically drowned
jungle, which is the "green hell" of the Brazilian writer,
Rangel. . . .

However, most of the Amazon country is *terra firma* and well
above the level of the yearly inundations. Going up the river
from Pará to Manaus, this fact soon becomes apparent after
leaving the Straits of Breves. Ranges of hills several hundred
feet in height begin to appear in the north. At Monte Alegre
the hills come down almost to the water's edge and behind the
first rise of ground there is a wide expanse of open *campos*
[grass country] lands with more ridges along their northern
edge. These natural *campos* are an interesting feature of the
Amazonian landscape and occur in many places. The largest of
them, the *campos gerais* of the Río Branco, are several thousand
square miles in extent.[4]

Moving south from the Amazon basin in eastern South America, we move to Dr. Preston James, a modern geographer with
much scientific field work in South America to his credit who
is today Chairman of the Department of Geography at Syracuse
University. In his book, *Latin America,* he says the following
about today's Paraguay:

The Paraguayans live in a natural paradise. They enjoy the
comfort of a mild climate, yet one which is not lacking in the
stimulating effects of moderate weather change. They have an
adequate supply of good soil for agricultural use. They possess
forests and grasslands. Their country is neither monotonously

---

4 William Lytle Schurz, *Latin America, A Descriptive Survey* (N.Y.: E. P. Dutton
and Co., 1941).

flat nor sharply separated into contrasting extremes of mountain and plain. . . .

The eastern third of Paraguay is an elevated plateau varying from one to two thousand feet in altitude. This is the western edge of the great Paraná Plateau.[5]

Most of today's population of Paraguay live in the plateau region between the Paraná and Paraguay rivers, where the early Spaniards carried out their conquest. East of the Paraguay is the so-called Chaco, which James deals with as follows:

> The Chaco, which lies west of the [Paraguay] river, is a world apart. As far as physical conditions are concerned, this great alluvial plain between the river and the base of the Andes bears a striking resemblance to the Ganges Valley of northern India. The climate of the two regions is similar; the scrub forests of both can be placed in the same general category of natural vegetation; and the similarity is increased by the presence in both regions of great, sprawling rivers, subject to annual floods and frequent shifts of channel. Only in detail do the two pictures differ. But the one is densely populated—more than a thousand rice- and wheat-growing farmers per square mile; and the other is one of the larger areas of very sparse population in Latin America.

South of Paraguay, James gives the following brief description of the lands comprising Argentina:

> The Argentine national territory includes a wide variety of kinds of country. Argentine geographers recognize four major physical divisions, each with numerous subdivisions. Except in the far south, the western border of the country is in the Andes. The first major division of the country, the *Andes,* includes the cordillera from the dry north to the heavily glaciated and ice-covered mountains of Patagonia. . . . The eastern piedmont of the Andes with its succession of oasis settlements may be included with this first major division of the country.
> The second major division is the North. . . . There is the vast alluvial plain of the Chaco, with its tropical scrub-forest cover. On the east and the south of the Río Paraná there is Argentine *Mesopotamia,* the land between the rivers [the Paraná and the Uruguay], composed partly of flood-plain, partly of gently rolling and well-drained interfluves. . . .

[5] Preston E. James, *Latin America* (N.Y.: The Odyssey Press, 1959).

The third major division of the country is the *Pampas*—the great plains which lie south of the Chaco and east of the Andean piedmont. Most of these plains were originally covered with a growth of low, scrubby trees, a vegetation-type known as *monte;* but toward the southeast of the *Pampas,* where the rainfall is heavier and the summers remain cool, tall prairie grasses were once probably more important than the *monte.* It is customary to divide the *Pampas* into a wetter eastern part and a drier western part. . . .

Finally, the fourth major physical division of Argentina is *Patagonia,* the region south of the Río Colorado. This is land of arid, wind-swept plateaus, crossed at wide intervals by strips of green vegetation along the valley bottoms. In the far south of *Patagonia* Argentina shares with Chile the land of continuously cool and stormy weather, where winters are never severe, but where there is never any summer.

Guiana

Proceeding northward, to the ancient Guiana Highlands which, before the Andes arose, comprised approximately half of today's South America, Dr. James gives the following description:

Guiana, as a regional name, is commonly applied to an area which is entirely surrounded by water. The several water bodies which form the outlines of Guiana are the Orinoco River, the Río Cassiquiare which drains water from the upper Orinoco southward to join a headwater of the Río Negro, the Río Negro itself, the Amazon, and the Atlantic Ocean. This territory is divided politically into Venezuelan Guiana, Brazilian Guiana, British Guiana, and French Guiana.

This region lies only a short distance north of the equator, and almost exactly on the heat equator, that is the part of the earth with the highest average annual temperatures. Behind a flat, swampy coast, the Guiana Highlands are composed of the same basic elements as the Brazilian Highlands on the southern side of the Amazon. Almost all the surface is covered with tropical rain forest except for narrow belts of wet savanna along the coast, and dry savanna which crosses the border from the Río Branco area of Brazil into the interior of British Guiana. With the exception of the fringe of settlement along the coast, most of Guiana is very scantily inhabited.

Even though they failed to penetrate into the heart of Venezuelan Guiana (Chapter XIII), the old El Dorado hunters were
in some ways correct in locating their golden dream city in that
difficult region. Today the Guiana Highlands are known to be
rich in gold and diamonds. Venezuela's "El Callao" gold mine,
located not far from the spot where Walter Raleigh placed El
Dorado, was opened in 1853 and was for decades the richest such
mine on earth. The Caroní River brings diamonds from some
source in the interior highlands. Most of them are lost, but
every ten or fifteen years, when the stream was exceptionally
low (and before hydroelectric developments stopped the practice), people by the hundreds once flocked in from many parts,
pitched camp along the banks, dug pits in the uncovered sand,
and panned it for gems, while dozens of diamond dealers from
New York, Amsterdam, and elsewhere came flying in to see
what they could buy. (If only Sir Walter Raleigh had known
about those diamonds! What little "exploring" he did in South
America did take him as far as the Caroní.)

Today the greatest economic importance of Venezuelan Guiana stems from its vast stores of some of the world's highest-grade
iron ores. Several mining companies are exploiting that ore and
sending prospectors by helicopters into the jungled interior to
look for more. Along the region's northern edge, on the Orinoco
River, the Venezuelan government, under President Romulo
Betancourt, developed the immense hydroelectric capacity of
such rivers as the Caroní and built at least one industrial city to
foster and carry forward new industrial developments.

In a discussion of this kind it is impossible to deal in detail
with all the geographic regions which, in their immense diver-
sity, make up the continent of South America. Suffice it to say
that the continent's exploration and conquest carried thousands
of men past and over towering mountains, through forbidding
deserts, swamps, and millions of square miles of dense jungles.
Far from completed as yet, that exploration opened to the
knowledge of men of European stock almost seven million
square miles of dramatically variegated land, stretching north
and south from the lower half of the north tropical zone, through
the south tropical and the south temperate regions—which in
South America deserve the appellation "temperate" far more
than do their often appalling counterparts in the north—into
sub-Antarctica.

❧ III ❧

THE INDIANS

The West Coast

PEDRO de Cieza de León, whose four-part *Chronicles of Peru* [1] comprises one of the most engaging and informative descriptive accounts ever written about South America, left Spain for the New World in 1532, at the age of fourteen. A soldier all his life, he was also an indefatigable observer and writer, whose first volume was published in Seville in 1553. In 1538 he became a member of an expedition which marched southward from the Gulf of Darien into the former Inca empire, as far as Lake Titicaca. Of the lowland Indians around the Gulf of Darien, he wrote as follows:

> These Indians . . . originally came . . . from the other side of the great river of Darien [Atrato]. The lords or caciques are obeyed and feared by the Indians, and their women are the prettiest and most lovable of any that I have seen in the Indies. They are clean in their eating, and have none of the dirty habits of other nations. These Indians have small villages and their houses are like long sheds. They sleep in hammocks and use no other sort of bed. Their land is fertile and is abundantly supplied with provisions, such as well tasted roots. There are also herds of small pigs which are good eating, and many great tapirs, said by some to be of the shape and form of zebras. . . .
>
> When the Spaniards occupied the villages of these Indians,

[1] The Cieza quotations in this chapter are taken from *The Travels of Pedro de Cieza de León, A.D. 1532–50, Contained in the First Part of his Chronicles of Peru*, translated and edited by Clements R. Markham (The Hakluyt Society, 1864).

they found a great quantity of gold in some small baskets, in
the form of rich ornaments. . . . The women wore mantles,
which covered them from the waist to the feet, and other mantles over their bosoms. . . . The men go naked and barefooted.
. . . These Indians are engaged in trade, and take pigs . . . to
sell them to other tribes more inland. . . . The Indians also
trade with salt and fish, getting in exchange their gold, cloth
and other articles. Their arms are bows . . . with very long
and sharp arrows, anointed with a juice which is so evil and
pestilential, that no man who is wounded with it so as to draw
blood, can live, although it should not be as much as would
flow from the prick of a pin. . . .

These Indians have no temples nor any form of worship, and
nothing has been discovered concerning their religion as yet,
except that they certainly talk to the devil, and do him all the
honor they can, for they hold him in great esteem. . . . Their
chiefs have many wives. When a chief dies, all his servants and
friends assemble in his house in the night, without any light;
but they have a great quantity of their wine made from maize
which they continue drinking while they mourn for the dead.
After they have completed their ceremonies and sorceries, they
inter the body with its arms and treasures, plenty of good food,
and jugs of *chicha,* together with a few live women. The devil
gives them to understand that, in the place where they will go,
they will come to life in another kingdom which he has prepared for them, and that it is necessary to take food with them
for the journey. As if hell was so very far off!

As Cieza traveled southward, he became increasingly impressed with the Indians' cannibalism. Modern ethnologists are
inclined to believe that true cannibalism, practiced for the purpose of allaying hunger, was never found in the Americas, and
that men and women were there eaten only for ritual purposes.
If that is true, Cieza de León makes the Indians of the Cauca
Valley out to be enthusiastically ritualistic. Of those near the
city of Antioquia, he wrote:

The lord or king of this country was one named Nutibara.
. . . When the lord went to war, he was followed by many
people with their arms. When he traveled through the country,
he sat on a litter inlaid with gold. . . . He had many wives.
Near the door of his house, and the same thing was done at the
houses of his captains, there were many heads of the enemies

whom he had eaten, which were kept there as trophies. All the natives of this country eat human flesh.

Again, of another group of Indians near Antioquia, he wrote:

> I heard it said that the lords or caciques of the valley of Nore collected all the women they could find from the land of their enemies, took them home, and used them as if they had been their own. If any children were born, they were reared with much care until they reached the age of twelve or thirteen, and, being then plump and healthy, these caciques ate them with much appetite, not considering that they were of their own flesh and blood.

The Indians whom he saw in today's Colombia were in general quite similar, each group to the others. They lived in wooden houses at one point built off the ground in trees, with thatched roofs and walls, had considerable gold, tilled the soil, fished, made war, ate their prisoners, traded from tribe to tribe, and wore cotton clothes. Virtually all of them, according to the young chronicler, talked with the devil who, with God's permission, gave them much bad advice. Cieza ascribes their bitter resistance to the Spaniards to the fact that they lacked a strong, unifying central government such as that of the Incas from Quito southward. Once the Incas fell, their entire great empire fell with them, offering relatively little resistance. In Colombia, each tribe, each nation of Indians, put up its own resistance.

As soon as he reached the lands which had formerly been ruled by the Incas (Cieza, and Markham after him, write the word "Yncas"; in this account it is changed to "Incas" for the sake of simplification) Cieza found marked improvement in the Indians. In Chapter XL, he was near the city of Quito, which had been conquered by the Incas in 1487, and by the Spaniards in 1533.

> The natives are in general more gentle and better disposed and have fewer vices than any of those we have passed. . . . They are a people of middle height, and very hard workers. They live in the same way as the people of the . . . Incas, except that they are not so clever, seeing that they were conquered by them, and now live by the rules which were ordered to be observed by the Incas. For in ancient times they were, like their neighbors, badly dressed and without industry in the erection of buildings.

The mighty Inca empire, which Pizarro had conquered only six years before Cieza saw its remnants, had stretched from north of Quito as far south as the Río Maule in Chile, including large parts of today's Ecuador, Peru, Bolivia, and Chile. Its size and wealth, its excellent organization and efficient government astonished all the early Spaniards, who disrupted it entirely and stole it for themselves. While Cieza devoted one of his four books entirely to the Incas (that book seems never to have been published and the manuscript seems to be lost), he has much to say about them in his first book. In Chapter XXXVIII, he says:

> From the accounts which the Indians of Cuzco have given us, we gather that, in ancient times, there were great disorders in all the provinces of that kingdom which we now call Peru, and that the natives were so savage and stupid as to be beyond belief; for they say that these early tribes were bestial, and that many ate human flesh, others taking their mothers and daughters for their wives. Besides all this, they committed other greater sins, having much intercourse with the devil, whom they served and held in high estimation. They had their castles and forts in the mountain fastnesses, and, on very slight provocation, they made war upon each other, killing and taking prisoners without mercy.
>
> Notwithstanding that they committed all these crimes and walked in wickedness, they are said to have been given to religion, which is the reason why . . . great temples have been found where they prayed to, adored, and had interviews with the devil, making great sacrifices before their idols. . . .
>
> While all the provinces of Peru were in this state, two brothers rose up, the name of one of whom was Manco Capac. The Indians relate great marvels and very pleasant fables regarding these men. . . . This Manco Capac founded the city of Cuzco, and established laws for the use of the people. They conquered and dominated over all the country, from Pasto to Chile, and their banners were carried to the south as far as the river Maule, and north to the Ancasmayu. These rivers were the boundaries of the empire of these Incas, which was so great, that from one end to the other is a distance of one thousand three hundred leagues.
>
> The Incas built great fortresses and in every province they had their captains and governors. They performed such great deeds, and ruled with such wisdom, that few in the world ever

excelled them. They were very intelligent and learned without having letters, which had not been invented in these Indies. They introduced good customs into all the provinces. . . . They thought much of the immortality of the soul, and of other secrets of nature. They believed that there was a Creator of all things, and they held the sun to be a god, to whom they built great temples; but, deceived by the devil, they worshipped among trees and on stones, like heathens. In the principal temples they kept a great quantity of very beautiful virgins, just as was done in the Temple of Vesta, in Rome, and the rules concerning them were almost the same.

They chose the bravest and most faithful captains they could find to command their armies. They were very astute and artful in turning enemies into friends without having to resort to war, but they chastised rebels with severity and cruelty.

According to Philip Ainsworth Means, in his monumental, engaging book *Ancient Civilizations of the Andes,* Manco Capac, who came from elsewhere and was married to his sister, passed himself off as a Son of the Sun, and by such means gained ascendancy over the people around Cuzco, whence the Inca empire was to expand in ever-widening circles. The first historic —as opposed to legendary—Inca was Sinchi Roca, a war chief who lived about 1105–40. When the Inca empire fell under the brutal and tricky assault of the Spaniards, it was therefore barely more than five centuries old.

After conquering a territory and people, the Incas forced the newly subjected people to speak their own (Inca) language— Quechua, which is still widely prevalent in those lands—just as the Germans once tried to "Germanize" the French people of Alsace-Lorraine and we Americans, after the Spanish-American War, tried to "Americanize" the people of Puerto Rico by ramming English down their throats. But the Incas seem to have been more successful.

While still dealing with the people near Quito, Cieza wrote:

These and all the other natives of the kingdom, over a space of more than one thousand two hundred leagues, speak the general language of the Incas, being that which is used in Cuzco. They generally speak this language, because such is the order of the Incas, and it was a law throughout the kingdom that this language should be used. Fathers were punished if they neglected to teach it to their sons in their childhood.

Cieza describes the system of settling people of known loyalty
in newly conquered lands, which the Incas employed for subduing and transforming the natives of those lands.

> As soon as a province was conquered, ten or twelve thousand
> men were ordered to go there with their wives, but they were
> always sent to a country where the climate resembled that from
> which they came. If they were natives of a cold province they
> were sent to a cold one; and if they came from a warm province
> they went to a warm one. These people were called *Mitimaes*,
> which means Indians who have come from one country and
> gone to another. They received grants of land on which to
> work, and sites on which to build their houses. The Incas de-
> creed that these *Mitimaes* should always obey the orders of the
> governors and captains who were placed over them, so that if
> the natives rebelled, the *Mitimaes*, who owed obedience to their
> captains, would punish them and force them into the service
> of the Incas; consequently, if there was any disturbance among
> the *Mitimaes* themselves, they were attacked by the natives. By
> this policy the Lords Incas kept their empire safe and free from
> rebellion.

The chronicler wrote again and again of the magnificent system of roads, constructed by order of the Incas for the purpose
of managing their vast empire.

> In the time of the Incas there was a royal road made by the
> force and labor of men, which began at this city of Quito, and
> went as far as Cuzco, whence another of equal grandeur and
> magnitude led to the province of Chile, which is more than one
> thousand two hundred leagues from Quito. On these roads
> there were pleasant and beautiful lodgings and palaces every
> three or four leagues, very richly adorned.

Later, dealing with matters of administration, he said:

> The chiefs looked to large stations, such as Quito, Tume-
> bamba, Caxamarca, Xauxa, Vilcas, or Paria, and others of the
> same rank for orders. . . . Nevertheless affairs of great difficulty
> or importance were not decided upon without reference to the
> . . . Incas. The transmission of these references was arranged
> with such skill and order that the post went from Quito to
> Cuzco in eight days. Every half league along the road there was
> a small house, where there were always two Indians with their
> wives. One of them ran with the news that had to be trans-

mitted, and, before reaching the next house, he called it out
to the other runner, who at once set off running the other half
league, and this was done with such swiftness that neither mules
nor horses could go over such rocky ground in shorter time.[2]

Such was the empire of the Incas which the Spaniards destroyed in 1532. Means characterized it as follows:

> Enormous, variegated, and somewhat feebly held together,
> the empire spread itself over many kinds of country and over
> many types of society. Through the matchlessly logical admin-
> istrative hierarchy which, since the days of the Inca Viracocha
> and of the still earlier Incas, had gradually grown to amazing
> efficiency, society was firmly welded vertically to the person of
> the supreme and absolute sovereign. . . . The flow of author-
> ity was ever from the Inca at the top down through the orderly
> sequence of ranks to the officials in charge of ten families. Each
> official's jurisdiction was an entity answerable only to him, just
> as he was answerable only to the official immediately above him
> in the scale. All power, grace, and privilege proceeded from the
> Sapa Inca. Thus, to capture the person of the ruler was, as we
> shall see, to capture all the authority of the empire.[3]

As stated above, the Inca empire was bordered in the south by
Chile's Maule River, beyond which lived the fierce Araucano
Indians who have never been truly conquered, either by the
Inca armies, by the Spaniards, or by the Chileans after they at-
tained their independence in 1818.

Pedro de Valdivia, the *conquistador* (Chapter IX) who won
Chile for Spain, had relatively little trouble with the native Indians as he made his way southward from Cuzco, through the
Atacama Desert, to Chile's central valley, where he founded the
city of Santiago under much harassment from the Araucanos.
Before he was killed by the latter, he had to fight them almost
constantly for a number of years, during which he wrote his

---

[2] The straight-line distance between Quito and Cuzco, scaled off on the map, is
some 1,050 miles. The actual distance by road must be a minimal 1,200 miles.
The eight days mentioned by Cieza therefore called for relay runs averaging
150 miles per day over extremely rough, mountainous country. The speed approaches that of the U. S. Pony Express, inaugurated in 1860, between San Francisco and St. Joseph, Missouri, run by swift horses and largely over plains country.

[3] Philip Ainsworth Means, *Fall of the Inca Empire* (N.Y.: Charles Scribner's Sons,
1932).

famous five letters to Emperor Charles V detailing his services, his troubles, and his just deserts.[4]

In the Atacama Desert, Valdivia found oasis-dwelling Indians who had already, for about a century, been conquered and ruled by the Incas. The fierce Araucano agriculturalists whom he encountered farther south lived in a relatively primitive fashion but had mastered the arts of war and were determined to maintain their independence. In his letter to the Emperor, dated September 25, 1551, Valdivia wrote:

> Their land abounds with all the foods that the Indians cultivate, such as maize, potatoes, yellow pumpkins, . . . pepper, and beans. The people are tall, fond of their houses, friendly and white, with handsome faces, both men and women. They are clad in wool though their clothes are somewhat coarse. They are very much afraid of horses. They are fond of their children, wives, and houses, which are well built, strong with great planks, and many of them very large and with two, four, and eight doors. They use them for storing food and wool as well as for living. They have many fine vessels of clay and wood. They are great husbandmen as well as drinkers. Their law lies in arms, which they have in all their houses, ready for defending themselves against their neighbors, and attacking the weaker.

The most famous chronicler of the Araucanians was Alonso de Ercilla y Zúñiga, who arrived in Chile in 1557 and spent a year fighting against the indomitable Indians. His admiration for those adversaries came to be expressed in his epic poem of 21,072 lines, called *La Araucana* and published in Spain in three parts, appearing successively in 1569, 1578, and 1589. There is debate as to whether or not that work is true literature or journalistic reporting in a verse which often seems to approach doggerel in quality; there is no debate, among the many scholars who have studied it, as to its accuracy. C. M. Lancaster and P. T. Manchester, who translated the work into English [5] write in their introduction: "The long discussion as to whether *La Arau-*

[4] J. T. Medina, *Cartas de Pedro de Valdivia que Tratan del Descubrimiento y Conquista de Chile* (Seville, 1929). The letters are available in English in the book *Pedro de Valdivia, Conqueror of Chile,* by R. B. Cunninghame Graham (N.Y.: Harper and Brothers, 1927).

[5] Charles Maxwell Lancaster and Paul Thomas Manchester, *The Araucaniad* (published for Scarritt College, Peabody College, and Vanderbilt University; Nashville, Tennessee: Vanderbilt University Press, 1945).

cana is an epic poem or a poetic journal of foreign wars bears today little interest, for the poem stands on its own merits as the first literary masterpiece of the New World."

In Canto I, after eleven verses of eight lines each, devoted to a description of Chile, Ercillo writes as follows about the province of Arauco, the home of the Araucanian Indians:

> At this district's demarcation
> Where 'tis broadest, lies the nation
> Thirty-six degrees projected.[6]
> Costly to itself and aliens,
> Toll it takes of strange usurpers,
> Fetters Chile in straight shackles,
> And with warfare undiluted,
> With sheer grit outrocks the earthquake.

The land seems to have been relatively small. Ercilla writes:

> 'Tis Arauco self-sufficient
>
> .   .   .   .
>
> Twenty leagues contain its landmarks
> Sixteen Toqui chiefs possess it
> Ten and six are lords and chieftains
> Who control the haughty nation,
> Those best versed in art of warfare
> Born of red barbaric mothers
> Bulwarks of the realm incarnate.
> None who governs boasts preferment.
> Other chiefs there are, but valor
> Proves and crowns their choice commanders.

On the training of children:

> As for children, those of talent,
> Those endowed with agile vigor
> Run a marathon of manhood
> Over slopes and stony hillocks,
> And the winner is rewarded,
> From the race at length returning,
> Strong of lung and nimble-footed
> Deer they overtake, unwinded.
>
> Elders, tending passion's vineyard,
> Teach them exercise from childhood.

[6] 36° S latitude.

Veterans drill them in adulthood
For a bellicose profession
They disqualify the weaklings
From the military practice
And bestow on brilliant soldiers
Rank according to their rigor.

.   .   .   .

Weapons used by them most often
Are comprised of pikes and halberds,
Lances, pointed arms long-handled
Of the shape and form of bodkins,
Hatchets, hammers, stout-ribbed bludgeons,
Darts and axes, sticks and arrows,
Rattan lassoes, thongs of osier,
Catapults, and throwing missiles.
Some of these are filched munitions
Seized of late from Christians' clutches.

.   .   .   .

Each brave has one weapon only
Which he skills himself to handle,
One on which since vernal nonage
He has hung his predilection.
He attempts with this one solely
To win mastery; the archer
Is untrammeled with the pikestaff;
Pikeman spurns the bow and arrows.

.   .   .   .

Beardless men, robust of gesture
Theirs are full-grown, shapely bodies.
Lofty chests and massive shoulders,
Stalwart limbs and steely sinews;
They are confident, emboldened,
Dauntless, gallant, and audacious,
Firm inured to toil, and suffering,
Mortal cold and heat and hunger.
Never has a king subjected
Such fierce people proud of freedom,
Nor has alien nation boasted
E'er of having trod their borders;
Ne'er has dared a neighboring country
Raise the sword and move against them;
Always were they feared, unshackled,
Free of laws, with necks unbending.

The East Coast

In general, Indians of the Atlantic coast in what today comprises the Guianas and Brazil were tropical-forest people, related —at least in the forms of their adjustment to their environment— to those of most of the Amazon basin. Assorted into several major stocks and literally hundreds of tribes, those Indians cannot be described either simply or briefly. For instance, Volume 3 of the Smithsonian Institution's *Handbook of South American Indians,* devoted to those people, comprises 986 pages (including a bibliography of 100 pages), and is as incomplete as it is often repetitive. The lacunae result from incomplete available knowledge and many unsatisfactory source materials; the repetitions stem from what Dr. Julian H. Stewart, in his preface to the volume, calls "the comparative uniformity of the Tropical Forest cultures and their environments."

Among the most important of the forest Indians were those of Tupi stock. The so-called Tupinamba, divided into numerous tribes that waged merciless war against one another, inhabited the Brazilian coastal regions from the mouth of the Amazon River to the southern part of today's state of São Paulo, a lordly stretch of nearly 2,000 miles of coast. An extremely interesting and valuable account of their life and customs in the sixteenth century has been left to us in a book published in Germany in 1557, by Hans Stade (at times also called Staden).[7] This man left

[7] The Hakluyt Society volume, from which the following material was taken, gives the author's name, throughout the text and in Burton's long introduction, as "Stade." However, its bibliography, which lists nine editions of the book in several languages (the Hakluyt Society prepared and published the first English translation) published between 1557 and 1859, gives other spellings. The first bibliographic reference includes most of the German title of the first edition, but gives the name as "Standen," in which the first "n" may well have been a typographical error. All the other references, except one, call him "Staden." The exception is the 1714 edition, published in Amsterdam, with a French title, in which he appears as "Jean Stade." The Smithsonian Institution volume mentioned above, gives the full German title of the first, 1557, edition. Not only does the spelling of a number of words in that title differ from that in the Hakluyt reference, but the author's name is given as "Staden," as it is in the second reference in the Smithsonian bibliography and throughout the text, wherever the name is mentioned. The present editor finds that "Staden" is more commonly used than "Stade." However, while bewildered and wishing he could find an explanation for the discrepancy, the editor also has an abiding faith in the Hakluyt Society's translators and editors. The name "Stade" is therefore used here, as it is in the Hakluyt volume.

his home state of Hesse in 1547 and made two voyages to America, the first in a Portuguese ship and the second in a Spanish. In 1553 he was wrecked on the Brazilian coast and captured by Indians. According to the custom of his captors, he was held for some time and treated reasonably well, though always intended for killing and eating. Finally, in 1554, he was ransomed by a French ship and taken back to Europe. The book,[8] which he published shortly after his return to Germany, became famous immediately and went into a number of editions. The book's second part consists of: "A veritable and short account of all the by me experienced manners and customs of the Tuppin Imbas, whose prisoner I was."

Of the houses of the "Tuppin Imba" Indians, Stade writes:

> They prefer erecting their dwellings in spots where they are not far from wood and water, nor from game and fish. After they have destroyed all in one district, they migrate to other places; and when they want to build their huts, a chief among them assembles a party of men and women (some forty couples) . . . and these live together as friends and relations.
>
> They build a kind of hut which is about fourteen feet wide, and perhaps a hundred and fifty feet long, according to their number. . . . They thatch them thickly with palm leaves, so that it may not rain therein, and the hut is all open inside. No one has his specially-prepared chamber; each couple . . . has a space of twelve feet on one side; whilst on the other, in the same manner, lives another pair. . . . The chief of the huts has also his own lodging within the dwelling. . . . Few of their villages have more than seven huts.

After some admiring accounts of the Indians' prowess as hunters and fishermen, Stade devotes a short chapter to describing them.

> They are a race of well-made body and figure, both women and men, like the people of this country, only that they are brown from the sun; for they all, young and old, go naked; also they wear nothing over their sexual organs, and they disguise themselves with painting. They have no beards, for they pull the hair out by the roots whenever it grows, and they pierce

---

[8] The quotations given below are from *The Captivity of Hans Stade of Hesse* . . . , translated by Albert Tootal, Esq., annotated by Richard F. Burton (The Hakluyt Society, 1874); republished 1960 [?] by Burt Franklin.

holes in the mouth and ears, wherein they hang stones, that are their jewels, and they deck themselves with feathers.

The author now describes the stone axes, and tools made of the teeth of peccaries, which the Indians had used before European ships had begun to bring them iron axes and the like. He deals with the processes used in preparing the poisonous manioc to make it edible, processes which can still be observed in many parts of the Amazon basin. He also describes the method for making dried meal from meat and fish. Lasting a long time without salt, that meal, together with manioc, was the warriors' travel ration, equivalent to the pemmican of the North American Indians. "There are many tribes of savages who eat no salt. Some of those amongst whom I was captive ate salt, of which they had learnt the use from the Frenchmen who traded with them."

On government:

> They have no particular government or laws; each hut has a head-man who is their king. For all their chiefs are of one tribe, one command and authority; thus they can do whatever they will. One may perhaps be more experienced than the others in war, so that . . . , when they go to war, more deference is shown to him than to the others. . . . Otherwise I have observed no particular authority among them, than that the youngest observe obedience to the eldest.

On fermented drinks:

> The womankind make the drinks; they take the mandioca root, and they boil great jars full. When it is boiled they take it out of the jars, pour it into other pots or vessels, and allow it to get cool. Then the young girls sit down to it and chew it in their mouths, and the chewed stuff they put into a separate vessel.

There follows a technical account of the manner in which a potent beer, approximately 12 percent alcohol, is prepared from the chewed-up roots. Today it is customarily the old women rather than the young who do the chewing among the Amazonian tribes, and a traveler who has managed to overcome his first revulsions and become fond of the native drink (called *caxiri* in Brazil and *chicha* in Peru), necessarily also develops feelings of real affection for the crones who have so laboriously prepared it.

> Each hut makes its own drink. And when a village wants to make merry with it, which generally happens once a month, the men first go all together to one hut, and drink out there. This is so carried out in succession, until they have drunk out the drink in all the huts. . . .
>
> The drinking lasts through the whole night; they also dance between the fires, shout and blow trumpets; they make a terrible noise when they wax drunk. They are rarely seen to become quarrelsome. They also behave generously to one another; whatever of them has more food than his neighbor, that he divides with him.

Stade now gives much space to vivid accounts of the various ornaments worn by men and women, to their customs of naming themselves and their children, the rare practice of polygamy, and the like. Chapter XXI, five lines long, is headed "What Their Greatest Honours Are."

> They hold in honour him who has captured and slain many enemies. For this is customary among them, so many enemies as one of them slays, so many names does he give himself. And those are the noblest among them who have many such names.

After a long discussion of soothsayers and religious beliefs, Stade goes on to cannibalism:

> Chapter XXV. *Why One Enemy Eats the Other.*
>
> They do this, not from hunger, but from great hatred and enmity, and when they are fighting, during war, one, impelled by great hatred, calls out to the other, *"Dete Immeraya, Schermiuramme, heiwoe";* or "May every misfortune come upon thee, my meat!" *"De Kanga Yuca eypota kirine";* or, "This day I will break your head!" . . . *"Yande soo, sche mocken Sera, Quora Ossorime Rire, etc.";* or, "Thy flesh shall this day, before the sun sets, be my roast!" All this they do from great enmity.

Concerning their weapons:

> They have bows, and their arrow-heads are of bone, which they sharpen, and bind thereon. They also make them of the teeth of a fish, which is called Tibeset Tiberaun [probably a shark], which are caught in the sea. They also take cotton-wool,

mix it with wax, tie it to the piles of the shafts, and set fire thereto; these are their burning arrows. They also make shields of the bark of trees, and others of wild beasts' skins, and they bury sharp thorns like our foot-hooks.

Having himself been a captive, being held for a cannibal feast which never came off, Stade goes into some detail on the treatment of such prisoners.

When they first bring their enemies home, the women and children beat them. Thereupon they paint the captive with gray feathers, shaving his eyebrows from above his eyes; they dance about him, tie him securely that he may not escape them, and give him a woman, who takes care of him, and who also has intercourse with him. And when she becomes pregnant they bring up the child until it is full grown; after which, whenever they take it into their heads, they slay it and eat it. They give him plenty of food, keeping him in this manner for a time; they prepare everything; they make many pots, wherein they keep the drinks; they bake peculiar vessels, wherein they put the compounds wherewith they paint him; they get ready feather-tassels, which they tie to the club with which they kill him, and then twist a long cord called Mussurana, wherewith they bind him before he is to die. When they have all the requisites together, they fix upon a time for his death, and they invite the savages from other villages to proceed thither at that time. They then fill all the vessels with liquor, and a day or two before the women make the drinks they lead the prisoner once or twice to the area, and they dance around him.

Still he is not ready to be dispatched. While apparently getting themselves royally drunk, the Indians continue to decorate the death club, dance, and go through other ritual ceremonies.

Now, as the drinking comes to an end, they rest the day after, and they make for the prisoner a hut on the place where he is to die. Here he lies during the night, well guarded. Towards the morning, some time before daylight, they begin to dance and sing about the club, wherewith they intend killing him, and they continue until day breaks. Then they take the prisoner out of the hut, which they pull down; they clear a space; they take the Mussurana from off his neck; and they tie it round his body, drawing it tight at both ends. He stands bound in the middle, many of them holding the cords at both ends. They let him stand thus for a while, and they place small stones close to him, that he may throw them at the women, who run around him and threaten to eat him. These same are now painted and ready, when he is cut to pieces, to run with his four quarters round the huts. In this the others find pastime.

Now, when this has been done, they make a fire about two feet from the prisoner; this fire he must see. Then a woman comes running about with the club Iwere Pemme; turns the feather-tassels in the air, and shouts, with joy, running before the prisoner that he may see it.

The privilege of bashing in the unfortunate's skull was a great honor. The man chosen to do the deed brandished the club while dancing around the victim, calling out: "Yes, here I am! I will kill thee, for thine have also killed and eaten many of my friends." Whereupon the prisoner was supposed to answer, and probably did: "When I am dead, I shall yet have many friends, who will revenge me well." Those were his last words before being dispatched.

Hereupon the other strikes him on the head from behind, so that his brains are dashed out. At once he is seized by the women, who drag him to the fire, scrape all his skin off, making him quite white, and stop up his posterior with a piece of wood, so that nothing of him may be lost.

There follows a meticulous description of the manner in which the corpse is butchered—apparently with more ritualistic precision than is followed by today's scientific meat-cutters— and the division of the various parts among the feasters. "All this," says Stade, "I have seen and have been present at."

Other Indians

Even the most cursory account of all the various and highly variegated Indians encountered by the explorers of South America would fill several volumes thicker than the present. However, a number of descriptions is found in the chapters to follow. The Indians encountered and described by Columbus (Chapter IV) and Vespucci (Chapter V), along the north coast of South America, were Arawaks, a relatively advanced, seafaring group who also inhabited many of the Caribbean islands (such as Puerto Rico) at the time of the conquest. Their traditional enemies were the fierce, warlike Caribs, with whom Berrio (Chapter XIII) had peaceful encounters on the Orinoco River, and whose raiding and trading expeditions took them all the way to the vicinity of today's New Orleans.

At the other end of the continent, both Pigafetta (Chapter VI) and Darwin (Chapter XVIII) give somewhat conflicting accounts of the world-famous Patagonian "giants," whose size, according to the available literature, ranges all the way from Darwin's approximate six-feet-plus-a-little, to 10 or 12 feet, depending on who did the describing, and perhaps on how much he had to drink. Carvajal (Chapter X), describes, somewhat superficially, the various Indians he and Orellana encountered along the Amazon River, as does Father Samuel Fritz (Chapter XV).

Suffice it here to say that the Indians encountered by South American explorers varied as greatly, one group from the other, as did the terrain, topography and climate. When one deals with a continent like South America, only one generalization can be applied to its physical nature as well as its flora and fauna (including the Indians), namely: *extreme variation.*

⚜ IV ⚜

COLUMBUS "DISCOVERS"
SOUTH AMERICA

BY THE customs of modern history, Christopher Columbus
is credited with the discovery of South America in 1498, in
the course of his third transatlantic voyage. Being personally
unable, or unwilling, to admit anything of the kind, he decided—
and reported—that he had actually located the site of Paradise
and the geographical gates thereto. It must be remembered that
Columbus had offered, and undertaken, to reach the Indies by
sailing west. Throughout his four voyages he held to that aim
with a singular, stubborn determination. His discovery of
America, blocking his way, proved to be a thoroughly frus-
trating bit of explorer's bad luck. He did not *want* to discover
America; he hated to admit that the "New World," which he
did so much to open for exploration and conquest, existed at
all.

As far as South America goes—and quite aside from the fact
that the Indians obviously got there ahead of him—there is now
little doubt and some evidence that the Polynesians preceded
him several centuries by crossing the Pacific to today's Peru.
There is also a growing group of students, diggers, scholars and
writers who maintain that a number of Europeans had preceded
Columbus across the Atlantic to South America by possibly
more than a millennium. Without entering into that fascinating
and at times emotional controversy, the present editor expresses
the personal opinion that it would have been strange if Europe
had in fact waited until the end of the fifteenth century to dis-

cover lands—not too far away and not too difficult to reach—the existence of which had been rumored for thousands of years.

Evidence brought out later in this chapter, which Columbus may or may not have suppressed, indicates that Spaniards may well have reached the South American mainland in 1494, four years before the great admiral reached the continent. However, since those men had been sent on a reconnaissance expedition by Columbus himself, from the island of Hispaniola and in the course of his second voyage, there seems no reason that he should not have claimed and won credit for their achievement, precisely as he was credited with every landfall made by his sailors from the mast tops.

Germane to the present inquiry is the fact that Columbus (or one of his men) certainly was the original discoverer of South America within the chain reaction set off by Europe's population explosion, touched upon in Chapter I. The large extent to which modern scholars and historians, with indisputable *written* proof as their only source material, confine the history of voyaging and exploration to the period of that chain reaction, is the extent to which Christopher Columbus undoubtedly deserves the kudos of having been the continent's unwilling discoverer.

The excerpts given below are from his curiously rambling, somewhat confused, and at times self-contradictory letter to Ferdinand and Isabella, dealing with his third expedition.[1] The letter reads like that of a man who had by then more or less lost interest in his job as an explorer. The bad treatment accorded to him in Spain after his return from his second voyage, plus his unwavering determination to reach Marco Polo's Asian lands, seems to have done something to take the heart out of him. Progressively, in the course of his work, he seems to have acquired serious and disturbing private doubts as to whether he had actually carried out that assignment. After his first voyage to the Antilles he believed—or at least tried to make the world believe—that he had reached islands lying off the Asian mainland. During his second voyage, which took him into the Caribbean Sea, he forced all his men to swear before a notary and four witnesses that they had reached Asia, stipulating heavy penalties

[1] *Select Letters of Christopher Columbus. . . . Relating to his Four Voyages to the New World*, translated and edited by R. H. Major (Hakluyt Society, 1847; republished [in both English and Spanish] New York: Corinth Books, Inc., 1961).

for those who might later, on their return to Spain, go back on their oaths. By the time of his third voyage he must have suspected strongly that he was still far from Japan, China, and India. The nonchalant manner in which he deals with his discoveries on that voyage may well have hidden a strong resentment against South America for being where it was and where Columbus didn't want it to be.

A number of scholars and writers have claimed that he was so uninterested that he didn't even bother to set foot on the new lands which he had discovered. As we shall see later, he seems to contradict himself on that point.

The letter was written in Española—the island of Haiti–Santo Domingo, commonly written "Hispaniola" in English—and was sent thence October 18, 1498, addressed to the "Most serene and most exalted and powerful princes, the King and Queen, our Sovereigns." After some pages of flattery for Ferdinand and Isabella, leading into a recital of his own accomplishments in the course of his two previous voyages, his just deserts resulting therefrom, and the abuse which he had reaped after his second venture, the Admiral wrote:

> I started from San Lucar, in the name of the most Holy Trinity, on Wednesday the 30th of May [1498], much fatigued with my voyage, for I had hoped, when I left the Indies,[2] to find repose in Spain, whereas, on the contrary, I experienced nothing but opposition and vexation. I sailed to the island of Madeira by a circuitous route, in order to avoid any encounter with the armed fleet of France, which was on the look out for me off Cape St. Vincent. Thence I went to the Canaries, from which islands I sailed with but one ship and two caravels, having dispatched the other ships to Española by the direct road to the Indies; while I myself moved southward, with a view to reaching the equinoctial line, and then proceeding westward, so as to leave the island of Española to the north.
>
> Having reached the Cape Verde islands (an incorrect name, for they are so barren that nothing green was to be seen there, and the people so sickly that I did not venture to remain among them), I sailed away four hundred and eighty miles, which is equivalent to a hundred and twenty leagues, toward the southwest. . . . The wind then failed me, and I entered a climate

[2] In 1496, at the conclusion of his second voyage to the New World.

where the intensity of heat was such that I thought both ships and men would have been burnt up, and everything suddenly got into such a state of confusion that no man dared go below deck to attend to the securing of the water-cask and the provisions. This heat lasted eight days; on the first day the weather was fine, but on the seven other days it rained and was cloudy, yet we found no alleviation of our distress. I certainly believe that if the sun had shone as on the first day, we should not have been able to escape in any way. . . .

At the end of these eight days it pleased our Lord to give me a favorable east wind, and I steered to the west . . . on the direct westward course, in a line from Sierra Leone, being resolved not to change it until the chance offered of more speedily reaching land on another tack. This I was very desirous to do for the purpose of repairing the vessels, and of renewing, if possible, our stock of provisions, and taking on what water we wanted.

At the end of seventeen days, during which our Lord gave me a propitious wind, we saw land at noon of Tuesday the 31st of July . . . when one of the sailors went up to the main-top and saw to the westward a range of three mountains. . . . I then . . . put in for the land, [reaching] a cape which I called Cape Galea,[3] having already given to the island the name of Trinidad. Here we found a harbor which would have been excellent but that there was no good anchorage. We saw houses and people on the spot, and the country around was very beautiful, and as fresh and green as the gardens of Valencia in the month of March.

I was disappointed at not being able to put into the harbor, and ran along the coast to the westward. After sailing five leagues I found very good bottom, and anchored. The next day I set sail in the same direction in search of a harbor. . . . When we had taken in a pipe of water, we proceeded onwards till we reached the cape, and there finding good anchorage and protection from east wind, I ordered the anchors to be dropped, the water-cask to be repaired, a supply of water and wood to be taken in, and the people to rest themselves from the fatigues which they had endured for so long a time. I gave this point the name of Sandy Point.[4]

On the following day a large canoe came from the east, containing twenty-four men, all in the prime of life, and well pro-

[3] Today called Cape Galeota, the most SE point of the island of Trinidad.
[4] "Punta del Arenal," today's Icacos, the most SW point of Trinidad.

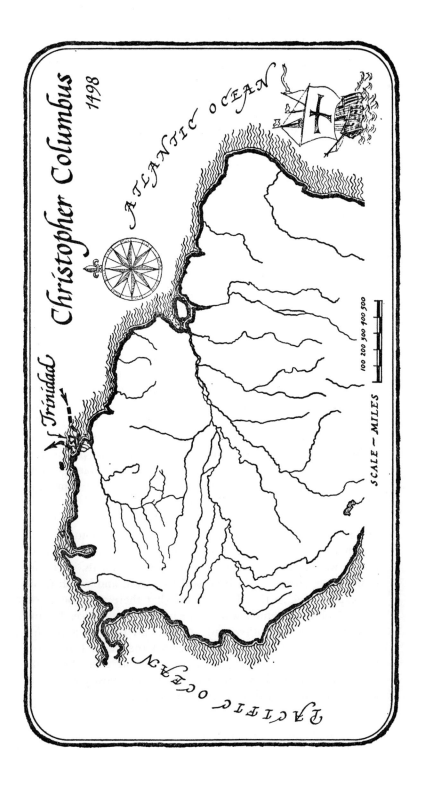

Christopher Columbus

1498

ATLANTIC OCEAN

Trinidad

PACIFIC OCEAN

SCALE — MILES

100 200 300 400 500

vided with arms, such as bows, arrows, and wooden shields. They were all young, well-proportioned, and not dark black, but whiter than any other Indians I had seen,—of very graceful gestures and handsome forms, wearing their hair long and straight, and cut in the Spanish style. . . .

The natives spoke to us from the canoe while it was yet at a considerable distance, but none of us could understand them. I made signs to them to come nearer to us, and more than two hours were spent in this manner. . . . I caused basins and other shining objects to be shown them to tempt them to come near; and after a long time they came somewhat nearer than they had hitherto done. . . . I caused a drum to be played upon the quarter-deck, and some of our young men to dance, believing that the Indians would come to see the amusement. No sooner, however, did they perceive the beating of the drum and the dancing, than they all left their oars, and strung their bows, and . . . they commenced discharging their arrows at us. I immediately stopped the playing and dancing, and ordered a charge to be made from some of our cross-bows.

They then left us and went rapidly to the other caravel, placing themselves under its poop. The pilot of that vessel . . . gave a coat and a hat to the man who seemed to be their chief, and it was arranged . . . that he should go to speak with him on shore. . . . The Indians immediately went thither and waited for him; but as he would not go without my permission, he came to my ship in the boat, whereupon the Indians got into their canoe again and went away, and I never saw any more of them or of any of the other inhabitants of the island.

When I reached the point of Arenal, I found that the island of Trinidad formed with the land of Gracia [the South American mainland] a strait of two leagues width from east to west, and as we had to pass through it to go to the north, we found some strong currents which crossed the strait, and which made a great roaring, so that I concluded that there must be a reef of sand or rocks which would preclude our entrance. Behind this current was another and another, all making a roaring noise like the sound of breakers against the rocks. I anchored there, . . . outside of the strait, and found that the water rushed from east to west with as much impetuosity as that of the Guadalquivir at its conflux with the sea.[5]

---

[5] The conditions described were caused by the flow of water into the sea from the mouths of the Orinoco River.

Columbus was badly frightened by the unfavorable conditions he found in the strait which is today known as the Serpent's Mouth. The next day, however, it "having pleased the Lord to give us a favorable wind," he negotiated the strait safely and headed north through the Gulf of Paria. Without seeing the mouths of the Orinoco, he detected the river's presence: "The men happened at this time to draw up some water from the sea, which, strange to say, proved to be fresh."

> I then sailed northward till I came to a very high mountain, at about twenty-six leagues from the Punta del Arenal. Here two lofty head-lands appeared, one in the east, forming part of the island of Trinidad, and the other in the west, being part of the land which I have already called Gracia. We found here a channel still narrower than that of Arenal, with similar currents and a tremendous roaring of water; the water here also was fresh.[6]

He did not, however, pass through this second strait but sailed "along the coast westward" within the gulf.

> When I had proceeded a considerable distance, I reached a spot where the land appeared to be cultivated. There I anchored and sent the boats ashore, and the men who went in them found that the natives had recently left the place. They also observed that the mountain was covered with monkeys. They came back, and as the coast at that part presented nothing but a chain of mountains, I concluded that farther west we should find the land flatter, and consequently in all probability inhabited. . . .
>
> I weighed anchor and ran along the coast until we came to the end of the cordillera. I then anchored at the mouth of a river, and we were soon visited by a great number of the inhabitants, who informed us that the country was called Paria and that it was more fully peopled farther west. I took four of these natives and proceeded on my westward voyage. When I had gone eight leagues further, I found on the other side of a point which I called the Needle [today Point Alcaraz], one of the most lovely countries in the world, and very thickly populated. . . .
>
> Some of the natives soon came out to the ship in canoes, to

---

[6] The names "Dragon's Mouths" for the entire strait leading northward out of the Gulf of Paria, and "Boca Grande" for one of its channels, were bestowed by Columbus and are still in use.

beg me in the name of their king to go on shore. When they saw that I paid no attention to them, they came to the ship in their canoes in countless number, many of them wearing pieces of gold on their breasts, and some with bracelets of pearls on their arms. . . . Much delighted, I made many inquiries with the view of learning where they found them. They informed me that they were to be procured in their own neighborhood and also at a spot to the northward of them.

Worried because his supplies were spoiling, or "nearly wasted," Columbus wanted to leave as soon as possible, but the sight and thought of those pearls and all that gold held him for a while longer.

I wished however to get some of the pearls that I had seen, and with that view sent the boats on shore. The natives are very numerous and for the most part handsome in person, and of the same color as the Indians we had already seen. They are, moreover, very tractable, and received our men who went on shore most courteously, seeming very well disposed toward us.

These men [the men whom Columbus had sent ashore] relate that when the boats reached shore, two of the chiefs, whom they took to be father and son, came forward in advance of the mass of the people, and conducted them to a very large house with façades, and not round and tent-shaped as the other houses were. In this house were many seats on which they made our men sit down, they themselves sitting on other seats. They then caused bread to be brought, with many kinds of fruits, and various sorts of wine, both white and red, not made of grapes, but apparently produced from different fruits. . . . The men remained together at one end of the house, and the women at the other. Great vexation was felt by both parties that they could not understand each other, for they were mutually anxious to make inquiries respecting each other's countries.

After our men had been entertained at the house of the elder Indian, the younger took them to his house, and gave them an equally cordial reception; after which they returned to their boats and came on board. I weighed anchor forthwith, for I was hastened by my anxiety to save the provisions which were becoming spoiled, and which I had procured and preserved with so much care and trouble, as well as to attend to my own health, which had been affected by long watching. . . . Never were my eyes so much affected or so painful as at this period.

These people, as I have already said, are very graceful in

form,—tall, and elegant in their movements, wearing their hair very long and smooth. They also bind their heads with handsome worked handkerchiefs, which from a distance look like silk or gauze. Others use the same material in a longer form, wound round them so as to cover them like trousers, and this is done by both the men and women. These people are of a whiter skin than any I have seen in the Indies. It is the fashion among all classes to wear something at the breast, and on the arms, and many wear pieces of gold hanging low on the bosom. Their canoes are larger, lighter, and of better build than those of the islands which I have hitherto seen, and in the middle of each they have a cabin or room, which I found was occupied by the chiefs and their wives.

I made many inquiries as to where they found the gold, in reply to which all of them directed me to an elevated tract at no great distance, lying westward on the confines of their own country. But they all advised me not to go there for fear of being eaten. At the time I imagined that they wished to imply that cannibals lived there, but I have since thought it possible that they meant merely that the country was filled with beasts of prey.

I also inquired where they obtained the pearls, and in reply to this question likewise, they directed me to the westward, and also to the north, behind the country they occupied. I did not put this information to the test, on account of the provisions, and the weakness of my eyes, and because the large ship that I had with me was not calculated for such an undertaking. The short time that I spent with them was all passed in putting questions; and at evening, as I have said, we returned to the ships, upon which I weighed anchor and sailed to the westward.

That "we returned to the ships" seems to imply that Columbus himself had after all gone ashore, whereas earlier he had written only about sending a delegation of his men to visit the Indians. It is almost impossible to imagine that he had not personally gone to visit such fine people, living in so beautiful a land. And why did he content himself with merely asking about the sources of the gold and the pearls? Didn't he acquire any to take home as trophies? Had he brought with him no trade goods, no knives, axes, fishhooks, mirrors, or cloth, with which he could undoubtedly have bought both gold and pearls? The editor finds the above account truly baffling.

I proceeded onwards on the following day, until I found that we were in only three fathoms of water; at this time I was still under the idea that it was but an island, and that I should be able to make my exit by the north. Upon which I sent a light caravel in advance, to see whether there was any exit, or whether the passage was closed. The caravel proceeded a great distance until it reached a very large gulf in which there appeared to be four smaller gulfs, from one of which there debouched a large river.[7] They invariably found ground at five fathoms, and a great quantity of very fresh water; indeed, I never tasted any equal to it.

I felt great anxiety when I found that I could make no exit, either by the north, south, or west, but that I was enclosed on all three sides by land. I therefore weighed anchor and sailed in a backward direction [i.e., eastward] with the hope of finding a passage to the north by the strait which I have already described, but I could not return along the inhabited parts where I had already been, on account of the currents which drove me entirely out of my course. But constantly, at every headland, I found the water sweet and clear, and we were carried eastward very powerfully toward the two straits already mentioned.

I conjectured that the currents and the overwhelming mountains of water which rushed into these straits with such an awful roaring, arose from the contest between the fresh water and the sea. The fresh water struggled with the salt to oppose its entrance, and the salt contended against the fresh in its efforts to gain a passage outwards. And I formed the conjecture that at one time there was a continuous neck of land from the island of Trinidad and with the land of Gracia, where the two straits are. . . . I passed out by this northern strait and found the fresh water even there. When, by the aid of the wind, I was able to proceed, I remarked, while on one of the watery billows which I have described, that in the channel the water on the inner side of the current was fresh, and on the outside salt.

There follow some pages of observations he had previously made at sea, about the ocean's nature and the behavior of the stars. Unable to explain those matters, Columbus arrived at a curious concept of the earth's shape.

---

[7] This is a description of the Gulf of Paria. The "large river" is Caño Mánamo, the northernmost of the many branches which flow around and through the Orinoco's delta. Since the Orinoco is a "white water" river, Columbus seems purposely to have omitted mention of all the mud and silt it pours into the sea.

> Ptolemy and the other philosophers who have written upon the globe, thought that it was spherical, believing that this hemisphere was as round as that in which they themselves dwelt. . . . But this western half of the world, I maintain, is like the half of a very round pear, having a raised projection for the stalk, . . . or like a woman's nipple on a round ball.

There follow a number of reports and speculations to support his thesis. Not only had he long had the feeling of sailing uphill as he proceeded westward in latitudes relatively near the equator, but the lands in the west were much more pleasant, their climate milder, and their people lighter, than they were on the African coast at equal latitudes. Such conditions must mean that in the western hemisphere the earth bulged upward into higher altitudes than in the eastern.

Now Columbus delves into theology.

> I do not find, nor have ever found, any account by the Romans or Greeks which fixes in a positive manner the site of the terrestrial paradise; neither have I seen it given in any map of the world, laid down from authentic sources. Some placed it in Ethiopia, at the sources of the Nile, but others, traversing all these countries, found neither the temperature nor the altitude of the sun to correspond with their ideas concerning it. Nor did it appear that the overwhelming waters of the deluge had been there. Some pagans pretended to adduce arguments to establish that it was in the Fortunate Island, now called the Canaries.

Now Columbus places "the earthly paradise" south of the Gulf of Paria, possibly in today's Brazil, near the mouth of the Amazon.

> I have already described my ideas concerning this hemisphere and its form, and I have no doubt that if I could pass below the equinoctial line, after reaching the highest point of which I have spoken, I should find a much milder temperature and a variation in the stars and in the water. Not that I suppose that elevated point to be navigable, nor even that there is water there. Indeed, I believe it is impossible to ascend thither because I am convinced that it is the site of the earthly paradise whither no one can go but by God's permission. But this land which your Highnesses have now sent me to explore is very

extensive, and I think there are many other countries in the south, of which the world has never had any knowledge.

Not that the Admiral, whose determination to reach China, Japan, and India by sailing westward had led him into exploration in the first place, *wanted* any such countries to lie between Europe and Asia. He was obviously worried about the immense volumes of fresh water poured by the Orinoco into the sea, which seemed to indicate the presence of a vast land mass behind the river's mouths. The presence of Paradise might give him an out as well as a means for keeping his great dream alive.

> I think that if the river mentioned does not proceed from the terrestrial paradise, it comes from an immense tract of land situated in the south, of which no knowledge has been hitherto obtained. But the more I reason on the subject, the more satisfied I become that the terrestrial paradise is situated in the spot I have described.

All this part of Columbus' letter is heavily larded with references to scholars, geographers, and theologians, which are of intense interest to students of ancient and medieval thought but would merely clutter up the present summary of South America's exploration. Near the end of his missive, he again begs the sovereigns' help against his enemies and detractors.

Now comes a sly hint about the rivalries between the kings of Portugal and Spain.

> Neither do they [Columbus' detractors] take into consideration the noble spirit of the princes of Portugal, who so long ago carried into execution the exploration of Guinea, and still follow it up along the coast of Africa, in which one half of the population of the country has been employed, and yet the King is more determined on the enterprise than ever. The Lord grant all that I have said, and lead them to think deeply upon what I have written; which is not the thousandth part of what might be written of the deeds of princes who have set their minds upon gaining knowledge, and upon obtaining territory and keeping it.
>
> Although we have not sent home ships laden with gold, we have nevertheless sent satisfactory samples, both of gold and of other valuable commodities, by which it may be judged that in a short time large profit may be derived.[8]

[8] Obviously, he here refers to former expeditions.

There follow a number of paragraphs establishing Columbus' just deserts and expressing his faith that the King and Queen will do right by him. The letter ends:

> And now, during the despatch of the information respecting these lands which I have recently discovered, and where I believe in my soul that the earthly paradise is situated, the *"Adelantado"* will proceed with three ships, well stocked with provisions, on a further investigation, and will make all the discoveries he can about these parts. Meanwhile I shall send your Highnesses this letter accompanied by a drawing of the country, and your Majesties will determine on what is to be done, and give your orders as to how it is your pleasure that I should proceed: the which, by the aid of the Holy Trinity, shall be carried into execution with all possible diligence, in the faithful service and to the entire satisfaction of your Majesties. Thanks be to God.

But Columbus never did carry out his expressed intention of continuing his third voyage after he had "discovered" the South American mainland by sailing through and exploring the Gulf of Paria. So many accusations had been raised against him and his lieutenants that he was sent home from Hispaniola in chains. By the time he arrived in Spain, however, the tide had turned and he was again in popular and royal favor.

In the course of his fourth voyage, with four ships and 150 men, from 1502 to 1504, he cruised along the Caribbean shores of today's Honduras, Nicaragua, Costa Rica, and Panama. Scholars disagree on whether he now, at last, believed that he had reached the Asian mainland or whether he was seeking a strait or passage through the inconveniently located American continent in order to bring his great dream to fruition.

Born some time between 1446 and 1451, the great navigator died May 20, 1506, a broken old man, rich but calumniated and bitterly disappointed.

The Probable Discovery of South America
by Spaniards in 1494

In an article in the *Geographical Review* [9] W. J. Wilson brings to light a letter written by one Angelo Trevisan to the king and queen of Spain, which was first published in that country in 1502 or 1504. While certain points about the letter remain to be cleared up, it seems probable that it is genuine and describes the discovery of South America and the exploration of its north coast by sailors whom Columbus had sent on a reconnaissance expedition, guided by some native Indians of Hispaniola, in 1494. The letter reads as follows:

By an oversight it was omitted, in the story about Columbus, how he sent five caravels from the island of Hispaniola to that neighboring country which they call Cuba, with orders to skirt the coast toward the south and southeast to a certain place where he had information that pearls were found.

Well, setting out and keeping close to land, they went through some intense and awful heat that they could hardly endure, and the water ran low in the barrels, and the hoops burst, so they decided to drop down more to the south and southwest. The farther they got away from the southeast, the more moderate they found the weather.

Just as they caught sight of land, a tremendous rain poured down on them. And the islanders from Hispaniola, who were with them, began to beat and bemoan themselves, declaring that they were lost and drowned. For where they were driving in toward land, all the banks were very steep and high, so that no one could escape. The crew of the caravels asked where these banks and cliffs ended. [The islanders] pointed out a cape where, they said, was the place in which they fished and got pearls. [The sailors] set their course sideways to the wind, or by the bowline, according to our fashion, so that they put that cape to leeward. And those islanders, where they had just been moaning, now began to cheer and show great joy and sing and cheer with their hands and with joyful faces.

Passing that cape, they came to a very good harbor, where two canoes came toward them with six men inside, fishermen,

[9] *The Geographical Review*, American Geographical Society, Vol. 31, No. 2 (April, 1941), pp. 283–99.

who came out to those caravels with pleasure, as if they had been there before, and they gave [the sailors] some of the fish they had caught. They saw on the beach men signaling that they wanted to come out to the ships. One of the ships' boats was launched in the sea. And when it put ashore, many persons came out to the ships, among whom there was one young man with a string of pearls on his neck and on his arms, and from the waist downward he had a covering of colored cotton cloth. And [the natives] gave [the sailors] pearls for little bells and certain other trinkets.

Then, through the interpreters from the Island of Hispaniola, who it seems understand a few words of that language, they said that not very far away there was a very populous village, and that this young man was one of the honored chiefs of that land. There the captain of those caravels decided to send some of his men, who went off with those people. And they went about three leagues and found a very fine village of about 150 to 200 houses. It was made in this manner: all the houses were joined all the way around, with an open square in the middle, and some trees in the middle of the square, where they made abundant shade. The houses were tall, made of timbers, covered around and up to a point, tent-fashion, with palms and with other leaves of trees. There they were led to a house formed in this manner: it was [not] made round, [but] with beams and two rooms; it was remarkably constructed.

And entering, they found an old man of advanced age, who, it was judged, was the father of that young man who came to the caravels, sitting on a chair wrought out of black wood, highly polished; and he had many others brought in, some black and some of various colors. I believe that the black was ebony, and the red ones were brazilwood. And when they were seated, he had twenty young men bring in plates wrought out of wood, and in them many sorts of fruits unknown to me, but sweet, good, and smooth; also bowls or cups wrought of wood, full of wine—not, however, from grapes, but from various sorts of very pleasing juices of fruits—and they banqueted sumptuously. And they talked a great deal but could not understand each other or give answers.

Afterward they went into a room and saw many women sitting on the floor, their shameful parts covered; they were beautiful with blue covering; their heads were combed, with their hair neatly parted. When they saw the old man and us, they all got to their feet and made a gesture of reverence. They took one another by the hand and began to make merry, to dance and sing, beating with their hands, all shouting. From the body downward they were covered with cottons of various colors, and their ears, arms and neck wtih pearls and certain objects— of wood, [the sailors] judged—in squares, in bits and long pieces, strung on their neck and arms. These were shining and well polished, said to look like glass and stones, yet they were nothing but wood, as I have said.

The houses were of timbers, but artfully fashioned with beams of various colors; and likewise the rooms were of boards that were certainly beautiful for a person to see who has had no experience of such things. There were in that square many men who seemed to be from different countries.

Pearls they obtained there in very great quantity. They have certain baskets with which they go down with cords of palm on to the bottom in the water, and with a weight inside, and they go fishing for the oysters just as we do, and they catch a great many, and eat them, and in them find pearls. But because they do not have any means of piercing them, they scatter and ruin them. Yet they are very beautiful "oriental" pearls, of which [the sailors] bought some for little bells and other trinkets and especially for pieces of mirror and bits of copper.

In that place we did not see any metal of any sort. We saw vessels baked from earth, of various sorts, of which [the sailors] took some for their own use. They did not see there any four-footed animal. They [the natives] live on roots made by the trees of the place that was mentioned above. [The visitors] saw millet larger and finer than ours, and panic grass. They saw many fruits and herbs, very good, but unknown to those who saw them.

They live, as I have said above, for the most part on fish and on the containers of the pearls and on flying birds, that is, geese, ducks, and other large birds like peacocks, very handsome, white, and with red necks, handsome beak, feet like the goose, the beak being sharp, pointed; [also] numberless parrots of every sort. They saw forests of the most beautiful trees, unknown to them, except locust trees and wild pines; meadows, very beautiful, which were all green and flowering, and it was the month of October, which seemed to be spring for them; the finest sweet water, and very large rivers. They saw much cotton, which [the natives] took to make themselves caps and to clothe themselves from the waist down.

The men, of light color, with long hair and beards, are of

fine stature, gentle, and show a desire for new things, and this was indicated by signs. And they indicated with the hand that the interior of the country was very populous and had various peoples; for when we asked them about both the chair and the utensils, they managed to indicate by signs with the hand that people came from inside the country and took shells of the pearls—or rather, of the containers [i.e., oysters] and pearls— for their garments. [Those natives] had also some clothes of cotton.

They received perfect hospitality. The day when they returned to the ships, they decided to depart and go back to the captain, Columbus, whom they had left on the island of Hispaniola. They sailed along that coast, where in many places they found the woods so thick that, even if they had wanted to go ashore, there was no way that they could enter. Still from the ships they could see smoke inside the forest, so that they believed there were habitations inside this forest. In certain other places where they wanted to go ashore, [the natives] suddenly fled, so that they had no speech with them or any sign of a word.

They said, moreover, that they sailed along that coast toward the west for 35 days, found beaches, bays, many ports and numerous islands, but did not go onto these because they were worried about shelves and insufficient depth; and they hesitated to approach the shore of the land because of such doubts, except where they saw, in their judgment, that they were safe in approaching the shore at a given place. And with fair weather they returned to Hispaniola, satisfied with what they had found, and especially with the pearls.

This voyage is connected with the third [second] voyage, because the Admiral had sent them on various routes that he might have knowledge of such unknown and unheard of land and people. From their departure to their return was 45 days. In this time they had every sort of weather, rainstorms, winds, and much sea, and also periods of calm with pleasant mildness of air, since it was the beginning, according to them, of their summer season, and [yet] it was in the month of October. They returned to the Island of Hispaniola on the 14th day of November. They said that they had sailed along that coast toward the west for approximately 2,500 miles, from the first glimpse of land that they had. They went to the south-southeast for 12 days, and 35 days to the west. They started from the Island of Hispaniola on the 28th day of September.

The letter has raised a great many speculations, and seems to clear up several "mysteries" which have bothered scholars for years. With regard to Columbus, the editor offers the following thoughts:

1. Columbus' letter about his second expedition, from which he returned to Spain in 1496, two years after the voyage reported by Trevisan, makes no mention of the latter's account. If the Trevisan letter is genuine and factual, then it seems impossible that Columbus did not have the report from his men. If he did, then the omission of it from his letter on the second voyage was not due to an "oversight" but was calculated. Quite possibly the Admiral didn't want his underlings to gain credit for a major discovery, while Trevisan wrote the letter for the purpose of remedying that fault.

2. The similarities between Trevisan's description of the Indians and that in Columbus' letter—the chiefs who were father and son, their entertainment of the Spanish sailors, the wines which were not made of grapes, the cotton turbans and skirts, etc.—are too striking to be ignored.

3. Nowhere in his letter on the third expedition does Columbus mention that he or his men had obtained pearls or gold from the South American Indians—an omission which can only mean that they did *not* obtain them. Since it is inconceivable that he should have failed to obtain such fresh evidence of the wealth of the Indies, the possibility looms that the entire story, quoted above, of his sending his men ashore on a social visit to the Indians was a fabrication, the details of which were adapted from the Trevisan report. Like the other explorers of that age, Columbus was no slouch when it came to claiming credit for himself.

4. After his return to Spain in 1496, he was impatient to set sail again for his third voyage, which was delayed two years through bureaucratic jealousies. The possibility exists that it was precisely the Trevisan report of 1494 which induced him to bear south four years later with a view to personally making the geographical discovery described in that account—which proved later to have been South America.

❧ V ❧

AMERICA IS MISNAMED

W HEN Columbus sailed to America on his second voyage, one member of his crew was Francisco Casas of Seville. Francisco's son was Bartolomé de las Casas, who came to the New World in 1502, where he eventually became a priest who labored so mightily against the maltreatment of the Indians that he came to be called "The Apostle of the Indies." Unable to make headway against Spanish brutality opposite the natives, he entered a monastery, where he spent his time in scholarship and writing. His monumental *Historia de las Indias,* first printed in 1875,[1] came to be highly valued for its account of the early Spanish colonies in America. According to Las Casas, Columbus first sighted the South American mainland August 1, 1498, and thereafter sent an "account of all these discoveries, with a painted outline of the land" to "the Sovereigns." Columbus' report "came into the hands of the Bishop Don Rodriguez de Fonseca, . . . who had charge of all business connected with the Indies." That bishop had a great friend and favorite named Alonso de Hojeda, "and when the report of the Admiral and the map arrived, Fonseca suggested to Hojeda to go and make more discoveries in the same directions as the Admiral had taken."

Hojeda thought it a good idea and got up an expedition, taking with him as many as he could of the officers and men who had been with Columbus on the latter's third voyage. "Hojeda

[1] Quotations from this and other sources, unless otherwise specified, are taken from *The Letters of Amerigo Vespucci and other Documents Illustrative of his Career,* translated, with Notes and an Introduction, by Clements R. Markham (The Hakluyt Society, 1894; reissued 1960 by Burt Franklin, New York).

also took with him Americo Vespucci, and I do not know whether as a pilot, or as a man instructed in navigation and learned in cosmography. For it appears that Hojeda puts him among the pilots he took with him."

This Amerigo [2] Vespucci was an Italian from Florence, a businessman who lived in Spain as representative of one of the great Florentine firms. While the general consensus among scholars is that he was—at least to some extent—an imposter, he also remains a highly controversial figure. The 1960 edition of the *Encyclopedia Americana* not only seems to accept his own account of his "four" voyages at face value, but also says of him: "He acquired in some fashion an excellent practical knowledge of astronomy. He was the greatest expert of his day in the determination of latitude and longitude." The author of the *Americana* article lists a considerable number of references on Vespucci, though omitting several which are at one and the same time the most scholarly and the most critical. While at least one of the references shows quite clearly that the 1497 voyage claimed by Vespucci was never made, the *Americana* article solemnly describes that voyage, which antedated Columbus' discovery of South America. As though in justification, its author says of the account of that voyage that "Vespucci scrupulously gives latitude and longitude." How scrupulously the author *examined* the Florentine's astronomical positions and the extent of Vespucci's alleged expertness in such matters will appear shortly.

To return to Hojeda's voyage of 1499, we find, unfortunately, that Hojeda seems to have written no firsthand account of his voyage; but he later testified at a famous law case, and his testimony is preserved. From such and other sources, Las Casas, as well as the famous writer Martín Fernández de Navarrete (1765–1844), pieced together the main story of Hojeda's voyage. Fernández [3] wrote as follows:

In December 1498 the news arrived of the discovery of Paria. The splendid ideas of the discoverer touching on the beauty

[2] The Italian version, which Markham uses throughout, is "Amerigo Vespucci." Spaniards wrote the first name "Americo." The Latin, from which "America" derived its name, is "Americus Vespucius."

[3] In the Hakluyt volume cited, Sir Clements Markham consistently calls him "Navarrete," as does the author of the above mentioned *Americana* article. His name, however, was Fernández. Navarrete was his birthplace.

and wealth of that region were presently made known, and the spirit of maritime enterprise was revived with renewed vigor.

The first who adventured with Alonso de Hojeda . . . Juan de la Cosa, a great mariner [who] . . . had been a shipmate and pupil of the Admiral in the expedition of Cuba and Jamaica . . . was the principal pilot of Hojeda. . . . Among the other sharers in the enterprise, the Florentine Americo Vespucci merits special mention. He was established in Seville, but became tired of a mercantile life, and entered upon the study of cosmography and nautical subjects, with the desire of embracing a more glorious career. . . .

With such useful companions Hojeda put to sea on the 18th or 20th of May 1499. . . . At the end of twenty-four days they came in sight of the continent of the new world, further south than the point reached by the Admiral, and apparently on the coast of Surinam. They sailed along in sight of the coast for nearly 200 leagues [N] . . . without landing. In passing, besides other rivers, they saw two very large ones which made the sea water to be fresh for a long distance, one . . . which should be the river now called Essequibo in Dutch Guiana. The . . . other . . . may have been the Orinoco. . . .

The first inhabited land seen by our navigators was the island of Trinidad, on the south coast of which they saw a crowd of astonished people watching them from the shore. They landed at three different places with the launches well provisioned, and twenty-two well-armed men. The natives were Caribs, or Cannibals, of fine presence and stature, of great vigor, and very expert in the use of bows and arrows, and shields, which were their proper arms. . . . Thence they entered the Gulf of Paria, and anchored near the river Guarapiche, where they also saw a populous village of peaceful Indians. . . . Hojeda says that they found traces of the Admiral having been in the island of Trinidad, near the Dragon's Mouths, which circumstances were carefully omitted by Vespucci.

Fernández here referred to Amerigo Vespucci's own letters concerning his claimed "four voyages," written five years after the return of the Hojeda expedition and dealt with later in this chapter.

Having passed the mouth of the terrible strait, Hojeda continued his discovery along the coast of the mainland. . . . He continued to coast along from port to port, according to the expression of the pilot Morales, until he reached the Puerto *Flechado,* now Chichirivichi [on the NE coast of today's Venezuelan state of Falcón], where he seems to have had some encounter with the Indians, who wounded twenty-one of his men, of whom one died as soon as he was brought to be cured.

Las Casas and others made much of that incident, coinciding almost exactly with one subsequently claimed by Vespucci in the course of *his* postulated first expedition.

From this place they shaped a course for the island of Curaçao. . . . They then crossed to a land which they judged to be an island, distant ten leagues from Curaçao, and they saw a cape forming a peninsula. . . . Having rounded the cape, they entered a great gulf, on the eastern side of which, where it is shallow and clear of rocks, they saw a great village, with the houses built over the water, on piles driven into the bottom, and the people communicated from one another in canoes. Hojeda named it the Gulf of Venice, from its similarity to that famous city in Italy . . . and we now know it as the Gulf of Venezuela.

This was another discovery which Vespucci was to claim for himself by way of trying to deprive Columbus of the honor of having discovered South America. The gulf is today "Lake Maracaibo," on whose eastern shore there are still pile villages whose rather farfetched similarity to Venice was to give the country of Venezuela its name.

Having explored the western part of the gulf, and doubled the Cape of Coquibacoa [Punta Gallinas], Hojeda and his companions examined the coast as far as the Cabo de la Vela, the extreme point reached on the voyage. On the 30th of August they turned on their homeward voyage for Española or Santo Domingo, and entered the port of Yaquimo [today's Jacmel, on the S coast of Haiti] on the 5th of September 1499, with the intention of loading with brasil wood, according to what Don Fernando Columbus says.

The last-mentioned, son of Christopher and governor of Hispaniola, took a dim view of anybody's doing any exploring in those parts without his special permission. Moreover, he resented hearing about a lot of Spaniards landing on the island without paying their respects to him. Finally, he wanted nobody to load up with the precious dye wood called *brasil,* or with anything else for that matter, since Hispaniola's wealth was his personal property. For such reasons he sent one Francisco Roldan with a body of men to what is now Haiti, to intercept Hojeda, forbid him to load brazilwood, and get his story. He spent considerable time with the expedition, obtaining a detailed account of where it had been and what it had done and experienced. Las Casas and Fernández were later to base their accounts of Hojeda's work and adventures largely on Roldan's reports.

Hojeda remained in the western part of Hispaniola more than two months, stirring up trouble among the Spanish settlers and at one time trying to lead them in a revolt against Governor Columbus, Roldan dogging him, finally causing him to depart for Spain, and sending regular reports to Columbus. In his account, based on the Roldan reports, Fernández added some further information, supplied some years after the Hojeda expedition by Vespucci, to the effect that they explored northward for 200 leagues (800 miles; Vespucci, like Columbus, used the four-mile league, corresponding to the German mile), discovered numerous islands, and seized "232 persons for slaves." "The truth of these events is not very certain," says Fernández, "but it is certain that the profit of the expedition was very small, . . . for, imitating badly the acts of the Admiral, the desire to push on for discovery was greater than that for the acquisition of riches."

Such, in general, is the story of the Hojeda expedition, as it was later pieced together by historians from random scraps revealed by members of Hojeda's crew and by the commander himself. There is no doubt that Amerigo Vespucci was a member in some capacity, but he kept quiet for five years after the expedition's return to Spain. According to his own claim, he was, after his return with Hojeda, invited by the king of Portugal to go to Lisbon to participate in a Portuguese expedition to America, returning to Lisbon in 1502. On his return, he wrote a letter to the head of the mercantile house to which he had belonged, Lorenzo Piero de Medici, giving his account of the voyage. On May 10th, 1503, he sailed from Lisbon on another voyage, returning on June 28th, 1504. According to Markham, in the introduction to the Hakluyt volume:

In the following September he finished writing the famous letter containing the account of his alleged four voyages. The original Italian version was sent to a magnificent Lord, who is supposed to have been Piero Soderini, Gonfaloniere of Florence, in 1504; and a French translation was sent to René, Duke of Lorraine. Soon afterwards Vespucci left the Portuguese service and returned to Spain.

Latin translations were also made of the letters, and scholars have found many contradictions in detail among the various versions. In describing his four alleged voyages, at least the first of which was palpably a clumsy piece of fiction, Vespucci failed to mention the names of the commanders or of any shipmates, so giving the—undoubtedly intended—impression that he, presumably as navigator, had been the explorer-discoverer. By claiming that he had sailed to South America in 1497, he gave the impression—also undoubtedly intended—of having antedated Columbus as the discoverer of the continent which later, unjustly, came to be named after him. The evidence, compiled from many sources by Markham, that the account of his "first" expedition was a fraud, is overwhelming. The first to attack Vespucci for mendacity was Las Casas. Markham writes: "The authority of Las Casas is alone conclusive. Modern investigators, such as Robertson, Muñoz, Navarrete, Humboldt, Washington Irving, and D'Avezac examined the question, and they all came to the same conclusion as Las Casas."

> The matter appeared to be finally settled until 1865. In that year M. F. de Varnhagen, Baron of Porto Seguro in Brazil [and Brazil's ambassador to Peru], published a book at Lima, . . . arguing that the story of the alleged voyage in 1497–98 was worthy of credit.

Varnhagen's book was the one which persuaded the Hakluyt Society to commission Markham to reopen the entire question, with the result that Vespucci again remains accused of having been a liar, seeking glory for himself.

After a flowery introduction, in which Vespucci told how he had gone to Spain "to engage in mercantile pursuits," but "decided upon leaving the mercantile career, and upon entering one that would be more stable and praiseworthy," he wrote that "time and opportunity offered themselves very conveniently."

The king Don Fernando of Castile, having ordered four ships to be dispatched for the discovery of new lands toward the west, I was chosen by his Highness to go in this fleet to help in the discovery. I left the port of Cádiz on the 10th of May 1497 [note from Chapter IV: Columbus didn't leave Spain for *his* discovery of South America until May 30th, 1498], and we took our way for the Great Gulf of the Ocean Sea, on which voyage I was engaged for eighteen months, discovering a great extent of mainland and an infinite number of islands, most of them inhabited, of which no mention had been made by ancient writers, I believe because they had not any clear information.

Since Vespucci has long been so controversial a character, a number of scholars have searched diligently in the voluminous old Spanish archives for some mention, however slight, of that expedition which Vespucci described as having been sent by the Spanish king. To date, nobody has succeeded.

According to Vespucci, the ships tarried eight days in the Canary Islands, whose latitude he gives approximately correctly. After taking on "wood, water, and other necessities," they set sail again.

Our progress was such that at the end of thirty-seven days we reached land which we judged to be the mainland. . . . For we found that the North Pole was above its horizon 16°, and more to the westward of Canaria, according to the observations of our instruments, 70°.

These coordinates would place him at 16° N. latitude and 88° W. longitude. His latitude placed him near the south shore of Guadalupe, about 200 miles north of South America's most northerly extension. The longitude given placed him in the Pacific Ocean, more than a hundred miles west of South America's most westerly cape. And he called himself a navigator! He didn't even take the trouble to look at other people's maps, crude as they were, before committing himself to paper!

We anchored with our ships at a distance of a league and a half from the shore. We got out the boats, and, filled with armed men, we pulled them to the shore. Before we arrived we had seen many men walking along the beach, at which we were much pleased; and we found they were naked, and they showed fear of us. . . . As night was coming on, and the ship was anchored in a dangerous place, off an open unsheltered coast, we arranged to get under weigh the next day and to go in search of some port or bay where we could make our ships secure. We sailed along the coast to the north, always in sight of land, and the people went along the beach.

That "to the north" is bothersome and typical of Vespucci's vagueness. According to his own given latitude, he was already far north of South America. Moreover, the next identifiable place he mentions could be reached only by sailing *west* along the continent's north coast. There follow seven pages of description of the Indians' customs, many of which, since Vespucci came to admit that "we did not know the language," must have been arrived at by the processes of intuition not unknown to travel writers, unless they had been taken from other travel accounts—another custom not unknown to travel writers. Next he had himself coming to a place which he was actually to see some years later, as a member of the Hojeda expedition.

We resolved to depart and to proceed onward, coasting along the land; in which voyage we made many tacks, and had intercourse with many tribes. At the end of certain days we came to a port where we were in the greatest danger, and it pleased the Lord to save us. It was in this way. We went on shore in a port where we found a village built over a lake, like Venice. There were about forty-four large houses founded on very thick piles, and each had a drawbridge leading to the door. From one house there was a way to all the rest by drawbridges which led from house to house. [In the settlement—La Ceiba—which the editor visited on the east shore of Lake Maracaibo in 1931, all the houses were still on piles, connected one with the other, not by "drawbridges," but at least by wooden walks, also built on piles.] The people of this little city showed signs that they were afraid of us, and suddenly they rose all at once.

After a time, the Indians "went on shore, and made signs to us that we should wait, and that they would soon return."

They went straight to a hill, and were not long before they came back, leading with them sixteen of their young girls. They got into the canoes and came to the ships, and in each ship they put four, and we were as much surprised at such a proceeding as your Magnificence will be.

After a while, however, the Indians set up a great commotion, and "a number of people came swimming over the sea and approached us without our feeling any suspicion whatever, having come from the houses." Indians also came in canoes, and suddenly the young girls jumped overboard and swam toward shore.

> As soon as we understood the treachery we not only defended ourselves from them, but also attacked them vigorously and sank many of their canoes with our ships. Thus we routed and slaughtered them, and all took to swimming, abandoning their canoes. Having suffered enough damage, they swam to the land. Nearly fifteen or twenty of them were killed, and many were wounded. Of our men five were wounded, and all escaped, thanks to God. . . . Next day we decided upon continuing our course onwards.
> We sailed constantly along the coast, and came to another tribe, distant about 80 leagues from the one we had left, and very different as regards to language and customs.

Again he is quiet as to directions. Eighty leagues from the stilt villages of Lake Maracaibo—which is the only place in South America where there were such villages—*could* have taken him to the northern edge of Colombia's Guajira Peninsula. He spent a number of pages describing the many Indians they encountered and the Christians' adventures with them. Then he said, "This land is within the Torrid Zone, *under the parallel which the tropic of Cancer describes*, where *the Pole is 23° above the horizon*." The italics seem to have been Markham's. His latitude places him north of Cuba, while he was exploring South America.

> We departed from this port. The province is called Parias and we navigated along the coast, always in sight of land, *until we had run along it a distance of 870 leagues, always toward the NORTH-WEST*, making many tacks and treating with many tribes.

That was one of the most epic voyages ever made! Presuming that he started from the north of Cuba, where his latest report of latitude had placed him, 870 leagues to the northwest took him (by ship) diagonally across the United States to Vancouver, British Columbia. Vespucci now gives long accounts of finding the "finest harbor in the world," of tarrying here and there for

many days to stock up and repair his ships, of visiting Indians
and of one battle which seems significant because the casualties
were almost exactly the same as those reported by Hojeda after
a similar encounter.

> Next day we saw a great number of the people on shore, still
> with signs of war. . . . It was then decided that we should do
> all in our power to make friends with them, and if they rejected
> our friendship we should treat them as enemies, and that we
> should make slaves of as many as we could take. . . . Forty of
> our men landed in four detachments, each with a captain, and
> attacked them. After a long battle, many of them being killed,
> the rest were put to flight. We followed in pursuit until we
> came to a village, having taken nearly 250 prisoners. We burnt
> the village and returned to the ships with these 250 prisoners,
> leaving many killed and wounded. On our side no more than
> one was killed and twenty-two were wounded, who all re-
> covered. God be thanked! . . . We made sail for Spain with
> 222 prisoners, our slaves, and arrived in the port of Cádiz on
> the 15th of October 1498, where we were well received and
> where we sold our slaves.

Such, without Vespucci's many dubious descriptions of the
Indians he encountered, is the account of his "first voyage,"
which had him discover South America a year or so before
Columbus did. Las Casas, after meticulously analyzing every one
of the Florentine's claims, did not hesitate to brand him an outright liar and give the credit for prior discovery to the "Admiral." The consensus is that Vespucci took a number of his
observations from his actual voyage with Hojeda, scrambled
them a bit, obfuscated them, and constructed out of them a
mythical prior voyage by himself, knowing nothing about the
Trevisan report on a voyage dated 1494 (Chapter IV).

Clements Markham has the following to say about Varnhagen's attempt to make sense out of Vespucci's account of his
"first voyage":

> Varnhagen accepts the Florentine's latitudes, and assumes
> that when in 23° N. he was near Tampico, on the coast of
> Mexico. But he rejects the impossible courses and distances of
> Vespucci, substituting an imaginary voyage of his own, by
> which he takes our contractor along the coast of North America,
> round the peninsula of Florida, and to Cape Hatteras, where

he confesses, "the finest harbour in the world" is not to be found.

Such a voyage is so contrary to all of Vespucci's descriptions that Varnhagen's theory is absurd, and the man after whom America came to be named remains the liar who was first openly branded as such by Las Casas.

In his two letters, Vespucci refers often to a book which he had written, entitled *Four Voyages*. Unfortunately, the book seems never to have been published.

The second voyage described by Vespucci in his long letter dealing with all four is obviously that of Hojeda, whose name is never mentioned by the Florentine. He deals with their departure from Cádiz "with three ships, on the 16th of May 1499." He had the date correct, but actually, according to Las Casas, there were four ships. Forty-four days after taking in supplies in the Canaries, they "came within sight of a new land, and we judged it to be the mainland, continuous with that of which mention has already been made. This land is within the Torrid Zone, and beyond the equinoctial line on the south side, over which the Pole rises from the Meridian 5°."

If he had there meant that the equator was five degrees south of them, placing the ships in latitude 5° north, he had them near Surinam, which checks with what is known about the Hojeda expedition. However, later he specifically said that they were 5° south of the equator, which checks neither with known facts about the Hojeda voyage nor with Vespucci's own ensuing account of trouble with an ocean current. At 5° north latitude, he was up against the South Equatorial Current. Moreover, the direction he now gives for their next procedure would have been correct for 5° north, but not for 5° south.

We weighed our anchors, and navigated between the east southeast, coasting along the land . . . and many times we made forty leagues, but all was time lost. We found on this coast that the current of the sea had such force that it prevented us from navigating, for it ran from south to north. The inconvenience was so great for our navigation that, after a consultation, we decided upon altering the course to north [northwest], and we made good such a distance along the land that we reached an excellent port, formed by a large island, which was at the entrance. Within, a very large haven was formed.

This was Trinidad and the Gulf of Paria. But Vespucci, characteristically, failed to mention that Columbus had been there the year before Hojeda reached the place, and six years before Vespucci wrote about it. He described various encounters with Indians, always vague about where he was. At one point, the natives opposed their landing.

> Seeing that they were such barbarians we departed thence, and, sailing onwards, we came in sight of an island which was fifteen leagues from the land. . . . We found on it the most bestial and the most brutal race that has ever been seen. . . . They were very brutish in appearance and gesture, and they had their mouths full of the leaves of a green herb, which they continually chewed like beasts, so that they could hardly speak; and each had around his neck two dry gourds, one full of that herb which they had in their mouths, and the other of white flour that appeared to be powdered lime. . . .
>
> These people, when they saw us, came to us with much familiarity, as if we had formed friendship with them. . . . We walked over the island for a day and a half, without finding a spring of water, and we saw that the water they drank was what had fallen during the night on certain leaves which looked like ass's ears. . . . They had no kind of meat, and no roots as on the mainland. They were sustained by fish caught in the sea, of which they had a great abundance, and they were very good fishermen. They gave us many turtles, and many large and excellent fish.

But Vespucci didn't seem to mind contradicting himself. In the following paragraph he said:

> The island contains many animals of various sorts, and much water in swamps, and seeing that it offered no profit whatever, we departed and went to another island.

The next island was identified by Markham as having been Curaçao—how he did it is not evident—and called by Vespucci "The Island of the Giants."

> We landed to see if there was water, and . . . we came upon very large foot-marks in the sand. . . . Going in search, we came to a road which led inland. There were nine of us. Judg-

ing that there could not be many inhabitants . . . we walked over it to see what sort of people they were. When we had gone about a league we saw five huts. . . . But we only found five women, two old, and three children of such lofty stature that, for the wonder of the thing, we wanted to keep them. . . . They were taller than a large man may well be tall, such as was Francisco degli Albizi, but better proportioned. Our intention was to take the young girls by force, and to bring them to Castile as a wonderful thing. While we were forming this design there entered by the door of the hut as many as thirty-six men, much bigger than the women, and so well made that it was a rare thing to behold them.

The inequality of thirty-six against nine made the whites change their minds about kidnapping children. Somewhat fearfully, they made their way back to the ships, followed by the natives, let go with "two bombard-shots" to scare the Indians, weighed anchors, and set sail.

We proceeded onwards along the coast, and there happened to be combats with the natives many times, because they did not wish us to take anything from the land. At length we became desirous of returning to Castile. . . .

For from the time that we had left the islands of Cape Verde, we had been continually navigating within the Torrid Zone, and twice we had crossed the equinoctial line; for, as I said before, we went 5° beyond it to the south, and now we were in 15° to the north.

Another error. The farthest north reached by the Hojeda expedition along the South American mainland was 13°. After spending about one and a half months with some friendly natives, obtaining supplies and exchanging trade goods for pearls, they set sail for Hispaniola.

Here we took many supplies on board, and remained two months and seventeen days. Here we endured many dangers and troubles from the same Christians who were in this island with Columbus. I believe this was caused by envy; but to avoid prolixity, I will refrain from recounting what happened.

Vespucci now said that they left Hispaniola July 22nd, and arrived in Cádiz September 8th, having both dates wrong according to Las Casas and Markham. Naturally, having already

used those incidents in his account of his "first" voyage, he said
nothing about the Hojeda expedition's encounter with the
Indians of Lake Maracaibo and about its battle with the Indians, resulting in one dead Spaniard and twenty-two wounded.

As stated above, Vespucci now described two voyages which
he made with the Portuguese, on invitation by the king of
Portugal. The first of those two, he described twice, once in
his letter to Lorenzo Piero de Medici, and again in his account
of the four voyages which he sent, in 1504, to "a magnificent
Lord." There are curious contradictions in those two accounts
of the same voyage.

The two accounts agree as to the expedition's approximate
South American landfall, being given as "5° to the south of the
equinoctial line" in the second, and "a point where the coast
turned toward the south" in that of 1503, both of which placed
them at Brazil's Cabo de São Roque. In both versions of the
expedition, Vespucci dealt at length with the Indians encountered, but what a difference he discovered between his two letters! In 1503, he wrote: "They are people gentle and tractable,
and all of both sexes go naked, not covering any parts of their
bodies." Later, he did mention cannibalism, stating, "I was once
in a certain city for twenty-seven days, where human flesh was
hung up near the houses, in the same way as we expose butcher's
meat." Throughout, however, he gave the impression that relations between the Indians and the invading whites were cordial.
By the time he wrote his next letter, the following year, he had
changed his mind.

They saw Indians shortly after their first South American
landfall, and the captain sent two men ashore to deal and trade
with them, instructing the two to remain away from the ships
no longer than five days. They never saw their two messengers
again.

> On the seventh day we went on shore, and found that they
> had arranged with their women; for, as we jumped on shore,
> the men of the land sent many of their women to speak with
> us. Seeing that they were not reassured, we arranged to send
> to them one of our people, who was a very agile and valiant
> youth. . . . He went among the women, and they all began to
> touch and feel him, wondering at him exceedingly. Things
> being so, we saw a woman come from the hill, carrying a great

stick. . . . She raised it, and gave him such a blow that he was felled to the ground. The other women immediately took him by the feet, and dragged him towards the hill. The men rushed down to the beach, and shot at us with their bows and arrows. . . . At last, four rounds from the bombard were fired at them, and they no sooner heard the report than they all ran away towards the hill, where the women were tearing the Christian to pieces. At a great fire they had made they roasted him before our eyes, showing us many pieces, and then eating them. The men made signs how they had killed the other two Christians and eaten them.

In his letter of 1503, he dealt at some length with astronomical matters.

> The sky is adorned with most beautiful signs and figures, in which I have noted as many as twenty stars as bright as we sometimes see Venus and Jupiter. I have considered the orbits and motions of these stars, and I have measured the circumference and diameters of the stars by a geometrical method, ascertaining which were the largest.

Many modern astronomers would dearly like to learn what that mysterious "geometrical method" was. Markham, at this point, added the following footnote: "He may mean their orbits, not the stars themselves; but in either case he is talking nonsense."

His letter of 1504 makes no mention of the "farthest south" attained. But there is a curious statement in that of the preceding year.

> Part of this continent is in the Torrid Zone, beyond the equinoctial line towards the South Pole. . . . We sailed along the coast so far that we crossed the Tropic of Capricorn, and found ourselves where the Antarctic Pole was 50° above our horizon. We went towards the Antarctic Circle until we were 17° 30' from it.

At this point Markham, as editor, made one of his rare mistakes. He thought that the latter figure placed the explorers at 73° 30' south latitude. If his interpretation of the words was correct, the latitude would have been 72° 30'. Either location would have placed Vespucci on the Antarctic Continent. However, he seems to the present editor to have said that they were

17° 30′ north of the *Antarctic Circle,* not of the pole. In that event, they were about at 40° south latitude. Since he had earlier placed himself at 50° south, or just north of the Falkland Islands, he could not possibly have sailed from there "towards the Antarctic Circle," meaning south, to reach a position which was actually 10° *north* of his starting point.

Vespucci's account of his fourth voyage is rather brief, but of the same pattern as was that of the third.

Summing up in his introduction, Markham wrote:

> The evidence against Vespucci is cumulative and quite conclusive. His first voyage is a fabrication. He cannot be acquitted of the intention of appropriating for himself the glory of having first discovered the mainland. The impartial and upright Las Casas, after carefully weighing the evidence, found him guilty. This verdict has been, and will continue to be, confirmed by posterity. . . . But he did not dare to publish his fiction in Spain, and, so far as we know, it did not reach Spain in print until after his death. He wrote well, and his stories about a new world excited the enthusiasm of those who read them. His Latin editor suggested that his new world should be called America, and the name was adopted by mapmakers.

One supposes that, even after the passage of all these centuries, it would be impossible to change the name to honor Columbus as the discoverer, without stirring up a dreadful pother in Vespucci's point of origin, the city of Florence.

❧ VI ❧

THE SOUTHWEST
PASSAGE

T HE westward route to Asia so ardently sought by Columbus
was not discovered until 14 years after his death. While
Spaniards were making their way across the Isthmus of Panama
and inching toward Peru along South America's west coast, their
king and his associates were in no way unconcerned with the
east coast and with the desirability of finding a route to the East
around America, as their Portuguese rivals had previously
found one around Africa. Some seven years after Vasco Nuñez
de Balboa (Chapter VII) had discovered a new ocean from a
peak in Darien, and named it the "South Sea," Magellan saw
the same ocean from the deck of his ship and called it the Pacific.

As Robert Thorne was to write King Henry VIII (Chapter I),
the Spanish authorities were particularly eager to prove that the
Moluccas, or Spice Islands, belonged to them under the terms of
the papal line of demarcation, rather than to Portugal. Ironi-
cally enough, they hired a Portuguese mariner to do the job for
them, a man who was angry at his own king and nation.

Ferdinand Magellan, whose Portuguese name was Fernando
de Magalhães, was born about 1480, of noble family. He served
his country well in India and elsewhere in the East between
1504 and 1512, returning that year to study navigation and sea-
manship in Portugal. In 1513 he was sent on an expedition
against the Moors in Morocco. In 1517 he went before his king,
Dom Manuel, with a petition for an advancement in rank as a
court noble as well as for service as an exploring mariner. When

the king refused him on both counts, Magellan took umbrage, gave up his Portuguese citizenship, and moved to Spain, where he married and petitioned King Charles to be sent on a westward voyage to the Spice Islands, "without touching any sea or land of the King of Portugal." In other words, he offered to prove that the Moluccas actually did belong to Spain. The Spanish king agreed to the proposal, and in 1518 five ships began to be fitted out for the voyage. They were the *Conception*, 90 tons; *Victory*, 85 tons; *St. Anthony*, 120 tons; *Trinity*, 110 tons; and *St. James*, 75 tons. (The names are here given in their anglicized form, as in the Hakluyt volume from which this account was taken.) The Portuguese king's representative in Seville wrote to his sovereign about them as follows:

> They are very old and patched up; for I saw them when they were beached for repairs. It is eleven months since they were repaired, and they are now afloat, and they are caulking them in the water. I went on board of them a few times, and I assure your Highness that I should be ill inclined to sail in them to the Canaries, because their knees are of touchwood.[1]

The same correspondent, Sebastian Alvarez, gave the king of Portugal a full account of preparations made for the voyage, including the names of 16 Portuguese who formed a part of the total of 243 members of the commander's crews. He tried unsuccessfully to talk Magellan out of the project, on the grounds of patriotism. His letter gave the general course which the fleet was to take, and added piously: "Please God the Almighty that they may make such a voyage as did the Cortereals,[2] and that your Highness may be at rest, and for ever be envied, as you are, by all princes."

In Portugal, Magellan was widely regarded as a traitor who had sold out to his country's bitter rival. Moreover, his Portuguese origin was held against him by a number of the expedition's jealous Spanish officers and men, who were to cause him considerable trouble on that account.

The best account of the voyage came to be written by Magellan's navigator and pilot, a Genoese named Anthony Pigafetta.

---

[1] This quotation and others in this chapter are from *The First Voyage Round the World*, by Magellan (Hakluyt Society, Volume 52, Series 1).
[2] Portuguese navigators, two brothers, both of whom were lost in American waters.

Ferdinand Magellan

1519

PACIFIC OCEAN

ATLANTIC OCEAN

SCALE — MILES   0   500

Having manned and provisioned his ships and distributed written orders to the captains of the other four vessels on how to signal to each other day and night in order not to become separated, Magellan set sail August 10, 1519, heading for South America by way of Tenerife. After considerable trouble in the doldrums off Africa, they finally made their landfall at South America's Cape St. Augustine, on November 23. The natives treated them well. Pigafetta wrote:

> The people of the said place gave, in order to have a knife, or a hook for catching fish, five or six fowls, and for a comb they gave two geese, and for a small mirror, or a pair of scissors, they gave so much fish that ten men could have eaten of it. And for a bell they gave a full basket of the fruit named battate; this has the taste of a chestnut, and is the length of a shuttle. For a king of cards, of that kind which they used to play with in Italy, they gave me five fowls, and thought they had cheated me.

On December 13 the expedition entered the bay of what is today Rio de Janeiro. Of the country, Pigafetta wrote:

> The said country of Verzin [Brazil] is very abundant in all good things, and is larger than France, Spain, and Italy together. It is one of the countries which the King of Portugal has conquered. Its inhabitants are not Christians, and adore nothing, but live according to the usage of nature, rather bestially than otherwise. Some of these people live a hundred, or a hundred and twenty, or a hundred and forty years, and more; they go naked, both men and women. . . . The men and women of this said place of Verzin are well made in their bodies. They eat the flesh of their enemies, not as good meat, but because they have adopted this custom. Now this custom arose as follows: an old woman of this place of Verzin had an only son, who was killed by his enemies, and, some days afterwards, the friends of this woman captured one of the said enemies who had put her son to death, and brought him to where she was. Immediately the said old woman, seeing the man who was captured, and recollecting the death of her son, rushed upon him like a mad dog, and bit him on the shoulder. However, this man who had been taken prisoner found means to run away, and told how they wished to eat him, showing the bite which the said old woman had made in his shoulder. After that those who were caught on one side or other were eaten.

They stayed at Rio de Janeiro 13 days. In March, 1520, they arrived at latitude 49° south and put in at what they called Port St. Julian, prepared to spend the winter. They had had contact with the "giant" Patagonians before, and here they encountered them again.

> One day, without anyone expecting it, we saw a giant, who was on the shore of the sea, quite naked, and was dancing and leaping, and singing, and whilst singing he put the sand and dust on his head. Our captain sent one of his men towards him, whom he charged to sing and leap like the other to reassure him, and show him friendship. This he did, and immediately the sailor led this giant to a little island where the captain was waiting for him; and when he was before us he began to be astonished, and to be afraid, and he raised his finger on high, thinking that we came from heaven. He was so tall that the tallest of us only came up to his waist; however, he was well built.[3] . . . When he was brought before the captain he was clothed with the skin of a certain beast [the guanaco], which skin was very skillfully sewed. . . . The captain caused food and drink to be given to this giant, then they showed him some things, amongst others, a steel mirror. When the giant saw his likeness in it he was greatly terrified, leaping backwards, and made three or four of our men fall down.

Magellan gave the giant "two bells, a mirror, a comb, and a chaplet of beads, and sent him back to shore, having him accompanied by four armed men." The escorting Spaniards returned to the ships with 18 more Patagonians, "men and women who brought with them four of those little beasts of which they make their clothing, and they led them with a cord in the manner of dogs coupled together." From time to time they had contacts with other Patagonians, all of them peaceful until the Spaniards decided to kidnap two of them to take them back to Spain as curios.

> Fifteen days later we saw four other giants, who carried no arrows, for they had hid them in the bushes, as two of them showed us, for we took them all four, and each of them was painted in a different way. The captain retained the two younger ones, to take them to Spain on his return; but it was done by gentle and cunning means, for otherwise they would

[3] See Chapter XVIII for a somewhat different account of the Patagonians' stature.

have done a hurt to some of our men. The manner in which he retained them was that he gave them many knives, forks, mirrors, bells, and glass, and they had all these things in their hands. Then the captain had some irons brought, such as are put on the feet of malefactors: these giants took pleasure in seeing the irons, but they did not know where to put them, and it grieved them that they could not take them with their hands, because they were hindered by the other things which they held in them. The other two giants were there, and were desirous of helping the other two, but the captain would not let them, and made a sign to the two whom he wished to detain that they would put those irons on their feet, and then they would go away: at this they made a sign with their heads that they were content. Immediately the captain had the irons put on the feet of both of them, and when they saw that they were striking with a hammer on the bolt which crosses the said irons to rivet them, and prevent them from being opened, these giants were afraid, but the captain made them a sign not to doubt of anything. Nevertheless when they saw the trick which had been played on them, they began to be enraged, and to foam like bulls, crying out very loud Setebos, that is to say, the great devil, that he should help them. The hands of the other two giants were bound, but it was with great difficulty; then the captain sent them back on shore, with nine of his men to conduct them.

The two tied Patagonians managed to get themselves untied. They reached their people, and eventually all of them fled.

Two of these giants being a rather long way off shot arrows at our men, and fighting thus, one of the giants pierced with an arrow the thigh of one of our men, of which he died immediately. Then seeing that he was dead, all ran away. Our men had cross-bows and guns, but they never could hit one of those giants, because they did not stand still in one place, but leaped hither and thither. After that, our men buried the man who had been killed, and set fire to the place where those giants had left their chattels. Certainly these giants run faster than a horse, and they are very jealous of their wives.

Obviously fascinated by the Patagonians, Pigafetta gave a large number of pages to descriptions of them, their customs, and the Spaniards' several encounters with them. Not until that was out of the way, and as though as an afterthought, did he go back to describing the aborted mutiny which had taken place immediately after their arrival at Port St. Julian.

Immediately that we entered into this port, the masters of the other four ships plotted treason against the captain-general, in order to put him to death. These were thus named: John of Carthagine, conductor of the fleet; the treasurer, Loys de Mendoza; the conductor, Anthony Cocha; and Gaspar de Casada. However, the treason was discovered, for which the treasurer was killed with stabs of a dagger, and then quartered. This Gaspar de Casada had his head cut off, and afterwards was cut into quarters; and the conductor having a few days later attempted another treason, was banished with a priest, and was put in that country called Patagonia. The captain-general would not put this conductor to death, because the Emperor Charles had made him captain of one of the ships.

One of our ships, named St. James [Santiago], was lost in going to discover the coast; all the men, however, were saved by a miracle, for they were hardly wet at all. Two men of these, who were saved, came to us and told us all that had passed and happened, on which the captain at once sent some men with sacks full of biscuits for two months. . . . The place where these men were was twenty-five leagues from us, and the road bad and full of thorns, and it required four days to go there, and no water to drink was to be found on the road, but only ice, and of that little.

In this port of St. Julian there were a great quantity of long capres [oysters] . . . , these had pearls in the midst. In this place they found incense, and ostriches, foxes, sparrows, and rabbits a good deal smaller than ours. We set up at the top of the highest mountain which was there a very large cross, as a sign that this country belonged to the King of Spain; and we gave to this mountain the name of Mount of Christ.

Departing thence, we found in fifty-one degrees less one third, in the Antarctic, a river of fresh water [the Coyle], which was near causing us to be lost, from the great winds which it sent out; but God, of his favor, aided us. We were about two months in this river, as it supplied fresh water and a kind of fish an ell long, and very scaly, which is good to eat. Before going away, the captain chose that all should confess and receive the body of our Lord like good Christians.

Discovery of the Strait
of Magellan

After going and taking the course to the fifty-second degree
of the said Antarctic sky, on the day of the Eleven Thousand
Virgins [October 21], we found, by a miracle, a strait which we
called the Cape of Eleven Thousand Virgins; this strait is a
hundred and ten leagues long, which are four hundred and
forty miles, and almost as wide as less than half a league, and
it issues into another sea, which is called the peaceful sea; it is
surrounded by very great and high mountains covered with
snow. . . . This strait was a round place surrounded by mountains, as I have said, and the greater number of the sailors
thought that there was no place by which to go out thence to
enter into the peaceful sea. But the captain-general said that
there was another strait for going out, and said that he knew
it well, because he had seen it by a marine-chart of the King
of Portugal, which map had been made by a great pilot and
mariner named Martin of Bohemia.[4]

The captain sent on before two of his ships, one named *St.
Anthony* [San Antonio] and the other the *Conception* [Concep-
ción], to seek for and discover the outlet of this strait. . . . And
we, with the other two ships, that is to say, the flagship named
Trinity [Trinidad], and the other, the *Victory* [Victoria], remained waiting for them within the bay, where in the night
we had a great storm, which lasted till the next day at midday,
and during which we were forced to weigh the anchors and let
the ships go hither and thither about the bay. The other two
ships met with such a head wind that they could not weather a
cape which the bay made almost at its extremity; wishing to
come to us, they were near being driven to beach the ships. But,
on approaching the extremity of the bay, and whilst expecting
to be lost, they saw a small mouth, which did not resemble a
mouth but a corner, and . . . they threw themselves into it,
so that by force they discovered the strait. Seeing that it was

---

[4] Magellan was here drawing the long bow to quiet his men. The editor of the
Hakluyt volume from which the present account is taken, Lord Stanley of
Alderley, has the following to say in a footnote: "Martin Behaim, who lived at
Fayal and Nuremburg. A globe was constructed at Nuremburg under the in-
structions of Martin Behaim, and given by him to the town of Nuremburg. This
globe disproves the idea that Martin Behaim or his maps had indicated to
Magellan any straits, for the whole continent of America is absent from it."

not a corner, but a strait of land, they went further on and found a bay, then going still further they found another strait and another bay larger than the first two, at which, being very joyous, they suddenly returned backward to tell it to the captain-general. Amongst us we thought that they had perished: first because of the great storm; next, because two days had passed that we had not seen them. And being thus in doubt we saw the two ships under all sail, with ensigns spread, come towards us: these, when near us, suddenly discharged much artillery, at which we, very joyous, saluted them with artillery and shouts. Afterwards, all together, thanking God and the Virgin Mary, we went to seek further on.

After they had resumed their exploration, Magellan, confused by the jumbled topography, again sent the *St. Anthony* and the *Conception* ahead to reconnoitre. Now, however, he lost the *St. Anthony*, which deserted the expedition and headed back to Spain.

The principal reason was on account of the pilot of the said ship being previously discontented with the said captain-general, because that before this armament was made, this pilot had gone to the Emperor to talk about having some ships to discover countries. But, on account of the arrival of the captain-general, the Emperor did not give them to this pilot, on account of which he agreed with some Spaniards, and the following night they took prisoner the captain of their ship, who was a brother of the captain-general . . . ; they wounded him and put him in irons. So they carried him off to Spain. And in this ship . . . was one of the two above-mentioned giants whom we had taken, and when he felt the heat he died. The other ship, named the *Conception*, not being able to follow that one, was always waiting for it, and fluttered hither and thither. But it lost its time, for the other took the road by night for returning.

While the *Conception* was fluttering hither and thither, Magellan, with the two ships left under his immediate command, continued his explorations and rediscovered the strait which they had lost. "We arrived at a river which we named the River of Sardines, because we found a great quantity of them. So we remained there four days to wait for the other two ships." It was during this time that the outlet to the Pacific Ocean was discovered.

A short time after we sent a boat well supplied with men and provisions to discover the cape of the other sea: these remained three days in going and coming. They told us that they had found the cape, and the sea great and wide. At the joy which the captain-general had at this he began to cry, and he gave the name of Cape of Desire [Cabo Deseado] to this cape, as a thing which had been much desired for a long time.

Having done that we turned back to find the other two ships which were at the other side, but we only found the *Conception,* of which ship we asked what had become of her companion. To this the captain of the said ship . . . replied that he knew nothing of her, and that he had never seen her since she entered the mouth. However, we sought for her through all the strait, as far as the said mouth, by which she had taken her course to return. Besides that, the captain-general sent back the ship named the *Victory* as far as the entrance of the strait to see if the ship was there, and he told the people of this ship that if they did not find the ship they were looking for, they were to place an ensign on the summit of a small hill, with a letter inside a pot placed in the ground near the ensign, so that if the ship should by chance return, it might see the ensign, and also find the letter which would give information of the course which the captain was holding. . . . So the people of the said ship did what the captain had commanded them, and more, for they set two ensigns with letters; one of the ensigns was placed on a small hill at the first bay, the other on an islet in the third bay, where there were many sea wolves and large birds. . . .

If we had not found this strait the captain had made up his mind to go as far as seventy-five degrees toward the antarctic pole; where at that height in the summer time there is no night, or very little: in a similar manner in the winter there is no day-light, or very little, and so that every one may believe this, when we were in this strait the night lasted only three hours, and this was in the month of October.

We called this strait Pathagonico [today, Strait of Magellan]. In it we found at every half league a good port and place for anchoring, good waters, wood all of cedar, and fish like sardines, *missiglioni* [mussels ?], and a very sweet herb named *apio* [celery]. . . . This herb grows near the springs, and from not finding anything else we ate of it for several days. I think that there is not in the world a more beautiful country, or a better strait than this one.

Pigafetta had evidently gotten on very good terms with the remaining of the two kidnapped Patagonians, who gave him a long list of Patagonian words which Pigafetta recorded with their Spanish equivalents.

> When he saw me write these names after him, and ask for others he understood [what I was doing] with my pen in my hand. Another time I made a cross and kissed it in showing it to him; but suddenly he exclaimed Setebos [Devil]! and made signs to me that if I again made the cross it would enter into my stomach and make me die. When this giant was unwell he asked for the cross, and embraced and kissed it much, and he wished to become a Christian before his death, and we named him Paul.

The explorers left the strait and entered the Pacific on Wednesday, November 28, 1520. Heading in general northwest, they encountered good weather but terrible hardships, remaining "three months and twenty days without taking in provisions or other refreshments."

> We ate old biscuit reduced to powder, and full of grubs, and stinking from the dirt which the rats had made on it when eating the good biscuit, and we drank water that was yellow and stinking. We also ate the ox-hides which were under the main-yard, so that the yard should not break the rigging: they were very hard on account of the sun, rain, and wind, and we left them for four or five days in the sea, and then we put them a little on the embers, and so ate them; also the sawdust of wood, and rats which cost half-a-crown each, moreover, enough of them were not to be got. Besides the above-named evils, this misfortune which I will mention was the worst, it was that the upper and lower gums of most of our men grew so much that they could not eat,[5] and in this way so many suffered that nineteen died, and the other giant, and an Indian from the country of Verzin. Besides those who died, twenty-five or thirty fell ill of divers sicknesses, both in the arms and legs, and other places, in such manner that very few remained healthy. However, thanks be to the Lord, I had no sickness.

The expedition reached the Philippines March 16th, stocked up on food and water, and sailed on. Magellan was killed in a

[5] The editor of the Hakluyt volume here adds a footnote: "Effects of scurvy. Gama's seamen suffered in the same way, after passing the Cape of Good Hope."

fight with the natives at Cebu. The *Conception* was abandoned and burned at the island of Bohol because not enough men were left to manage three ships. They were now in Portuguese waters and were attacked by Portuguese and natives alike. The *Trinity,* grown old, clumsy and leaky, was abandoned with her crew. The *Victory* set sail across the Indian Ocean with a captain and 60 men, 47 of them Spaniards and 13 natives. Of the 60 men, some died of disease, some were killed as punishment for one misdeed or another, some were killed by natives. Finally, on Monday, September 8th, the *Victory* reached Seville after a voyage that had lasted almost three years. Of the five ships and 243 men that had originally left that city, one ship and 18 men returned. But the *Victory* carried a cargo of cloves which sold for more than enough to defray the cost of the entire venture.

❧ VII ❧

SOUTH FROM PANAMA

AFTER Columbus' first voyage, the Spaniards overran large areas of the New World with astonishing speed and energy. They colonized Hispaniola (Haiti and Santo Domingo) in 1493, Puerto Rico in 1508, and Cuba two years later. Hispaniola became not only the center of regional government, but also a way station and point of departure for further expeditions. Panama was first explored by a European—Rodrigo de Galván Bastidas—in 1501, and revisited the following year by Columbus in the course of his fourth and last voyage to America. In 1510, Diego de Nicuesa founded the settlement of Nombre de Dios on Panama's north coast, departing shortly thereafter to be killed by Indians. A few years later plans began to be formulated for the conquest of Peru. Philip Ainsworth Means wrote as follows in 1932:

> When, in 1513, the first real step towards the Spanish conquest of Peru was taken, Spain had been acquainted with America during some twenty years, each of which had seen a considerable increase in the sum of geographical knowledge brought home by Columbus and other emissaries of the Crown of Castile. The incident destined to lead up to the first real step in question took place on the Atlantic side of the Isthmus of Panama. It befell thus: Vasco Nuñez de Balboa, a young gentleman-adventurer of respectable abilities and, on the whole, of good character, was supervising the weighing-out of some gold recently found among the Indians by his soldiers. A youthful Indian chief named Panciaco, who was looking on, was astonished by the, to him, abnormal interest of the strangers in every-

89

thing relating to gold and, moved perhaps by some idea of ridding his own bailiwick of of their presence, he told them of vague rumors which had reached him concerning a mysterious land far in the south where gold in huge quantities was to be found.

This hint presently led Nuñez de Balboa to turn his steps southwards in company with about 190 soldiers—among whom was numbered one Francisco Pizarro—and with a number of Indian servitors and auxiliaries. . . . At length, . . . after sundry adventures with the natives, the weary explorers reached, on September 25th, 1513, a mountain-top whence they could see the southern ocean of which they had heard. Four days later they were on its shore, and Nuñez de Balboa was wading in its waters, brandishing a banner and a sword and taking possession of it for his king. . . . Very soon thereafter confirmation of Panciaco's words was given by two chiefs on the southern shore of the Isthmus. . . . The wanderers were convinced that at last they were on the track of something really worthwhile.[1]

Balboa, whose name was Nuñez though he is commonly called Balboa, had taken charge of the Darien colony upon its abandonment by its founder, Nicuesa. While he was apparently an excellent ruler and an exceptionally energetic explorer, he made many enemies, some of whom carried slanderous tales about him to Spain. His crossing of the Isthmus and discovery of the South Sea—which continued to be so called long after it was renamed the Pacific by Magellan in 1520—seem to have been undertaken as a last-minute effort to gain royal favor. But the effort was made too late. When he returned to the north coast he received word that a new governor, Don Pedro Arias de Avila —usually called Pedrarias—was en route from Spain to take over the governorship of Darien. Means writes:

> Pedrarias, a thoroughly objectionable old man, arrived in Darien or Panama on June 30th, 1514, bringing with him some 1,500 young blades eager for wild adventure and for sudden wealth. The little colony, thus violently inflated in numbers, soon fell prey to terrible famine so that, in less than a month, some 700 men died of hunger.

Writing in 1865, Clements R. Markham said:

[1] Philip Ainsworth Means, *Fall of the Inca Empire* (N.Y.: Charles Scribner's Sons 1932).

Pedrarias was accompanied by many learned clerks and gallant knights. Among them were Quevedo the bishop, Oviedo the future historian, Enciso the learned geographer and spiteful enemy of Vasco Nuñez, Espinosa the subtle lawyer, Benalcazar the destined conqueror of Quito, Hernando de Soto the discoverer of the Mississippi, and Pascual de Andagoya.[2]

Andagoyas' narrative begins:

In the year 1514 Pedrarias de Avila, who had been appointed governor of the mainland called Castilla de Oro, by the Catholic king of glorious memory, embarked in Seville, with nineteen ships and fifteen hundred men—the most distinguished company that had yet set out from Spain.

After recounting several adventures with cannibal Indians on the island of Dominica and elsewhere, he wrote:

Continuing his voyage, he arrived at a province called Darien, which is at the end of the gulf of the same name. Here he found a certain quantity of Spaniards, who had Vasco Nuñez de Balboa for their captain and alcalde mayor.

The author now gives an account of certain historic events before Pedrarias' arrival as well as of the famine which killed seven hundred Spaniards in one month. Then he goes on to Balboa's journey to the South Sea.

It was but a short time since Vasco Nuñez had reached a point near the South Sea where he had seen it. The captains and troops who went forth in that direction, where the country is healthier and more peopled, brought back great troops of captive natives in chains, and all the gold they could lay their hands on [apparently after Balboa had blazed the trail]. This state of things continued for nearly three years. The captains divided the captive Indians among the soldiers, and brought the gold to Darien. . . . In this manner the land suffered for a distance of more than a hundred leagues from Darien. All the people who were brought there, and there was a great multitude, were immediately sent to the gold

2 From the Introduction to *Narrative of the Proceedings of Pedrarias Davila*, by the Adelantado Pascual de Andagoya, translated and edited, with notes and an introduction, by Clements R. Markham (London: The Hakluyt Society, 1st series, No. 34, 1865).

mines . . . ; and as they had come from a great distance, and
were worn out and broken down by the great burdens they had
to carry, and as the climate was different from their own, and
unhealthy, they all died. In these transactions the captains never
attempted to make treaties of peace, nor to form settlements,
but merely to bring Indians and gold to Darien, and waste
them there.

After describing the conquest of the provinces of Careta and
Acla in the eastern part of Panama, the chronicler mentions the
first Spanish navigation of the Pacific Ocean.

At this time a captain named Gaspar de Morales set out to
discover the South Sea, and he went out on it as far as the
Islands of the Pearls [in the Gulf of Panama], where the lord
was friendly and gave him rich pearls.

In a footnote, however, quoting Balboa, Markham described
the terrible atrocities practiced by the Spaniards on the Indians.

On his return he murdered the Indians, stole their women,
and caused twenty chiefs to be torn to pieces by his dogs. . . .
He afterwards seized many Indian men and women on this rich
island, and sold them as slaves at Darien, without any conscience.

Francisco Pizarro served as second in command in this infamous expedition of Morales. The invaders entered the territory of the Cacique Birú, whose name supplied the Spaniards
with an erroneous designation for the great empire of the Incas.
It was here, possibly, that Pizarro first heard faint rumors respecting the scene of his future conquest, and here Andagoya
afterwards collected fuller information on the same subject.

After some pages of description of the Indians in eastern
Panama, Andagoya touches on the subject of Christianity.

Wishing to know whether these people had any notion of
God, I learned that they knew of the flood of Noah, and they
said that he escaped in a canoe with his wife and sons; and
that the world had been peopled by them. They believed that
there was a God in heaven, whom they called *Chipiripa,* and
that he caused the rain and sent down the other things which
fall from heaven. . . . There was a principal woman of this
land who said that there was a belief among the chiefs (for the

common people do not talk of these things), that there is a
beautiful woman with a child in heaven; but the story goes no
further.

In 1516, Andagoya was to accompany Vasco Nuñez de Balboa
on another crossing of the Isthmus, this time a laborious undertaking to carry two ships to the Pacific in pieces and reassemble
them on the other side for the exploration of the South Sea.
Pedrarias and the unfortunate Balboa had had several serious
quarrels, but in the end the disreputable governor promised the
other his daughter in marriage, "who was then in Spain."

Having thus received Vasco Nuñez as his son-in-law, Pedrarias
sent him to the province of Acla [at the east end of today's
Panama] to form a settlement. . . . Thence Vasco Nuñez sent
people to the Río de la Balsa, and made two ships, that he
might embark on the South Sea, and discover what there might
be in it.

. . . In this river we made two ships; and we brought many
Indians to Acla, to carry the materials for the ships, and the
food for the carpenters and other workmen. [Markham states
in a footnote that as many as five hundred Indians died in this
service.] We conveyed these ships down to the sea [on the other
side of the Isthmus] with great labor, for we met with many
torrents forming hollows which we had to cross. Having got
down to the Gulf of San Miguel, there was a high tide, and,
as the carpenters did not know the wood, it proved to be such
that all the planks were eaten through and honeycombed. Thus
there was much trouble before we could pass in the ships to
the Islands of Pearls, where they came to pieces, and we made
others of good timber, which were larger and better.

Vasco Nuñez was to be absent on this expedition for a year
and a half, at the end of which time he was to send an account
of what he had done to the governor. . . .

As Vasco Nuñez had never paid much respect to the officials,
nor sent them any of the Indians that he had captured, as the
other captains did, they bore him no good will, and they said
to the governor that he had rebelled. They persuaded the
governor to go to Acla, that he might get news of Vasco Nuñez
and send for him, and the officials accompanied the governor.

At this time Vasco Nuñez, having built the ships, came to the
Gulf of San Miguel, where he remained for two months, seizing
Indians and sending them to Acla for more cordage or pitch,

which were required for the ships. Here we received news that
Lope de Sosa had been appointed in Castile to come out to
this land as governor.

Alarmed, Balboa sent a small force of Spaniards to Acla with
the Indians, instructed to check the rumor, and, if it turned out
to be true, to return to the Gulf of San Miguel posthaste. Determined to sail south toward the land of Peru about which everybody had heard by now, the great Nuñez de Balboa wanted to
take no chances on some new governor's calling off the expedition. But the man he had sent to Acla for information was
apprehended as a spy. The officials around Pedrarias accused
Balboa of rebellion and persuaded the governor to send for him
and arrest him. The man sent to do the arresting was Francisco
Pizarro, who undoubtedly had his own mind and heart set on
the conquest of Peru and was glad to eliminate a rival. In Acla
a process was drawn up against Balboa and three others. All
four were beheaded in 1517, when the discoverer of the Pacific
Ocean was forty-two years old.

Pedrarias now took Nuñez' two ships and sailed for the
Islands of the Pearls "with all the troops that were at Acla."

The ships were there, with the people who had remained in
the South Sea. Thence he went in the ships to Panama, where
he founded the present city, the rest of the people going round
by land with the licentiate Espinosa. The governor divided the
land amongst the four hundred citizens who then settled in
Panama, leaving a certain portion of the province of Cueva for
the citizens of Acla. But as the captains, who had made many
incursions into the country from Darien, had carried off great
numbers of Indians, and as the land was of small extent from
one sea to the other, there were very few Indians at the time
that the land was divided, and the governor could give only
ninety Indians, in *repartimiento* [allotment], or fifty or forty.
And as each cacique had to give nearly all his Indians, who
were required to till the ground and to build houses, and as
those that remained were taken off to the gold mines, where
they died, in a short time neither chiefs nor Indians were to
be found in all the land.

Panama was founded in the year 1519, . . . and at the end
of that year a certain captain named Diego Alvites founded
Nombre de Dios [on the Atlantic coast near the site of today's

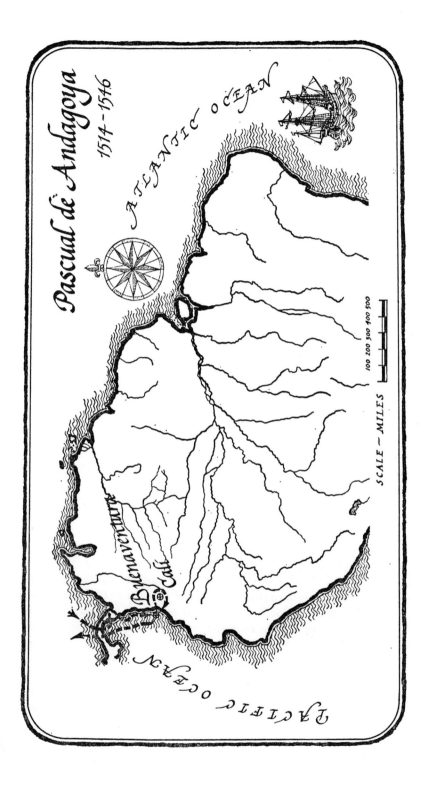

Pascual de Andagoya
1514–1546

ATLANTIC OCEAN

PACIFIC OCEAN

Buenaventura

Cali

SCALE — MILES

100 200 300 400 500

Colón] [3] by order of Pedrarias. In Nombre de Dios there was a certain race of people called *Chuchures,* with a language different from that of the other Indians. They came to settle in this place in canoes from Honduras, and as the country was unhealthy their numbers decreased, and there were few of them. Of these few none survived the treatment they received after Nombre de Dios was founded.

Andagoya now gives an account of an expedition, which he seems to have accompanied, toward the west and as far as Nicaragua—another greedy slaving and looting venture in which the Christians seem to have suffered considerable—well-deserved—damage from the fighting Indians. In the end, however, they were successful—to a certain extent.

From this expedition we returned to Darien with a great number of persons, so that, in order to make a day's journey of three or four leagues, we had to cut two roads for the people to pass along. These people, with all the others who went to Darien, ended their days there. It was seen that in Darien there were no Indians, unless they were brought from other distant provinces; and as they all died there, the settlement was moved to Acla, and thus Darien was abandoned.

There follow more accounts of the conquest and settlement of Nicaragua, of which land Pedrarias was eventually appointed governor, fortunately—for all concerned—to die in 1530. Then the chronicler gets around to the question of Peru.

In the year 1522, being inspector of the Indians, I set out from Panama to visit the surrounding territory to the eastward. . . . [He mentions "a province called Birú, the name of which has been corrupted to Pirú," and describes defeating its soldiers in battle.] After this defeat and the capture of the fort, the people did not dare show themselves in arms again; but several chiefs came to treat for peace, and went through the acts and ceremonies which are required from those who become vassals of his Majesty. Afterwards others came; and seven important chiefs became friendly, among whom one of them was like a king over the others, and was recognized as such by them all.

In this province I received accounts both from the chiefs and from the merchants and interpreters, concerning all the coast,

---

[3] Andagoya seems to have been mistaken here. Nombre de Dios was founded in 1510 by Diego de Nicuesa.

and everything that has since been discovered, as far as Cuzco;
especially with regard to the inhabitants of each province, for
in their trading these people extend their wanderings over
many lands. Taking new interpreters, and the principal chief
of that land, who wished of his own accord to go with me
and show me other provinces of the coast which obeyed him,
I descended to the sea. The ships followed the coast at some
little distance from the land, while I went close in, in a canoe,
discovering the ports. While thus employed I fell into the water,
and if it had not been for the chief, who took me in his arms
and took me on the canoe, I should have been drowned. I remained in this position until a ship came to succour me, and
while they were helping the others, I remained for two hours
wet through. What with the cold air and the quantity of water
I had drunk, I was laid up next day, unable to turn. Seeing
that I could not now conduct the discovery along the coast in
person, and that the expedition would thus come to an end,
I resolved to return to Panama with the chief and interpreters
who accompanied me, and report the knowledge I had acquired
of all that land.

So ended the first Spanish venture southward along the Pacific
coast of Colombia, and so, also, ended Andagoya's high hope of
being the discoverer and conqueror of Peru, reports of which
had already begun to inflame men's minds, as its eventual discovery was destined to set off the frantic, centuries-long search
for El Dorado.

As soon as Pedrarias heard the great news which I had
brought, he was also told by the doctors that time alone
could cure me, and in truth it was fully three years before I was
able to ride on horseback. He therefore asked me to hand over
the undertaking to Pizarro, Almagro, and Father Luque, who
were partners, in order that so great a discovery might be followed up, and, he added, that they would repay me for what I
had expended. I replied that, so far as the expedition was
concerned, I must give it up, but that I did not wish to be paid,
because if they paid me my expenses they would not have
sufficient to commence the business, for at that time they had
not more than sixty dollars.

Accordingly, these three, and Pedrarias, which made four,
formed a company, each partner taking a fourth share. Guided
by the narrative and the interpreters given them by me, they
set out on the expedition with a ship and two canoes.

At this point, Clements Markham adds a footnote: "The agreement between the partners was dated March 10th, 1526. Pizarro and Almagro could not write. One Juan de Panes signed for Pizarro, and Alvaro de Quiro for Almagro. When Pedrarias was superseded (as governor of Panama), he retired from the partnership, to which he had never contributed a farthing."

Andagoya goes on with his own account of Pizarro's four years of groping, fighting, exploring down the South American coast, as far as the island of Gallo, a small island at about 2° N, near today's Tumaco, Colombia.

> At this time, Pedro de los Ríos came to Panama as governor, who, moved by avarice, wished to displace Pizarro from the command of the expedition, and he sent a captain in search of him. The captain found the followers of Pizarro at Gallo, and he took them back, Pedro de los Ríos having ordered that they should return to Panama.
>
> Pizarro, seeing himself ruined by this, determined to remain there with ten men [actually thirteen] who wished to accompany him. He sent the vessels, with only sailors on board, to search the coast ahead, and they reached as far as a land which was level and open. The vessels returned to the island of Gallo, where Pizarro had been for seven or eight months. Pizarro then sailed along this coast in the vessel, and discovered Tumbez and Payta.

The next fifteen pages of Andagoya's chronicle contain his secondhand, but surprisingly accurate, account of the conquest of Peru, the nature of the Inca empire, and the disputes between the *conquistadores* of that land.

For some reason, Andagoya's Panamanian property was taken away from him in 1536, and he was sent to Spain in disgrace. However, according to Markham, "he was eventually acquitted and honored with favours by the Emperor, for his long and faithful services." Later, Markham's introduction reads: "Andagoya happened to be at the Spanish court in 1538, when news arrived of the death of the licentiate Gaspar de Espinosa at Cuzco, who had been appointed Governor of New Castile. The government of this territory was, therefore, granted to Andagoya. . . . His new government was to extend along the Pacific coast from the Gulf of San Miguel on the isthmus to the river of San Juan; but, unfortunately, its inland boundary was not defined." Andagoya now fitted out an expedition and embarked for further explorations and conquests, which were to take him into Colombia from the Pacific side.

I started from Toledo in the year 1538, and embarked at San Lúcar in the beginning of 1539, taking sixty men with me from Spain. I arrived at Nombre de Dios on the day of San Juan, and began to prepare my expedition to Panama, having collected two hundred men. I was thus engaged until the 15th of February, having made three ships and two brigantines. I left Panama on the 15th of February, and, doubling Cape Corrientes [on the coast of today's Colombia], sailed along the coast as far as the island of Palmas [off Colombia, about 4° N], where I disembarked all the men and horses. I found here five Indian huts, with some maize.

He sent the brigantines "to seek inhabited parts."

Eight leagues from this island, the port of Buenaventura was discovered, and a road descended through a very dense forest to the sea, by which the Indians came to get salt. The Indians came down by these forest-covered mountains, which are the highest and the most rugged that have been seen in the Indies. Leaving fifty men with the ships, I entered this road with all the rest of the men and horses, which I conveyed to a distance of nine leagues from the sea with great labor; but from that point onwards the country was and is so rugged that many dogs, not being able to go on with the men, returned to the sea.

At a distance of fourteen leagues from the sea I came to a province called Atanzeta, a very rugged country, but well peopled. The Indians came out prepared for war, but as we gave no occasion for it, and entered their villages without seizing or robbing anyone, they all became friendly. Here I learned that, in a province called Lili [the Cauca Valley] ten leagues further on, there was a town of Christians, which Benalcázar [4] left there when he departed from this land. The town is called Cali [today an important Colombian city of some 100,000], and was subject to the Marquis Don Francisco Pizarro.

In such manner Andagoya made contact with the northern edge of the vast territory claimed by Pizarro. Things had been

[4] Andagoya and his translator-editor, Markham, spell the name "Belalcázar." For convenience' sake, their spelling has been changed to that used here, which was used by Means and is today more commonly accepted.

happening in that territory during the preceding years. Pizarro's officer, Sebastián de Benalcázar, commander of the garrison of the port of San Miguel, today's Piura, had in 1534 been instructed to march north to Quito for the purpose of subduing that Indian city and claiming it for Pizarro. Before he started, however, Don Pedro de Alvarado de Contreras, a hero in Cortés' conquest of Mexico and now governor of Guatemala, arrived in San Miguel and persuaded some of Benalcázar's men to go with *him* to take Quito. According to Means, he had ample royal authority for the venture—though not for stealing Pizarro's men—while Quito plainly lay beyond the latter's realm.

While Alvarado was proceeding north from San Miguel by sea, Benalcázar moved by land to forestall him in Quito, and word of the entire matter flew south to Pizarro in Cuzco—probably via the superb Inca system of Indian runners. Possibly not quite trusting Benalcázar, the Marquis sent Almagro to follow him. The three, Alvarado, Benalcázar, and Almagro, met in Quito, where the governor of Guatemala was bought off by the other two with what was reputed to be a tidy sum.

Recounting what had happened after all that, Andagoya wrote:

> This Juan de Ampudia and Pedro de Añasco set out from Quito in the year 1536, with the troops that had been left there by Don Pedro de Alvarado, and marched through this province until they arrived at Lili, where Juan de Ampudia formed a settlement, which he called the town of Ampudia. In 1538 Benalcázar marched against them from Quito, in disobedience of the express orders of his governor. When he arrived in Lili, he caused the town which Juan de Ampudia had formed, to be abandoned, and founded Cali and Popayán. In 1539, as soon as Benalcázar heard that the licentiate Espinosa was governor of that land, he abandoned those two towns, with few men in them, and went thence to the province of Bogotá, where he found the licentiate Jiménez and Federman, captains from Santa Marta and Venezuela. Leaving a brother of the licentiate Jiménez there as captain, they all went to Spain.

Jiménez was Gonzalo Jiménez de Quesada, who had in 1536 proceeded up the Magdalena River and conquered Colombia's highland Indians. Nicholas Federman, whose name Andagoya first wrote "Filaymana," but later as here given, was a German knight and lieutenant of the German governor of Venezuela, George of Spires.

Returning to Andagoya's contact with Benalcázar's men in Cali:

> On the tenth day of May, 1540, I arrived at this town, and found thirty men in it, eighteen of whom were disabled. I learnt how the Indians of a province, ten leagues distant, had killed the captain, Pedro de Añasco, and the captain Osoria, with upwards of fifty Spaniards, and as many horses, and were besieging a town called Timana, which Pedro de Añasco had founded. The besieged had sent for help to the captain Juan de Ampudia, who was at Popayán, and he had sent to pray for succor from Lili. The force which was prepared to set out from these two towns of Popayán and Lili amounted to sixty men. Two days after I arrived at Lili [he seems to confuse the province of Lili with the town of Cali], news arrived how that the Indians had defeated and killed Juan de Ampudia, with other soldiers; that the survivors were flying by night through the forests; and that the Indians, following up their success, had appeared before Popayán. I made haste to march and resist their entry, and on my arrival they halted. As soon as I arrived at Popayán, I sent a captain with fifty arquebusiers and crossbowmen, by a secret road, to succor Timana, and they arrived at a time when the greater part of the inhabitants were on the road, with the intention of going to Bogotá. Thus I restored peace to the province of Popayán.

There follows a somewhat confusing account of parties sent out by Andagoya to help other Spaniards, newly arrived from Spain in search of Peru, of fights with Indians, of the founding of the town of Santa Ana, and the like. Returning to his own immediate activities, he writes:

> On arriving at Lili, I found that the road by which I came was so rugged that it was impossible for horses to pass; so I presently sent a party to discover another road which should avoid the mountains. The new road came to the seaside, in the bay of Zinzy . . . , where I ordered the city of Buenaventura to be founded. On that coast a large river opens out into a bay, three leagues across, where ships, laden with all their cargo, may approach so near the land as to disembark their horses in the very square of the town. The land is wooded, and there are many fruits; and pig hunting. This city is twenty-two

leagues from that of Lili, east and west; and that of Lili is
nearly twenty from that of Popayán, north and south.[5]

On the ten leagues of road toward Popayán [from Lili]
there was . . . a chief, called Jamindi, . . . [with] many villages with five hundred to eight hundred houses; of which,
when I arrived, no memory remained except the ashes; for all
had been destroyed, and the inhabitants killed by Benalcázar.

Describing the environs of Popayán, he writes:

The whole is a very beautiful land, with plains, rivers full of
fish, and abundant hunting of deer and rabbits. This land, now
laid waste, was a most populous and fertile country, abounding
in maize, fruit, and ducks. When I arrived, it was so laid waste
that there was not a duck fit to breed, to be found throughout
the land; and where there had been over one hundred thousand
houses, . . . I did not find ten thousand men. And the principal cause of their destruction was that they received such
evil treatment, without having faith kept with them. In
Popayán, the Christians never sowed during the whole time
they were there, having the crops of the Indians to live on,
and they gathered these crops, and turned their pigs and horses
into the fields. So the Indians determined not to sow, and
there was no maize for eight months, which caused so great a
famine that many ate each other, and others died. Benalcázar
also took many out of the country.

The few that remained were friendly, and I wished to
convert them to our holy faith, and to learn whether they had
any religion. They had none whatever, and did not even
worship the sun, like those of Cuzco.

After some energetic proselytizing and preaching, he converted a hundred local Indians, plus 50 whom Benalcázar had
earlier brought up from Quito.

Mass was solemnly said, and . . . they all ate with me, and
I ordered that the captains and officers of his Majesty should
serve them, at which they were astonished. After eating, I
gave them to understand that on that day they had merited
to be changed from beasts to sons of God and heirs of his kingdom. I ordered a tournament and a great festival to be celebrated, and they held it to be very grand; and after four or

[5] Buenaventura, one of the rainiest spots on earth, is still the seaport for Cali
and its Cauca Valley district. In a straight line it lies about 50 miles northwest
of Cali, which, in turn, is some 70 miles north of Popayán.

five days there were three hundred more for whom the same festival was celebrated.

Encouraged by his success at Popayán, Andagoya roamed neighboring territories on missionary expeditions which seem to have been remarkably successful. In the "province of the Jitirigites, three conversions were made in three different parts, and four or five thousand persons were converted." All such conversions were followed by feasts and joyful parties, while the indefatigable chronicler also saw to it that the matter of wives was straightened out, each Christianized Indian being reduced—and legally married—to only one. Such activities, going hand in hand with Andagoya's generally mild treatment of the Indians, paid handsome dividends. A number of chiefs, with their people, who had previously been bitterly hostile to the Spaniards, declared themselves to be Andagoya's friends, helped him all they could, and embraced Christianity.

But the well-meaning new governor was not to enjoy his rule long. Markham's introduction reads:

> While Andagoya was thus quietly taking possession of the fruits of the labours of Benalcázar, that bold conqueror was successfully urging his suit at court. Charles V granted him the government of Popayán with the title of Adelantado, chiefly with a view to checking the ambition of the Pizarros in Peru. The new governor went to Panama, fitted out an expedition, and sailed down the coast to Buenaventura, in the wake of Andagoya. . . . The new Adelantado was allowed to land . . . , and to march towards Cali. Andagoya prepared to resist, but some friars and leading citizens interposed, and it was agreed that they should decide upon the rival claims of the two Adelantados. The assembly declared in favor of Benalcázar, who immediately arrested Andagoya, and sent him in chains to Popayán.

After some time, Andagoya was allowed to set out for Buenaventura, whence he sailed for Panama and, eventually, Spain, having lost his government and a sum of money which Markham estimates at the equivalent of more than 700,000 dollars. In 1546 he returned to America as a member of a force which had been sent to Peru to put an end to the civil war stirred up there by Gonzalo Pizarro. But Andagoya died en route. He was never to see the Peru whose conqueror he might have been, had it not been for the ducking which had laid him up for three years.

VIII

THE CONQUEST
OF PERU

THE conquest of the great empire of the Incas along South America's west coast forms one of the great, heroic, if also disreputable, chapters in South America's opening to Europeans. In his book, *Fall of the Inca Empire*,[1] Means has the following to say about the empire's extent on the eve of the Spanish conquest, about 1528:

> At this period . . . the territory occupied by the Inca Empire was very great. It reached from the Ancas Mayu (Blue River, now known as Patía River) in what is now southern Colombia down to the Maule River in Chile, and it ran eastwards from the Pacific Ocean over the coastal zone, into and across the lofty highlands of the Andes, and down their eastern slope until it faded away among the hot and humid shadows of the Amazonian jungles, the width of the empire varying from some 150 miles to more than 400 miles. The empire therefore contained some 380,000 square miles, or about as much territory as that now occupied by the Atlantic Seaboard states of our country. In a sense, however, it was greater by far than they because of the immense diversity of climates, topography, and environmental conditions within it, and in customs on the part of the inhabitants, who probably numbered over 16,000,000, or about twice the present-day population of the same territory.

Just before the arrival of the Spaniards, that great territory was ruled by the Inca Hayna Capac, whose capital was in Cuzco,

[1] Philip Ainsworth Means, *Fall of the Inca Empire* (N.Y.: Charles Scribner's Sons, 1932).

Peru, but who also liked to dally with his astonishing number of concubines in the Indian city of Quito, Equador, and in "his sumptuous palaces at Tumipampa, in what is now the southern highlands of Ecuador." While at the latter place, about 1528, Hayna Capac "received news of the arrival at Tumbez (a Peruvian port on the south coast of the Gulf of Guayaquil) of Francisco Pizarro and his small group of adventurous followers."

This was the advance group of the Spanish *conquistadores*. For reasons to be set forth later, their conquest of the Inca empire was not truly to get under way for several years. Meanwhile, the empire itself began to fall to pieces in a manner which was greatly to facilitate the work of the Spaniards when finally they did arrive.

During Hayna Capac's reign, the northern part of the empire, with Quito as its capital, had revolted, forcing the Inca to march north from Cuzco with "an army of 200,000 warriors and of a great many *yanaconas* (hereditary servitors) and women, including a harem of 2,000 for his own pleasure." Having put down the revolt with some difficulty and settled down for a time to rule the land from Ecuador, the ailing Inca prepared for his death. About 1524 he decided to divide the empire between two of his offspring, Atahualpa, an illegitimate son by a Quito woman "who, almost certainly, was a daughter of the last independent King of Quito," and Huáscar, his legitimate son in Cuzco, whose mother was the Inca's sister-wife, Coya (Empress) Mama Rahua Ocllo. Atahualpa was to receive the Kingdom of Quito as a separate dominion, while to Huáscar was willed the southern four-fifths of the overgrown empire. The half brothers agreed to the arrangement but fell out soon after their father's death in 1528 or 1529. Immediately after assuming the throne in Quito, Atahualpa set out to do away with Huáscar and to usurp the entire empire for himself. His army of 30,000 warriors "under the able leadership of his three generals, Calcuchima, Quizquiz, and Rumi Ñahui, marched south to Cuzco, where it defeated Huáscar's forces, butchering the Inca's followers and taking the latter prisoner. Hence, when Pizarro definitely entered Peru in 1530, Atahualpa had achieved his ambition of becoming the empire's sole ruler, although it seems, from the Pedro Sancho account quoted below, that his soldiers under Quizquiz, remaining in the Cuzco part of Peru as an army of occupation, were far from popular. Pizarro, a skilled if ruthless and unprincipled diplomat, was to make full use of the unpopularity.

Of the partnership between Pizarro, Almagro, and Father Ferdinand de Luque, mentioned in Chapter VII, Means writes as follows:

> The understanding between the three active partners was . . . tolerably clear as to the tasks to be performed by each one. Father Luque was to remain in Panama and look after the financial side of the affair; Pizarro was to lead the first exploring expedition southwards; and Almagro was to act as liaison and supply officer, going back and forth between the expedition and its base at Panama.

Pizarro set sail with one ship and some 112 Spaniards and Indian servants in November, 1524, followed and eventually joined by Almagro with a supply ship, coasting southward to the San Juan River at about 4° north latitude. Their hardships were appalling. Food gave out and some of the men died. The expedition, depleted and disheartened, returned to Panama in 1525. The governor of Panama was in a truculent mood and "raised a fearful pother about the men who had died of hunger." Father Luque had considerable difficulty in quieting him and in raising money for further explorations. In November, 1526, three ships set sail, one commanded by Pizarro, another by Almagro, and the third by the expedition's chief navigating officer, Pilot Bartolomé de Estrada. The vicissitudes of that expedition, masterfully described by the American William H. Prescott in his *Conquest of Peru*, do not belong in the present narrative. Suffice it to say that Pizarro disembarked with his men at the San Juan River while Almagro returned to Panama for more supplies, and the expedition's chief navigator, Bartolomé Ruiz de Estrada, reconnoitred southward. In the course of his journey he fell in with a large and sumptuous balsa raft, loaded with finely dressed people who had much gold. These were the first subjects of the Inca to be seen by the Spaniards, and Ruiz took some of them prisoner in order to teach them Spanish and later use them as interpreters. The news brought back by him to Pizarro and his men, camped in a region of endless mangrove swamps and insects, decimated by starvation, disease, and

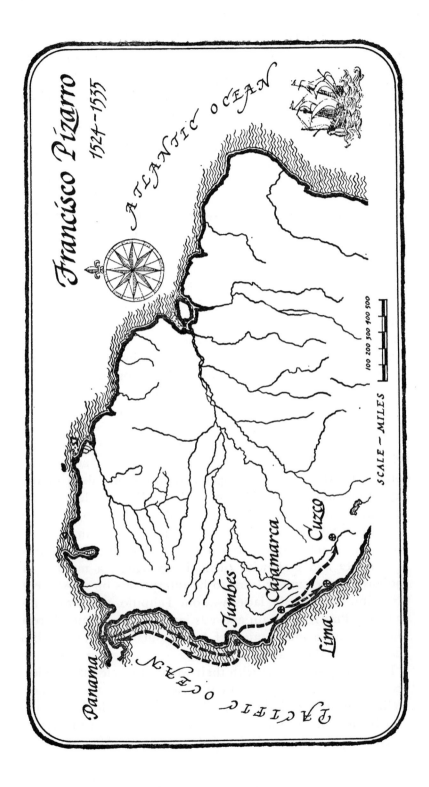

Francisco Pizarro
1524–1535

ATLANTIC OCEAN

PACIFIC OCEAN

Panama

Tumbes

Cajamarca

Cuzco

Lima

SCALE — MILES

100 200 300 400 500

the poisoned arrows of the Indians, was like a breath of fresh air to the discouraged Pizarro group. Soon thereafter they were joined by Almagro, arriving from Panama with supplies and 80 new recruits.

While they continued their explorations, however, the governor in Panama became apprehensive and decided to call off the entire venture, holding Almagro when that stalwart returned to Panama and sending orders to Pizarro, with one Pedro Tafur and two ships, to give up and go back. It was at this point on the island of Gallo, that Pizarro drew his famous line with his sword, stepped south of it, and invited all who had the courage for great deeds to join him. Thirteen "immortals" volunteered to stay with their commander, the rest sailed back to Panama with Tafur. While Pizarro and his small force of heroes remained camped on the coast, under fearful conditions, Father Luque, in Panama, succeeded in placating the governor sufficiently to send the stranded *conquistadores* a small ship with supplies. That ship and its crew were seized by the indomitable Pizarro and used for further southward gropings. It was during the course of that voyage, early in 1528, that the Inca, Hayna Capac, heard of the Spaniards' arrival at Tumbez. The whites were overjoyed at the wealth and civilization they found at Tumbez and elsewhere along the Peruvian coast. They were received hospitably, feted, dined, and wined by the Indians. According to Means, "the younger and lustier members of the expedition were greatly drawn to the Indian maidens whom they saw, and Pizarro had some difficulty in inducing them to desist from taking up their permanent abode upon that coast." Nevertheless, on their way back north they left several Spaniards at Tumbez and took with them, in exchange, a number of Indians "so they might learn to be interpreters on subsequent occasions." Among the latter was one Felipillo, who was to accompany Pizarro to Spain and was later, at the conquest's real onset, to make much mischief for Atahualpa by telling lies about him to the Spaniards.

Returning to Panama with their wonderful tales, the explorers were greeted with popular enthusiasm, though the governor, feeling the pangs of jealousy, made more trouble for them than ever before. On agreement with his partners, Pizarro therefore sailed for Spain to enlist the king's direct support. After some difficulties and many delays, on July 26th, 1529, he received the famous "Capitulación" or Agreement for the Conquest of Peru, which gave the partners more or less of a free hand. That document was to be the cause of much subsequent trouble. As Almagro and Luque had feared, it gave the lion's share of the loot, lands, and powers, to Pizarro, whose return to Panama was followed by much recrimination and bickering among the partners.

Finally, in January, 1531, Pizarro set sail again for Peru. "With him," writes Means, "went all his kinsmen, a few ecclesiastics . . . and not more than 200 men, some of whom had horses. As on previous occasions, Almagro was left behind to gather additional forces, supplies, and munitions, it being understood that he would follow after." On their previous foray the Spaniards had been friendly, inquisitive, and delighted by the hospitality shown them. This time they made fierce war on all the Indians they encountered, journeying slowly down the coast for a year or so, suffering horribly from hunger, disease, and death in various forms. In May, 1532, on the site of today's Piura, they founded San Miguel, the first Spanish city in Peru, which was for some years to be used as the Spaniards' chief port of entry in that country. Sebastián de Benalcázar, who was later to become active in the conquest of Ecuador, was left to hold San Miguel, together with a number of Spaniards who chose to settle there.

By this time Pizarro was in communication with the Inca Atahualpa, who was camped with his army near the inland mountain city of Cajamarca. With fewer than 200 men, he set forth on an epoch-making march to that city, exchanging messengers, gifts, and declarations of friendship with the Inca as he traveled. However, no sooner had the Spaniards reached Cajamarca, on November 15th, 1532, and received Atahualpa, who visited them on a mission of goodwill, than they imprisoned the Inca, holding him as a hostage to assure their not being attacked by the thousands of soldiers in his army.

Means writes:

> The Inca's first idea seems to have been that Pizarro and his men were partisans of Huáscar and that they would kill him and place his brother, then held in captivity at Antamarca, upon the seat of power. He soon learned his mistake, however, and rightly gauged his adversaries' overwhelming lust for gold

and silver. Accordingly he made an offer of ransom, promising to fill with gold a certain good-sized chamber in his palace and another large space with silver. On November 18th or 20th, 1532, the terms were formally set down in a notarial document wherein it was agreed that all the Spaniards then in Cajamarca should partake of the resultant treasure and that, if he refrained from "treasonable" actions, the Inca would be set free.

While the treasure flowed into Cajamarca from all parts of the empire, Francisco Pizarro's brother, Hernando, led an important exploring expedition which left Cajamarca January 5 and returned there April 25, after scouting the country between that city and the holy city of Pachácamac, near today's Lima. During his absence, Almagro arrived in Cajamarca with a fresh force of men, most of whom he had dredged from Panama's gutters. Dissensions between those men and Pizarro's original force, squabbles over the division of the treasure, and differences of opinion as to what should eventually be done with the Inca prisoner Atahualpa, stirred up so much ill-will in the Spaniards' camp that Francisco Pizarro (hereinafter also referred to as "the Governor") decided to prepare a case for himself for submittal to the Spanish court, in the form of a "true" account of all that happened, to be written by Pedro Sancho, his secretary and "scrivener general of these kingdoms of New Castile." [2]

Curiously enough, while the Sancho document was intended to present Pizarro's actions in the best possible light, and was signed by the Governor as an official document, its author did not hesitate, from time to time, to accuse his employer of double-dealing in his relations with the Indians. However, such statements on what a Puritan like Prescott would, and did, regard as treachery, were possibly quite acceptable to Pizarro and the Spanish crown as revealing a skilled and zealous type of diplomacy, exercised for the purpose of enhancing Spain's greatness and wealth. It must be remembered that Pizarro found himself with a very small force of men, in a large, populous, and well-organized country, skilled in the arts of war. He must have presumed that the king would not only understand his free use

[2] Pedro Sancho, *An Account of the Conquest of Peru* translated into English and annotated by Philip Ainsworth Means (New York: The Cortes Society, 1917).

of lies and deceptions but would even applaud them as means of preventing too much armed conflict, and so also as means of saving Spanish lives.

Sancho's account begins at a time when a large part of the treasure had arrived in Cajamarca and Hernando Pizarro had been sent to Spain with the king's share, via San Miguel and Panama.

> The Captain Hernardo Pizarro had departed with the hundred thousand pesos of gold and the five thousand marks of silver which were sent to His Majesty as his royal fifth; after that event, some ten or twelve days, the two Spaniards who were bringing gold from Cuzco arrived, and part of the gold was melted at once because it was in very small pieces; [the remainder included] five hundred odd plates of gold torn from some house-walls in Cuzco; and even the smallest plates weighed four or five pounds a piece; other, larger ones weighed ten or twelve pounds, and with plates of this sort all the walls of that temple were covered.

The king's treasurer, who accompanied Pizarro to make sure that the crown's rights be protected, took charge of the royal fifth of that part of the loot which had arrived after Hernando Pizarro's departure for Spain.

> All that remained, beyond the royal fifth, was divided among the soldiers and companions of the Governor. He gave to each one what he conscientiously thought he justly merited, taking into consideration the trials each man had passed through and the quality of his person, all of which he did with the greatest diligence and speed possible in order that they might set out from that place and go to the city of Xauxa.[3]
>
> And because there were among those soldiers some who were old and more fit for rest than for fatigues, and who in that war had fought and served much, he gave them leave to return to Spain. He procured their good will so that, on returning, these men would give fairer accounts of the greatness and wealth of that land so that a sufficient number of people would come thither to populate and advance it. For, in truth, the land being very large and very full of natives, the Spaniards

[3] Jauja, approximately 400 miles more or less south of Cajamarca, on the Mantaro River, in the Huancayo Valley of Central Peru. This important Indian settlement had been scouted by Hernando Pizarro in the course of his reconnaissance expedition from Cajamarca to Pachácamac.

who were in it then were all too few for conquering it, holding it and settling it. . . .

The melting of the metals completed, the Governor commanded the notary to draw up a document in which it said that the cacique Atabalipa [Atahualpa] was free and absolved from the promise and word which he had given to the Spaniards, who were to take the house full of gold in ransom for himself. This document the Governor caused to be proclaimed publicly and to the sound of trumpets in the plaza of that city of Cajamalca [Cajamarca], making it known, at the same time, to the said Atabalipa, in the same proclamation, that, because it suited the services of H.M. and the security of the land, he wished to maintain the cacique as a prisoner with a good guard, until more Spaniards should arrive who should give added security.

In other words, having publicly granted that the Inca had honorably fulfilled his part of the ransom agreement, the Spaniards were still afraid to release him. Moreover, according to Means, the interpreter, Felipillo, invented and told many tales, later disproved, about Atahualpa's perfidy in organizing from his place of captivity a concerted attack through which the Christians were to be wiped out. Sancho, in his account, repeats those tales as facts and in detail. Pizarro therefore called a council in which:

after there had been much debate and discussion over the harm and the profit that might follow upon the continued life or the death of Atabalipa, it was resolved that justice should be done upon him. And . . . he was finally taken from the prison in which he was, and, to the sound of a trumpet, his treason and perfidy were published, and he was borne to the middle of the plaza of the city and tied to a stake, while the religious was consoling him and teaching him, by means of an interpreter, the things of our Christian faith, telling him that God wished him to die for the sins which he had committed in the world, and that he must repent of them, and that God would pardon him if he did so and was baptised at once.

On learning that if he permitted himself to be baptised he would not be burned at the stake but would be garroted instead, the Inca embraced the Christian faith while also recommending to the Governor "his little sons, so that he might take them with him."

While the Spaniards who stood around him said the creed for
his soul, he was quickly throttled. May God take him to his holy
glory, for he died repentant of his sins with the true faith of a
Christian. After he was thus hanged, in fulfilment of his sentence, fire was cast upon him so that a part of his clothes and
flesh was burnt. . . . On the next day the Governor ordered
that all the Spaniards should be present at his interment, and,
with the cross and other religious paraphernalia, he was borne
to the church and buried with as much solemnity as if he had
been the chief Spaniard in our camp. Because of this all the
principal lords and caciques who served him received great
pleasure, considering as great the honour which was done them,
and knowing that, because he was a Christian, he was not
burned alive, and he was interred in church as if he were a
Spaniard.

Having disposed of Atahualpa, the Governor stayed in Cajamarca long enough to appoint a successor for the Inca. This was
a brother of Atahualpa, another son of Hayna Capac, whom
Sancho called Gucunacaba. Sancho, who was often careless
about proper names, called the new ruler also Atabalipa. Since
Hayna Capac's legitimate sons were named Huáscar, Manco,
Paullu, and Titu Atauchi, scholars have had a difficult time in
trying to determine just who this Atabalipa the Second might
have been. He was installed in office in a great ceremony, attended by a crowd which included "as many as fifty caciques and
chiefs," to whom Pizarro preached a sermon on the Christian
faith going hand in hand with service and loyalty to the Spanish
king.

Then the Governor took in his hands the royal standard
which he raised on high three times, and he told them that, as
vassals of the Caesarian Majesty, they ought to do likewise, and
the Cacique took it, and afterwards the captains and the other
chiefs, and each one raised it aloft twice; then they went to
embrace the Governor who received them with great joy
through seeing their good-will, and with how much content-
ment they had heard the affairs of God and of our religion. The
Governor wished that all this be drawn up as testimony in
writing, and when it was over, the caciques and chiefs held great
festivities, so much so that every day there were rejoicings such
as games and feasts, usually held in the house of the Governor.

Having finished the business, together with the distribution of gold, Pizarro set out for "the city of Xauxa where he [the Governor] intended to found a colony of Spaniards on account of the reports he had of the good surrounding provinces and of the many cities which were there about it." First, however, he dispatched "ten cavalrymen and a captain" to San Miguel to reinforce the garrison at that important point until more soldiers should arrive from Panama.

Sancho's account of the march to Jauja is a somewhat pedestrian story of journeys, of capturing and holding various bridges, for the construction of which the Incas were famous, of impressing Indians to carry the Spaniards' supplies and baggage, including the Cajamarca treasure. Shortly after the journey's beginning, they were informed of the murder of one Guaritico, a brother of Atahualpa, by order of Atahualpa II. This Guaritico, whom Means presumes to have been Huáscar, the deposed Cuzco Inca, was, according to Sancho "a very important person and a friend of the Spaniards, and he had been sent by the Governor from Caxamalca to repair the bridges and the bad spots in the road."

Evidently Almagro had by now joined his companion in arms instead of sailing back and forth between San Miguel and Panama. At one point Sancho writes that "the Governor commanded a captain of his, who was the Marshal D. Diego de Almagro, to go with troops to take a bridge two leagues from Guaiglia, which bridge was built in a manner that will soon be related."

Pizarro had with him an Indian officer named Chilichuchima [4] who had accompanied Hernando Pizarro on the latter's scouting expedition to Pachácamac. The Governor, however, did not altogether trust the Indian, taking extra precautions lest "the captain Chilichuchima . . . would hatch some treasonable plot, all the more so on account of the suspicion he felt owing to the fact that neither in Caxatambo [5] nor in the eighteen

[4] Means writes of this man: "Properly Challcuchima or Calicuchima. This remarkable Indian general was the son of Epiclachima, younger brother of Cacaha, last Caran Scyri of Quitu. Cacaha was conquered by Hayna Capac about 1487, and Calicuchima entered the service of Atahualpa who was his kinsman through Paccha his cousin, Hayna Capac's wife."

[5] Cajatambo. In a straight line, the invaders were by now about 260 miles approximately South of Cajamarca, having traveled the distance in something less than a month, through the valleys and over the passes and rivers of Peru's Andean spine.

leagues after it had he met with any warriors, nor were his fears lessened during a halt in a village five leagues beyond because all the people had fled without leaving a living soul." At that point they received a warning of trouble ahead.

> When he had arrived there, a Spaniard's Indian servant, who was from that land of Pambo distant from here ten leagues and twenty from Xauxa, came to him saying that he had heard that troops had been assembled in Xauxa to kill the Christians who were coming, and that they had [four important] captains . . . and the servant added that they had placed a part of this force in a village called Tarma five leagues from Xauxa in order to guard a bad pass that there was in the mountain and to cut and break it up in such a way that the Spaniards could not pass by. Informed of this, the Governor gave orders that Chilichuchima should be made a prisoner, because it was held to be certain that the force had been made ready by his advice and command, he thinking to flee the Christians and join it.

The Spaniards crossed a disagreeable, snowy pass and camped on bare fields near a place called Pombo, where they waited for word from their scouts.

> One came who told how the warriors were five leagues from Xauxa on the road from Cuzco and were coming to burn the town so that the Christians should not find shelter, and that they intended afterward to return to Cuzco to combine under a captain named Quizquiz who was there with many troops who had come from Quito by command of Atabalipa for the security of the land. When this was learned by the Governor, he caused to be made ready seventy-five light horse, and with twenty peones who guarded Chilichuchima, and without the impediments of baggage, he set out for Xauxa, leaving behind the treasurer with the other troops who were guarding the camp baggage and the gold of H.M., and of the company.
>
> The day on which he set out from Pombo, he traveled some seven leagues, and he halted in a village called Cacamarca, and here they found seventy thousand pesos of gold in large pieces, to guard which the Governor left two Christians from the cavalry. . . . Then, in the morning, he set forth with his men in good array, for he had word that three leagues from there were four thousand men.

The *conquistadores* managed to negotiate the bad pass about which they had been warned, though without finding Indians in it, and came to Tarma, a mountain village surrounded by steep slopes, where they camped and spent a miserable night drenched by heavy rains, having left their tents and blankets behind in order to travel light. The next day they entered Jauja without at first finding hostile Indians in the town.

> The natives all came out along the road in order to look at the Christians, celebrating much their coming because they thought that, through it, they would issue forth from the slavery in which that foreign army [the Incas] held them.

Seeing no armed warriors, the Spaniards started to enter the city but were halted by an Indian, "running toward them at great speed with a lance erect." This proved to be a servant of a member of an advance guard of two Spanish soldiers who had been ambushed by a large number of armed Indians but had managed to rout them. On receipt of this news, Pizarro and his small body of men spurred their horses and charged into the city and beyond. Sancho now describes a melee in which some 15 or 20 Spaniards routed a force of 600 Indians, of whom "not more than twenty or thirty, who took to the mountains before the other captain with his fifteen men could arrive, saved themselves."

Resting after the engagement, the Spaniards learned that

> the main body [of Indians] were encamped six leagues down the river from Xauxa, and that, on that very day, they had sent those six hundred men to complete the burning of the city of Xauxa, having already burned the other half of it seven or eight days before, and that they had burned a great edifice which was in the plaza, as well as many other things before the eyes of the people of that city, together with many clothes and much maize, so that the Spaniards should not avail themselves of them. The citizens were left so hostile to those other Indians that if one of the latter hid, they showed him to the Christians so that they would kill him, and they themselves aided in killing them, and they would even have done so with their own hands if the Christians had permitted it.

That night, after a short rest, Pizarro dispatched 50 light horsemen to dislodge the main body of Indian troops, beyond Jauja on the road to Cuzco, keeping 15 horsemen and 20 "peones" with him. Five days later the captain of the sally returned to Jauja with the message of mission accomplished.

> He related . . . how, on the night he left Xauxa, he journeyed some four leagues before dawn, with much eagerness to attack the enemy's camp before they were warned of his coming; and being now near [the enemy] at dawn, they saw a great mass of smoke in the place of their encampment, which seemed to be two leagues further on. And so he spurred on with his men at great pace, thinking that the enemy, warned of his approach, had fled and that the buildings . . . in a village were burning. And so it was, because they had set fire to that wretched hamlet. Arrived at that place, the Spaniards followed the footsteps of the warriors through a very broad valley.
>
> . . . As they overtook them they collided with the enemy who were going more slowly with many women and children in their rear-guard, and the Spaniards, leaving these behind them in order to catch up with the men, ran more than four leagues, and caught up with some of their squadrons. As some of them [the Indians] saw the Castilians, from some distance, they had time to take shelter on a mountain and save themselves; others, who were few, were killed, leaving in the power of the Spaniards— who, because their horses were tired, did not wish to go up the mountain—many spoils and women and children. And as it was already night, they returned to sleep in the village which they had left behind. And the following day these Spaniards determined to follow them as they fled back to Cuzco so as to take from them certain bridges of net-work and to prevent their crossing. But, because of lack of pasturage for their horses, they found themselves obliged to fall back, to the dissatisfaction of the Governor because they had not at least followed and taken those bridges so as to prevent those Indians from returning to Cuzco.

In summarizing Chapter V of his report, Sancho wrote as follows:

> They name new officials in the city of Xauxa in order to establish a settlement of Spaniards, and, having had news of the death of Atabalipa, with great prudence and much craftiness in order to keep themselves in the good graces of the Indians, they discuss the appointment of a new lord.

After the battle, Pizarro brought up the men he had left behind at Pombo, with the baggage and gold. He offered help to any Spaniard who wanted to settle in Jauja but found no takers; they all wanted to keep on fighting as long as hostile Indians were to be encountered. Having attended to the business of appointing a successor to Atabalipa, playing one chief off against the others, but actually playing for time until enough new Spanish soldiers should arrive to permit him to subdue *all* the Indian chiefs, Pizarro appointed 30 light horsemen to stay in Jauja as the city's garrison and as guards for the newly appointed civil officials and the king's treasurer who was keeping close guard over the royal share of the gold. Extraordinarily busy, he sent men to the port of San Miguel with instructions for managing it, sent messengers to Quito and Cuzco to advise any hostile Indians in those centers to think twice before attacking the Spaniards, and reinforced the guard around Chilichuchima, "because that captain was the key [the possession of which ensured] having the land quiet and subjected."

> This precaution taken, and the troops who were to go with the Governor toward Cuzco being made ready, the number of whom was one hundred horsemen and thirty peons, he [the Governor] ordered a captain to go ahead with seventy horsemen and some peones in order to rebuild the bridges which had been burned, and the Governor remained behind while he was giving orders for many matters touching on the welfare of the city and Republic which he was to leave already well established, and in order to await the reply of the Christians whom he had sent to the coast in order to examine the ports and set up crosses in them in case someone should come to reconnoitre the land.[6]

The captain sent to repair the bridges left Jauja with his men on a Thursday, "and the Governor with the rest of the troops, and Chilichuchima with his guard left the following Monday. In the morning they were all ready with their arms and other necessary things; the journey they were to make being long, they were to leave all the baggage in Xauxa, it not being convenient

---

[6] This remark seems to reflect Pizarro's impatience for reinforcements to bolster the small force with which he was trying to subdue and hold the entire Inca empire. One imagines that the crosses were meant to be markers, beacons to attract the attention of any Spaniards who came coasting down from Panama. However, from having too few men, as at this stage, it did not take Pizarro long to have too many, as attested by the civil wars which followed the first conquest.

to carry it with them on that journey." After two days "down the valley along the banks of the Xauxa River, which was very delectable and peopled in many places," Pizarro arrived at the first of the bridges which the enemy's fleeing troops had destroyed but his own advance guard, "forcing local Indians to do the work," had again repaired. There follows Sancho's description of the bridges of which the present was an example. The Inca bridges have caught the attention of a number of commentators of the time as well as of later writers. Suffice it here to say, since detailed descriptions are too long to be included in an account of this kind, that they were suspension bridges, constructed of vines and the like, ingeniously hung between stone abutments on the banks.

Having crossed the river, and a bridged tributary farther down, "he [the Governor] began to climb a very steep and long mountain all made of steps of very small stones.[7] Here the horses toiled so much that, when they had finished going up, the greater part of them had lost their shoes and worn down the hoofs of all four feet."

Exhausted, the *conquistadores* came to a village in the evening, only, again, to find themselves victims of the Incas' "scorched-earth policy." The canal which had brought water to the site had been destroyed. The next day they came to another, larger settlement and were dismayed to find that it, too, contained no food.

> The Governor wondered greatly with his men at finding here neither food nor anything else, because this place belonged to one of the lords who had been with Atabalipa .. ., and he had come in their company as far as Xauxa, [where] he said he wished to go ahead in order to prepare in this land his victuals and other things necessary for the Spaniards.

Evidently the man had done a thorough job of preparing the land. Pizarro now began to worry about his advance guard, consisting of "the captain who had gone ahead with the seventy horsemen," from whom he had had no word for some time. But the next day, early, "they . . . arrived at a village called Tarcos,

[7] In addition to wide roads, the Incas constructed many foot trails, with steps hacked into the steeper slopes. Even today the Indians living in the more remote, mountainous parts of Peru cut or build steps wherever their mule trails and foot paths encounter steep grades.

where they met the cacique of the district . . . who told them of the day on which had passed that way some Christians who were going to fight with the enemy who had established their camp in a neighboring settlement."

The following evening, after having had to ford a wide river whose bridge had been destroyed, and cross a large, steep, exhausting mountain, Pizarro and his men camped in a partially burned village, where couriers reached them from the advance guard. At and near a place called Bilcas, the 70 advance horsemen, divided into two groups of 40 and 30 respectively, had encountered the enemy troops and fought two battles, leaving behind "more than six hundred men . . . dead." The Indians had managed to kill a horse and had "cut off his head and put it on a lance which they bore before them like a standard." The officer advised Pizarro that, after a few days' rest, he intended to set out "to take . . . a bridge of net-work which was near there, so that the fugitive enemies should not cross it and go to join with Quizquiz [8] in Cuzco and the garrison of troops he had there, which was said to be waiting for the Spaniards in a bad pass near Cuzco." The letter delivered by the messenger stated that the advance force planned to go on to the pass to demolish the enemy there, so preparing the way for Pizarro to enter the Incas' capital.

Overjoyed, Pizarro sent the report to Jauja to the end of maintaining morale there, sent instructions to the advance force, and then set out for Bilcas.

> This city of Bilcas is placed on a high mountain and is a large town and the head of a province. It has a beautiful and fine fortress; there were many well-built houses of stone, and it is half-way by road from Xauxa to Cuzco.
>
> Scarcely had the Governor arrived here, when he received a letter from the captain who was reconnoitring in which the latter informed him that the enemy had gone on five leagues and were in waiting on the slope of a mountain in a land called Curamba, and that there were many warriors there, and that they had made many preparations and had arranged great quantities of stones so that the Spaniards would not be able to

[8] According to Means, Quizquiz, like Chilichuchima, had been a general of Atahualpa before the coming of the Spaniards. He fought long against the invaders, but at length his unavailing efforts caused him to be murdered by his own followers.

go up. The Governor . . . at once ordered the Marshal D.
Diego Almagro to get ready with thirty light horsemen, . . .
[and] not to delay for anything until he should come up with
the captain who was ahead with the others. . . . The Governor
likewise started on the following day, with ten horsemen and
the twenty peones who were guarding Chilichuchima, and he
quickened his pace so much that day that of two days' marches
he made one. . . . On the next day, they arrived at the village
of Airamba from where the captain had written that he was
with the armed troops waiting for them upon the road.

In the village the men "found two dead horses, from which it
was suspected that some misfortune had befallen the captain."
But a letter arrived, informing Pizarro that the advance force,
which had evidently not yet been reached by Almagro and his
men, had fought a difficult battle, had lost some men and horses,
and was now on a plain, halfway up a mountain, surrounded by
jeering Indians who were certain that they would receive reinforcements the following day and that the Spaniards would be
wiped out to a man.

> This news reached the Governor . . . and he . . . communi-
> cated it to the ten horsemen and twenty peones whom he had
> with him, consoling them all with good words which he spoke
> to them, although they were greatly disturbed in their minds,
> for they thought that if a small number of Indians, relatively
> to the number anticipated, had maltreated the Christians in
> such a manner in the first action, they would bring upon them
> still greater war on the following day when their horses were
> wounded and when the aid of thirty horsemen, which had been
> sent to them, had not yet arrived among the Spaniards.

The men broke camp and set out but had to camp two days
by a swollen river where a bridge had been burned. Here "a
Christian was seen coming," and brought the welcome news that
Almagro had finally joined the besieged men with his reinforcements and that the Indian enemies had retreated on seeing the
augmented forces.

> At this juncture, a thousand Indians in a squadron com-
> manded by Quizquiz arrived in aid of the Indians who, seeing
> the Christians on horseback and so warlike, judged it time to
> withdraw into the mountains. At the same time the Christians
> assembled in their [the Indians'] fort, whence the captain had

sent this messenger to the Governor to tell him that he would await him there until he should arrive.

The same messenger warned Pizarro to be careful because four thousand men had split off from Quizquiz' force to waylay the Governor's small force, and also that Pizarro "should . . . be very sure that Chilichuchima was arranging and commanding all this and was giving advice to the enemy as to what they were to do, and that, on this account, he should bear himself with caution."

Pizarro now began to upbraid Chilichuchima, reminding him how "well" he had always been treated, how he had been groomed for an important government post in Cajamarca, accusing him of treason, and promising to burn him at the stake as soon as the Spanish forces were reunited. Chilichuchima's protestations of innocence were ignored.

> Then, having crossed the river in the afternoon, the Governor went forward . . . and arrived by night in a village called Rimac [9] a league from the river. And there the Marshal arrived, with four horsemen, to wait for him, and after they had talked together, they set out the next day for the camp of the Spaniards where they arrived in the afternoon, the captain and many others having come out to meet them, and all rejoiced greatly at seeing themselves all together again.
>
> . . . The Captain and the Marshal urged the Governor to do justice on Chilichuchima, because he ought to know that Chilichuchima advised the enemy of all that the Christians did, and that it was he who had made the Indians come out of the mountains of Bilcas, exhorting them to come and fight with the Christians who were few and who, with their horses, could not climb those mountains save step by step and on foot, and giving them, at the same time, a thousand other counsels as to where they were to wait and what they were to do, like a man who had seen those places and who knew the skill of the Christians with whom he had lived so long a time.

Pizarro then gave orders that Chilichuchima "was to be burned alive in the middle of the plaza."

---

[9] The modern Limatambo, a settlement with many ruins of Inca fortifications, about 35 miles from Cuzco and approximately halfway between that city and the famous ruins of Machu Picchu.

The religious tried to persuade him to become a Christian, saying to him that those who were baptized and who believed with true faith in our saviour Jesus Christ went to glory in paradise and that those who did not believe in him went to hell and its tortures. . . . But he [Chilichuchima] did not wish to be a Christian, saying that he did now know what sort of thing this law was, and he began to invoke Paccamaca and captain Quizquiz that they might come to his aid. This Paccamaca the Indians have as their god and they offer him much gold and silver, and it is a well-known thing that the demon is in that idol and speaks with those who come to ask him something. . . . In this way this captain paid for the cruelties which he committed in the conquests of Atabalipa, and for the evils which he plotted to the hurt of the Spaniards and in disservice of H. M. All the people of the country rejoiced infinitely at his death, because he was very much abhorred by all who knew what a cruel man he was.

Means, in a footnote, calls the last statement "another obvious fabrication." The present editor, remembering that Chilichuchima had been one of the generals from Quito, sent to Cuzco to subdue the forces of Inca Hayna Capac there, is not certain that it need have been a fabrication. One of the reasons that Pizarro had a relatively easy time in reaching and taking Cuzco was the fact that in that part of Peru the Quito generals were none too popular.

Here the Spaniards rested that night, having set good guards, because they were given to understand that Quizquiz was close by with all his men. And on the following morning, came to visit the Governor a son of Guainacaba [10] and a brother of the dead cacique Atabalipa, and the greatest and most important lord who was then in that land; and he had ever been a fugitive so that those of Quito might not kill him. This man said to the Governor that he would aid him to the extent of his power in order to drive from that land all those of Quito, who were his enemies and who hated him and did not wish to be the subjects of a foreign people.

Pizarro assured his visitor that he had marched from Jauja for no other purpose than that of liberating him (Manco) and the

[10] Hayna Capac. Pizarro's visitor was Manco Inca, Atahualpa's legitimate half-brother, and the brother of the Inca Huáscar, whom Atahualpa's forces had defeated and captured just before the arrival of the Spaniards in Peru.

people of Cuzco from the Quito forces commanded by Quizquiz. The two pledged friendship and mutual assistance, and Manco said: "I am going to fish because I know that tomorrow the Christians do not eat flesh, and I shall encounter this messenger who tells me that Quizquiz is going with his men to burn Cuzco and that he is now near at hand, and I have wished to warn you of it in order that you may fix upon a remedy."

Alerted, Pizarro set out for Cuzco immediately with all his men. There was a skirmish that afternoon, in which two Spanish captains "with some forty horsemen" killed two hundred Indians and sent the rest fleeing into the mountains.

> And the next day, at the first ray of dawn, the Governor arranged the troops, horse and foot, and he took the road to Cuzco, with good understanding and caution, believing that the enemy would come to attack him on the road, but none of them appeared. In this way the Governor and his troops entered the great city of Cuzco without any other resistance or battle on Friday, at the hour of high mass, on the fifteenth day of the month of November of the year of the birth of our Saviour and Redeemer Jesus Christ MDXXXIII.

The entire journey from Cajamarca to Cuzco, a straight-line distance of nearly 650 miles, through strange, rugged, and often hostile country, harassed and often beset by enemy troops, with time out for establishing a Spanish government in Jauja, had taken two months.

> The Governor caused all the Christians to lodge in the dwellings around the plaza of the city, and he ordered that all should come forth with their horses to the plaza and sleep in their tents, until it could be seen whether the enemy was coming to attack them. This order was continued and observed for a month. On another day, the Governor created as lord that son of Guainacaba, for he was young, prudent and alive and the most important of all those who were there at that time, and was the one to whom the lordship came by law. And he did it so soon in order that the lords and caciques should not go away to their own lands which were divers provinces, and some very far away, and so that the natives should not join those of Quito, but should have a separate lord of their own whom they might reverence and obey and not organize themselves into

bands. So he commanded all the caciques to obey him [Manco] as their lord and to do all that he should order them to do.

With honeyed words Pizarro now again assured his new Inca that the Spaniards had come to Cuzco solely to free him from the Quito forces, though at one point he also made Manco and all his chiefs swear allegiance to the Spanish king. At the Spaniards' instigation, Manco now raised a fighting force which eventually came to number 24,000 picked warriors, and sent it forth to fight against the forces of Quizquiz, aided by some fifty Spanish horsemen. After some skirmishes near Cuzco and several months' delays caused by the seasons' heavy rains, these troops arrived at Jauja, which the men from Quito were besieging, and managed, with the help of the Spanish garrison of that city, to drive the besiegers off.

Meanwhile, Pizarro and the troops remaining with him in Cuzco looted the city of vast quantities of gold and silver, melting it all down to portable size, setting aside the royal fifth and dividing the rest among themselves and the Jauja garrison. "Truly," writes Sancho, "it was a thing worthy to be seen, this house where the melting took place, all full of so much gold in plates of eight and ten pounds each, and in vessels, and vases and pieces of various forms with which the lords of that land were served, and among other very sightly things were four [llamas], and ten or twelve figures of women of the size of the women of that land, all of fine gold and as beautiful and well-made as if they were alive."

This was the Spaniards' bonanza in the New World, the mainspring of the El Dorado dream which was to drive men forth for centuries in search of another Cuzco, another "golden city" called "Manoa." This, too, was the lure which soon came to draw hundreds and thousands of more *conquistadores* to Peru from Spain, to create disturbances and serious social problems, because they had come too late to get in on the conquest and the loot, and an unemployed *conquistador*, poor and disgruntled, is a dangerous man to have around.

Having divided the treasure, and having "set aside twelve thousand-odd married Indians . . . near the mines, in order that they might take out gold for H. M. from which, it is understood, there will be great profits, considering the great wealth of the mines," Pizarro proceeded to "found . . . 'the very noble and great city of Cuzco,' " marking out the site "for the church which was to be built, appointing civil officers, and giving to all Spaniards who were to stay in the city presents of numbers of Indians, "in order that they might instruct them in the things of our holy Catholic faith."

> When these things were done, the Governor set out for Xauxa, taking the cacique with him, and the citizens remained guarding the city [according] to orders which the Governor left them so that they might govern themselves until he should command something else.

Having been informed by a message from Jauja that the enemy forces under Quizquiz had fortified themselves at a difficult pass some 40 leagues from Jauja, along the road to Cajamarca, he ordered the cacique, Manco, to send to Cuzco for another 2,000 picked warriors, telling him that "it would be better were they few and good than if they were many and unserviceable, because the many would destroy the food in the land through which they were to pass without necessity or profit." While waiting in Jauja for the reinforcements to arrive, Pizarro received word that the Spaniard Pedro de Alvarado had landed at San Miguel with some 250 soldiers, and that the officer whom he, Pizarro, had left to guard that port had left with 200 men "to the provinces of Quito in order to conquer them." The messenger, as quoted by Sancho, said:

> "And in order to bring more quickly the news of what had happened there I returned . . . without going to the city of San Miguel, knowing for certain that the captain would have departed with his men and would already be near Cossibamba.[11] Turning back on my road, I met, on Easter, the Marshal D. Diego de Almagro near Cena which is where the road to Caxamalca branches off, and to him I related how things were going and how some suspected that the captain who was going to Quito was not going with good intentions. As soon as the Marshal heard this, he set off in order to catch up with the captain who was taking these soldiers on the march to Quito, in order to detain him until together they could arrange the

---

[11] In Ecuador; possibly, according to Means, Riobamba, Tumebamba, or some other place in the "Kingdom" of Quito.

necessary provisions for this war. This, then, sir, is what happened to me on this journey, during which I tried to get information about those ships, but could not learn anything else about them. Of Alvarado nothing more is known [than] that he has already embarked on these shores or has passed further on, as letters inform me."

Pizarro's affairs were getting out of hand; his officers, in undertaking the conquest of Ecuador on their own, without orders from the supreme command, were beginning to worry the Governor. Having sent letters of instruction to Almagro and the defecting commander of the San Miguel garrison, he laid out the site for a church in Jauja, which the district's caciques were ordered to build.

> In the meantime there arrived the four thousand Indian warriors whom the cacique had called from Cuzco, and the Governor caused to be made ready fifty Spanish cavalrymen and thirty peones to go [with the Indians] in order to drive the enemy from the pass where they were, and they set out with the cacique and his soldiers, who loved the Spaniards better every day.

After dispatching the force to pursue Quizquiz' army, Pizarro "received a letter from San Miguel which two Spaniards brought him, and he learned . . . how the Adelantado de Alvarado had gone up to Puerto Viejo three months before with four hundred men [on foot] and one hundred and fifty cavalry and with them he entered the interior in the direction of Quito, believing that he would arrive there at the same time that the Marshal Don Diego de Almagro would enter those provinces from the other side." This news of a rival *conquistador* entering the game to snatch Ecuador from him worried Pizarro considerably.

> As a result of all this information concerning the justice and government of the city of S. Miguel and of other places, the Governor entered upon the control of it [himself]. And in order to mend matters . . . he sent his messengers in a brigantine by sea, and with them he sent orders to the Marshal, that, in the name of H. M., he should lend him [Pizarro] aid, and should conquer, pacify and settle those provinces of Quito with the troops he had with him and with those who were in readiness

in the city of San Miguel. At the same time he arranged other matters in this connection, so that Alvarado should do no harm in the land.

After sending his orders to Almagro, Pizarro sent a dispatch to Spain, informing the King of what had happened and no doubt complaining of Alvarado's invasion of what he, Pizarro, regarded as his personal province and property, according to the royal "Capitulación" which had been given him.

At this point, Sancho ends his narrative proper, and devotes four chapters to a description of the land, of Cuzco, "of the province of Collao and of the qualities and customs of its people, and of the rich gold mines that are found there," and finally to the position of the Inca in Cuzco, amounting almost to godhood.

This relation was finished in the city of Xauxa on the 15th day of the month of July, 1534. And I, Pedro Sancho, Scrivener general of these kingdoms of New Castle and secretary of the Governor Francisco Pizarro, by his order and that of the officials of H. M. wrote it just as things happened, and when it was finished I read it in the presence of the governor and of the officials of H. M., and, as it was all true, the said governor and officials of H. M. sign it with their hand.

FRANCISCO PIZARRO

ALVARO RIQUELME   ANTONIO NAVARRO

GARCIA DE SALCEDO

SANCHO

By order of the Governor and Officials

IX

THE CONQUEST
OF CHILE

HAVING conquered Peru, Pizarro installed Atahualpa's
half brother, Manco Capac, as his puppet-Inca in Cuzco,
and proceeded to parcel out the land's vast wealth among his
Spaniards. Temples were stripped of their gold. Landed estates,
including thousands of enslaved Indians to work them, were
given away with a lavish hand, together with town houses in
Cuzco and other urban centers. Mines were divided among the
caballeros and worked by captive Indians and their wives. Naturally, the Indians disliked the arangements and became restive.
A number of the Spaniards, too, were dissatisfied with their
shares and began the grumbling and plotting which was eventually to erupt into civil wars.

Then a serious dilemma confronted Pizarro. While he had
too many Spaniards for the available loot, with each claiming
a veritable lion's share, he had too few for the purpose of policing the Indians and keeping them in check. It did not, for instance, take Manco Capac very long to raise an army and besiege
Cuzco. Pizarro sent to Panama for help; fresh *conquistadores*
responded by the hundreds, drawn by tales of Peru's fabulous
wealth. They kept arriving in a steady stream, to constitute a
dangerous threat to the peace. Out of that situation developed a
great deal of exploration and conquest in search of a much-
discussed, but always elusive, second Peru somewhere in South
America.

The first embittered Spaniard to leave the land in search of a better one—or one at least as good—was Pizarro's companion-in-arms, Diego de Almagro, who had first begun to grumble in 1529, when Pizarro returned from Spain, loaded with honors, promises, and royal appointments for himself, but with nothing for his two partners. After the conquest's end, Almagro still considered himself slighted. King Charles V believed that he settled the matter when he gave Pizarro a territory to be called "New Castile," running 200 leagues along the coast and from there eastward indefinitely as far as the Pope's line of demarcation, which nobody was able to locate. Almagro was given another 200 leagues, called "New Toledo," extending southward from the southern boundary of Pizarro's realm. The trouble, again, was that nobody could tell for certain just where that southern boundary was placed and so to which of the two rivals the golden city of Cuzco belonged. No matter what the Governor himself may have felt about the matter, his brothers were certainly not going to relinquish that rich plum.

Furious, joined by a number of captains who held grudges against Pizarro, Almagro hastened to the ancient Inca capital and had himself proclaimed governor. Francisco Pizarro hastened toward Cuzco from "The City of the Kings," today's Lima, which he had founded. In the small town of Mara, the two met for a stormy session at which one Pedro de Valdivia acted as mediator. The question of Chile was raised. Regardless of whether or not his claim to Cuzco was justified, it was certain that Almagro's New Toledo reached far into that land, whose wealth—doubtlessly for the purpose of draining Spaniards away from Peru—had long and enthusiastically been proclaimed by Manco Capac and other Incas. The upshot of the meeting was an agreement whereby Almagro was to explore and conquer Chile while Pizarro was to have a free hand in consolidating the conquest of Peru.

Using all the money which had accrued to him from Atahualpa's treasure, Almagro got together a force of about 550 Spaniards, plus 15,000 Indian burden-bearers. Since the Incas had conquered half of Chile a century earlier, as far as the River Maule, and were therefore still the land's nominal rulers, Almagro took with him for diplomatic and prestige reasons the Inca Paullu, brother of Manco Capac. The high priest of Cuzco's

Temple of the Sun was also forced to go along for the purpose of making friends and influencing Indians.

Virtually all commentators say, as though by rote, that there were two southward roads into Chile in those days, one by the mountains and the other by the coast. The editor can testify from firsthand experience that the latter road did not exist. It would have been virtually impossible to travel from Peru to central Chile "by the coast," through the rugged coastal cordillera, cut only here and there by rivers. Moreover, accounts of Valdivia's subsequent march on the so-called coastal road make it abundantly clear that his route lay about a hundred miles inland, through the reasonably level land between the coastal cordillera in the west and the towering Andes in the east. It was the shorter mountain road, however, that Almagro chose for his southward march, returning some months later via the "road by the coast," terribly buffeted, bitterly disappointed, and in a violent rage.

Caught in midwinter (June) in the high altitudes, the men suffered and died. R. B. Cunninghame Graham writes:

> In this high altitude the miserable Indians, clad in the unsubstantial clothes that they wore in Peru, perished like flies. Even the Spaniards suffered terribly. Garcilasso puts the Indians' loss at ten thousand, and that of the Spaniards at one hundred and fifty, who sank and died amongst the snows. All baggage had to be abandoned, and the miserable remnant of the army pushed on for life, taking no notice of those who fell behind.[1]

The expedition seems to have inspired as many tall tales as did the twentieth-century winter war between the Soviet Union and Finland, in which thousands of dead Russians seem never to have bothered to fall after being shot unerringly through their foreheads by the brave Finns, being instantly frozen stiff and upheld in their vertical positions by the bitter cold. Five months after Almagro's passage he was followed by reinforcements who traveled the same mountain road. Solemnly it was reported then, and evidently repeated by all later writers and commentators, that these men, "reduced almost to the last gasp . . . , had been forced to eat the flesh of the horses that

[1] R. B. Cunninghame Graham, *Pedro de Valdivia, Conqueror of Chile* (N.Y. and London: Harper & Row, 1927).

had been frozen and left stiff, standing upon their feet, during Almagro's passage through the hills. Although five months had passed, the intense cold and the high altitudes had preserved their flesh as fresh as the day they had died." [2] Six years later, a Spaniard reported having found upon the road "a Negro standing propped up against the rocks without having fallen, and his horse also still standing [frozen] as if cut out of wood, and the decaying reins still in the Negro's hands."

Since this editor knows the region well, and has climbed its highest peak (Auconquilcha, 20,500 feet) to find men working a reeking sulphur mine at the top, he can unhesitatingly brand such reports as folkloric trimmings on a tale sufficiently horrible without them.

Almagro's men finally descended to warmer and lower lands, to be received hospitably by the local Indians, who flocked to pay obeisance to the Inca Paullu and to the high priest from Cuzco. Those two persuaded the Indians to give the Spaniards a large quantity of gold as well as of provisions. Moving south, however, Almagro's force soon ran into a different breed of Indians, the Araucanians, whom even the Incas had been unable to subdue a century earlier. They blocked the invaders at every turn, fighting more fiercely in every engagement. This was more difficult and discouraging than had been the conquest of Peru, whose Indians had been relatively tame and submissive. Almagro decided to turn back in order to establish his "rightful" claim to Cuzco and its surrounding rich lands.

This time they avoided the high mountains and traveled through the Atacama Desert, sending small parties from waterhole to waterhole, since large forces would have depleted the water in short time.

Since the Pizarros had no intention of letting Almagro have Cuzco, a war now broke out between the two factions. Almagro's forces were beaten decisively at the "Battle of the Salt Flats"; Almagro himself was captured and subsequently executed. One of the men on Pizarro's side who distinguished himself in this war was Pedro de Valdivia.

Born in Estremadura, Spain—nobody knows the date for certain—Valdivia had for some years served his emperor as a professional soldier in several European wars. There is considerable

[2] *Ibid.*

difference among modern writers on the question of when, and under what circumstances, he had come to the New World, but he himself was to write Charles V as follows, on October 15th, 1550:

> After having served Your Majesty as was my duty, in Italy, in winning the State of Milan, and taking prisoner the King of France in the time of the famous Colonna, and of the Marquis de Pescara, I came to this part of the Indies in the year 1535. After laboring at the exploring and conquest of Venezuela following my wishes, I went on to Peru in 1536, where I served in the subduing of those provinces to Your Majesty with the post of maestre de campo general [Chief of Staff?] to the Marquis Pizarro, of good memory, until they were at peace both from the differences among the Christians and from the rebellion of the Indians.[3]

To reward him for his valiant help in the civil war against Almagro, the Marquis Pizarro gave Valdivia a large estate with many Indians, plus a silver mine. But Don Pedro could evidently not be content with the life of a country gentleman. An ambitious man, he wanted to conquer lands of his own and rise to a governorship. Undoubtedly his paramour, the Spanish Inés de Suárez, spurred and fed his ambitions. Famous today as one of the heroines of early Chile—in the conquest of which she played an important role—that lady was quite naturally not mentioned by Valdivia in his letters to the king, partly because the *conquistador* had left a wife behind him in Spain. Nor does she appear in Cunninghame Graham's book, though she was sufficiently real and important to have had at least one Spanish and one English book written about her.

Valdivia applied to Pizarro for permission to conquer and rule Chile. Considerably surprised, since the ill-fated Almagro expedition had given that country an execrable reputation, the Marquis argued for a time but gave in at the end.

In his letter of October 15th, 1550, Valdivia gave the following account:

[3] From the third of Valdivia's five letters to King Charles V, dealing with the conquest of Chile. In Spanish, the letters were published in Seville in 1929. Cunninghame Graham's book, *op. cit.*, includes what seems to be a literal translation of all five. The present quotations were taken from that source. Here and there, however, for the purpose of readability and clarity, the text has been altered somewhat from that given by Cunninghame Graham.

The Marquis, being so zealous in Your Majesty's service, and knowing my disposition for it, opened me the door thereto under a letter and grant he held from your Majesty . . . to send to conquer and settle the government of New Toledo and the province of Chile. [The project] having been abandoned by D. Diego de Almagro who came thither, [the Marquis appointed] me for this purpose to fulfil it and hold the land as governor, and all the others that I might discover, conquer, and settle, until Your Majesty's pleasure should be known. I obeyed and gave up my mind to the task of winning for you such a land as this. And this though it was . . . [an] ill-famed expedition, owing to Almagro having come away from the land and left it, though he took with him so many and so good men. And in Peru I also left food [4] behind, as the Marquis had it, and that was the valley of Canela in Charcas, which was given [after being relinquished by me] to three *conquistadores* . . . , and a silver mine which has since been worth over two hundred thousand *castellanos*, without [my] having any profit of it, nor did the Marquis give me such toward the expedition.

In an earlier letter, dated September 4, 1545, he had mentioned his troubles in recruiting men for the enterprise:

Your Majesty shall know that when the Marquis D. Francisco Pizarro entrusted this expedition to me, there was none that cared to come to this land, and those that most shunned it were they whom the frontier-governor, D. Diego de Almagro, [had] brought with him. When he left it got so evil a name that it was shunned like the plague. Moreover, many of those that were friendly to me and were deemed men of sense, did not hold me for such a one when they saw me spending the substance I had on an undertaking so far away from Peru, . . . where the frontier-governor had not held on, he and those that came in his company having spent over five hundred thousand gold pesos, and all he got by it was to give twice as much heart to these Indians.

[But] when I saw the service that could be done to Your Majesty by entrusting oneself to it, settling and upholding it, so as by its means to make discoveries as far as the Strait of Magellan and the North Sea,[5] I set to sharpening my wits, and I raised money among the merchants. With what I had of mine,

---

[4] Being given *de comer*, "to eat," meant to the *conquistadores* obtaining a landed estate.
[5] The Atlantic Ocean.

and with the help of friends, I raised up to one hundred and fifty men, mounted and on foot, with whom I came to these lands, all of us on the way going through great toil, fighting with the Indians, and such other evil haps as there have been in these parts in abundance to this day.

One hundred and fifty was the number of men in his initial force at its greatest strength, but most of them joined him at various points along the route. In her meticulous, scholarly work on the conqueror, Mrs. Ida Vernon says [6] that when he finally managed to leave Cuzco, in January, 1540, his "army" consisted of himself, the veteran Alvar Gómez de Almagro, Diego's brother and Valdivia's invaluable camp-master who was very soon to fall from his horse and die, six young and untried soldiers, and Doña Inés de Suárez. That sorry-looking little troop, however, rode herd on a force of a thousand *yanaconas* (Indian burden-bearers) and 30 pack-horses, all overloaded with supplies for the expedition, plus a quantity of chickens, pigs, seeds, tools, and other things they would need once they arrived in central Chile and settled down as colonists.

Valdivia was ready to leave Cuzco in December, 1539, but was delayed a month through the unexpected—and unwelcome— arrival from Spain of Pedro Sancho de Hoz, who, as Pizarro's secretary, had earlier been the official chronicler of the conquest (Chapter VIII). Claiming to have been commissioned by the king to conquer, settle, and rule New Toledo, Sancho proposed to take charge of the expedition, offering Valdivia a place in it as his, Sancho's lieutenant. The resulting dispute was taken before Pizarro in Lima, the upshot being that the two disputants signed a formal agreement as partners. Valdivia, however, regarded the partnership as purely a commercial arrangement, in no way infringing on his own rights as commander and governor of New Toledo. After arranging for the other to remain behind for the purpose of obtaining more supplies and recruiting more men with whom to join his own body along the way, he finally managed to leave Cuzco.

Little is known about Valdivia's southward march through the great Chilean desert; no detailed firsthand account of it seems ever to have been written. In the first of his letters to the

[6] Ida Stevenson Weldon Vernon, *Pedro de Valdivia, Conquistador of Chile* (Austin: University of Texas Press, 1946).

king, that of September 4th, 1545, Valdivia himself mentioned only the local Indians' bothersome scorched-earth policy.

> From Indians taken on the way as I came hither I knew that the Inca, Manco, the native lord of Cuzco and a rebel against your Majesty's sway, had sent to warn the chiefs of this land of our coming, and to tell them that if they wanted us to go back again like Almagro, they should hide all the gold, llamas, clothing, stuffs and food, for since we sought all this we should go away if we did not find it. And this they did so thoroughly that the llamas were eaten . . . and the gold and all the rest burnt. They did not even spare their very clothing, but left themselves bare, and so they have lived, are living, and will live till they come into obedience.

Mrs. Vernon, who examined literally hundreds of authoritative scraps in almost as many reference works, gives us his route, while also committing a few common geographical errors, such as having him head for the west shore of Lake Titicaca and then taking the "coastal route." After leaving Cuzco the force, picking up more men as it went until it numbered 150, marched first to Arequipa, which is about 120 miles west of Lake Titicaca and some 60 miles east of the Pacific coast. The next stop was Tacna, still 30 miles inland. Their trek through the desert, from waterhole to waterhole, took them through the pleasant oases of Pica and Matilla, 60 miles inland from today's Pacific port of Iquique, and thence to the two settlements which were called Atacama la Chica and Atacama la Grande, identified by Mrs. Vernon as today's Chiu Chiu and San Pedro de Atacama. At nearly ten thousand feet altitude, on the Río Loa and a hundred miles from the Pacific coast, Chiu Chiu is today a small village near the ruins of a former Indian town whose ancient cemetery has yielded artifacts dating back to before the land's conquest by the Incas, to the century of Inca rule which preceded the invasion by Spaniards, and finally, in the form of scraps of velvet and copper horseshoe nails, to Valdivia's day. San Pedro de Atacama lies 80 miles southeast of Chiu Chiu.

The expedition camped at Chiu Chiu while Valdivia rode to San Pedro with eight or ten men, to forage for food and to pick up a body of 25 more Spaniards, "fifteen horsemen and ten arquebusiers," who were waiting for him there. While in San Pedro, Valdivia received an urgent message, informing him that

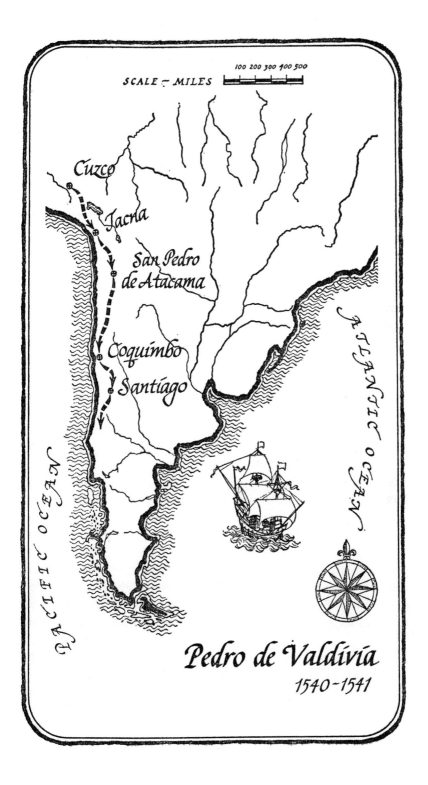

SCALE — MILES

100 200 300 400 500

Cuzco

Tacna

San Pedro
de Atacama

Coquimbo

Santiago

PACIFIC OCEAN

ATLANTIC OCEAN

Pedro de Valdívia

1540~1541

Pedro Sancho de Hoz had arrived in Chiu Chiu with evil intentions and a small group of friends. Taking ten horsemen with him, Valdivia is reported to have galloped back to Chiu Chiu "in one night," a report which the present editor, having required three days to cover the distance on muleback, permits himself to doubt.

There was no doubt, and plenty of evidence, that Sancho had intended to kill Valdivia in Chiu Chiu and take command of the expedition. A gallows was erected for hanging Sancho and his companions, but in the end they were given a conditional pardon. The men were sent back to Peru "without arms and without horses." Sancho, however, broke down and begged to be pardoned, "promising to continue the journey as an ordinary soldier if only he were allowed to continue it at all." Valdivia finally relented and agreed to take Sancho with him, though under guard. For seven years the conspirator stayed with the company, without, however, being able to break himself of the conspiracy habit. He was caught in one plot after another, imprisoned and forgiven again and again. At one point he was even awarded a landed estate in central Chile with Indians to work it. Finally, on December 3, 1547, that one-time favorite of Emperor Charles V was caught in the last of his plots with discontented Spaniards to kill Valdivia and make himself governor, and was beheaded in the city of Santiago.

Slowly, combatting hunger, thirst, dust, hostile Indians, and incredible fatigue, the Spaniards made their way south through the worst part of the Atacama Desert. At last, when they were on the verge of eating the animals which they would later need as settlers, they came to the green valley of Copiapó, which marked the southern boundary of the desert. Here the *conquistadores* rested some two months. Mrs. Vernon wrote that Valdivia "ordered Luis de Cartagena, the scribe, to write an account of all that had happened," but gives no inkling of where that account is today.

After leaving Copiapó, the Spaniards found the Indians to be both more numerous and fiercer than had been those farther north. December 13, 1540, after weeks of constant fighting in which every valley was hotly contested by followers of the great cacique Michimalongo, they finally reached the fertile and beautiful valley of the Mapocho River, "where they could pitch their tents permanently." They had been 11 months on the way after leaving Cuzco. Battles and other causes had by now reduced their number from 150 to 136, the survivors including Inés de Suárez and Sancho de Hoz, and Valdivia himself.

Still beset by Indians, they could not found the city of Santiago until February. Wrote Valdivia in 1545:

> I reached this valley of Mapocho towards the end of 1540. I at once set about coming to speech with the chiefs of the land, and owing to the diligence with which I moved about it—whereby they believed that we were many Christians—most of them came in peacefully and served us well for five or six months. They did this in order not to lose the provisions which they got in the camp. In this time they built us our wood and grass houses on the plan I gave them, on a spot where I founded this city of Santiago del Nuevo Extremo in Your Majesty's name in this said valley, when I came there on the 24th of February, 1541.

But they were not to occupy their new city in peace.

> I . . . got news that the Indians were making a levy of the whole land in two parts to come and make war on us. I, with ninety, went to attack the greater one, leaving my lieutenant to guard the town with fifty, thirty being horsed. And while I was dealing with the one part, the others came down on the town and fought the whole day through with the Christians. They burned down the whole town, the food and clothing and all that we had, so that we were left but with the tattered clothes we had for fighting, and with the arms at our sides, and two small pigs, a suckling-pig, a cock and a hen, and about two handfuls of wheat. In the end, when night came, the Christians got so much courage . . . that, although all wounded . . . they put the Indians to flight and killed very many of them. . . .
>
> Seeing the plight we were in, it seemed to me that, if we were to cling to the land and make it Your Majesty's forever, we must eat of the fruit of our hands as in the beginning of the world, and I set about sowing. . . . When the seed had been sown, some kept guard over it and the town . . . while I, with the others, moved all the time eight or ten leagues around it, breaking up the bands of Indians where I knew them to be, for they surrounded us on every side. And with the Christians and the people we brought from Peru in our service, I built up the town again, and we . . . sowed to feed themselves. It was no easy thing to find maize for seeds, and it was got with great risk.

I also had the two handfuls of wheat sown, and from them that year twelve *fanegas* [nineteen bushels] were harvested, whereof we provided ourselves with seeds.

Sowing, harvesting, hungering because every grain of seed, every pig, hen, and egg, had to be nurtured carefully for purposes of multiplication, fighting Indians, the Spaniards had a busy and terrifying time, with the indomitable Inés de Suárez always active in both leadership and fighting. Eventually, however, things were put into sufficient order that Valdivia could leave Santiago with eighty men on a scouting and exploring expedition. His dual purpose, beside wanting to teach better manners to the hostile Indians, was to search for the gold which the *conquistadores* had always uppermost in their minds, and to find a spot by the ocean where he could build a ship for sea communication with Peru.

The expedition seemed phenomenally successful. In a battle with the Indians they captured the great chief, Michimalongo himself. He couldn't pay an Atahualpa ransom, but he showed them his gold mines instead. Overjoyed, the Spaniards put a hundred of their *yanaconas* from Peru to work in the mine, while Michimalongo added 1,200 of his own Indians. Ten Spaniards were left there to guard the mine and keep the natives working. The men proceeded to the coast, where they found a good spot and put men to work building the vessel, while Valdivia remained there with eight horsemen. Things seemed to be working out fine; the vessel was almost completed early in August, 1541; and the happy Spaniards had already begun to count their share of the gold together with their prospering crops. But then a messenger arrived from Santiago with the news that another plot to assassinate the commander had been uncovered.

I received a letter from the Captain Alonso de Monroy, wherein he gave me news of a certain plot on foot to kill me among some of the soldiers belonging to the frontier-governor's party. . . . When I got this letter I came away to this town [Santiago]. . . . I made my enquiries here, and found many guilty, but with the straits in which I was I hanged [only] five and said nothing to the others. . . . They [apparently the five] confessed in their statements that they had made arrangements in the provinces of Peru with the persons advising D. Diego to kill me here about this time, for so they were to do there [in Peru] to the Marquis Pizarro in April or May. And this was their resolve, to go and live an easy life in Peru with those of their party, and to leave the land if they could not administer it.

His force being as small as it was, Valdivia could not afford to hang too many men. Even the incorrigible Sancho de Hoz escaped execution but was imprisoned. Valdivia had heard earlier reports from the Indians of the assassination of Pizarro—without quite believing them. "For they lie," he wrote. Actually, the Marquis had been killed in Lima, June 26th, 1541.

While Valdivia was busy with the treason plot in Santiago, two messengers rode in from the shipbuilding site with the news that Michimalongo's 1,200 Indians at the mines had revolted, had killed all the Spaniards' *yanaconas* together with their Spanish overlords, had taken the gold to the sea, dumped it, burned the almost completed ship, and killed all but those two of the force which Valdivia had left at the site.

Now they had to start all over again, while it was obvious that they were in desperate need of more men.

> I resolved to send the Captain Alonso de Monroy to . . . Peru with five men and the best horses I had (I could not give him more), and he offered himself for so manifest a danger to serve Your Majesty and bring me help. . . . I knew that no men would stir to come to these lands owing to their ill repute unless someone should go from here to bring them and take gold to buy men withal.

Monroy stayed away more than two years. After losing four of his five original men on the northward march, to warlike Indians who also took away all the gold he had as well as his dispatches—though Monroy took from them a Spaniard he found in their settlement, a member of Almagro's earlier expedition who had deserted to live with the natives—he reached Peru. There, after borrowing money, urging and cajoling men to go to Chile with him, he at last returned with 60 horsemen. He also managed to have a ship sent south with supplies, including wine which seems to have been badly needed. Valdivia wrote his king, "for four months divine services had not been held for want of it, nor had we heard Mass."

During Monroy's absence, the small force based at Santiago

planted, harvested, and fought, "seeing the great shamelessness and boldness shown by the Indians," fought again and again, planted and harvested, and built an adobe wall around their little settlement, which was destined to grow—through their astonishing energy and industry and from three pigs, a rooster and hen, plus two handfuls of wheat—into today's splendid capital of Chile.

In his letter of September 4, 1545, Valdivia stated that it had taken Monroy "nearly three years' time" after his departure to return to Chile with reinforcements. In that of October 15th, 1550, which repeated, and enlarged upon, many of the accounts given in the first letter, he made the time almost exactly two years.

Says the letter of 1545:

> The toils of war, ever-victorious Caesar, men can bear, since it is the soldier's boast to die fighting; but if those of hunger are added to them, they must be more than men to bear them. . . . Up to the last of these three years, when we have sown very well and had food in plenty, we went through the two first in very great want. . . . Many of the Christians had to go sometimes to dig up roots for food. . . . When these came to an end, things were as before, and all the women, our servants, and children lived thus, and there was no meat, and the Christian who got fifty grains of maize a day thought himself well off. . . . And in this manner have we lived, and the soldiers would have been very satisfied had I left them in their houses with this subsistence; but I chose to have thirty or forty mounted men always about the plain in winter. . . . And so we went about like ghosts, and the Indians called us *Cupais*, which is the name they give to their devils, for whenever they came in search of us—for they know how to attack at night—they found us awake, armed, and, if needful, on horseback. And so great was the care I took in all this all the time that, though we were a few and they many, I had them in hand, and Your Majesty may know that we did not do it with folded hands.

Later in the same letter he painted a glowing picture of the wealth of Chile—which he called "Nueva Extremadura" because of the bad repute in which "Chile" was held as a result of Almagro's failure there—its timbers, gold, amazing fertility. Obviously he wrote in that manner in order to win royal favor and attract more settlers. To prove the point that "in this land all that are here and that may come can be fed," he wrote:

> In three months from now, in December (which is mid-summer), there will be harvested in this town ten or twelve thousand fanegas [16,000 or 19,000 bushels] of wheat, and any amount of maize, and from the two small pigs and suckling-pig we saved when the Indians burned down the town there are now eight or ten thousand head, and of the cock and hen-fowl as many as blades of grass, breeding in abundance in summer and winter.

On the arrival of the badly needed supplies and reinforcements:

> In September, 1543, Lucas Martínez Vegazo's ship reached the harbor of Valparaiso of this town, and the Captain Alonso de Monroy came with his men from mid-December onwards; and from that time the Indians did not dare to come any more, nor did they come within four leagues round this town, and they all withdrew to the province of the Promaocaes. [But] they sent me messengers daily, bidding me to come to fight them and bring the Christians that had come, for they wanted to see whether they were as brave as we were, and if they were, they would submit to us, but if not, they would do as they had done before. I sent them answer that I would do so.
>
> When the men and horses had recovered—for they had arrived all weak through not having seen one peaceful Indian from Peru to here, suffering much hunger through finding everywhere the food taken away, I went forth with all the men that had come very well equipped and on horseback . . . and went to seek the Indians. When I came to the strongholds, I found them all fled . . . leaving all their villages burned down and deserting the best stretch of land in the world, so that it looks as if it had never had any Indians in it.

In April, 1544, another ship came south with supplies, but the Indians of Copiapó lured its crew ashore, killed all but "three men and a Negro and plundered and burned the vessel." But in June of that year still another ship arrived, sent by Peru's governor, Pizarro's successor, Vaca de Castro.

> The rage of the winter being over, in mid-August, when spring begins, I went to the harbor. Learning the wishes of the captain [Juan Bautista de Pastene], which were to serve Your

Majesty here as I should order him, and learning what a person he was . . . I made him my lieutenant-general by sea, and sent him to explore this coast as far as the Strait of Magellan, giving him another ship and a very good crew for both, that he might take possession of the land in Your Majesty's name.

The Spaniards left in Santiago now pushed as far as the River Maule, a hundred miles south, where the Incas, a century earlier, had been stopped by the Araucano Indians.

I have Francisco de Aguirre, my captain, on this side of the River Maule . . . with men holding the frontier. He does not allow the Indians there to cross to the other side, and if they are caught, he punishes them; and he will be there till I go forward. The Indians, seeing themselves so followed, and that we stay on the land, and that ships and men have come, have their wings clipped, and now, being wearied of going about through snow and mountains like animals they are resolved to give in. Last summer they began to rebuild their villages, and each cacique has given his Indians seed, both maize and wheat, and they have sown for seed and to feed themselves. From now on henceforward there will be a great abundance of food in this land for there are two sowings in the year, the maize being gathered in April and May, and then wheat is sown; and in December it is harvested, and maize sown again.

By such means, at terrible cost in hardship and loss of men, brutality and the butchery of thousands of Indians, was Chile's central valley finally secured. But there was to be no peace for years to come. The Araucanian Indians, south of the River Maule, made war implacably, not only on Valdivia and his men, but on one after another of his successors. Governor after governor was to come out from Spain, determined to win glory by finally defeating those fierce fighters. Nobody ever succeeded. Unbeaten in war, the Araucanians finally signed a treaty of peace with the Republic of Chile in 1850. They still live in Chile's south, preserving their language and many of their ancient customs.

One Lautaro, Valdivia's stableboy, escaped from the Spaniards, returned to his people, had them steal horses, taught them to ride and breed the animals, organized a cavalry, and led them in relentless warfare against the invaders. Valdivia crossed into their territory, looted it, founded cities only to have them burned by his enemies, returned and founded new cities. Finally he was captured, on Christmas Day, 1553, and was executed a week or so later. A legend was to arise in later years that the Araucanians, taunting him with his lust for precious metals, offered him all he wanted and killed him by pouring melted gold down his throat. Actually, he seems to have been clubbed to death after some days of fearful torture.

X

THE FIRST DESCENT
OF THE AMAZON

THE conquest of the Andean regions with their wealth in minerals, fertile lands, and Indians to work those lands, required a mere 41 years, though the "exploration" of those regions, their systematic examination, is not yet completed. Between 1500 and 1541, the entire stretch of 3,500 miles, from Colombia's Caribbean coast to Chile's River Maule, had been conquered and divided among the avid conquerors. Meanwhile, however, more *conquistadores* and would-be *conquistadores* arrived on the west coast, threatening to become serious social problems because all the land, all the wealth, all the Indians in sight had already been divided by their predecessors. Before the conquest of the Andean regions had been completed, the stream of epic exploration turned eastward, over the Andes and into the Amazon basin, while rumors of vast wealth to be found in those regions were kept alive as lures to draw men away from lands along the coast.

The first recorded expedition eastward over the Andes was that of Gonzalo Pizarro, half brother of the great conqueror, who set out in February, 1541, to seek El Dorado and the forests of cinnamon trees which were reputed to exist on the other side of the mountains. His second-in-command was Francisco de Orellana who was to win acclaim for being the first European to cross South America via the world's greatest river, while also being accused of treason and desertion by his commander as well as by a long string of scholars, dramatists, and historians during the ensuing centuries.

The mouth of the Amazon River had been discovered and explored in 1500 by a Spanish expedition commanded by Vicente Yáñez Pinzón, who had accompanied Columbus on his first voyage. To Orellana goes the honor of having been the first to travel most of its course from the headwaters of one of its major tributaries. The epic journey, however, was unplanned and unintended. When the large and cumbersome Pizarro expedition found itself in difficulties and short of supplies near the headwaters of one of the Río Napo's tributaries, Orellana was dispatched downstream with 60 men to forage for food, which meant, according to the custom of those days, to scout for Indians from whom food could be taken. However, they came to discover that it was much easier to travel downstream than up; they decided, in fact, that an upriver return to the expedition's main body was impossible and that there was nothing for them to do but continue their eastward voyage to wherever the stream might carry them.

Though their failure to return caused Pizarro later to accuse Orellana of desertion, it also taught a valuable lesson to Peru's authorities. On at least one subsequent occasion, in 1559, those authorities fanned into flame the rumors of an El Dorado sighting far down the Amazon and north of the river, and organized an expedition, primarily for the purpose of ridding their country of some 300 discontented, turbulent latecomers (see Chapter XI).

Francisco de Orellana, a kinsman of the Pizarros, was born in Trujillo, Estremadura, about 1511 and came to the New World when still in his teens. In his own words, he participated "in the conquest of Lima and Trujillo and Cuzco and in the pursuit of the Inca and in the conquest of Puerto Viejo and its outlying territory," losing an eye in the course of those activities. Since the cities of Lima and Puerto Viejo had both been founded by the Spaniards in 1535, Orellana's claim to have participated in their "conquest" must have referred to the land on which they are situated. He settled for a time in Puerto Viejo, but soon went off to the wars again, marching to Lima with a body of men to aid in the relief of that city from Manco Capac's revolting, besieging Indians. In 1538 he participated in the battle of Las Salinas between the forces of Pizarro and those of Almagro.

According to José Toribio Medina, writing in 1894,[1] the destruction of the Almagro party left "many captains who had served under the banners of Pizarro . . . without occupation. To leave them inactive was extremely dangerous when the leaven of civil disturbances was latent and might ferment at the least threat; and, besides, it was necessary to reward them in some manner for their services in the cause of Pizarro." The governor therefore scattered those men in all directions, commissioning them to explore and conquer lands which were still unknown. "In this distribution there fell to Orellana the Province of Culata, which was picked out for him with the special commission that he should found a city there."

The city founded by Orellana to provide an outlet to the sea for the ancient inland Indian city of Quito and its surrounding lands is today's Guayaquil, on Ecuador's coastal plain. He conquered the Culata territory and built the city at his own expense, with the help of a group of men he had picked up near Lima. Pizarro was so pleased over his success that he appointed Orellana "captain-general and lieutenant-governor in the new city and in Puerto Viejo."

In December, 1540, Orellana was informed that his kinsman, Gonzalo Pizarro, had arrived in Quito to replace Sebastián de Benalcázar as governor of the Provinces of Quito, which included Guayaquil, and that Pizarro was preparing to lead a great expedition over the Andes to search for El Dorado and the cinnamon forests. Orellana immediately went to Quito to see his new chief, and at the same time "to offer to accompany him on the proposed expedition," offering to take his friends along and to bear the cost of his participation from his own pocket. Having been accepted, he hurried back to Guayaquil to wind up his affairs and then returned to Quito. Friar Gaspar de Carvajal, the chronicler of Orellana's Amazon voyage, has the following to say about the first stage:

[1] The materials for the present account, including the quotations from Medina, Friar Gaspar de Carvajal, and Gonzalo Pizarro, are from *The Discovery of the Amazon, According to the Account of Friar Gaspar de Carvajal and Other Documents,* with an introduction by José Toribio Medina, translated from the Spanish by Bertram T. Lee, edited by H. C. Heaton (New York: American Geographical Society, 1934).

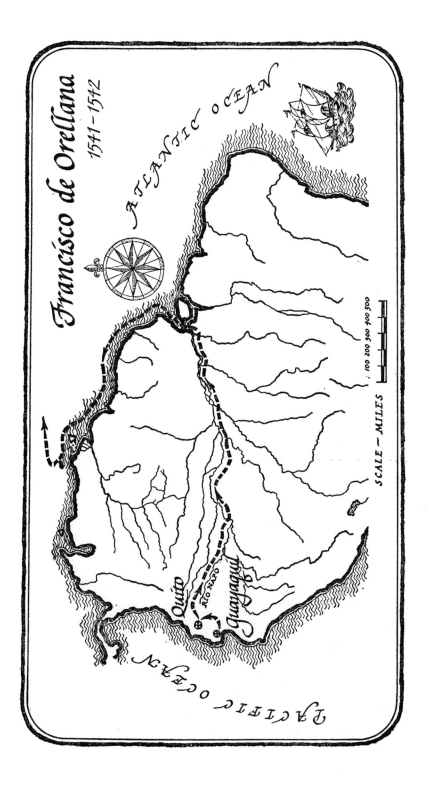

Francisco de Orellana
1541-1542

ATLANTIC OCEAN

PACIFIC OCEAN

Quito

RIO NAPO

Guayaquil

SCALE — MILES

100 200 300 400 500

He departed for the town of Quito, where he had left the said Gonzalo Pizarro, and when he arrived there he found that he had already started out, for which reason the Captain was somewhat embarrassed as to what he should do, and he determined to press forward and follow him . . ., although the Spaniards dwelling in the country tried to dissuade him from doing so because he would have to pass through a hostile and rough country and because they feared that they [the natives] would kill him as they had done others who had gone [there] with a very large force of men; yet notwithstanding this, for the sake of serving His Majesty, he determined in spite of all this risk to go and catch up with the said Governor; and so [he did], suffering many hardships both from hunger and from fights which the Indians forced upon him, for he, not having more than twenty-three men wtih him, many times they placed him in such straits that they considered themselves doomed to destruction and death at their hands; and in spite of these hardships he journeyed [about thirty] leagues from Quito, before the end of which [journey] he had lost all that he had started out with, so that when he overtook the said Gonzalo Pizarro he had still left only a sword and a shield, and his companions likewise.

Orellana's journey to catch up with his commander was made doubly difficult by the fact that Pizarro's large and cumbersome force had virtually swept the country clean of provisions while also enraging the resident Indians. Acccording to Medina, Pizarro had left Quito with nearly 4,000 Indians, as well as 220 Spaniards.

He assembled also almost an equal number of horses . . . ; arquebuses, crossbows, munitions of all kinds in abundance; llamas as beasts of burden, destined also to serve as food; more than two thousand live hogs,[2] and almost as many dogs, efficient aids for hunting, as well as, whenever the occasion should present itself, for turning loose on hostile Indians.

Pizarro was delighted to receive Orellana and "promptly made him his lieutenant-general." Exhausted from the privations

[2] Other accounts place the number of hogs at 5,000. The availability of those animals, as well as of the expedition's many horses, so soon after the country's conquest, attests to the Spaniards' energy in settling and transforming their new American possessions. The availability of nearly 4,000 unfortunate Indians attests to Pizarro's personal foresight. His first act on taking command in Quito was to have them rounded up and put in irons to make sure that they would be on hand when needed.

endured, Orellana and his men, together with a part of the Pizarro body, remained in camp while the commander set out with 80 men to search for the cinnamon forests. Traveling on foot because the terrain was unsuitable for horses, they searched for more than 70 days, suffering from torrential rains, hunger, and fevers, as a result of which several Spaniards died. They did find some trees "which bear cinnamon," but they were so scattered and inaccessible that their exploitation for profit was impossible. The indomitable Spaniards asked innumerable questions of the Indians they met, refusing to accept unsatisfactory answers. Medina writes: "Irritated when these Indians could not give him the kind of answer that he wanted, he delivered some of them over to be torn to pieces by the dogs, while others he caused to be burned alive." They came to a large river, "dotted with canoes manned by Indians," some of whom they lured to shore with promises of presents and good treatment. Their chief told Pizarro, "fully conscious that he was lying, that farther on there were great settlements and regions very rich, ruled over by powerful overlords; and, by way of rewarding the chief for what he had related, Pizarro ordered him to be held prisoner for such services as he might later furnish as a guide."

After more wanderings along the river, and several skirmishes with Indians, Pizarro pitched camp on a small savanna surrounded by dense forests, and sent for Orellana with the expedition's main body. When the men were again united, the camp master was sent on an exploration trip with 50 companions. In his letter to the king, dated September 3, 1542, Pizarro wrote that "he was fifteen days going and coming and he brought back a story that he had found a great river, that there were houses right on the edge of the water, and that on the river he had seen many Indians wearing clothes, going about in canoes, and that it seemed to him that the province was a thoroughly settled one, because the Indians whom he had seen wore clothes and [were] quite civilized."

The Spaniards set out to reach the great river, probably the Coca, though the going was difficult in part because all the Indian slaves whom they had taken from Quito had by this time died. Being highland Indians, they were unduly susceptible to lowland fevers. Moreover, while the soldiers now had to do their own carrying, they also began to suffer from hunger, all their swine and llamas having been consumed.

According to Friar Carvajal's account, they followed the river "twenty leagues, at the end of which we found some settlements not very large, and here the said Gonzalo Pizarro decided that a boat should be built to cross from one side of the river to the other for food, for that river was now half a league wide." Orellana oposed the construction of the boat, urging that the expedition return to the savannas to "follow the roads that led to the settled country," but Pizarro "would consent to nothing save that work on the said boat be started, and so Captain Orellana, seeing this, went throughout the camp securing iron for nails and apportioning to each one the timbers that he was to bring, and in this manner and with the labor of all the said boat was built."

According to Carvajal, Pizarro "placed a certain amount of baggage and some sick Indians [in the boat] and we went down the river another fifty leagues, at the end of which we found no more inhabited regions, and we were now suffering very great privation and lacked food, for which reason all of the companions were greatly dissatisfied and talked of returning and not going ahead any farther, because it was reported that there was a great uninhabited region [ahead]."

Orellana now volunteered to proceed downstream to search for food. Pizarro accepted the offer, turning over to his lieutenant the boat, which he called a brigantine, some canoes, and 60 men, including the friar who was to become the chronicler of Orellana's voyage. While that force proceeded downstream in the brigantine and some canoes, Pizarro was to go overland with the main body of men, to an agreed-upon rendezvous point where the foragers were to meet them with food. When he arrived there, however, he found that Orellana had gone on downstream.

> When the members of the expeditionary force, having gone that far, saw the junction and realized [that there was no relief] for them in the way of food, because he had gone on and there was no way of finding any food whatsoever, they became greatly discouraged, because for many days the whole expeditionary force had eaten nothing but palm shoots and some fruit stones which they found on the ground which had fallen from the

trees, together with all the various kinds of noxious wild beasts which they had been able to find. They had eaten in this wild country more than one thousand dogs and more than one hundred horses, without any other kind of food whatsoever, from which cause many members of the expeditionary force had become sick, and some were weak, while others died of hunger and from not being in a condition to go on any farther.

Pizarro managed to steal a few canoes from the Indians. Foraging brought him a certain amount of food, but he came by now to consider his quest hopeless. He turned back with his force and finally, near the end of June, 1542, reached Quito with 80 emaciated men, no Indians, no horses and no dogs. Of the original 220 Spaniards, 60 had gone with Orellana, which means that about 80 had died in the expedition's course, some of them probably having been killed by hostile Indians.

The Orellana party had set out with very little food, which was gone within five days, but was traveling rapidly, "at the rate," as reported by Carvajal, "of some twenty to twenty-five leagues [a day], for now the river was high and [its power] increased owing to the effect of many other rivers which emptied into it." They found themselves traversing a large stretch of uninhabited country where no food was to be found. Returning upstream against the swift current might have been physically possible, but with no food on hand or available they could not have made the journey in any event. After consultations and some arguments, and after the good friar had commended their souls to God in a solemn mass, they decided to proceed downriver on what was probably the Napo. Carvajal writes:

It was decided . . . to go forward and follow the river, . . . trusting in our Lord that he would see fit to preserve our lives until we should see our way out; and in the meantime, lacking other victuals, we reached a [state of] privation so great that we were eating nothing but leather, belts and soles of shoes, cooked with certain herbs, with the result that so great was our weakness that we could not remain standing, for some on all fours and others with staffs went into the woods to search for a few roots to eat and some there were who ate certain herbs with which they were not familiar, and they were at the point of death, because they were like mad men and did not possess sense; but, as Our Lord was pleased that we should continue our journey, no one died.

On New Year's Day, 1542, some of the men believed that they heard Indian drums, but throughout the following week they neither heard nor saw anything of human inhabitants. Not until January 8, "while eating certain forest roots they heard drums very plainly very far from where we were." Orellana now ordered his men to be on the alert and have weapons ready for a possible attack. The next morning, after a night spent in worried vigilance, "we saw coming up the river to look over and reconnoitre the land four canoes filled with Indians, and, when they saw us, they turned about at great speed, giving the alarm, in such a manner that in less than a quarter of an hour we heard in the villages many drums that were calling the country to arms."

By the time the Spaniards had reached the first village, its inhabitants had fled, leaving a welcome supply of food behind. About two in the afternoon a few Indians began to return on the river. Orellana lured two of them ashore, gave them presents, and asked them to go and fetch their "overlord," who "came right away, very much decked out, to where the Captain and the companions were and was very well received by the Captain and by all. . . . The Chief ordered his Indians to bring food, and in a very short time they brought, in abundance, all that was needed, including meats, partridges, turkeys, and fish of many sorts."

Orellana sent the Indian chief home, asking him to return the next day with all the other chiefs, of whom there were said to be 13. (According to Carvajal, Orellana spoke the Indians' language, though where he could have learned it is hard to imagine.) It required several days to bring all the chiefs together, after which Orellana "took possession of them and of the said land in the name of His Majesty."

The Spaniards stayed in the village nearly three weeks, on friendly terms with the Indians, who brought them much food "with as much orderliness as if all their lives they had been servants; and they came wearing their jewels and gold medallions." It was at this spot that the Spaniards first heard of the Amazons, said to live far down the river, and also of "another overlord who lived at some distance from the river, far inland, who . . . possessed very great wealth in gold."

In order not to waste time, Orellana had his men begin to gather materials and make nails for another boat, larger than the one they had. Though inexperienced in that kind of work, they made bellows out of buskins, cut wood, made charcoal, gathered all the iron they could produce among them, and managed to make some two thousand nails as well as a number of other things which they would need for the new boat. They left the settlement on February 2, in part because food was again running short while the Indians seemed to be growing restive. The next day, after some dangerous adventures with powerful currents, they reached another settlement of peaceful Indians, who treated them well and gave them much food, "consisting of turtles and parrots in abundance," and sent them to the other side of the river to an uninhabited village. Mosquitos drove them out of the latter place, and the Spaniards proceeded downstream, from village to village. On February 12 they reached a confluence with a great river, undoubtedly the main-stream of the Amazon. Finally, on February 26, they arrived at the village of a famous and powerful overlord named Aparia the Great. There were some tense moments when it seemed that the Indians might attack, but, according to Carvajal, they were saved by the fact that Orellana knew the Indians' language, understood what they said, and convinced them of his peaceful intentions. Aparia, accompanied by his court of lesser chiefs and nobles, asked for a conference and "ordered to be brought from his canoes a great quantity of foodstuffs, not only turtles, but also manatees and other fish, and roasted partridges and cats and monkeys." Carvajal reports:

> The Captain, perceiving the polite manners of the over-lord, addressed a few words to him, giving him to understand that we were Christians and worshipped a single God, who was the creator of all things, and that we were not like them who walked in the paths of error worshipping stones and images made [by man]; and in this connection he told them many other things, and explained to them also how we were servants and vassals of the Emperor of the Christians, the great King of Spain, and [that] he was called Don Carlos our master, to whom belonged the territory of all the Indies and many other dominions and kingdoms existing throughout the world, and that it

was by his command that we were coming to that land, and that we were going to make a report to him on what we had seen in it.

The Spaniards stayed in the village almost two months, building their second boat. "Such great haste was applied to the building of the brigantine," writes Carvajal, "that in thirty-five days it was constructed and launched, calked with cotton and tarred with pitch, all of which the Indians brought." They were well treated by Aparia and his subjects, who urged them to remain in the village instead of proceeding downstream where the fierce Amazons, "whom they call 'Coniupuyara' in their tongue, which means 'grand mistresses,'" were likely to kill them. Nevertheless, having spent Easter in the village, they departed on Monday, April 24, happy about their new boat, which was large enough to be used at sea after they had come to the river's mouth. Carvajal writes:

> We came on down past the settlements belonging to that dominion of Aparia, which extended for more than eighty leagues, without finding a single warlike Indian; on the contrary, the Chief himself came to talk and to bring us abundant food. . . .
> Within a few days the Indians ceased to appear, and by this we recognized that we were [now] outside the dominion and tribal domains of that great overlord Aparia; and the Captain, fearing what might come to pass on account of the small food supply, ordered that the brigantines proceed with greater speed than had been the custom.

On May 13, they arrived "in the provinces belonging to Machiparo, who is a very great overlord and one having many people under him, and is a neighbor of another overlord just as great, named Omagua, and they are friends who join together to make war on other overlords who are [located] far inland, for they [i.e., the latter] come each day to drive them from their homes."

Carvajal writes that Machiparo had under his command 50,000 warriors, aged between thirty years and seventy, "because the young men do not go to war."

> Before we had come within two leagues of this village, we saw the villages gleaming white, and we had not proceeded far

when we saw coming up the river a great many canoes, all equipped for fighting, gaily colored, and [the men] with their shields on, which are made out of the shell-like skins of lizards and the hides of manatees and of tapirs, as tall as a man, because they cover them entirely.

There was a battle, in the course of which the Spaniards managed to take the first village, though still beset by Indians. They found "a great quantity of food, such as turtles in pens and pools of water, and a great deal of meat and fish and biscuit, and all this in such great abundance that there was enough to feed an expeditionary force of one thousand men for one year."

However, the Indians did not allow them to rest, coming back at them constantly on land and on the river.

They followed us for two days and two nights without letting us rest, for it took us that long to get out of the territory occupied by the subjects of this great overlord named Machiparo, which in the opinion of all extended eighty leagues, for it was all of one tongue, these [eighty leagues] being all inhabited, for there was not from village to village [in most cases] a crossbow shot, and the one which was farthest [removed from the next] was not half a league away, and there was one settlement that stretched for five leagues without there intervening any space from house to house, which was a marvellous thing to behold.

Having passed the domain of Machiparo, the Spaniards came to that of a chief named Oniguayal, where they captured a fortified village, well supplied with food. After a few days' rest they resumed their voyage, now passing the domain of Omagua.[3]

There were numerous and very large settlements and very pretty country and very fruitful land: . . . because the villages were so numerous and so large and because there were so many inhabitants, the Captain did not wish to make port, and so all that day we passed through settled country with occasional fighting, because on the water they attacked us so pitilessly that they made us go down mid-river; and many times the Indians started to converse with us, and, as we did not understand them, we did not know what they were saying to us.

At the hour of vespers we came to a village that was on a high bank, and as it appeared small to us the Captain ordered

[3] Carvajal mistakenly took "Omagua" to be the name of a chief. Actually, a large, powerful, and remarkably advanced Indian tribe or nation was called "The Omaguas."

us to capture it, and also because it looked so nice that it seemed as if it might be the recreation spot of some overlord of the inland. The Indians put up a defense for more than an hour, but in the end they were beaten and we were masters of the village, where we found very great quantities of food, of which we laid in a supply.

In this village there was a villa in which was a great deal of porcelain ware of various makes, both jars and pitchers, very large . . . and other small pieces such as plates and bowls and candelabra of this porcelain of the best that has ever been seen in this world, for that of Málaga is not its equal. . . . Here the Indians told us that as much as there was made out of clay in this house, so much there was back in the country in gold and silver, and [they said] that they would take us there, for it was near. . . . In this village also there were gold and silver; but, as our intention was merely to search for something to eat and see to it that we saved our lives and gave an account of such a great accomplishment, we did not concern ourselves with, nor were we interested in, any wealth.

From this village there were many roads, and fine highways to the inland country.

Their next stopping place, after having passed the dominion of Omagua "for more than one hundred leagues," was the first settlement in the realm of a chief named Paguana. Of this village Carvajal writes that it

> must have been more than two leagues long [and] in which the Indians let us go to them in their houses without doing us any harm or damage. . . . From this village there were many roads leading to the interior, because the overlord does not reside on the river. . . . In this country the overlord has many sheep of the sort found in Peru, and it is very rich in silver, according to what all the Indians told us, and the country is very pleasing . . . and very plentifully supplied with all kinds of food and fruit, such as pineapples and pears, which in the language of New Spain are called *"aguacates,"* and plums and custard apples and many other kinds of fruit and of very good quality.

It took the Spaniards four days to pass through Paguana's country, which was densely populated. When they traveled along the river's right bank they could not see the left, and vice versa. On May 29 they reached the territory of a large number of warlike and troublesome Indians. On June 2 they passed the mouth of the Río Negro, flowing into the Amazon's north bank.

> This same day, . . . pursuing our voyage, we saw the mouth of another great river on the left, which emptied into the one which we were navigating [and] the water of which was black as ink, and for this reason we gave it the name of Río Negro, which river flowed so abundantly and with such violence that for more than twenty leagues it formed a streak down through the other water, the one [water] not mixing with the other.

On June 4, after several encounters with hostile Indians, they came to their first indication of the nation of the Amazons, of whom they had heard from Aparia.

> On Monday, we continued our way from there, all the time passing by very large settlements and provinces, procuring food as best we could whenever we lacked it. On this day we made port at a medium-sized village, where the inhabitants let us come right up to them. In this village there was a very large public square, and in the center of the square was a hewn tree trunk ten feet in girth, there being represented and carved in relief a walled city with its enclosure and with a gate.
>
> At this gate were two towers, very tall and having windows, and each tower had a door, the two facing each other, and at each door were two columns; and this entire structure . . . rested on two very fierce lions, . . . holding between their fore-paws and claws the entire structure, in the middle of which there was a round open space. In this center of this space there was a hole through which they offered and poured out chicha for the sun, for this is the wine which they drink, and the sun is the one whom they worship and consider as their god.
>
> In short, the construction was well worth seeing, and the Captain and all of us, marvelling at such a great thing, asked an Indian who was seized there [by us] what that was, or as a reminder of what they kept that thing in the square. The Indian answered that they were subjects and tributaries of the Amazons and that the only service which they rendered them consisted in supplying them with plumes of parrots and macaws for the linings of the roofs of the buildings which constitute their places of worship, and that [all] the villages which they had were of that kind, and that they had that thing as a reminder, and that they worshipped it as a thing which was the emblem

of their mistress, who is the one who rules over all the land of the aforesaid women.

The Spaniards continued through densely populated territory, several times being forced to fight against large hordes of Indians. Running short of food, they stormed a village, where they thought to have obtained news of the Diego de Ordaz expedition, which had been shipwrecked and lost near the mouth of the Amazon in 1531. While most critics do not take Carvajal's story of the "lost white explorers" seriously, there is no reason why it should not be true. Captivities, or even voluntary sojourns of white men and women among the Amazonian Indians as dramatized in the twentieth-century stories about Colonel Fawcett, have been common through the centuries, as they remain to this day.

> There was captured in this village an Indian girl of much intelligence, and she said that nearby and back in the interior there were many Christians like ourselves and that they were under the rule of an overlord who had brought them down the river; and she told us how there were two white women among them [as the wives of two of these Christians], and that others had Indian wives, and children by them; these are the people who got lost out of Diego de Ordaz' party, so it is thought from the indications which were at hand regarding them, for it was off to the north of the river.
>
> We proceeded on down our river without seizing any village, because we had food on board, and at the end of a few days we moved out of this province, at the extreme limit of which stood a very large settlement through which the Indian girl told us we had to go to get to where the Christians were. But as we were not concerned with this matter, we decided to press forward, for as to rescuing them from where they were, the time for that will come.

On June 24, rounding a bend, they saw ahead "many villages, and very large ones, which shone white."

> Here we came suddenly upon the excellent land and dominion of the Amazons.
>
> These said villages had been forewarned and knew of our coming, in consequence whereof the inhabitants came out on the water to meet us, in no friendly mood. When they had come close to the Captain, he would have liked to induce them to

accept peace, and so he began to speak to them and call them, but they laughed, and mocked us, and came up close to us and told us to keep on going, and that down below they were waiting for us, and that they were to seize us all and take us to the Amazons.

The Captain, angered at the arrogance of the Indians, gave orders to shoot at them with the crossbows and arquebuses, so that they might reflect and become aware that we had wherewith to assail them. In this way damage was inflicted on them and they turned about toward the village to give the news of what they had seen.

The Spaniards followed the Indians to shore, and in the village there ensued a fierce battle, lasting more than an hour.

I want it to be known why these Indians defended themselves in this manner. It must be explained that they are subjects of, and tributaries to, the Amazons, and, our coming having been made known to them, they went to them to ask for help, and there came as many as ten or twelve of them, for we ourselves saw these women, who were there fighting in front of all the Indian men as women captains, and these latter fought so courageously that the Indian men did not dare to turn their backs, and anyone who did turn his back they killed with clubs right there before us, and this is the reason why the Indians kept up their defense for so long. These women are very white and tall, and have hair very long and braided and wound about the head, and they are very robust and go about naked, [but] with their privy parts covered, with their bows and arrows in their hands, doing as much fighting as ten Indian men, and indeed there was one woman among them who shot an arrow a span deep into one of the brigantines, and others less deep, so that our brigantines looked like porcupines.

The little band set out again, beset by Indians, and in one of the battles Friar Carvajal lost an eye. Constantly followed and harassed by Indians, they stayed in the middle of the river in order to avoid the settlements. They were glad when they had finally passed beyond the stretch where the bank was densely populated.

That night we managed to get to a place to sleep, now outside of this whole settled region, in an oak grove which was on a large flat space near the river, where we were not without fearful apprehensions, because Indians came to spy on us, and toward the interior there were many well-populated districts and [there were] roads which led into it [i.e., the interior], for which reason the Captain and all the rest of us stayed on guard waiting for whatever might happen to us.

In this stopping-place the Captain took [aside] the Indian who had been captured farther back, because he now understood him by means of a list of words he had made, and asked him of what place he was a native: the Indian answered that he was from the village where he had been seized; the Captain asked him what the name of the overlord of this land was, and the Indian replied that his name was Couynco and that he was a very great overlord and that his rule extended to where we were. . . .

The Captain asked him what women those were [who] had come to help them and fight against us; the Indian said that they were certain women who resided in the interior of the country, a seven-day journey from the shore, and [that] it was because this overlord Couynco was subject to them that they had come to watch over the shore.

The Indian, who had often visited the Amazons, having been sent by his overlord to carry tribute to them, said that they were very numerous and that he knew by name 70 of their villages. They lived in stone houses and not in huts of palm thatch. Every once in so often they went on the warpath, captured men from a neighboring tribe, and brought them back to their own country, sending the men back unharmed after the women had become pregnant.

Afterwards, when the time came to have children, if they gave birth to male children, they killed them and sent them to their fathers, and, if female children, they raised them with great solemnity and instructed them in the arts of war.

He said furthermore that among all these women there was one ruling mistress who subjected and held under her hand all the rest, which mistress went by the name of Coñori. He said that there was [in their possession] a very great wealth of gold and silver and that [in the case of] all the mistresses of rank and distinction their eating utensils were nothing but gold or silver, while the other women, belonging to the plebeian class, used a service of wooden vessels, except what was brought in contact with fire, which was of clay.

He said that in the capital and principal city in which the ruling mistress resided there were five very large buildings which were places of worship and houses dedicated to the sun, which they called *"caranain,"* and [that] inside, from half a man's height above the ground up, these buildings were lined with heavy wooden ceilings covered with paint of various colors, and that in those buildings they had many gold and silver idols in the form of women, and many vessels of gold and silver for the service of the Sun; and these women were dressed in clothing of very fine wool, because in this land there are many sheep of the same sort as those in Peru; their dress consists of blankets girded about them [covering their bodies] from the breasts down, [in some cases merely] thrown over [the shoulders], and in others clasped together in front, like a cloak, by means of a pair of cords; they wore their hair reaching down to the ground at their feet, and upon their heads [were] placed crowns of gold, as wide as two fingers, and their individual colors.

He said in addition that in this land, as we understood him, there were camels that carried them [i.e., the inhabitants] on their backs, and he said that there were other animals, which we did not succeed in understanding about, which were as big as horses which had hair as long as the spread of the thumb and forefinger, measured from tip to tip, and cloven hoofs, and that people kept them tied up; and that of those there were few.

He said that there were in this land two salt water lakes, from which the women obtained salt. He related that they had a rule to the effect that when the sun went down no male Indian was to remain [anywhere] in all of those cities, but that any such must depart and go to his country; he said in addition that many Indian provinces bordering on them were held in subjection by them and made to pay tribute and to serve them, while other [provinces] there were with which they carried on war, in particular with the one which we have mentioned, and that they brought the men [of this province] there to have relations with them: these were said to be of very great stature and white and numerous, and [he claimed that] all that he had told here he had seen many times as a man who went back and forth every day.

All that this captive Indian told us and more beside had been told to us 6 leagues from Quito, because concerning these women there were a great many reports. In order to see them many Indians came down the river 1,400 leagues. . . .

The country, the captive Indian said, was cold and there was very little firewood there, and [it was] very rich in all kinds of food.

The scholars who have attacked Carvajal as a liar have based their charges largely on the above account, going on from there to dismiss as untruths other sections of the friar's narrative and descriptions. They did him an injustice. Throughout his narrative, Carvajal was careful to differentiate between the things which he and his companions had seen and those which had been reported to them. His report that in one of their battles they had seen women fighting, and had killed several of them, is completely credible. Many travelers have reported, as late as the 1930's, having observed women in the Amazonian regions participating in battles. Since Carvajal and his companions had heard about the nation of women all the way across the continent, beginning "6 leagues from Quito," it was natural for him to take it for granted that the women in the battle had belonged to that nation.

While language difficulties must have prevented the captive Indian's account from being entirely and correctly understood, it is also true that even today, when a white man asks questions of a tribal Amazonian Indian, the latter usually gives the answer which he believes his questioner wants to hear, regardless of truth or untruth. All the way down the river the Spaniards had undoubtedly asked many leading and specific questions about El Dorado and the Amazons, which, in the report given by Carvajal, were fused into one account. As Carvajal stated at one point, word of their coming ran ahead of them. There can be no doubt that with that word ran descriptions of them, of how they behaved, what they were looking for, what questions they asked. The Indian whom they questioned had been reasonably well prepared by the excited gossip and accounts which preceded Orellana downstream. Moreover, word of Pizarro's action at the expedition's outset, in having the dogs tear Indians to pieces for not telling him what he wanted to hear, could well have traveled thousands of miles from mouth to mouth, while it is not inconceivable that Orellana himself tortured Indians whose answers failed to satisfy him.

As stated above, in searching for El Dorado the *conquistadores* were actually searching for another Peru. The land described to Orellana by the captive Indian, in terms which had probably been put into his mouth by Orellana himself, throughout thousands of miles of travel, was unmistakably Peru, with Cuzco now inhabited by women and with a few understandable fancy touches added. The two saltwater lakes may by the same token have been a distortion of the memory of Lake Titicaca. Cuzco was a populous city, rich in gold and silver, near a large lake. Virtually every account of El Dorado, through the centuries down and into von Humboldt's day early in the 1800's, gives precisely the same general description, give and take a few such details as filling the lake with salt water in place of Titicaca's fresh water.

Continuing his narrative, Carvajal writes:

> The next day, in the morning, we departed from this stopping-place in the oak grove, not a little delighted, thinking that we were leaving all the settled country behind us and that we were going to have an opportunity to rest from our hardships, past and present; and so we started off again on our customary way; but we had not gone far when on the left we saw some very large provinces and settlements, and these lay in the pleasantest and brightest land that we had seen and discovered anywhere along the river, because it was high land with hills and valleys thickly populated, from which said provinces there came out toward us in midstream a very great number of pirogues to attack us and lead us into a fight.

The Indian prisoner who had told them about the Amazons said that

> that land and the settlements which were in sight, together with many others that we could not see, belonged to a very great overlord whose name was Arripuna, who ruled over a great expanse of country. . . . It is he who holds under his control and in his country the Christians whom we had learned about farther back, because this said Indian had seen them; and he said that he [i.e., the overlord] possessed and controlled a very great wealth of silver . . . but [that] gold they were not familiar with.

Carvajal's narrative contains the first account to come out of the Amazonian regions of curare, the famous arrow poison of the Indians.

We went on pursuing our course down the river, and at the end of two days we came upon a small village where the Indians offered resistance to us, but we routed them and seized their food supplies and [then] continued on, and [we captured] another [village] that was close to it, a larger one: here the Indians put up a resistance and fought for the space of half an hour, so well and with such bravery that before we had a chance to leap on land they killed on board the larger brigantine a companion whose name was Antonio de Carranza, a native of Burgos. In this village the Indians were familiar with some kind of poisonous plant, for this became evident from the wound of the aforesaid man, because at the end of twenty-four hours he surrendered his soul to God.

. . . The village was captured and we collected all the maize that the brigantines could hold, because, when we saw [the effects of] the poison, we proposed not to put foot on land in a settled district unless it was from sheer necessity, and so we proceeded with more prudence than we had been exercising up to now.

It was at about this time, however, that the Spaniards were cheered by discovering that they were in tidewater.

Here we recognized that we were not very far from the sea, because the flowing of the tide extended to where we were, whereat we rejoiced not a little in the realization that now we could not fail to reach the sea.

In another fight, a few days later, another Spaniard was killed by a poisoned arrow.

As we started to move on, as I have said, within a short time we discovered an arm of a river not very wide, out of which we saw coming forth two squadrons of pirogues with a very great clamor and outcry . . . and [they] began to attack us and to fight like ravenous dogs; . . . but . . . with the damage that our crossbowmen and arquebusiers did to them, we managed, with the help of Our Lord, to defend ourselves; but after all we did not escape without damage, because they killed another companion of ours, named García de Soria . . . ; and in truth the arrow did not penetrate half a finger, but, as it had poison on it, he did not linger twenty-four hours and he gave up his soul to Our Lord. . . .

We went on fighting in this manner from the time the sun

came up until it was somwehat past ten o'clock, for they did
not let us rest one moment. . . . [They] kept following us . . .
to the point where they were now close to the brigantines. Here
there were fired two remarkable shots with the arquebuses,
which had the effect of inducing that devilish mob to abandon
us; and one of them was fired by the Lieutenant, who killed two
Indians with one shot, and from fright at this thunderclap many
fell into the water, of whom not one was saved, because they
were all slain from the brigantines; the other [shot] was fired by
a Biscayan named Perucho. This was a thing worth seeing, in
consequence of which the Indians left us and turned back without helping those that were in the water; not one of those, as
I have said, escaped alive.

They crossed to the river's other side in order to avoid settlements. Exploring inland from the uninhabited bank, two scouts
reported that a little less than a league from the river "the country kept getting better and better because it was all savannas
and woodlands . . . and there had been seen many traces of
people who came there to hunt game." On hearing this news
of Indians, possibly nearby, Orellana decided to push on downstream. Now they reached the Amazon's delta.

Here we began to leave [behind us] the good country and the
savannas and the high land and began to enter into low country
with many islands, although not so thickly inhabited as those
farther back. . . . Owing to the fact that the islands were numerous and very large, never again did we manage to reach the
mainland either on the one side or on the other, all the way
down to the sea, during which part [of our voyage] we covered,
in and out of the islands, a distance of some two hundred
leagues, over the full length of which, and a hundred more, the
tide comes up with great fury, so that in all there are three hundred of tidewater and one thousand five hundred without tide;
consequently the total number of leagues that we have covered
on this river, from where we started out as far as the sea, is one
thousand eight hundred leagues, rather more than less.

Continuing on our journey in our customary way, as we were
getting to be very weak and in great need of sustenance we
set out to capture a village which was situated on an estuary; at
the hour of high tide the Captive gave orders to steer the large
brigantine toward that place; he succeeded in making port in
good form and the companions leaped out on land; [those on

board] the smaller one did not see a log that was covered by water and it struck such a blow that a plank was smashed to pieces, so badly that the boat was swamped.

No sooner had the men of the large boat leaped ashore than a large force of Indians arrived to give battle, forcing the Spaniards back to the brigantines. However, with the small ship stove in and swamped, the large one had by this time been left high and dry by the receding tide. Orellana divided his force into two parties, one to fight the Indians and the other to repair the small ship and push the large one into the water. Some three hours were required for floating the ships, "and at this very same instant [that the repairing was completed] the warriors took to flight, and during the three hours that the said task had required they had not ceased fighting."

> The following day we made port in a wooded section. Here we set to work repairing the small brigantine in order that it might be fit for navigation. . . . We were held up by the said task eighteen days, and once again, in this place, they made nails, where once more our companions toiled with no little amount of endeavor; but there was a very great shortage of food; we ate maize in rations counted out by grains. [However] . . . one day . . . there was seen coming [i.e., floating] down the river a dead tapir, the size of a mule. . . . It was divided up among all the companions in such a way that for each one there turned out to be enough to eat for five or six days. . . . This tapir had been dead for only a short time, because it was [still] warm, and it had no wound whatsoever on it.

Pushing on after the small boat had been completed, they looked for suitable ground on which to beach the large one for repairs and preparations for ocean travel.

> We found the said beach that we were looking for, where both brigantines were entirely repaired and rigging for them was made out of vines . . . and sails out of the blankets in which we had been sleeping, and their masts were set up: the said work took fourteen days of continuous and regular penance due to the great hunger [that we were enduring] and to the little food that was to be had, for we did not eat anything but what could be picked up on the strand by the water's edge, which was a few snails and a few crabs of a reddish color of the size of frogs.

On the eighth of August they set out again.

> From here on we proceeded under sail, watching the tide,
> tacking from one side to the other, for there was a very con-
> siderable tide when one took into consideration the fact that it
> was a place where the river was wide, although we were passing
> among islands; . . . we were in no small danger whenever we
> expected the tide; but as we had no irons [i.e., anchors], we
> would fasten to stones . . . and we held on so poorly that it
> happened to us very frequently to drag our [stone] anchors along
> the bottom and go back upstream in one hour a greater distance
> than we had covered the whole day.

At the mouth of the Amazon they reached some villages of
docile Indians from whom they obtained food, and who "gave
us to understand by signs that they had seen Christians [before]."

> We passed out of the mouth of this river . . . on the twenty-
> sixth of the month of August . . . and we [always] had such
> good weather that never in our course down the river or on the
> sea did we have squalls. . . .
> We began to proceed on our way with both brigantines at
> times in sight of land and then again [so far out that] we could
> see it, but not so [plainly] that we could determine where we
> were. . . . On the very day of the beheading of St. John, at
> night, one brigantine got separated from the other, so that never
> again did we succeed in sighting each other.

Following the coast, they rounded South America's northeastern bulge, until, finally, they:

> made port on the island of Cubagua and in the city of Nueva
> Cádiz, where we found our company and the small brigantine,
> which had arrived two days before, because they arrived on the
> ninth of September and we arrived on the eleventh of the month
> with the large brigantine, on board which was our Captain: so
> great was the joy which we felt, the ones at the sight of the
> others, that I shall not be able to express it, because they con-
> sidered us to be lost and we them. . . .
> From this island the Captain decided to go and give an ac-
> count to His Majesty of this new and great discovery and of this
> river, which we hold to be the Marañón.

While his men returned to Peru to take part in one of the
civil wars which were tearing that country to pieces, Orellana

made his way to Spain, where he succeeded after much difficulty in being appointed governor of the Amazonian countries and fitted out a major expedition to return there for the purpose of conquest and settlement. Writing during the period 1546 to 1549, Gonzalo Fernández de Oviedo, one of Orellana's bitterest critics, says the following about Orellana's death, in his *Historia de las Indias:*

> This Captain Francisco de Orellana went off with something over four hundred men and an excellent military organization and equipment, having been appointed adelantado and governor [of a stretch of territory along the course] of the Marañón River; and he touched at the Cape Verde Islands, where, partly as a result of sickness of various sorts, partly in consequence of his poor leadership, he lost a large part of the men that he was taking along. And as [best] he could, notwithstanding the hardships that befell him, he pushed on in search of those Amazons whom he had never seen and whom he had talked so much about throughout Spain, whereby he had deprived of their senses all those covetous individuals who followed him; and finally he reached one of the mouths through which the Marañón River empties into the sea. And there he died, as did the greater part of the company that he had brought with him; and those few who were left over, later, [though now] ruined men, reached a port of safety on our Island of Hispaniola.[4]

[4] Gonzalo Fernández de Oviedo y Valdés, *Historia General y Natural de las Indias Occidentales.* [Orellana's note.]

XI

THE SECOND CROSSING
OF THE CONTINENT

THE dream of an "El Dorado," hidden somewhere in the continent's mazes, was a powerful incentive to South American exploration. While failing to reveal a second Cuzco, that exploration did open thousands of square miles of "unknown" territory to the knowledge of European man. Except for a few sporadic individual efforts, the actual search for a physical golden city has long since petered out, though the term "El Dorado" itself—dramatizing man's relentless, romantic, tragic quest for the unattainable, for the pot of gold at the rainbow's end—remains established in a number of modern languages.

The term means "the gilded man," and scholars tend to believe that he once existed. Near Lake Guatavita, in the highlands of Colombia, a priest-king staged an annual religious ceremony. On the appointed day he had himself smeared with "turpentine," rolled in gold dust, was transported by boat to the lake's center, and jumped in to wash off the gold. The ablutions completed, his subjects, crowding the shores, threw golden objects into the lake as further appeasements of Guatavita's god. Spaniards in Ecuador heard the story in 1535, and scholars have an explanation for the fact that the priest-king eluded their subsequent efforts to find him.

Dr. V. T. Harlow, who wrote one of the best modern condensed accounts of the search for El Dorado,[1] said that Baron

[1] Sir Walter Raleigh, *The Discoverie of the large and Bewtiful Empire of Guiana*, with an introduction by V. T. Harlow (London: The Argonaut Press, 1928).

Alexander von Humboldt (Chapter XVII) found partial veri-
fication of the tale when he personally examined Lake Guatavita. There is no reason to differ with either Harlow or
Humboldt in their belief that the gilded man had once existed,
or to disbelieve Harlow's word that the ceremony was discon-
tinued after 1480. But there *is* strong reason to doubt his specific statement that the king had greased himself with turpentine
—at any rate, oftener than once—to cause the gold to adhere to
his body. If that was the substance used, the king was mighty
happy to jump into the lake as quickly as possible, and the
colder the water the better, to quench the intolerable burning
of his more sensitive parts.[2]

As a will-o'-the-wisp to lure men on, the gilded man was soon
transformed into an elusive rich city by a great lake. Though it
was a dream, an illusion which drew hundreds of men into bitter disappointment, it was also useful in a hard, practical sense.
If the Spaniards had not heard about El Dorado, they would
have had to invent him. In at least one instance high Spanish
authorities in South America seem to have done precisely that.

The early exploration and conquest of South America was
accelerated immensely by the hysterical publicity over the conquest of Peru and its fabulous wealth. Highborn and low, Spaniards flocked into Peru in a veritable gold rush, determined to
share the loot. So great was the pull and yearning that Spanish
authorities elsewhere felt compelled to take action to prevent
or stop the human flow. Puerto Rico, for instance, had been
colonized by Spaniards in 1508. But Puerto Rico was and is
dramatically poor in all natural resources, including gold, and
the old *conquistadores* were notoriously allergic to poor countries. When Puerto Rico's settlers heard about Pizarro's Peruvian bonanza, they all wanted to leave their island and head
south. To prevent the abandonment of an important military
position, Puerto Rico's Spanish authorities threatened the death
penalty for anybody caught trying to leave the island. Undoubtedly, Spanish governors in other parts of the New World, less
rich than Peru, had orders to take similar action to prevent the

---

[2] Repeated efforts to drain Lake Guatavita, for the purpose of recovering the accumulated gold on its bottom, have failed. However, modern technology may yet
lead to a renewal of the quest. For the benefit of adventurous skin-divers willing
to brave the cold mountain water, it may be stated that the lake is located at approximately 5° N latitude, and 74° W longitude, not far from the city of Bogotá.

abandonment of established colonies. Nevertheless, too many Spaniards managed to boom into Peru to become surplus to the economy and society established by Pizarro.

The latter's policy, followed by his successors, was to send the unwanted elsewhere on voyages of conquest of their own. The results were not always happy. Almagro, for instance, while not exactly a latecomer, was certainly a discontented *conquistador* who was persuaded to go and conquer Chile for himself (Chapter IX). When that land failed to come up to his expectations, he returned to Peru to start a civil war, as did the marquis' brother, Gonzalo Pizarro, after discovering that the cinnamon forests and El Dorado—beyond Ecuador's high eastern mountains—were illusions.

Many of the Spaniards who continued inconveniently to pour into Peru were men of low birth with no money and less credit, unemployed *conquistadores* who created serious social problems. In 1559, to rid themselves of those troublesome persons, the land's authorities did something unprecedented. Possibly they invented, and certainly they exaggerated and spread, an exciting report of an El Dorado sighting far down the Amazon River. Then—and *that* was the action which was without precedent in an age when expedition leaders serving their king were commonly required to finance themselves—they provided government money to organize and equip an expedition to go forth and follow up on the report.

However, not all Spaniards shared the widespread, naïve belief in a hidden, far-off golden city. Many of the three hundred-odd men who permitted themselves to be recruited for the new venture seem from the start to have had no faith in the El Dorado report. They plotted only to leave Peru in order to return by another route to make war on the authorities who had so conveniently supplied them with ships and arms. Their plan was to wrest Peru from the king of Spain and set up an independent kingdom of their own. As a result, their expedition turned into one of the bloodiest dramas in the history of the conquest.

The opening sentence of Sir Clements Markham's introduction to his translation of the expedition's story reads as follows:

> The blood-stained cruise of the "tyrant Aguirre," the translated narrative of which, from the text of the old chronicler

Simon is now printed for the first time, is by far the most extraordinary adventure in search of El Dorado on record. The dauntless hardihood of those old Spaniards and Germans, who, undismayed by the reverses and sufferings of numerous predecessors, continued to force their way for hundreds of miles into forest-covered wilds, is sufficiently astonishing; but in this cruise of Aguirre all that is wildest, most romantic, most desperate, most appalling in the annals of Spanish enterprise seems to culminate in one wild orgie of madness and blood.[3]

The expedition's criminal archfiend was one Lope de Aguirre, who is still remembered on Venezuela's island of Margarita, for reasons set forth below, as *el tirano*. He and his companions were in the field during the years 1560–61. The account of their deeds which Markham translated was written during the 1620's by Fray Pedro Simon, of whom Markham wrote:

His principal authority was the manuscript of Francisco Vazquez, one of the companions of Aguirre, from whom he copies largely, and without any acknowledgement. He could not have taken his narrative from a more authentic source; and it is possible that he may have conversed with other followers of Aguirre, or with men who were engaged in the campaign which ended in the traitor's death.

In 1558, Peru was stirred by the arrival of news of an El Dorado sighting, brought by Indians who had completed an epic transcontinental trek up the Amazon from the Atlantic coast. Father Simon wrote as follows about the matter:

Certain rumors prevailed in those times, both in the city of Lima and throughout the provinces of Peru (which had been spread by Indians from Brazil), respecting rich provinces, which they had seen, as they said, when on their road from the coast of Brazil, whence more than 2,000 Indians had set out, with the intention of settling in other lands, which might be more agreeable to them, as their own were too crowded. Others declare that the Indians set out on this expedition to enjoy human food in those parts. At length, after travelling for ten years with two Portuguese in their company, some by the River Marañón, and some by land, they reached the provinces of the Motilones [4] in

---

[3] Sir Clements Markham, translator, editor, and annotator, *The Expedition of Ursúa and Aguirre* (London: The Hakluyt Society, Publication No. 28, 1861).
[4] A tribe on the Huallaga River, also called Lamistas.

Peru, by way of a famous river [5] which flows thence and enters the Marañón.

These Indians brought news respecting the provinces of the Omaguas, mentioned also by Captain Francisco de Orellana, when he descended this river Marañón after deserting Gonzalo Pizarro, in the Cinnamon country.

In these provinces, of which the Indians spoke when they reached Peru, dwelt the gilded man, at least this name was spread about in the land, taking its origin in the city of Quito. It so excited the minds of those restless spirits with whom Peru was full, and who were ever ready to credit these rumors, that the viceroy thought it prudent to seek some way by which to give employment to so large a body of turbulent men.

In his above-mentioned introduction to Sir Walter Raleigh's account of Guiana, Harlow gave the name of the chief of the arriving Indians as Virarutu, repeated much of Simon's account, and added:

> In their travels the Brazilian Indians had come upon a great lake, some distance from the river, and in the middle of a vast plain which was dotted about with populous villages and surrounded by high mountains. The invaders were driven off by the lake folk and pursued back to the Amazon, which they ascended until they eventually reached the province of the Motilones in Peru by way of the Huallaga River. The story created such interest that Virarutu was sent to the viceroy in Lima, the Marquis of Cañete. . . . Considering that the Brazilian spoke by means of an interpreter, the viceroy probably received a garbled version of an already exaggerated story. But the circumstances of a great lake with a numerous population and surrounding mountains was quite sufficient evidence from which to adduce El Dorado, and to identify it with the Omaguas described by Orellana. . . . Moreover, whether he himself believed it or not, the Marquis of Cañete was glad enough, as Simon suggests, to use the opportunity for ridding Peru of some of the turbulent spirits who had just taken part in the rebellion of [Francisco] Hernández Girón.

There is room for doubt as to whether or not Virarutu and his companions had actually seen the lake which they described on their arrival in Peru. But there can be no doubt that they

[5] The Huallaga.

knew about the Spaniards' disagreeable habit of using savage dogs to tear to pieces any Indians unwise enough to withhold information desired by the whites, that they knew about the Spaniards' immense thirst for word of El Dorado, and that they may well have invented the story of their "discoveries" in answer to eager, leading questions. Either way, directly or indirectly, Peru's Spaniards created the new El Dorado report. If they didn't exactly make it up out of whole cloth, they at least embroidered it to make it more enticing as a real-estate come-on. Having decided to organize a great expedition for the purpose of getting rid of their country's troublesome elements, they began to look for a reliable leader, whom they found in the person of Pedro de Ursúa.

The latter arrived fortuitously in Lima in 1558, just when the El Dorado excitement was beginning to build up. According to Simon, he was about thirty-three years old and had proved his valor by spending some of the preceding years as a conqueror, explorer, city-founder, and El Dorado hunter in Colombia and Venezuela. He had also proved his loyalty to the crown by helping to put down a slave revolt in Panama while passing through that country en route to Peru. He was known to be a fanatical, intensely loyal servant of the crown, ready for any task or adventure on behalf of the king. Those circumstances, which merited reward, plus the fact that he was himself a latecomer in Peru, made him the logical candidate for command of the projected expedition. When the offer was made to him, he accepted enthusiastically, in part as public service, in part to prove his valor, and in part because of the wealth, kudos, and political advancement which the success of such an expedition promised.

On Ursúa's acceptance, the viceroy, according to Simon, gave him

> the title of Governor of the Provinces which he might discover and conquer, with power to appoint officers, to reward his companions according to their merits, recommending him to have a care of the conquered Indians, to form settlements consisting of such Spaniards as he might think proper, and to do this for the good of the church and the crown of Spain. He was promised, after having founded such settlements, that he should be rewarded as the kings of Spain were accustomed to reward those who had discovered and settled new lands.

Ursúa was appointed in 1559 and immediately went to work to organize his expedition. He ran into difficulties from the very beginning. The funds made available by the viceroy—not without incurring bitter criticism—were not nearly enough to meet Ursúa's needs. Nevertheless, he put agents to work, mostly in and near Lima, to recruit members for the expedition, while he had tools and the like made for building ships. He then hurried across the Andes to the Huallaga River, taking with him 25 shipbuilders and "ten Negro carpenters." Having put those people to work, with instructions as to what ships to build, Ursúa hurried back to Lima, "from which place he could despatch the people and soldiers collected by his captains." However, he was desperately short of funds and therefore could not get away for the better part of a year, a fact which his mutinous men were later to hold officially against him. Finally the people of Lima, undoubtedly eager to be rid as soon as possible of the people of "corrupt blood" for whom the expedition had been organized, "supplied him with more money for the equipment of his soldiers, purchase of powder, rope, muskets, horses, arms and ammunitions, cattle, ship-provisions, and other things."

Ursúa hurried back to Moyobamba, but his money troubles were far from over. There was a priest in the town, a man named Pedro Portillo, who, according to Simon,

> had hoarded five or six thousand dollars. Portillo, hearing flattering accounts of Ursúa's expedition, and seeing the great number of gallant followers, anxious also to increase his fortune and dignity, by becoming a bishop in the new lands to be discovered, offered to lend Ursúa two thousand dollars, on condition that he would promise to appoint him cura and vicar of the expedition. Ursúa gladly accepted the cura's proposal, and felt no difficulty in acceding to Portillo's wishes for ecclesiastical preferment.
>
> But the priest soon repented his offer, and began to feel but little faith in the success of the expedition. He intimated that the loan of the two thousand dollars would be inconvenient to him; but Ursúa could not do without money, for he had ordered many articles for which it was necessary to pay. Ursúa, finding himself in an awkward position, called into his councils Juan de Vargas, who was afterwards his lieutenant, Fernando de Guzmán, Juan Alonso de la Vandera, Pedro Alonzo Casco, and Pedro de Miranda, a mulatto, all fighting men and of elastic con-

sciences; telling them his present trouble, and that he was most desirous that the money should be obtained from the priest. His friends saw no difficulty about the matter, even if a little violence was resorted to;—so one night they reported that Juan de Vargas (who was then quartered in the church on account of two wounds), was dying, and one of them went for the cura Portillo, urging him to lose no time in going to confess Vargas. On leaving his house the cura was seized by Ursúa's friends, and was forced to sign an order for two thousand dollars on a merchant of the town, who was the keeper of the cura's wealth. The cura went to Vargas, who was in an apartment of the church. On his arrival fire-arms were pointed at his breast, and, without waiting for the morrow, they took him to the town of Santa Cruz de Capacoba. Here the greater portion of the expedition was encamped. At this place they forced from him the other three or four thousand dollars of his fortune. This system of things did not stop here; for during the progress of the expedition there was much disturbance, and the turbulent paid for their misdeeds by terrible deaths, as we shall see further on.

The expedition of Governor Pedro de Ursúa (Simon remarks wryly: "He already took this title without knowing where the country lay that he was to be governor of") was by this time being discussed throughout Peru and had given rise to many grave fears. Simon writes:

> The Viceroy and Oidores [the royal court—Audience], as well as the inhabitants of Lima, began to entertain fears for the success of the Ursúa expedition, for there were in it so many mutinous and turbulent persons, who had been in the rebellions of Gonzalo Pizarro, Francisco Hernández Girón, Don Sebastián de Castilo, and that of Contreras; and the number of Ursúa's followers was large, amounting to nearly three hundred men.
>
> These suspicions increased daily . . . until a stop was put to them by the news of the execution of Arles and Frías by Pedro de Ursúa. The Marquis and the Oidores then became more tranquil, and praised the decisive act of the execution; and Governor Ursúa's management, promising to themselves great success on account of the expedition.

The details of that execution were as follows: because he had to feed so many mouths, and before he himself was ready to

leave his base camp, Ursúa sent a party downstream to forage
for supplies—which means to steal them from the Indians—
under the joint command of his old friends and campaign associates, Francisco Diáz de Arles and Diego de Frías. The two,
however, had been rivals for the post of his second-in-command
and were therefore united in their dislike of the "Corregidor
Pedro Ramiro," whom Ursúa had appointed to the post. At the
last minute, Ursúa appointed Ramiro over Arles and Frías as
commander of the foraging detail, which annoyed the other two
and led them to plot the corregidor's death. Downriver, they
managed to do away with him, sending word to Ursúa that they
had arrested him for plotting to usurp the post of commander
in chief, and asking for instructions as to what to do with the
prisoner. But Ursúa had already been appraised of the true state
of affairs. He lured the two with honeyed words of friendship
to come to where he could catch them, had them tried, and sentenced them to be beheaded, friendship or no friendship. That
was the act which gave the people of Peru faith in the ultimate
success of one of the most bloody and terrible expeditions in the
history of exploration.

> Pedro de Linasco, a settler of Chachapoyas, and a friend of
> Ursúa's, accustomed to such expeditions, and well acquainted
> with many of those who were with Ursúa, wrote him a letter, in
> which he notified to him the suspicions of people in Peru that
> many of his soldiers were turbulent and mutinous, and that they
> might be troublesome to him, and might even kill him. . . .
> [Among the dozen or so whom Linasco mentioned by name was
> one Lope de Aguirre. He begged Ursúa to] separate those he
> had named from being his followers. Even should he have com-
> passion on them in consequence of their poverty, such feelings
> should have no weight with him; that Ursúa should send them
> to him, and he would take care of them until the Governor
> should discover the lands he was in search of, and if he thought
> it opportune, he could send for them, and do with them as he
> thought best.
> He begged of him, as a friend, not to take Doña Inez de
> Atienza with him, who was the daughter of one Blas de Atienza,
> an inhabitant of the city of Trujillo, and widow of Pedro de
> Arcos, an inhabitant of Piura. Ursúa had taken her, with the in-
> tention of marrying her, as she was a spirited and beautiful
> woman. Linasco said that it did not look well, and that it was

setting a bad example to his followers; that greater evils would succeed than he could possibly suppose; and that if he determined to leave her, he would give orders that she should be taken care of; and this should be done in such a way that Doña Inez should not know who had been the cause of her remaining behind, or that Ursúa had even consented to it. This friendly letter had not the desired effect on the governor; who, although a man of great ability, was young, and without much experience. Thus he did not follow the advice of his friend, excepting that he sent back Don Martín; neither did he reply to the letter, or do what was advised therein. Had he done so he might have been saved from death by the hands of those whose names had been given to him.

The expedition began to get under way on the Huallaga River, piece by piece, in July, 1560. If ever, in its early stages and before it had begun to fall to pieces, it was assembled in one place—all the ships, the brigantines, the flatboats, the canoes and rafts, the soldiers, the men and women, the Indian servants, all assembled against the backdrop of olive-green jungles—it must have been a sight to inspire a modern producer of technicolor spectaculars. By the same token, its descent on a settlement of relatively peaceful Amazonian Indians, like a vast swarm of locusts, ravenous for provisions, must have struck terror into the natives. There is no record of how many souls were involved at the beginning or what happened to the majority of them. It is known that the original organization included about 300, of whom only a small handful were knights who could be expected to side with the commander for reasons of rank and social status; the rest were common folks, many of whom jealously resented the nobles. It is also known that Doña Inez, Ursúa's fiancee, was a member of the expedition, with two maids, and that Lope de Aguirre had his marriageable daughter on board. The records state that those people had horses and cattle with them and that they enslaved Indians whenever they could, to act as servants. Moreover, before Ursúa himself finally managed to depart from his base at the settlement of Motilones, his eloquence got the better of him. So glowing a picture did he paint of the El Dorado where they were going to find new homes, that he persuaded virtually the entire population to join him, taking their horses and cattle along.

Later in the Simon account it appears that the expedition also included a number of "guides," among them several men who had accompanied Orellana years earlier and some of the Brazilian Indians whose El Dorado tale had set off the venture.

There is no record of how many craft they built or filched from the Indians. What is known is that two brigantines fell to pieces quite early during the voyage, because they had been built of green, unseasoned wood, and had to be replaced by something else which floated, and that, of the horses and cattle which had embarked at Motilones, the greater part had soon to be turned loose on shore to run wild, much to the distress of their owners, who developed a burning desire to give up the search for El Dorado and return to Peru. Indeed, almost from the start the expedition members proper showed marked signs of discontent and began to talk *sotto voce* about some kind of mutiny. Had they been able to agree among themselves, Ursúa's end might have come much earlier than it did. Some wanted to kill the leader and his supporters and return to Peru. Others wanted to desert him at some convenient spot, take all the boats, and keep on exploring downriver. There were others who, regardless of whether the top leaders were killed or marooned, wanted to proceed downriver to the Atlantic and then sail around South America's northeast and begin to attack Spanish authorities on Margarita Island, working their way, victory by victory, across the Isthmus of Panama and down to Peru. The expedition was not noted for its morale.

Scouting parties were sent ahead to forage for food, and when, for weeks at a stretch, they failed to find it—meaning that they failed to find Indians—their morale sank still lower. Some Spaniards and many Indian servants died of hunger and diseases. Parties were separated, wandered in bewilderment, and came together again weeks later. The explorers met friendly Indians but alienated them almost immediately with brutal treatment and their habit of stealing canoes and food. Ursúa attempted to control his soldiers to make them behave well toward the Indians, but the going was hard.

It took Ursúa four months to reach the mouth of the Ucayali, where he was awaited by an advance party of a hundred men, commanded by Juan de Vargas. Eight days later they arrived at an island where another advance party of 30, commanded by

García del Arce, was waiting for them impatiently in a fort they
had built against Indian marauders.

> The people were allowed to go on shore for eight or ten days,
> so as to rest the soldiers and rowers; and also to take the horses
> on shore to exercise them, for they had not been landed since
> they first went on board. . . .
>
> The name of the principal Indian in this place was Papa. The
> natives were tall and strong, clothed in well-woven cotton shirt-
> like coverings, painted various colors. No gold was found, which
> produced dissatisfaction amongst the Spaniards, seeing that they
> had journeyed so far without meeting with the least sign of
> precious metal. The food of the natives was mostly maize of
> which they make much chicha. They also prepare chicha of the
> yucca, taking so much that they get drunk, the great sin of the
> Indians of those lands. They have batatas [sweet potatoes] and
> other roots; beans and other vegetables; but their chief food is
> fish.

They went on down the river, often suffering from hunger,
and arrived near the mouth of the Putumayo about Christmas-
time. Although Ursúa's guides were unable to tell him where
they were, he decided that they must be close to the land of the
Omaguas and that it was time for him to form a government to
help him rule the as yet unconquered province. His one ap-
pointment, however, that of vicar general, proved unpopular
and increased the grumbling among the men. Disaffection was
growing at an alarming rate. Many of the men felt that they had
been led astray, having as yet seen no sign of gold. There was
grumbling over hard duty at the oars and a number of men
charged that Doña Inez was the expedition's real leader, dominating Ursúa completely. The leadership was blamed for im-
providence when the expedition spent some days passing through
"desert" country where no Indians were to be seen and therefore no food could be obtained. There were secret councils and
bitter arguments as to what should be done about the situation,
but finally the most mutinous among them agreed to elect a new
leader to take Ursúa's place. Having decided on a young man of
twenty-five, Don Fernando de Guzmán, because "he was held to
be of noble blood and well disposed toward the soldiers," they
persuaded him to fall in with them in the interest of patriotic
service to the king, and to take over the expedition's leadership.

Don Fernando did not dislike the arguments of the mutineers, nor was he deterred either by the grave embarrassments which might follow, nor by the loyalty which (he being a knight) should have bound him to protect Ursúa, after the honours he had received from him, and the consideration with which he had always been treated by him. He believed all that had been told him by the mutineers, and, swelled up by the wind of ambition, he gave them thanks for what they had offered him, and assented to all their projects; so that it appeared to the messengers that they now had all that was necessary, in order to put their designs into execution. The mutineers, and Don Fernando among them, as their chief, conferred together, and began to offer various opinions (children of tyranny and heresy) respecting the mode of proceeding; to some it seemed best to leave Pedro de Ursúa, with some of his friends in that place (as had been suggested to Don Fernando) and, taking all the boats and canoes, to return up the river to Peru; others, among whom were Don Fernando, said that they would only do that which had been originally proposed, namely, return to Peru by descending the river, with the whole expedition, leaving Ursúa behind; but there was a third party, among whom were those two good souls, Lope de Aguirre and Lorenzo Salduendo, who declared that all they had heard was unwise, but that the only plan was to kill Pedro de Ursúa and, with all the people, return to Peru, and make Don Fernando the lord of the country. Don Fernando, giving reins to an ambition which he was already relishing, and promising to himself the enjoyment of the riches of Peru, also because it was of little avail to say anything else, gave out that the opinions of the two [Aguirre and Salduendo] appeared good to him; and the rest consenting, it was agreed that Ursúa and his lieutenant Don Juan should die. From this time they sought for an occasion to commit the deed, and busied themselves in gaining over the soldiers, that they might be on their side, when it became necessary.

On New Year's Day, 1561, while resting in an Indian village whose inhabitants had fled at the approach of the Spaniards, Ursúa sent some of his close associates to scout "a broad road" which led inland from the village. Taking the opportunity, a group of conspirators invaded his house and stabbed him to death. After leaving the house, with shouts of "Liberty, liberty! Long live the king! The tyrant is dead!", they ran into Ursúa's lieutenant and close associate, Juan de Vargas, who had left his own quarters to see what the commotion was about. They dispatched him with "so severe a thrust that the sword went through and through his body, the point wounding his companion badly, who was behind the lieutenant."

The next few days, the conspirators were extremely busy, winning the expedition's rank and file to their side and persuading Ursúa's scouting expedition, on its return from the trip up the "broad road," to at least seem to side with them. Don Fernando, as the expedition's head, had a deposition drawn up to be signed by all,

> stating why the governor Ursúa had been deprived of life, inasmuch as he had been most negligent and unmindful in his search after the new lands, that he had not taken the necessary steps, and that he had no intention to settle even if he should find them; that he was intolerant and severe to the soldiers, and that to preserve the men in the service of the king, as well as to discover the unknown lands, his death was a necessary act; for had he been allowed to govern them much longer, without doubt [his rule] would have been violently taken away from him, and that the people would have returned to Christian lands [Peru], leaving him on the river, without discovering the vast provinces which were before them.

He had the entire camp sign the document, arguing that if they discovered El Dorado the king would be so pleased that he would forgive them the murder of Ursúa and Vargas. Lope de Aguirre, however, said that the argument was nonsense, and that they would all be hanged in any event if and when caught. Accordingly, and defiantly, he wrote the word "traitor" after his signature, a matter which stirred up considerable argumentative heat.

Five days after Ursúa's death the expedition proceeded downriver, arriving the same day "at another village on the cliffs of the river, so totally abandoned that they did not even find earthen vessels to cook their food in." But since the place seemed well supplied with timber they spent three months there, building several brigantines in which they could go to sea after leaving the river, living on fruits, horses, and dogs.

> This was not unpleasing to Aguirre (who had no intention of conquering new lands), for in this case the others would find it

impossible, being without horses and dogs, to commence their conquests by land. They also consumed all their poultry, without leaving any for the new settlements it was pretended they were to form, in the provinces they were to discover.

Without consulting the governor, Aguirre continued his assassinations, having four men strangled, largely because they had been friendly to Ursúa. His personal followers called themselves the "Marañanos," and a wild lot they were. The expedition was threatened with being divided between Aguirre's men and Don Fernando's but the latter placated his rival for a time with promises of promotion and with the pledge that on their return to Peru his brother, Martín de Guzmán, would marry Aguirre's daughter. He called the latter "Doña" and treated her as a sister-in-law.

The bickering, plots and counterplots, and murders continued throughout their stay in the camp, tensions growing greater among the survivors as one man after another was done away with as a result of mere rumors or unsubstantiated accusations. As a means of holding the expedition together, Don Fernando was not only reelected its head but was even made "Prince and King of all Tierra Firme." Delighted over his new honors, he thereafter signed all his decrees: "Don Fernando de Guzmán, by the Grace of God, Prince of Tierra Firme, and of Peru, etc." and eventually came to distribute Peruvian estates among his expedition mates in an abandoned Indian village 1,500 miles or so up the sinister, jungled Amazon River. The men accepted their new estates gladly, the main problem still to be solved being the one of how to reach them and conquer Peru itself. After many councils of war they finally agreed to head for the Atlantic and then for Peru via Margarita Island and Panama.

> In these and other visionary schemes they passed the three months, during which the two brigantines were building, and getting ready for sea. The brigantines had no upper works nor decks, but such strong hulls that they might have been armed as vessels of war of three hundred tons.

They set sail again, spending Easter Week in another Indian village, in which Aguirre had two more men killed, "in order that Easter might not pass without glutting his infernal appetite for human blood." There was still dissension as to whether to keep exploring and to conquer any good new land they found, and whether to go along with Aguirre in his designs for the conquest of Peru. A plot was cooked up to kill Aguirre, and another to kill Don Fernando, the "Prince of Peru, etc." Then came the death of Doña Inez, which was later to stir up considerable controversy among poets and scholars as to whether she was a pure and noble woman, a position which Sir Clements Markham was to defend passionately three centuries later, or was a wanton, as charged in the original chronicle and copied later by Simon. According to the latter version, she had, after the murder of Ursúa, become the mistress of Lorenzo Salduendo, captain of Don Fernando's guard, her immediate female companion being the mistress of another expedition member. Salduendo wanted some mattresses placed on one of the brigantines for the two women. Aguirre maintained that these would take up too much room. The ensuing argument resulted in the murder of Salduendo, followed by that of Inez. Shortly thereafter, Aguirre had Don Fernando murdered and made himself the undisputed head of the expedition.

The rest of the chronicle meticulously describes one unmitigated horror after another, murder after murder, dissensions, deep suspicions, and rumor-mongering which resulted in more murders. All dreams of El Dorado seem to have evaporated, and germane to the present account is primarily the argument of scholars as to the sanguinary expedition's route.

There seems to be good indication that the ships did get up the Río Negro a considerable distance, but the belief, shared by Markham, that they kept on up that stream and then reached the Atlantic via the Cassiquiare and the Orinoco, seems to be mere guesswork, without foundation. The upstream navigation of the Negro would have involved the passage of a very difficult rapid at today's São Gabriel, with no portage road around it. On the middle Orinoco the portage around, or passage over, the Maipure-Atures rapids would probably have been impossible for ships "of three hundred tons," and would in any event almost certainly have been recorded by Francisco Vazquez, the expedition member whose account was later copied by Simon. There is, however, no notice of any rapids being negotiated, while the travel account mentions only downstream progress. "They continued their voyage and got amongst a large number of islands, which confused them. They now had to row, particularly as the coming in of the tide made the water contrary for them." Wherever they were at this point, whether at the mouth of the Orinoco or that of the Amazon, the second crossing of South America from west to east had been accomplished. Aguirre finally managed to reach Margarita with "his . . . well-armed soldiers in good order for battle."

Of the expedition's end, Harlow writes:

> At last, on 1 July 1561, they reached the open sea and sailed for the Island of Margarita, thus completing in 5,000 miles one of the most remarkable journeys in the early history of South American exploration. At Margarita, which they captured, they inaugurated a reign of terror: all the Spanish officials were massacred, their wives and daughters outraged, and their houses and the Royal Treasury robbed and burned. After landing at Burburate in Venezuela, where he wrote the famous letter of warning and defiance to King Philip . . . Aguirre set off into the interior with the intention of conquering New Granada. But his bloody career was nearly at an end. Early in September he was met in battle and completely defeated by a Spanish force under Gutierrez de la Peña. The last act of this madman was to turn upon his own daughter. "Commend thyself to God, my daughter, for I am about to kill thee, that thou mayest not be pointed out with scorn, nor be in the power of any one who may call thee the daughter of a traitor," and, so saying, he plunged a poniard into her bosom. He himself was shot down and then beheaded. According to von Humboldt, the natives of Barquisimeto believe that the will-o'-the-wisp is the tyrant's soul wandering in the savannahs, like a flame fleeing the approach of man.

In his famous letter to King Philip, mentioned above by Harlow, Aguirre complained of the many injustices done to him and his companions in Peru, and wrote:

> I firmly believe that thou, O Christian king and lord, hast been very cruel and ungrateful to me and my companions for such a good service, and that all those who write to thee from this land deceive thee much, because thou seest things from too far off. I, and my companions (whose names I will mention presently), no longer able to suffer the cruelties which thy judges and governors exercise in thy name, are resolved to obey thee no

longer. We regard ourselves no longer as Spaniards. We make a cruel war on thee, because we will not endure the oppression of thy ministers, who, to give places to their nephews and their children, dispose of our lives, our reputations, and our fortunes.

After listing a number of valiant men whom the Peruvian viceroy had hanged, he made a passionate plea:

Hear me! O hear me! thou King of Spain. Be not cruel to thy vassals, for it was while thy father, the emperor Charles, remained quietly in Spain, that they procured for thee so many kingdoms and vast countries. Remember, king Philip, that thou hast no right to draw revenues from these provinces, since their conquest has been without danger to thee. I take it for certain that few kings go to hell, only because they are few in number; but that if there were many, none of them would go to heaven. For I believe that you are all worse than Lucifer, and that you hunger and thirst after human blood; and further, I think little of you, and despise you all, nor do I look upon your government as more than an air bubble. Know that I, and my two hundred arquebus-bearing Marañones, have taken a solemn oath to God, that we will not leave one of thy ministers alive. We consider ourselves, at this moment, the happiest men on earth, because, in this land of the Indians, we preserve the faith and the commandments of God in their purity, and we maintain all that is preached by the Church of Rome. We expect, though sinners in this life, to endure martyrdom for the laws of God.

On leaving the river of Amazons, which is called Marañón, we came to an island inhabited by Christians, called Margarita, where we received news from Spain of the great conspiracy of the Lutherans, which caused us much terror and alarm. In our company there was one of these Lutherans, named Monteverde, and I ordered him to be cut to pieces. Believe me, O most excellent king, that I will force all men to live perfectly in the faith of Christ.

After recounting the vice and corruption found among the king's priests and judges in the New World, Aguirre summarizes the Ursúa expedition as follows:

In the year 1559, the marquis of Cañete entrusted the expedition of the river of Amazons to Pedro de Ursúa, a Navarrese, or rather a Frenchman, who delayed the building of his vessels until 1560. These vessels were built in the province of the Motilones, which is a wet country, and, as they were built in the rainy season, they came to pieces, and we therefore made canoes, and descended the river. We navigated the most powerful river in Peru, and it seemed to us that we were in a sea of fresh water. We descended the river for three hundred leagues. This bad governor was capricious, vain, and inefficient, so that we could not suffer it, and we gave him a quick and certain death. We then raised a young gentleman of Seville, named Don Fernando de Guzmán to be our king, and we took the same oaths to him as are taken to [thy] royal person, as may be seen by the signatures of all those who are with me. They named me maestre del campo; and, because I did not consent to their evil deeds, they desired to murder me. I therefore killed this new king, the captain of his guard, his lieutenant-general, four captains, his majordomo, his chaplain, who said mass, a woman, a knight of the Order of Rhodes, an admiral, two ensigns, and five or six of his servants. It was my intention to carry on the war, on account of the many cruelties which thy ministers had committed. I named captains and sergeants; but these men also wanted to kill me, and I hung them. We continued our course while all this evil fortune was befalling us; and it was eleven months and a half before we reached the mouths of the river, having travelled for more than a hundred days, over more than fifteen hundred leagues. This river has a course of two thousand leagues of fresh water, the greater part of the shores being uninhabited; and God only knows how we ever escaped out of that fearful lake. I advise thee not to send any Spanish fleet up this ill-omened river; for on the faith of a Christian, I swear to thee, O king and lord, that if a hundred thousand men should go up, not one would escape, and there is nothing else to expect, especially for the adventurers from Spain.

The captains and officers who are now under my command in this enterprise, and who promise to die in it, are Juan Jerónimo de Espindola, a Genoese, captain of infantry, admiral Juan Gómez, a Spaniard [then follows a long list], and many other gentlemen. They pray to God that thy strength may ever be increased against the Turk and the Frenchman, and all others who desire to make war against thee; and we shall give thanks, if, by our arms, we attain the rewards which are due to us, but which thou hast denied us; and, because of thine ingratitude, I am a rebel against thee until death.

[Signed] LOPE DE AGUIRRE, THE WANDERER

XII

CONQUEST OF
THE RIVER PLATE

THE Plate River is a bay of the Atlantic Ocean as well as an estuary shared by the rivers Paraná and Uruguay, with some minor streams thrown in. The first European on record as having visited it was Juan Díaz de Solís, sent by Spain in 1516. He went ashore with a party of men and was promptly killed, and possibly eaten, by the Indians. Disheartened, his men sailed back to Spain. Four years later, in 1520, Ferdinand Magellan sailed into the great estuary but soon sailed out again, convinced that it was not a part of the elusive southwest passage to Asia. Next came Sebastian Cabot, son of John Cabot. Sent by the king of Spain, Emperor Charles V, he came to the River Plate in 1526, with four ships. Cabot sailed up the Paraná and Paraguay rivers and believed that he had discovered another Mexico when the Indians received him with presents of silver trinkets and ornaments. Hence the name "Río de la Plata," or Silver River. While there, he met one Diego García, who had been a member of the Solís expedition and had now returned on his own to try his luck at sailing to Asia. The country was not large enough to hold both explorers; they quarreled and sailed back to Spain. Before leaving, however, Cabot established a small fortified settlement, Espíritu Santo, near the junction of the rivers Paraná and Paraguay. But this was wiped out by the Indians very soon after Cabot's departure.

Pizarro's conquest of Peru inflamed all Europe a few years after Cabot's return. Mindful of the silver which the latter had brought back from the Silver River, Charles V decided to try for another Peru on South America's east coast, and hired an able nobleman named Pedro de Mendoza to conquer and settle the lands adjoining the Plate, naming him governor in reward. Mendoza sailed with a large expedition of 14 ships (as reported by Ulrich Schmidt, who was often wrong), carrying many men, horses, and other materials for settlement. In February, 1536, he landed at the site of today's Buenos Aires, where he founded the city of Puerto de Santa María del Buen Aire (Port of St. Mary of the Good Breeze). However, famine, pestilence, and trouble with the Indians soon forced him to look for a better place and try his fortunes farther up the Río Paraná. But he had little luck and lost many men. Finally he abandoned the expedition in despair and sailed for Spain; he died on the voyage home.[1]

Left in charge of the expedition on Mendoza's departure was Juan de Ayolas, who was to lose his life during a search for gold. He was succeeded as commander by Domingo Martínez de Irala, who ruled in the newly founded settlement of Asunción, today the capital of Paraguay. Martínez was to control the tiny community, except for a short interval, until his death in 1557. He undertook to build up the colony by granting new lands to his followers, at the same time assigning them control over captive Indians. Thus was established the unhappy *encomienda* system, the form of vassalage which was to persist in the provinces of western Argentina until the break with Spain.

The "short interval" (1541 to 1544) during which his governorship was interrupted comprised the governorship of Álvar Núñez Cabeza de Vaca, whose commentaries, written by his secretary, Pedro Hernández, and published in 1555, form the second part of the remarkable Hakluyt Society volume on the conquest of the River Plate.[2] The first part is the personal narrative of a German, Ulrich Schmidt, a member of Mendoza's expedition who served Irala until his departure for Europe in December, 1552.

Schmidt's narrative is in part an account of Álvar Núñez

---

[1] This material is from Natalie Raymond, *Argentina* (Vol. III of *New World Guides to the Latin-American Republics*, edited by E. P. Hanson; N.Y.: Duell, Sloan and Pearce, 1950).
[2] *The Conquest of the River Plate (1535-1555)* (London: Hakluyt Society, 1891).

Cabeza de Vaca's actions as seen from Irala's side. That Martínez de Irala did not relish the arrival of a new governor to supersede him may, of course, be taken for granted. Moreover, the two men were diametric opposites in many of their views. Martínez was the ruthless *conquistador,* greedy, brutal toward the Indians. Núñez tried at all times to be correct, humane, and fair toward the Indians and was therefore resented for what might today be called "interfering with free enterprise." He was overpowered by Martínez and his followers; serious charges were trumped up against him, and he was sent back to Spain in chains to stand trial.

The drama's beginning, Mendoza's departure from Spain, is described by Schmidt at the start of his narrative.

> In the first place, when setting forth from Antorff [Antwerp], I came in fourteen days to Hispania, to a town called Calles [Cádiz], to which one reckons four hundred miles by sea. . . . [Schmidt reckoned in German miles, each comprising about four English miles and so corresponding to Columbus' "league."]
>
> Near the said town of Calles there were fourteen great ships, well provided with all ammunitions and necessaries, which intended to voyage to Riodellaplata [Río de la Plata] in India. Also there were two thousand five hundred Spaniards and one hundred and fifty Germans, Netherlanders, and Saxons. And our chief captain was called Petrus Manchossa [Pedro de Mendoza].[3]
>
> Among these fourteen ships, one belonged to Messrs. Sebastian Neidhart and Jacob Welser, from Nürnberg, who had sent their factor, Heinrich Paeime, with merchandise to the Plate River. With these and others, as Germans and Netherlanders, about eighty men, armed with arquebuses and muskets, I went to Río de la Plata.

The expedition stayed some two weeks at the site of today's Rio de Janeiro, which Schmidt called "Riogenea," and where

[3] Schmidt's rendering of proper names and place names was horrendous. The corrections given in brackets above are given in footnotes in the Hakluyt volume. From here on, to save confusion, such names will be given in their correct, rather than Schmidt's garbled, form. The Hakluyt editor, Don Luis L. Dominguez, Argentina's minister to England at the time, also warns against Schmidt's statistics. Other accounts give the number of Mendoza's ships as eleven, and his men as ranging from 800 to 1,700. As for the North Europeans on the voyage, Dr. Dominguez reminds us that Emperor Charles V, while King of Spain, was also King of Germany and the Netherlands.

Mendoza saw fit to have his "sworn brother," Juan Osorio, put to death for treason. Then they made their way to the Plate estuary.

> So by the grace of God we arrived at Río de la Plata, Anno 1535, and found there an Indian place inhabited by about two thousand people, named Charúas, who have nothing to eat but fish and meat. These on our arrival did leave the place, and fled away with their wives and children, so that we could not find them. This Indian people go quite naked, the women having only their privities covered, from the navel to the knees, with a small piece of cotton cloth.

Mendoza moved the expedition to the other side of the Plate, and "there we built a new town and called it Bonas Aeires, that is, in German, *Guter Wind*."

The country was inhabited by Quirandis Indians, whose life and nomadic habits Schmidt describes. For two weeks the Indians brought the Spaniards daily supplies of fish and meat, but then they missed a day and Mendoza sent a judge with two foot soldiers to find out what was the trouble.

> When they came near to them [the Indians] they were all three beaten black and blue, and were then sent back to our camp. Pedro de Mendoza, our captain, hearing of this from the judge's report (who for this cause raised a tumult about it in our camp), sent Diego de Mendoza, his own brother, against them with three hundred foot-soldiers and thirty well-armed mounted men, of whom I also was one, straightway charging us to kill or take prisoners all these Indian Quirandis and to take possession of their settlement. But when we came near them there were now some four thousand men, for they had assembled all their friends. And when we were about to attack them, they defended themselves in such a way that we had that very day our hands full. They also killed our commander, Diego de Mendoza, and six noblemen. Of our foot-soldiers and mounted men over twenty-seven slain, and on their side about one thousand. Thus did they defend themselves valiantly against us, so that indeed we felt it.

The Spaniards had won a difficult victory, but of the Pyrrhic kind. The surviving Indians cleared out with their women and children, and without Indians to feed them it was notoriously difficult for the *conquistadores* to stay alive. A hundred of them were put to work fishing, but accomplished little to allay the hunger. Resolutely the men undertook to build the city of Buenos Aires, but it was slow work because they were weak from hunger, which "became so bad that the horses could not go. Yea, finally, there were neither rats, nor mice, nor snakes to still the great dreadful hunger and unspeakable poverty, and shoes and leather were resorted to for eating and everything else."

It happened that three Spaniards stole a horse, and ate it secretly, but when it was known, they were imprisoned and interrogated under the torture. Whereupon, as soon as they admitted their guilt, they were sentenced to death by the gallows, and all three were hanged.

Immediately afterwards, at night, three other Spaniards came to the gallows to the three hanging men, and hacked off their thighs and pieces of their flesh, and took them home to still their hunger.

A Spaniard also ate his brother, who died in the city of Buenos Aires.[4]

Mendoza now had the men build four brigantines and three smaller boats, and sent one George Lujan with 350 armed men up the Paraná River on a foraging expedition "in order to find out the Indians and so obtain victual and provisions."

But as soon as the Indians were aware of us, they wrought us the most abominable piece of knavery, by burning and destroying all their victual and provisions and their villages, and then all took to flight; in consequence whereof we had nothing to eat but three ounces of bread a day. One half of our men died during this voyage through hunger, therefore we had to return to the said place, where was our chief captain. . . .

After all this we remained still another month together in great poverty in the town of Buenos Aires, until the ships were prepared.

At this time the Indians came in great power and force, as many as twenty-three thousand men, against us and our town Buenos Aires.

During the fighting the Indians burned down most of the town by shooting fire arrows into the thatched roofs. They also

[4] Schmidt's translator and editor here adds the following footnote: "All this is exaggerated and incredible, though accepted as true by the pseudo-poet, Barco Centenera, in his *Argentina* poem."

succeeded in setting fire to four of the expedition's ships but were finally routed when the Spaniards shot at them with cannon from the other ships. Mendoza, who was tired and ill, now turned over the command of the expedition to Juan de Ayolas, who mustered the people and "found no more than five hundred and sixty men who were yet alive, out of two thousand five hundred, the others being dead and having been starved for hunger." Leaving 160 men "in the four great ships to guard them, Ayolas embarked with the other four hundred, including Mendoza, in the brigantines and boats, to ascend the Paraná River." After two hungry months' travel, during which 50 more Spaniards died, they reached a horde of friendly Indians who were happy to receive the white men's presents (a shirt, a red cap, a hatchet, and several other things for the Indian chief), and gave them in return "fish and meat in abundance."

> In this said place we abode four years, but our chief captain, Pedro de Mendoza, who was full of infirmities, and was unable to move his hands or his feet, and who had spent during this voyage forty thousand ducats of his own in cash, could not remain any longer with us, and he sailed off in two brigantines to Buenos Aires to the four great ships, and took two of them with fifty men and sailed for Spain. But when he was come nearly half-way, the hand of the Almighty so smote him that he died miserably. May God be merciful to him.
>
> But before his departure he had promised to send two other ships to the Plate River, as soon as he himself or the ships should arrive in Spain, and this was faithfully laid down in his will. Accordingly, when the two ships arrived in Spain, and the councillors of His Imperial Majesty were informed of this, they speedily, in the name of His Majesty, sent two ships with people, provisions, and merchandise, and all necessaries, to the Plate River.
>
> The commander of these two ships was called Alonzo Cabrera, who brought with him also about two hundred Spaniards and provisions for two years.

After the Cabrera force had joined that of Ayolas on the Paraná River, the total body numbered 550 men, plus the 160 who had been left in Buenos Aires. While a ship was immediately sent to Spain to report on the expedition's affairs, Ayolas with 400 men ascended the Paraná and Paraguay rivers, sometimes fighting but most of the time dealing with friendly Indians whom Schmidt describes in some detail. On the Paraguay they came to the land of the Carios Indians, which was extremely well supplied with food and pleased the Spaniards greatly.

> These Carios have a large country, nearly three hundred miles in length and breadth; they are men of short stature, and more able to endure work and labor than the other natives. . . .
>
> This people, men and women, young and old, go completely naked as God created them. Among these Indians the father sells his daughter, the husband his wife if she does not please him, and the brother sells or exchanges his sister. A woman costs a shirt or a bread knife, or a small hoe, or some other thing of that kind.
>
> These Carios also eat man's flesh if they can get it. For when they make prisoners in war, male or female, they fatten them as we do swine in Germany. But if the woman be somewhat young and good-looking, they keep her for a year or so, and if during that time she does not live after their desires, they put her to death and eat her, making a solemn banquet of it, and often times this is combined with a marriage. Only old persons are put to work until they die.

The Carios had a town named Lambaré, which the Spaniards took. Of the Indians Schmidt writes:

> Not being able to hold out any longer, and fearing besides for their wives and children whom they had with them in the town, they prayed for mercy, promising that they would do anything for us if only we would spare their lives. Also they gave to our commander, Juan de Ayolas, six women, the eldest of whom was only eighteen years old.
>
> They also gave him six deer and other wild beasts, and besought us to remain with them, and they gave to every soldier two women to wait on him, and to wash and cook for him. Besides which they gave us food and all the necessaries of life; so that peace was then concluded between us and our enemies.
>
> After that the Carios were compelled to build us a great house of stone, earth, and wood, in order that if in the meanwhile they were to revolt against us we Christians might have a place of refuge in which to defend ourselves.
>
> We took this town on the feast of Assumption, in the year

1539, and therefore it is called Nuestra Señora de la Asunción.[5]

According to Schmidt, after resting at Asunción two months, Ayolas took 300 Spaniards and 8,000 Carios, and went off downstream to punish another nation of Indians, the Agazés, who had treated the Christians badly in the course of the latter's ascent.

> We found them at the same place where we had left them, and we fell upon them by surprise in their houses while they were asleep, between three and four o'clock in the morning, for the Carios had sought them out and watched them, and we killed everybody, young and old, for it is the custom of the Carios, when they make war and are victorious, to kill all without any mercy or pity whatsoever.

After spending six months in Asunción, Ayolas loaded and provisioned five river ships.

> All things having now been arranged, and the ships provided with victual, our commander ordered all the people to assemble, and out of the four hundred men, took three hundred well armed; and the remaining one hundred were left in the aforesaid town [Asunción]. . . . And then we went up the river and found at a distance of five [20] miles from these Carios a village on the river Paraguay. The people here brought to us Christians victual, in the shape of fish, meat, hens, geese, Indian sheep, and ostriches.

They reached the land of the Payaguás Indians, about whom Ayolas had heard from the Carios, and who gave him much hearsay information about the Guaycurús, of whom it was said that "they dwelt far away in the country, and that they had much gold and silver, but that they, the Payaguás had never seen any of them."

Having heard the Guaycurús described as "wise men, like as we Christians are," plentifully supplied with fine foods as well as precious metals, Ayolas impressed 300 Payaguás as burden-bearers and set out, overland, westward, in search of that particular El Dorado. First he sent three of his brigantines back to

[5] At this point Schmidt's translator and editor has the following to say: "Schmidt's chronology is often mistaken. Lambaré, with its population, was taken by Juan de Ayolas on the 15th of August 1536. Asunción was founded the following year by Juan de Salazar."

Asunción, leaving two in the land of the Payaguás, with 50 men on board, including Ulrich Schmidt, with instructions to wait five months for Ayolas' return. According to Schmidt they waited six months without word from the commander, ran out of food, and returned to Asunción under the leadership of Domingo Martínez de Irala. Mystery still shrouds the fate of Ayolas. Some scholars are inclined to believe that he reached Peru, loaded up with gold and silver, and was massacred with all his men during his return. Schmidt, reporting rumors which filtered into Asunción and a report which was wrung from two Indians under torture, writes that the Spaniards were killed to a man by their own Payaguás burden-bearers, acting in league with the Yapeurús, a tribe of the Payaguás.

> Meanwhile it seemed good to us Christians to elect Domingo Martínez de Irala for our chief commander (especially because he had behaved so well against the war-people), until H. I. Majesty should give further orders.

After waiting another year in Asunción, Martínez fitted out an expedition of 150 soldiers, with four brigantines, for a down-river trip to Buenos Aires, to fetch "the one hundred and sixty Spaniards left [there] in the two ships, and bring them to the town of Asunción."

After considerable difficulties, including a disastrous attack by Indians, the Spaniards were finally reunited at Buenos Aires, where, after five days, "a ship called a *caravel*, came from Spain, and brought us fresh tidings to wit, that a ship had arrived at Santa Catarina, whose captain was called Alonzo Cabrera, and he had brought with him two hundred soldiers from Spain."

A ship was sent to Santa Catarina island, off Brazil, to escort Cabrera and his ship to Buenos Aires. The two vessels sailed south together, but they were beset by a bad storm and the ship to which Schmidt had been assigned "was broken into many thousand pieces, and fifteen of our men and six Indians were drowned. Some taking hold of large pieces of timber swam out, and I with five of my companions escaped on the mast."

Martínez de Irala now ordered the complete evacuation of Buenos Aires, which was not to be reestablished as a permanent settlement until 1580, under Juan de Garay.

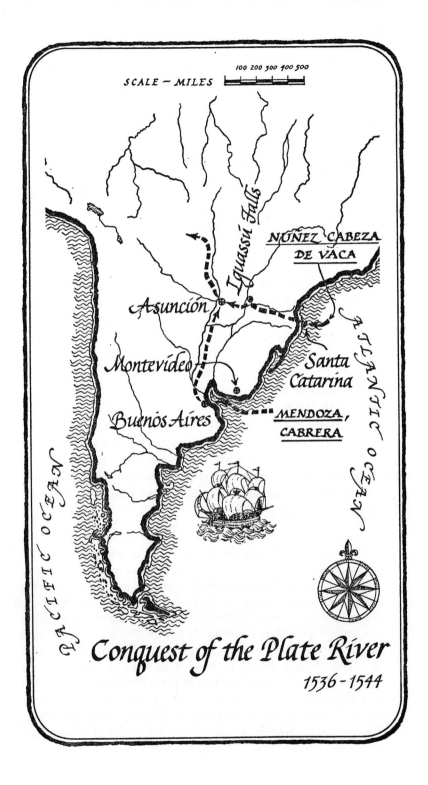

Conquest of the Plate River

1536-1544

All the people being together at Buenos Aires, our chief captain ordered that the brigantine ships should be made ready, and that all the soldiers should be in them together, and that they should burn the great ships; preserving, however, the iron tackling. After this had been done, we sailed once more up the River Paraná, and came to the town of Asunción, where we remained two years, awaiting further orders from H. I. Majesty.

Meanwhile, another chief commander named Alvar Núñez Cabeza de Vaca, came from Spain, appointed by H. I. Majesty, with four hundred men and thirty horses, in four vessels, two of which were large ships, and the other two caravels.

Núñez, whom the emperor sent as the new adelantado, or governor, of the Plate River country, was already famous for his adventures in North America. In 1527 he had sailed to Florida as treasurer of a colonizing expedition, sent to hold the country which Ponce de León had discovered in 1513 and had failed to colonize in 1521. But the expedition had bad luck and was shipwrecked, Núñez eventually being captured by Indians. In 1536, after years of wanderings as a captive, in the course of which he crossed Mexico to the Pacific, he ran into some Spaniards and sailed back to Spain. The fact that he had been treated reasonably well during his captivity had much to do with the humane attitude toward the Indians which he was to display in the Plate River country. Members of his family are today numerous and noted in New Mexico, where "Cabeza de Vaca" has been simplified to "Baca." His commentaries, written by his secretary, Pedro Hernández, begin as follows:

Since it pleased God to deliver Alvar Núñez Cabeza de Vaca from captivity and from the troubles that he underwent for ten years in Florida, he came to these kingdoms in the year of our Lord 1537, where he remained till the year 1540; in which year there came to this court of His Majesty some persons from the River La Plata to inform His Majesty of what had happened to the army which Don Pedro de Mendoza had taken there, and of the danger those were in who had survived, and to supplicate that His Majesty would be pleased to aid and succour them before they perished (as but few of them remained). And when His Majesty knew of it, he ordered that a certain arrangement and capitulation should be made with Alvar Núñez Cabeza de Vaca, in order that he might go to their relief. This arrangement and capitulation was there affected, the said Cabeza de

Vaca offering to go to their assistance, and undertaking to expend for that journey and relief, in horses, arms, apparel and provisions, as well as other things, eight thousand ducats. And in consideration of this treaty thus entered into, His Majesty favoured him with the governorship and general captaincy of that land and province, and with the title of Adelantado.

Núñez hurried to Seville, where he bought two ships and two caravels.

He equipped these vessels very well and supplied them with plenty of commodities, and engaged pilots and sailors, and four hundred soldiers well trained to the use of arms, and such as were wanted for that relief; and all that volunteered for that expedition were provided with a double set of arms.

After long and aggravating delays in Spain, the expedition weighed anchor for the transatlantic voyage on November 2, 1540. The voyage was troublesome. They suffered bad weather; leaking ships and other ills delayed them in La Palma and the Cape Verde Islands. After many reverses, they anchored off the island of Santa Catarina (off modern Brazil's state of the same name; site of today's city of Florianopolis) on March 29, 1541.

While there, they were visited by nine Spaniards "who came in a boat, having fled from the colony of Buenos Aires because of ill-treatment used towards them by the captains residing in the province." According to the account of those Spaniards, Juan de Ayolas and his men had been massacred after their return to the Paraguay River from their westward expedition. The men claimed that he had been treacherously abandoned by those whom he had left on the Paraguay to wait for him with two brigantines, who had sailed back to Asunción without waiting for him, and it was that desertion which had led to his being killed by the Indians. They ascribed the treason directly to Martínez de Irala. Núñez also heard from those nine Spaniards about the founding of Asunción.

To those nine Christians, who came naked, the governor gave clothing, and took them under his protection in order to bring them back with him to the province, for they were useful men, good sailors, and one of them was a pilot who knew the navigation of the river.

Álvar Núñez now decided to send his ships to Buenos Aires while he and the main body of men plunged westward, through unexplored territory, heading directly for Asunción.[6] First, however, he sent a reconnaissance patrol of "one hundred Spaniards and some Indians who acted as guides," to spy out the land, waiting three months on Santa Catarina Island for the expedition's return.

After provisioning and giving instructions to the 140 men who were to go to Buenos Aires by sea, Núñez, with the rest of the men and 26 horses "went on his way into the interior of the land, where he and his people underwent many troubles."

> In nineteen days they crossed great mountains, cutting roads through forests, to enable the men and the horses to pass, for all the land was uninhabited. And at the end of these nineteen days, having exhausted . . . [their] provision . . . it pleased God that without the loss of a man, they discovered the first inhabitants, who are called "del campo," where they found certain villages of Indians . . . and at one day's journey there was another. . . . And beyond this people there was a third tribe of Indians. . . . And when the Indians knew of the arrival of the governor and his people, they went out to meet him laden with plenty of provisions, showing great joy at their arrival. The governor received them affably, and, besides paying the value of the provisions into the hands of the chiefs, he graciously gave them many shirts and other things, with which they remained satisfied. This is a people and tribe called Guaranís; they are cultivators, sowing maize twice in the year, and also cassava. They rear fowls as in our Spain, and geese; keep many parrots in their houses, and occupy much land, and the whole are of one language.[7] They eat human flesh, as well that of their Indian enemies as of Christians; they also eat one another. This people is very fond of war; they are vindictive. Of this people and their territory the governor took possession, in the name of His Majesty, as newly discovered land, and called it the province of Vera.

The explorers reached the Iguazú River, a large tributary of the Paraná, which they followed downstream. Their reputation

---

[6] In the Hakluyt translation, this is spelled "Ascension" throughout. It is here written "Asunción" to avoid confusion.

[7] Guaraní is today one of Paraguay's two official languages, the other being Spanish.

had preceded them; Indians everywhere came forth to meet them with supplies, for which they were well paid, "so that they were never short of food, and had sometimes even more than they could take, and left it on the road." At one point "there arrived a newly converted Indian whose name was Miguel, who came from the town of Asunción, where the Spaniards resided who were to be relieved." The Indian was headed for the coast of Brazil but offered to turn back and guide Álvar Núñez to Asunción.

> Then the governor discharged the Indians that came with him from the island of Santa Catarina, and ordered them to return. These Indians, owing to the good treatment and many presents they had received, returned well satisfied and merry.

The Christians marched from one Indian settlement to the next, always meticulous in their treatment of the native people, always well received with plenty of provisions.

> Since entering the inhabited region they had found the country to be very pleasant, with large plains, forests, and many rivers, streams, and rivulets, with an abundance of good drinking water. In fact, it is a land very suitable for cultivation and stock-raising.

Only occasionally, when crossing uninhabited mountains, did they suffer hunger.

> The first of January of the year A.D. 1542, the governor and his people left the Indian settlements, and advanced across a mountainous region, through dense thickets of reeds, where our people underwent much trouble, because, up to the fifth of the month, they met with no settlement, and had to suffer much from hunger; and they kept themselves alive with great difficulty, besides having to open roads through the reed jungle. In the hollows of these reeds there were some white worms, about the length and thickness of a finger; the people fried these for food, obtaining sufficient fat from them to fry them in very well; all ate of them, and thought it excellent food.[8]

[8] At this point the translator adds a footnote: "The 'reeds' of the text must certainly be bamboos, and the larva or grub found in them answers to that of the *Calandra palmarum,* a species of weevil which is still cooked and eaten in the way here described."

On the last day of January, having been warned of hostile Indians ahead, Núñez split his force, one group of men with the horses proceeding down one bank of the Iguazú River, while he, with 80 men, embarked in canoes and followed the other bank. They had some difficulty in portaging their boats around the Iguazú falls, today a famous tourist attraction about eight miles from the river's mouth, but eventually the entire force was reunited on the banks of the Paraná River, which they crossed on rafts. Some time earlier Núñez had sent a courier to Asunción, with letters announcing his imminent arrival there and giving certain instructions to Martínez. Now, on the Paraná, his chronicler wrote:

> When the governor had passed [i.e., crossed] the river Paraná he was greatly disappointed at not finding the two brigantines which he had ordered by letter the two captains who were at Asunción to send, these vessels being much needed to protect the passage for the transport of the sick and those who were fatigued with the long journey. As there were many incapable of marching who could not safely be left behind in the midst of so many enemies, who might soon pluck up courage to attempt some of their treasonable practices, he arranged to send the sick down the Paraná on the rafts, entrusting them to the care of an Indian chief named Yguaron, to whom he gave presents.

There were about 30 incapacitated, "and he sent with them fifty arquebusiers and crossbowmen for their protection." The rafts were to proceed downstream to the village of a Christianized Indian, where the brigantines would perhaps be waiting. Álvar Núñez, with the rest of the force, made his way overland along the bank of the Paraná. The Indians along the way continued to cooperate with food and other help.

> Travelling in this way, it pleased God that on the eleventh of March, being one Saturday, at nine o'clock in the morning, in the year of grace 1542, we arrived at the city of Asunción, where we found the Spaniards living whom we had come to relieve. . . .
>
> The governor received them all at an interview, spoke very kindly with them, and informed them that he had come by His Majesty's orders to succour them. Thereupon he showed his credentials and powers to Domingo de Irala, and [the other officers]. . . . These documents were read out to the clergy and

soldiers present, and by virtue of them they recognized him as governor, and signified their obedience as to a captain-general of the province, appointed by His Majesty. The insignia of justice were given up to him, and were redelivered, in the name of His Majesty, to the magistrates who should administer civil and criminal law in the said province.

Ulrich Schmidt, presenting Martínez' point of view, tells a somewhat different story. First he complains about the length of time it had taken the relief expedition to reach Asunción. Then he accuses Núñez of holding back his credentials.

> This Commander was eight whole months on his way, for the distance is reckoned to be five hundred miles from Asunción to . . . Santa Catarina.
>
> He also brought with him from Spain his commission from H. I. Majesty, and required that Domingo Martínez de Irala should yield up the whole government to him, and that all the men should be obedient to him in every respect. The commander . . . Irala, and all the people declared that they were ready to obey, but with this understanding, that he, Cabeza de Vaca, should show and lay before them some document to prove that he had received from His Imperial Majesty such powers and authority.
>
> But this the whole assembly could not obtain from him; only the priests and two or three of the captains affirmed it, that Álvar Núñez Cabeza de Vaca ruled and commanded; but we shall see hereafter how things went with him.

The Spaniards whom Núñez had sent down the Paraná on rafts, "both sick and sound," arrived in Asunción a month later, after a troublesome voyage in the course of which they had been attacked by Indians for fourteen days.

The new governor now sent four brigantines with many men downriver to Buenos Aires, for the relief of the 140 men he had sent to that place from Santa Catarina Island and with instructions to begin immediately rebuilding that port. "He gave special injunctions to the captains of those . . . vessels to treat the natives of the Paraná with kindness, and induce them by fair means to acknowledge the sovereignty of the King." Having seen them off, he called together all the monks and clergy, and ordered them to see that the Indians were treated well, to win them to Christianity by gentle means, and to report to him,

Álvar Núñez, any abuses of the Indians that they might run into. He spent much time and energy in straightening out a number of evils. He concluded a treaty of peace with the warlike Agazés Indians who had long pillaged and harassed the Guaranís. He helped the poor among his Spanish settlers, and abolished oppressive taxes, "lately imposed [by Martínez and his officers] on fisheries, butter, honey, maize, and other commodities; on the skins with which they clothed themselves, and which they bought of the Indians." Such measures did not endear him to the Martínez faction.

Complaints came to Asunción from Guaranís living upriver, to the effect that the savage Guaycurús were waging a relentless war against them. After hearing much testimony from Indians and Spaniards, and asking his priests to investigate further, Núñez sent "two Spaniards who knew their language . . . with an escort of fifty Spaniards, to go in search of the Guaycurús, and summon them to submit to His Majesty, and desist from making war against the Guaranís, that these might freely go about their land, and enjoy their chase and fisheries." But the peace mission was greeted with hoots of derision and peppered with arrows, which wounded many men. Having received the news, "the governor . . . ordered two hundred arquebusiers and crossbowmen to be in readiness, and twelve horsemen, and with these he left . . . Asunción on Thursday the twelfth of July 1542." He also ordered two brigantines to ascend the Paraguay River, the meeting place being designated as the Indian village of Tapuá, four leagues above Asunción.

> All the soldiers and the horses marched to Tapuá by land, . . . passing, on the way, large troops of the Guaranís, who had orders to rendezvous at the same place, and accompany the governor on his expedition. It was wonderful to see the order they kept, and their preparations for war, all of them armed with bows and arrows, adorned with parrots' feathers, and painted with divers colors. They had musical instruments, which they use in battle, such as timbals and trumpets, cornets, etc. All arrived on the same day at Tapuá, and found here large numbers of Guaranís, bivouacking under the trees along the river bank.

They sent out scouts, who returned the following day, reporting that the Guaycurús were hunting some five or six leagues

inland, and seemed to be unaware of the approaching expeditionary force. The next day, having given orders not to light
fires or otherwise give away their presence to the enemies, Núñez
set out at the head of a relatively large army, including women
burden-bearers, in pursuit of the enemy. En route they had a
mishap with a "tiger" (jaguar).

> The governor and his army were marching through the skirts
> of a thick forest, and night was approaching, when a tiger passed
> through the midst of the Indians, causing a great panic and
> confusion among them, so that the Spaniards took to their arms,
> and, thinking the Indians were in revolt, fell upon them, calling
> on Santiago. In that affray several Indians were wounded, and
> their companions, seeing the attack made upon them, fled to the
> mountains. The governor himself narrowly escaped being
> wounded by two gunshots, the bullets having grazed the skin of
> his face; and these shots were certainly fired maliciously with
> intent to kill him, and to please Domingo de Irala, whom he
> had deprived of the command of the province.
>
> Álvar Núñez, seeing the Indians had fled, and anxious to put
> an end to the disorder, dismounted and rushed into the forest
> after them. He called to them that it was nothing more than
> a tiger had caused the confusion, and that he and his Spaniards
> were their friends, and that they were all brothers and subjects
> of His Majesty, and that all should advance together and drive
> the enemy from the country.

After some difficulty he managed to rally the Indians, and that
night, before daybreak, the whole force advanced on the Guaycurús, who, fortunately, had not heard the commotion over the
tiger. The punitive expedition seems to have been a complete
success. Since the Guaranís showed marked signs of fear, Núñez
arranged that a charge should be led by the Spaniards.

> He ordered the breastplates to be put on the horses, and, thus
> arrayed in order of battle, our forces charged the enemy with
> cries of "Santiago!" The governor, on horseback, led the van,
> and cut down all that opposed him. When the enemy saw the
> horses for the first time, a great fear fell upon them, and they
> fled to the mountains as quickly as they could. Passing through
> their village, they set fire to their houses, and these being made
> of mats of rushes and grass, caught fire at once, the flames
> spreading to the others, about twenty in number, all portable,

and each having a length of five hundred paces. Their owners, numbering about four thousand warriors, retired behind the smoke caused by the burning houses, and whilst so concealed killed two Christians, and decapitated twelve of our friendly Indians.

After pursuing the enemy a while, the Spaniards and their allies turned back and headed for Asunción, taking with them "four hundred prisoners, men, women, and children." However, Núñez had difficulty in keeping his Guaraní Indians from straggling off by themselves. "In this way it happened that one thousand of the Guaranís were killed singly by about twenty Guaycurús."

> During the return march the horsemen speared a number of deer, and the Indians were surprised to see the swiftness of the horses, which could overtake the deer. They, too, killed very many with their arrows. At four o'clock in the afternoon a halt was made under some large trees, and they passed the night there, having stationed sentinels to keep a good watch.
>
> The following day, in broad daylight, they set out in good order, hunting as they marched, and a number of deer and ostriches were killed. . . . It was a strange and pleasant sight to see the chase that day. One hour-and-a-half before nightfall they arrived on the River Paraguay, where the governor had left the two brigantines and the canoes.

After spending the better part of a day in ferrying his force to the river's east bank, "the governor and his people marched on to the town of Asunción, where he had left a garrison of two hundred and fifty men, under the orders of Gonzalo de Mendoza," who, during his governor's absence, had had his own troubles with attacking Indians.

Álvar Núñez now had all the Guaycurú prisoners brought together for a lecture to inform them that the Spaniards were the Indians' friends, and that his majesty the emperor did not want them to be enslaved.

> Among the captives was one of superior breeding and appearance, whom the governor ordered to be set free, desiring him to summon all his fellow tribesmen, because he had something to say to them in the name of the king, and that if they wished he would protect them, and give them presents, and so he let him go, giving him some presents; and he departed, well satis-

fied, to his own people. Four days afterwards, he returned accompanied by all his tribe, many of whom were badly wounded; all came, leaving none behind.

The chiefs of the Guaycurús, acknowledging the military power of the Spaniards, accepted the latter's rule and offered to become their slaves. But Núñez treated them well, returned all their prisoners without ransom, and admonished them to become Christians and loyal subjects of the King of Spain.

> Since then they have always kept the peace, and whenever the governor sent for them, hastened to obey his commands. Every eighth day they came laden with venison and wild boar. . . . They also brought much fish and plenty of other provisions, such as grease, linen mantles woven of a kind of teasel, dyed in bright colours; and skins of the tiger and tapir, deer and other animals. When they came, the markets for the sale of all these commodities lasted two days.

While all that was going on, Ulrich Schmidt was a member of a foraging expedition of "one hundred and fifteen soldiers," which the governor had sent out, "to go as far as they could, in order to find Indians who had manioc and Turkish corn [maize?]." These men went up a way and then turned back, "to a nation called the Aracarés," where they "found a letter from our chief captain, Álvar Núñez Cabeza de Vaca, to the effect that we should hang the chief of these Indians. . . . Our commander at once complied with this order, out of which afterwards a great war broke out, as will be seen hereafter."

Returning to Asunción, they were given a force of 2,000 Guaraní Indians and ordered again to proceed upriver, after being warned by the Guaraní chief that they were headed for country inhabited by bad and dangerous Indians. Martínez de Irala, undoubtedly to get him out of Asunción, was sent to head that expedition. They went back and forth, in and out of Asunción, and while Schmidt's account of the marching, sailing, and fighting makes entertaining and illuminating reading, it is too long and complex for a narrative of this kind. They did come to a nation of Indians called "Scherues" by Schmidt and "Xarayos" by his translator, whose king received them well and gave them a quantity of silver and gold, explaining that those things "were the spoils which in time past he had won in war from the Amazons." Schmidt now gives the common account of those fighting women, this time adding the ancient Greek touch that they cut off one breast in order to have that arm more free for fighting. The Spaniards impressed Indians as burden-bearers and set off after the Amazons, but were turned back by floods. Killing, looting, and plundering, they made their way back to Asunción, where Núñez took away their loot and arrested their commander, Hernando de Ribera, threatening to hang him for having maltreated the Indians. But the soldiers raised so great a howl that the prisoner was released and the booty was restored to the rebellious men. The new governor was developing difficulties in holding his forces together.

Word of Núñez' success against the dread Guaycurús spread through the country, and other Indians, notably a tribe called the Apirús, came in to make peace and seek protection. A revolt of the Agazés, who had earlier concluded peace but had been emboldened to revolt during the governor's absence from Asunción, was punished by hanging 13 Indians who had been languishing in prison in Asunción.

> Peace and tranquility being now established, the governor sent a party to the relief of Buenos Aires and Captain Juan Romero, who had been previously dispatched with two brigantines and some men with the same purpose. For this new relief the governor decided on sending Captain Gonzalo de Mendoza and two other brigantines and one hundred men. These dispositions having been taken, he sent for the monks, clergy, and officers, and spoke to them of the measures to be adopted for the discovery of the province, especially with the object of finding a route by land by which the Spaniards might be supplied with provisions in passing through desolate uninhabited tracts, of which there were many in that country.

The unanimous opinion of the council was that the conquest should be started without delay, and three Spaniards who were sent north on the river some 70 leagues, accompanied by 800 Indians, with instructions to strike inland from there and scout the country. However, no sooner had they left the river for their overland voyage than Aracaré, the local chief, a bitter enemy of the whites, began to set fire to his fields, and to incite the Spaniards' Indian guides to rebel. The three Spanish scouts were deserted by all their 800 Indian companions and had a terrible time making their way back to the river and thence to Asunción.

> About this time the governor sent in search of timber in order to build brigantines for the voyage of discovery he proposed making, and a caravel to send to Spain, to report to His Majesty how things were going in the province with reference to its discovery and conquest . . . and within the space of three months sufficient wood had been prepared for the construction of one caravel and ten rowing vessels [i.e., brigantines] for the navigation and exploration of the river. All this wood was transported by the natives to Asunción, and the construction of the brigantines was at once begun.

A new and larger scouting expedition was sent upriver and inland to explore the land where the three Spaniards had failed. These men returned after 45 days, during which they had suffered greatly from hunger and depredations at the hands of the chief, Aracaré.

> The governor having learned of the outrageous conduct of Aracaré, which had now become notorious, ordered an act of accusation to be drawn up against him, and to be notified to this chief—a somewhat dangerous commission, because Aracaré came out with arms in his hands, followed by a number of friends and relations, with the intent to kill the Spaniards sent to him. The process, however, was duly served according to law, and Aracaré was sentenced to death and executed, the natives being made to understand the just cause for which this had been done.
>
> On the 20th of December the four brigantines, sent by the governor to the river Paraná to the relief of the Spaniards who had come by ship from the island of Santa Catarina, arrived at Asunción, together with the ship's boat. In these craft came all the people, who soon disembarked.

The men sent from Santa Catarina had found Buenos Aires completely evacuated and had found, in a hollowed-out log, a letter from Martínez de Irala, telling why the site had been abandoned. Suffering starvation, constantly attacked by the Indians, "all must have perished . . . had not timely succour arrived." Together with the reinforcements from Asunción, they had tried to rebuild Buenos Aires on a better site, but were prevented by the advent of the rainy season. Finally they had decided to set out for Asunción.

To add to the troubles of the little colony, "on the fourth of February the following year, 1543, one Sunday morning, three hours before daybreak, a straw house in the city of Asunción took fire, and the flames spread so rapidly that in a short time the conflagration was awful to see."

> Upward of 200 houses were burnt down, only fifty being saved, these being separated from the rest by a stream of water which ran between them. Upwards of 5,000 measures of maize were burnt in grain. . . . A quantity of maize-flour, and other provisions, such as poultry and pigs, were destroyed, and the Spaniards were reduced to such a state of destitution that they had no clothes to wear. The fire continued for four days.

A few days later, while the town was being rebuilt, Domingo Martínez de Irala returned from his four-month scouting expedition, reporting his encounter with prosperous and friendly Indians who had "shown him specimens of their gold and silver," had told him that "the way to the interior of the country lay through their territory," and had offered to guide the Spaniards into the interior. In this customary fashion, the governor immediately called a conference of "the monks, the clergy, and the officers," who stated in writing that they were all for following up on Martínez' discoveries and getting on with the conquest. Captain Gonzalo de Mendoza was therefore dispatched up the Paraguay with three brigantines, to gather supplies for the projected military operations. However, he sent back word of more trouble, caused by hostile Indians who needed punishing because they made war on Indians friendly to the Spaniards. Martínez was therefore sent out again with 150 men, instructed to bring the bad Indians to terms by peaceful means if possible but to subdue them by war if necessary. He managed to bring them to terms peacefully, but no sooner had he accomplished his mission than Núñez had trouble with his clergy.

> Now when the brigantines were on the point of sailing, and everything was ready for the voyages of exploration as recommended by the council, the friars Bernaldo de Armenta and Alonso Lebron his companion were silently and secretly induced to proceed to the coast of Brazil by the route explored by the governor, bearing certain letters for His Majesty, acquainting him with the bad use the governor was making of the powers

and authority graciously conferred upon him. This was done out of jealousy and hatred towards the governor, and in order to hinder his exploration and discovery of the country so that his service to the king might be of no effect.

The monks, according to the governor's chronicler, belonged to the Martínez faction which was incensed over Núñez' humane Indian policies, his objections to looting the Indians, and his abolition of the profiteering taxes which the Martínez group had levied on the settlers. The absconders had sworn everybody to secrecy about their departure, but they had also carried off a number of Indian girls for the purpose of "Christianizing" them; the girls' fathers went to the governor to object, and the latter sent soldiers to bring back the friars with their companions and female retinue.

> In order that he might not be detained in his voyage of exploration, he deputed the cause to a judge, and bade him investigate the whole matter as to the misdeeds of the accused persons and the charges brought against them. Two of them he took with him on bail, leaving the others in prison in the city, suspended from office till such time as His Majesty should ordain as to what further should be done in the matter.

Álvar Núñez Cabeza de Vaca had his troubles. They were to come to a boil after he finally managed to get off on his long delayed voyage of exploration and conquest.

> All preparations being now completed for the voyage of discovery, and the ten brigantines having been laden with provisions, the governor selected 400 arequebusiers and archers to accompany him on that journey. Half of these embarked on the brigantines, the others, together with twelve horsemen, went by land along the river bank . . . keeping constantly among settlements of the friendly Guaranís. . . . Two hundred soldiers—arquebusiers and archers—and six horsemen remained behind to protect the city. . . . He set out [September 8, 1543] from Asunción with twenty brigantines and 120 canoes. In these were 1,200 Indian warriors, whose strange appearance, armed with bows and arrows, produced a wonderful effect, in their war paint adorned with plumes and feathers, and wearing on their brows plates of metal, so that when the sun shone they glittered marvellously. . . . When the governor departed from the city he left word with Captain Salazar [his deputy] to use every effort

to complete the caravel, which he had ordered to be built, so that he might then send his report to Spain of all that had happened in his voyage of exploration. Having made all necessary dispositions, and the weather being favorable, he reached the port of Tapuá, where he was received by the chiefs. These he told that he was about to undertake a voyage of discovery of that land; he therefore begged them always to live in peace and concord with their neighbors. If they obeyed him they would always be as well, and better, treated than heretofore, and he gave presents to be distributed among their sons and relatives, and left them well pleased and satisfied.

October 12, "the governor arrived at the port of Candelaria [today's Corumbá, Brazil], and the country of the Payaguás."

> It was here that Captain Juan de Ayolas [had] entered with his Spaniards, and hither he returned after his exploration, expecting to find Domingo de Irala, whom he had left in charge of the brigantines. . . . Here he remained four months awaiting their arrival, during which time he and his men suffered terribly from hunger.

Finally, seeing how weak the Spaniards were, the Indians "slew Captain Juan de Ayolas and eighty Spaniards, being all that remained of the one hundred and fifty who had gone on that expedition. . . . Domingo de Irala [had] acted with bad faith, to the intent that Juan de Ayolas might be slain, and that he might raise a revolt in the land against God and the king."

Shortly after Núñez' arrival at Candelaria, the local chief of the Payaguás, who had killed Ayolas, sent word to the Spaniards that he wanted to make peace, that he regretted having killed the Ayolas group, and that he wanted to return to Núñez all the loot he had taken from Ayolas.

> The governor then asked him how much gold and silver they had taken from Juan de Ayolas, and he showed them, by signs, that it would amount to sixty-six loads such as the Chamés Indians are accustomed to carry, and that it was all in plates, bracelets, crowns, and axes; also that there were small vases of gold and silver.

It was the account of that treasure which convinces many scholars that Ayolas, after striking west from Corumbá, had reached Peru. However, the treasure was never acquired by Núñez. The day after his first fine conversation with the chief, who had also promised the Spaniards guides and interpreters to help them retrace the westward Ayolas route in search of gold and silver, the latter was found to have decamped with all his people. Núñez followed them up the Paraguay River, but failed to catch them.

> As we were now approaching the country of the Guaxarapos Indians, who inhabit the bank of the Paraguay, and are neighbors and traffic with the port of Los Reyes,[9] for which we were bound, and as these Indians might have been alarmed at such a multitude of people and canoes, and might have fled inland, the governor . . . divided his flotilla into two parts, and, taking five brigantines and half the canoes, led the advance, leaving Captain Gonzalo de Mendoza to follow with the other vessels, canoes, and people, charging him to govern all the people kindly and not to abuse his authority.

Exhorting Indians all along the way to become Christians and obey the king, Núñez made his northward way to the mouth of a river flowing from the east, which must have been the Cuyabá and from which, some years earlier, a Portuguese leader (unidentified) named García had entered the Paraguay "at the head of a large number of Indians, fought many battles, and destroyed many tribes, having only five Christians with him." He had withdrawn, however, and had never returned.

> That morning the Guaxarapos . . . came . . . in two canoes with supplies of fish and meat. . . . He [Núñez] told them of the other vessels, canoes, and soldiers that were behind, and begged them to receive them kindly and treat them well . . . : this they promised they would do, but did not keep their word. The cause of this was certainly a Christian, who was punished for it, as I shall presently relate.

Ascending the Paraguay past settlements of agricultural Indians, the Spaniards came, on October 25, to a river they called the Yguatu, which was probably the Jaurú, in today's Brazilian Matto Grosso. There they erected three crosses as beacons for

[9] So named by Martínez de Irala, who had landed there on January 6, or Three Kings' Day, in the course of his earlier reconnaissance expedition, and who, "during the whole of his voyage . . . did not see a more convenient or better country by which to penetrate into the interior." At 18° N. latitude, the port was a little above the mouth of the Cuyabá River.

Gonzalo de Mendoza. Finally they arrived at "the port of Los
Reyes," the center of a large population of agricultural Indians,
where Núñez had a church built and a large cross erected, while
he took possession of the land in the name of his king (though
later it was to revert to Portugal and become part of today's
Brazil). Here they were in the country of the Xarayos, enemies
of the Guaranís. They were willing to serve Núñez but would
not go with him into Guaraní country except to make war.

Having made diligent inquiries, Núñez now struck westward
to "find the road leading to the interior." But they ran into uninhabited country when their own supplies were low, and his
officers forced him to return to Los Reyes. "Once there, it would
be easy to take fresh supplies and recommence the discovery.
Such was their advice, and, they added, if necessary, they would
require the governor in the name of His Majesty to conform
with it." The growing spirit of rebellion is expressed at about
this time by Ulrich Schmidt, who seems to have been a member
of a party sent out to scout the land ahead:

> Now our chief commander, after the report we had made of
> [the country], would have marched with all his people to that
> country to which we had just been; but we soldiers would not
> agree thereto. . . .
> Moreover, most of the people were very feeble and ill, besides
> which our chief commander Álvar Núñez Cabeza de Vaca, com-
> manded no great respect or favour among the soldiers, for he
> was a man who had never held a command nor any important
> post whatsoever.

On his return to Los Reyes, Núñez found the place not only
full of tensions between the white garrison he had left there
and the Indians, but also dangerously short of food. He therefore sent Gonzalo de Mendoza with a force of 120 Spaniards
and 600 Indians to a people called the Arianicosies, about nine
leagues away, who were reported to have plenty to eat, ordering
his officer to secure food in a nice, peaceful fashion. At the same
time, Captain Hernando de Ribera was sent upstream in a
brigantine, with 52 men, to contact the Xarayos Indians, obtain
food, and ask questions about the country beyond. Very soon,
however, Núñez received a letter from Gonzalo de Mendoza to
the effect that the Arianicosies Indians would have none of his

peaceful overtures, that they had called in their neighbors, and that fighting had broken out between the Indians and Mendoza's men. The governor sent him a message, ordering him to return to Los Reyes.

> On the 30th of January 1543, Captain Hernando de Ribera returned with the vessel and men entrusted to him for the exploration of the higher reaches of the river. But when he returned he found the governor and all his people sick with fever and shivering fits, so he could not make his report.

Later, however, on March 3, 1545, in Asunción, de Ribera dictated an account of his expedition to Pedro Hernández, notary and secretary to Álvar Núñez. With his brigantine "and a certain number of men," he had ascended the Ygatu River and had reached the Xarayos.

> And having pursued my journey past many Indian settlements, and obtained from their inhabitants and other natives who came to see me, full reports touching the land, I examined and sifted these statements, in order to learn the truth, being moreover, acquainted with the language of the Carios, and therefore able to hold intercourse with those tribes.

From the land of the Xarayos he had marched westward, overland, to the Urtueses and the Aburuñes, all of whom told him much about the country farther inland. First, as though in compliance with a tribal ritual of the *conquistadores,* he tells about the Amazons, whose existence and customs cropped up with astonishing regularity in the old chronicles.

> All these Indians told me that at ten days' march from there, towards the west-northwest, there were women inhabiting large villages, who possessed a large quantity of white and yellow metal, and all their domestic utensils and vessels were of this metal and their chief was a woman. . . . At a certain time of the year these women unite with their neighbors, and cohabit with them. And if the children born of this intercourse be girls, the mothers keep them; if they are boys, they send them as soon as they are weaned to their fathers.

Living beyond the Amazons, some 15 days' travel from where de Ribera obtained the information, were reported "other large nations of black people . . . negroes . . . eagle-faced, with

pointed beards like the Moors." Then the Spaniards' informants
talked about what was unmistakably Peru.

> Farther to the west there is a large lake, so wide that it is
> impossible to see from shore to shore, and by its side dwells a
> nation who wear clothes, and possess much metal and brilliant
> stones. . . . They have large villages, are agriculturalists, and
> have stores of provisions, besides an abundance of geese and
> other birds. . . .
> I also formally declare that the Indians showed me by signs
> that in that direction west, one quarter south-west, there are
> large towns, with houses built of earth, inhabited by a good
> people, clothed, very rich, and possessing plenty of metal. They
> rear a large number of great sheep, using these for agriculture
> and transport. . . . Among those people they said there were
> other Christians, and great waterless deserts of sand. . . . The
> Indians living in that neighborhood had been heard to say that
> as they were passing the desert they met many white people,
> clothed, with beards, and they had certain animals with them,
> (evidently, according to their showing, horses), and riders on
> their backs, and that, owing to the want of water they had
> returned, and many had died on the way.[10]

Ill, beset by floods and swarms of mosquitoes, Álvar Núñez
remained at Los Reyes three months before his officers insisted
that he abandon the port and return to Asunción. At the time of
departure he again decreased his popularity by making another
of his drastic, unheard-of rulings.

> Yet he would not allow the Christians to take with them about
> a hundred girls, whom the natives of Los Reyes, upon the gov-
> ernor's arrival, had offered to the captains and officers of dis-
> tinction, leaving them to do what they pleased with the girls.
> . . . He ordered, at the moment of departure, the fathers of
> these girls to receive them back into their houses until our
> return, being unwilling that their parents should be dissatisfied
> and the country scandalized because of this. . . . The natives
> were well satisfied with this measure, but the Spaniards were
> greatly discontented, . . . and from that time he was detested
> by the majority.

[10] This seems to have been a hearsay account of Diego de Almagro's ill-fated expedition into Chile, in 1535.

The descent to Asunción required 12 days during which they were attacked by the Guaxarapos, who killed a Spaniard and wounded a number of Indians.

> On the 8th of April . . . we arrived at . . . Asunción with our troops, our Guaranís, and our vessels. The governor and the Christians that were with him were all sick and weak. . . . We found the caravel ordered by the governor nearly finished. He had intended sending it, as soon as it was ready, to bear information to His Majesty of all that has happened in his voyage of discovery and all that had passed in the country. . . .
>
> Fifteen days after the arrival of the governor at Asunción, the officers of His Majesty who hated him . . . conspired with their friends on St. Mark's Day to take him prisoner that night. . . . In order to carry out their plan . . . they told a hundred men they knew the governor was about to take from them their property, their houses, and their Indian girls, and would distribute these among the men who had returned from the exploring expedition.

Having so stirred up a number of the settlers (many others objected to their high-handed procedure, and the town came close to civil war), the rebels then arrested Álvar Núñez and several of his close associates, crying "Liberty, liberty! Long live the king!" and put them in irons.

> They then went to the house of the governor, where he kept his property, papers, and the letters he had received from the king appointing him governor of the province, as well as the acts by which his authority had been recognized. . . . They also opened a chest, locked with three keys, containing the public indictments against officers charged with crimes referred to the king for final sentence. They took also his goods, stuffs, provisions, oil, steel, and irons, besides a number of other things. . . . They denounced him as a tyrant, and abused him in every way.

Schmidt's account of the disgraceful affair reads as follows:

> But our people being for the most part feeble and ill-affected towards our chief commander, the latter could not do anything with them, so he ordered a ship to be prepared and we all went down the River Paraguay and came to Asunción, where we had left the other Christians. There our chief commander fell sick again of a fever, and kept indoors for fourteen days together.

It was, however, more out of pride than out of weakness, for he did not please the people; but showed himself unseemly towards them more than it behooved a lord or commander who would govern a country; for such a man should always give good counsel to everyone alike whatever their rank or station, and should be wiser and cleverer than those whom he commands. . . .

But here there has been no regard as to persons, but our commander has in all things only followed his arrogant and vain inspiration.

Thereupon it was resolved by all, noble man and commoner, to meet in council, with a view to take prisoner this chief commander, Álvar Núñez Cabeza de Vaca, and to send him to H. I. Majesty, and to report to His Majesty about his nice virtue, and how he had behaved towards us, and how, according to his reason, he had governed; and other things besides.

According to the resolution come to, . . . three gentlemen, . . . taking with them two hundred soldiers, went to his lodging, and arrested our commander in chief when he least expected it. . . . They held prisoner the said Álvar Núñez Cabeza de Vaca for a whole year, until a ship called a caravel, provided with victual and a crew, had been prepared. And on board this ship the often-mentioned Cabeza de Vaca, with two other officers on behalf of H. I. Majesty, were conveyed to Spain.[11]

Having arrested Núñez, the soldiers elected Martínez de Irala acting governor "until H. I. Majesty had time to designate one himself."

The colony was in turmoil during the year of Núñez' imprisonment, those who clamored for his release being badgered constantly by those who demanded his beheading. Under Martínez' leadership, atrocities against the Indians were resumed full force.

While the governor was in this situation, the officers and Domingo [Martínez] de Irala gave public permission to all their friends and partisans to go into the villages and huts of the Indians and take by force their wives, daughters, hammocks, and other of their possessions. . . . While this was going on they would scour the country, strike the Indians blows with sticks,

[11] The caravel which had been built, and almost completed, by Núñez' orders, was burned a few days after his arrest, to prevent news of the insurrection from reaching Spain.

carry them off to their houses, and oblige them to labour in their fields without any remuneration. . . . The natives withdrew to the mountains, and concealed themselves where the Christians could not find them. A large number were Christians, together with wives and children. When they left the settlement they lost the religious teaching of the monks and clergy.

On discovering a plot to free Núñez, the insurgents arrested a large number of men, "whom they put to the torture. . . . Many were deprived of the use of their limbs by these tortures."

Utterly unable to keep peace in the settlement, Martínez at last decided to send the deposed governor back to Spain. The insurgents prepared a memorandum, addressed to the king, accusing their prisoner of a long, trumped-up list of crimes. Núñez' friends, however, "arranged with the carpenters [preparing the ship] to hollow a timber . . . and place inside it a general act of accusation which the governor had addressed to His Majesty, and other important papers collected by his friends when he was arrested."

In the course of the voyage, the ship put in at the Azores and the insurgent officers embarked for Spain, where they "arrived eight days before the governor, who was delayed by contrary winds. Being the first to present themselves at court, they gave out that Cabeza de Vaca had gone to the King of Portugal to inform him about those countries beyond the sea."

However, in one mysterious way or another, virtually all of Núñez' accusers died before the case came up in the Madrid court. There seems to have been no formal trial, but Álvar Núñez Cabeza de Vaca fared badly nevertheless.

> After keeping him eight years under arrest at court, he was set at liberty and acquitted. He was relieved of his governorship for divers reasons; for his enemies said that if he returned to punish the guilty, he would have occasioned more troubles and dissentions in that country. He therefore lost his appointment, besides other losses, without receiving any compensation for all the money he had spent in relieving the Spaniards, and in his voyage of discovery.

Ulrich Schmidt remained in Martínez de Irala's service until 1552, when he was permitted to return to Antwerp. His narrative, after the departure of Álvar Núñez, is an account of virtually endless campaigns against the Indians, one of which took the Spaniards to the eastern border of Peru. It is also a narrative of murder, butchery, and wholesale enslavement. While the king appointed a successor to Álvar Núñez, as governor of the Plate River territory, the man died before he could reach that land. The traitor Domingo Martínez de Irala remained governor until his death in 1557.

✺ XIII ✺

THE SEARCH FOR
EL DORADO

HISTORIANS calculate that the frenetic search for El Dorado lasted for about two and a half centuries, but old legends, old habits of thought die slowly, and isolated individuals still uncover clues and reports—now and then and here and there—and move into the Amazonian realms in search of the golden city. The two and a half centuries recognized by historians cover the period during which known and recorded expeditions, sanctioned by governments or organized private society, tore the country apart, acquiring much geographic knowledge, influencing European mapmakers, but invariably discovering where El Dorado is NOT. The golden city, the fantastic dream of so many doughty and avid men, was necessarily shifted all over northern South America, always farther back into the "unexplored" regions, until at last it came to rest for some hundreds of years in a land which remained virtually inaccessible until well into the twentieth century. That region is the southern part of Venezuelan Guiana, west of Mount Roraima, east of Mount Duida, between British Guiana and the Orinoco River, north of the Brazilian cattle plains at the headwaters of the Rio Branco.

Reputedly rich in gold and diamonds, the region is today famous in Venezuela as the "Gran Sabana." Along its northern edge it is guarded by a great escarpment which no man had ever been known to scale until the 1960s, when the revolutionary Venezuelan government of Romulo Betancourt blasted a southbound, zigzagging road across it into the Gran Sabana diamond country. During the 1920s, however, it began to be crossed by airplanes which long connected the Gran Sabana with the rest of Venezuela. At that time a swashbuckling American pilot named Jimmy Angel, having completed his work in the famous World War I aviation picture *Hell's Angels,* is said to have gone to Panama, where he acquired a map of Venezuelan Guiana showing the location of a mountain of gold. As a pioneer bush pilot, he subsequently did much valuable work, helping to open the country for settlers and prospectors and making some dramatic geographic discoveries, among them the famous Angel Falls, which is ranked as the highest single-drop waterfall on earth. Those who knew him, however, report that he was forever on the lookout for the "lost" golden city, on a number of occasions thinking to have spotted it only to find that what he had seen was a distant mesa, which, with the proper cloud effects, could look amazingly like a ruined city.

While the escarpment along its northern edge and the general, forbidding nature of the country to the north kept explorers for centuries from entering the Gran Sabana country from that direction, there is every reason to suspect that the Portuguese long ago penetrated it overland from the south, from their cattle plains on the upper Rio Branco. Since the way is passable from that direction, it is more reasonable to believe that they did than that they did not. However, the Gran Sabana country was claimed by Spain, and any Portuguese who penetrated it were trespassing; they could therefore be expected to keep prudently quiet about the venture, especially since they also failed to discover El Dorado. What is known is that the Spanish explorer Nicolas Martínez, working as late as 1772, came close to solving the knotty problem of overland accessibility, even though he was as far from El Dorado's discovery as had been all the rest. He struck south and attempted to enter the Gran Sabana country from that direction. However, now he had to deal with the Portuguese, who claimed that he was encroaching on their territory. They promptly chased him out again, holding 19 of his men as prisoners.

Esmeralda—a settlement on the upper Orinoco which was not finally given up until 1931, when it was entirely deserted by all but roving Indians—was first established as a seventeenth-century mission station but was also for some centuries the jumping-off place for El Dorado expeditions, working eastward toward today's Gran Sabana. One after the other, those expeditions failed to reach their nonexisting objective. Not until 1949–50, when the journey was made by a group of literate, artistic Frenchmen who tamed the wild savages with a recorded Mozart symphony, did a white explorer manage to journey overland from the Orinoco to the Rio Branco cattle country.

In 1596, Laurence Keymis, a one-time lieutenant of Raleigh's, sent a pinnace up the Essequibo River in today's Republic of Guayana, in an effort to reach the promised land from the east. Like subsequent and more persistent efforts by the Dutch on the same river, his expedition failed to find El Dorado.

By the time El Dorado had finally settled in that locale, one of the continent's least accessible, it had attained a quite definite character in men's minds, while growing richer in every great dream spun by explorers, who were virtually forced to equate the riches sought with the hardships endured in the seeking. What had more or less begun as "another Cuzco," the goal of those who, coming too late to share the wealth of Peru's ancient capital, desperately sought something similar in some other location, was now the golden city of Manoa, which had been established, according to many eager rumors, by Peruvian Incas who had left their homeland with many people and untold quantities of gold, either because of their Spanish conquerors or because they had quarreled with other Incas before the white men's arrival. Named after the nation of Indians who were eventually to give their name to the important commercial city of Manaus (formerly Manáos), Manoa was located by the shore of a great lake, called "Parima." Just as Manoa had evolved out of the Inca city of Cuzco, so Lake Parima may well have been the dream equivalent of Lake Titicaca, between Peru and Bolivia, from the islands of which the Incas, the "Children of the Sun," had sprung according to ancient mythology. To be sure, Titicaca is a freshwater body while Parima was said to contain salt water, but the earlier El Dorado seekers were not particular about the waters' chemical analysis when they heard of some great lake in the unknown distance.

Beginning in the late sixteenth century, and through the late seventeenth, virtually every map of the Guiana country showed Lake Parima as an established reality, as did Father Fritz's famous map of the Amazon River, published in 1707 (Chapter XV). The earlier the map, the larger the lake, which had perforce to be reduced in size and shifted hither and yon as explorers succeeded in discovering where it was NOT. As told in Chapter XVII, Baron von Humboldt, visiting Esmeralda on the upper Orinoco in 1800, was there told as "fact" about the great Lake Parima, lying far to the east, with the ruins of golden Manoa on its shore.

The doughty explorer who finally "established" the location of El Dorado in southern Guiana, spending the last tragic years of his life in obsessed but always thwarted attempts to reach it, was Spain's Antonio de Berrio. The man who broadcast Berrio's travels and achievements to the non-Iberian world, having first kidnapped the Spaniard and pumped him dry, was England's Sir Walter Raleigh. Indeed, throughout several centuries, Raleigh's account was the only one through which North European scholars were informed of Berrio and his work. It might still be the only such account, had it not been for the fact that during the second half of the nineteenth century England became embroiled with Venezuela in a bitter dispute over the two nations' common boundary in Guiana (Chapter XXI). Late in the century, in connection with that dispute, England sent scholars to Seville to examine old records. Among many other things of great historic value, these scholars found, in Seville's General Archives, Berrio's three letters to the king of Spain, giving his own account of his searches for El Dorado. The letters were copied for the British Museum and were eventually translated by Dr. V. T. Harlow and published by the Argonaut Press.[1]

Born in Segovia, Spain, about 1520, Berrio regarded himself all his life as a loyal and valiant servant of his king. He did not start his dogged search for El Dorado until he was well over sixty years old, and did not relinquish it until he died twelve years later, bitterly disillusioned about his fellow men but never for a moment abandoning his shining dream of Manoa. About the first four decades of his adult life, he wrote as follows (May 24, 1585) to his king, Philip II:

> For forty years I have served our Lord the Emperor and your Majesty in the wars in Germany, Barbary, Italy and Flanders, and more recently under your Majesty's command in the

[1] Sir Walter Raleigh, *The Discoverie of the Large and Bewtiful Empire of Guiana,* with an introduction by V. T. Harlow (London: The Argonaut Press, 1928).

Granada war in Spain. . . . When advancing age demanded rest, I came to the Indies to inherit the estates of the Adelantado of the new Kingdom of Granada.

The Adelantado referred to was Gonzalo Jiménez de Quesada, the great conqueror of Colombia, whose niece Berrio had married. He had willed his great estates in New Granada to the niece and her husband, but when the latter arrived at Santa Fé, New Granada, in 1580, with his wife, six daughters and two sons, he found a proviso in the will. Having devoted much time and money to the search for El Dorado, the Adelantado had demanded that his heir do likewise. There is no indication that the old war-horse resented the demand. He lost no time in fitting out his first expedition and plunging eastward into the unknown.

That first of three ventures involved a hundred men, of whom 20 soon deserted while eight died in the expedition's course. It kept him away from home for 17 months, during which, after crossing the Andean cordillera to the plains of eastern Colombia, south of the Meta River, he made his way to the Orinoco River. In his letter of January 1, 1593, in which he summarized all his expeditions, he wrote:

> I collected a large force of men and a great quantity of horses, cattle, munitions and other necessary stores; and with this equipment, which cost me a great sum of gold, I set out from the New Kingdom and crossed the plains, travelling through them for more than three hundred leagues by a way never previously traversed by any Spaniard, until I came to the cordillera on the other side, which twenty-three different captains, who have attempted this conquest, have so eagerly sought for.

By "the other side," Berrio meant the eastern side of the middle Orinoco River. Before reaching it, but long after seeing the mountains, he had been stopped for four months by the winter floods. Hostile Indians attacked the Spaniards during that period, but some captured natives gave welcome news of the mountains and what lay beyond. In his letter of May 24, 1585, giving an account of the first expedition, Berrio wrote as follows about the information received:

> They all, although for different reasons, agreed in one thing, the same as had been told us by many Indians on the way, that in the mountains there is a very large laguna, and that on the

other side are great towns and a vast population, with gold and precious stones.

Obviously, his problem now, and the one to which he devoted the last 12 years of his life, was to find some means of penetrating the Guiana Highlands, which lie east of the middle Orinoco and south of the lower. In his letter of 1585, he wrote of the Orinoco (which he called the "Baraguan"):

> It was the greatest river I had seen in my life. . . . Within a distance of two leagues, four other big rivers enter this one, and their entrance is hardly noticeable. This river, be it understood, enters the sea in front of Trinidad, from whence the voyage to Spain will be short.

That passage in the first letter to the king presages Berrio's later intense obsession with Trinidad, which was to get him into trouble because it was shared by Sir Walter Raleigh. Berrio built a boat with which to cross and navigate the Orinoco, but when the time for departure arrived, he found that all but 13 of his men were too ill to proceed. On the eastern side of the river, he and the healthy among his companions tried unsuccessfully to find a pass into the mountains. Of the venture he wrote later:

> With these 13 companions (14 with myself) I set out on foot and travelled for ten days towards the mountains, and owing to the height of the rocky crags, I was unable to reach the cordillera, but arrived at a rocky and lofty eminence at two leagues distance from it, and on this journey I took certain pieces [of gold?] which confirmed the information which I had; and with these, knowing that the road and the narrows were lower down, I turned back and descended the river in the boat for about two leagues from where I was then encamped, and found a small and very strong island, upon which were over a thousand Indian warriors; and being unable to approach it because of the strong current, I drew into a backwater at about musket range. I sent a canoe with one soldier and the interpreter, who understood the language, with gifts to offer peace and friendship. They accepted the gifts and sent back food and I felt certain that this island in the narrows was the limit between the plains and the mountains, and that on the farther side lay the open road to the cordillera, and with this certain knowledge I returned to the place of our encampment, and found there not one single soldier

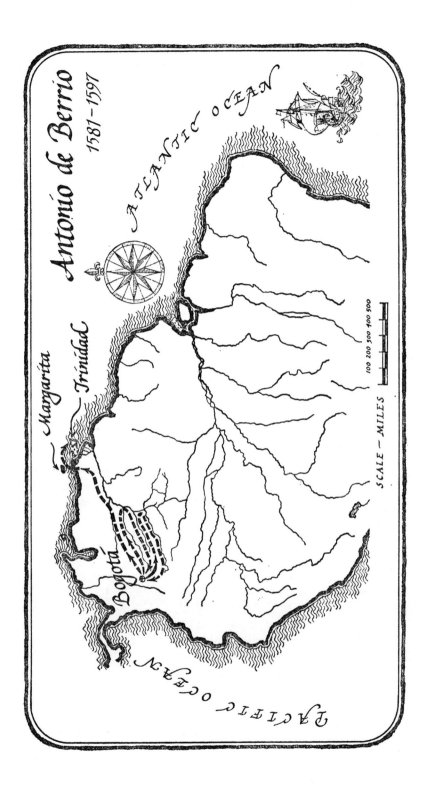

Antonío de Berrío

1581–1597

ATLANTIC OCEAN

Margarita

Trinidad

Bogotá

PACIFIC OCEAN

SCALE — MILES

100 200 300 400 500

fit for duty; nor could the pieces [of gold?] be put to any use. So in view of this disaster and the danger of being attacked by the Indians (in which event they would without pity inflict serious damage upon me), I decided that it would not be right, after having seen and discovered the cordillera, and considering the valuable knowledge I had gathered concerning it, to venture further to sacrifice my people and myself along with them, and the object of so many years' search and which by the mercy of God I had found. So after reflection I came back . . . with all the people, not losing on this journey more than eight Spaniards, three only killed by the Indians and five who died of sickness. I returned after an absence of seventeen months.

I returned by a different route, which was found shorter and drier and very populous. I came by the margins of the River Meta, and crossing this river travelled along the banks of another called Cazanar which rises in the cordillera of this new Kingdom of Granada, so that I have discovered the navigation of the rivers named and a short and dry land route. The distance from the cordillera of this Kingdom to the other beyond the plains is one hundred and twenty leagues more or less. There will be necessary for this expedition, that is to say, to start it, three hundred Spaniards, and to finish it more than three thousand because the territory and its population reach to the Marañón.

The 1585 letter describing the first expedition, mentions previous exploratory journeys, reaching the Guiana country by different routes, whose commanders called it variously "New Andalucía" and "El Dorado." After pointing out that the country should be known by "its true name" of Guayana, Berrio writes:

In order to populate these large provinces it will be of great importance that the Island of Trinidad should be peopled, because it is near to them and the island is near to Spain and a suitable latitude for going thither, and there is no cape to double. This island will be able to provide people and things necessary to those provinces, and in the meantime this can be done from the Island of Margarita up the river Orinoco.

His preoccupation with Margarita, too, was to contribute to his eventual disaster.

On his return to his home in Santa Fé, Berrio lost no time in outfitting a new expedition, which set out within a few months after the return of the first. The second venture was in the field more than two and a half years, during which Berrio worked farther down the Orinoco, convinced that the northern edges of the Guiana Highlands offered passes through which the mountains could be penetrated to Lake Parima and El Dorado. The letter of 1593 had this to say of the second expedition:

> This time I went much lower than on the first occasion, and obtained accurate and more detailed information. I made a series of attempts to cross the mountains, traversing the lower slopes for more than two hundred leagues; and in all this length it was impossible to cross them although I tried many times, for they are broad and rocky, full of high peaks and wholly uninhabited. I came upon large navigable rivers and gathered numerous reports to the effect that down the Orinoco the mountains came to an end. While I was having canoes made in order to travel down this river, a captain mutinied and fled with the majority of the men, so that I was obliged to start after him; nor could I overtake him until I had come to the Kingdom [of New Granada].

On his return to Santa Fé in the spring of 1588, he found a royal commission waiting for him, appointing him governor of the province of El Dorado, otherwise called Guiana, and investing him with ample powers. According to Dr. Harlow's essay, "a more powerful expedition than either of the two previous ones was accordingly prepared, which, after assembling on the banks of the Cacanare, set out from thence on 19 March 1590. The force consisted of a hundred and twelve Spaniards, a few native attendants, two hundred and twenty horses, twenty canoes, twenty rafts, and a large supply of stores."

> With this force, [wrote Berrio in 1593] I arrived at the great River Baraguan which is called the Orinoco lower down. Then I tried once more to cross the mountains at many points, but despite my utmost endeavor was not able to do so. Thereupon, I tried to travel down along the banks of the Orinoco; but this region also failed to afford me any place from which to make the crossing, although I deviated ten or twelve leagues from the river. For the whole land is without natives by reason of the fleets of Caribs who go up the river and have eaten so many of the populations that the others have fled the plains and betaken themselves to the mountains.

By this time the canoes had been lost, and three troops of Spaniards, thirty-four men in all, had fled from me, carrying off many horses; and a disease almost like the plague had killed all my carriers and more than thirty Spaniards. It was now eighteen months since I had left the Kingdom, and as I lacked supplies and the canoes were lost, I determined to make others and to kill the remaining horses as food for the men and to go down the Orinoco. For all the Indians assured me that on travelling down the Orinoco I should come across large Carib villages, and that further down I should find a great river called the Caroní which comes down from Guiana and which cannot be navigated because of a great waterfall; but that a little higher up, where a chief called Moriquita lived, the mountains ended and the provinces of Guiana began, behind which in turn came those of Manoa and El Dorado and many other provinces. Provided with this information, I embarked as the canoes were now ready; and God was served in that the very day I began to travel, his Divine Majesty sent us guides in the form of two canoes full of Caribs, who were going on a kid-napping expedition to supply their shambles [meat market]. These men, who were Caribs of Barima, accompanied me in return for presents. In their company I travelled down the Orinoco as far as the river Caroní, which is said to be more than three hundred and fifty leagues in length. We had much friendship in this journey; two of their chiefs came into my canoe and I handed one Spaniard over to them. They revealed great secrets about the land and confirmed all the information which I had received higher up; all that they had told me I found to be true. I asked these Caribs why, when they were so numerous and so brave and had Guiana so near, they went up such a long way and with so much labour. They answered me that the Guianians were numerous and very near and might make war [upon them] by land, and so for that reason they preferred to have them as friends. These Caribs came with me to the river Caroní, where I gave them [presents] from what I had with me and letters for the Governor of Margarita, asking him to help me. I had written on leaving the New Kingdom informing him of the circumstances and of the great riches which the expedition promised, and that he was to reply to Trinidad. [I told him that] I had written to Your Majesty and to Your Royal Council urging that the island should be settled if it had not been done already, and that if he wished to do a great service to Your Majesty, who might be anxious, he should come to my help on having this news of me; and this he might easily do by means of the traders who set out from that island.

Actually, according to his letter of October 26, 1591, dealing exclusively with his third journey, Berrio spent his two months' waiting time in "a province called Moriquito, which is also on the borders of Guiana." At the mouth of the Caroní he had heard that the river was not navigable because of a "great fall" a little above the mouth. At Moriquito (actually, the name was that of a chief, and is more commonly spelled "Morequito") he was told that "it was only four days' journey from there to the great cities and riches [of El Dorado]." He did not strike inland because only 15 of his men had remained healthy, leaving him with insufficient men for guarding his precious canoes while he went south, overland, with a small force.

At this time the Indians, seeing the soldiers so ill, rose and carried off the provisions, so that I was compelled, in order not to lose the canoes, to travel down the river for another twenty leagues to a province called Barguicana, where they willingly submitted to Your Majesty and gave us food. Here I spent another two months, waiting to see if help was coming. But knowing that Trinidad was not inhabited [by Spaniards] and that the letters had not gone on to Margarita, and that I had not ten men who could fight, necessity compelled me to go down to the sea and from there to Trinidad, which is only a day's journey. I was determined to remain there and to settle the island, as it so greatly concerns Your Majesty's service, and to re-assemble the men there in order to enter Guiana once more. God and my fortune so willed that at the moment when I began to travel by sea we became separated from one another, as the vessels were small and the soldiers ill and inexperienced and unable to row: and we had no sight of one another until near Margarita. I arrived in Trinidad with twenty men, and spent eight days there, although all of them were ill. I realised that it was a very easy matter to people it, but a very laborious one to maintain it without Your Majesty's favour because of the English. Nevertheless, it is expedient to occupy it, because it is only one day's journey from there to the mouth of the Orinoco, from there to Barguicana four days, and from Barguicana to the borders of the great provinces of Guiana less than eight. Wherefore the whole of this matter remains evident and is very certain. Having seen this, I returned to Margarita where I rejoined my companions. On my arrival there I learnt that the Governor, Don Juan Sarmiento, without receiving my letter, but merely on the strength of news which reached him concerning me, had sent thirty-six soldiers to my aid. It was not God's will that I should fall in with them, nor since my return have I yet done so. Don Juan received me and my men, and did us many kindnesses. He is beginning to help me to collect men to return and settle that region which I have been seeking for so many years, and which now lies open [to us]. If I can gather together a company of people I will leave Trinidad inhabited, for I have to pass through it.

Before very long, however, Berrio was to change his mind about Sarmiento. The small force which the latter had dispatched under one Lucas Fajardo to meet Berrio had turned its junket into a slaving expedition, stealing about three hundred Indians from Morequito, a business which distressed Berrio greatly when Fajardo returned to Margarita. Not only did Sarmiento fail to punish Fajardo, except with a token sentence of two days in prison, but he consistently evaded all of Berrio's requests for help in proceeding to El Dorado. Rumors and apparently trustworthy accounts reached the frantically impatient Berrio at Margarita, but Sarmiento's evasions prevented him from following up on them. Then he fell in with one Domingo de Vera Ybarguen, whom he sent to Caracas to ask the governor of Venezuela for men and money. Much to his delight, the mission was at least partially successful. Vera was then dispatched to Trinidad with the few available men to take possession of the island for Spain. He founded the city of San José de Oruña, made a survey of population and resources, and began to prepare the island as a new base from which Berrio might continue his search for El Dorado.

On Christmas Eve, 1592, while Berrio was directing his Trinidad operations from Margarita, a man turned up from Spain with a royal commission instructing him (Berrio), among many other things, to colonize Trinidad within six months of his arrival. However, Sarmiento still refused to help him. Bitterly disappointed over his failure to obtain the support he needed, Berrio set sail immediately for Trinidad with another twenty soldiers whom he had received from the governor in Caracas. On arrival he scoured the land for provisions and divided it up into estates for his soldiers. The need for speedy action to fore-stall his rivals then prompted him to send Domingo de Vera up the Orinoco, in April, 1593, to accomplish the discovery of Manoa and take possession of the city and its gold-rich territory. The latter returned after about a month, with fascinating, en-couraging accounts and a quantity of gold ornaments. Over-joyed, Berrio sent him to Caracas to ask his ally, the governor of Venezuela, for more supplies and men to permit him to com-plete the conquest. But again he was double-crossed. Jealous rivals wanted to conquer Manoa themselves. Governor Osorio now refused to help the doughty old explorer but sent a force of his own to conquer El Dorado. During the many long months which followed, Berrio was frustrated and hampered at every turn. Letters arriving for him from Spain and delivered at Mar-garita were withheld from him. Ten of his few remaining men, plus a friar, were attacked and killed on the Orinoco. The Caribs and English ships harassed him in Trinidad. On the mainland his agents were ordered "on the pain of death" to stop their ceaseless efforts to enlist recruits for the great El Dorado adventure. Finally Berrio sent his son with an older man to New Granada with a plea for help, and commissioned Domingo de Vera to go to Spain on a similar mission. These efforts brought some scant results, but they were too little and too late. On April 4, 1595, Sir Walter Raleigh arrived at Port of Spain, Trinidad, with five ships, and on the eighth of that month he took the settlement of San José, killed some twenty Spaniards, burned the town, and took Berrio and a companion prisoner.

For more than two months, Berrio was the Englishman's pris-oner, treated like an honored guest, Raleigh constantly pump-ing him for information about El Dorado, while also indulging in piracy on the Spanish Main. On June 22 Raleigh tried unsuc-cessfully to storm Cumaná, Venezuela, but left Berrio behind when he sailed away. Doggedly, the latter tried for another two years to realize his great El Dorado dream. Thwarted by refusals of help and the machinations of jealous rivals, by treachery and desertions, by mutinies, by attacks from Indians, he died in 1597, a bitterly disappointed, broken man, nearly eighty years old.

☙ XIV ☙

THE ENGLISH DISCOVER SOUTH AMERICA

JUDGED purely from the geographical point of view, in terms of lands traversed which had not previously been seen by Europeans, Sir Walter Raleigh was no great shakes as an explorer in South America. In fact, he was no shakes at all; his South American journeys took him to Trinidad, where he kidnapped Berrio, and later up the Orinoco as far as the Caroní River, through territories already held, if weakly, by the Spaniards. Nevertheless, Raleigh's vision, his great dream of an English empire in South America—in the beginning poorly appreciated by his sovereigns and government—came to inflame much of northwestern Europe and to set loose on the Guianas a long string of English, Dutch, and French explorers, conquerors, pirates, and would-be colonizers.

The indefatigable Walter Raleigh, poet, dreamer, man of action, colonizer, occasional pirate, was a one-man challenge to Spain's empire and hegemony in the Americas. V. T. Harlow writes of him as follows: "The idea that dominated Raleigh's mind for the last thirty years of his life was the complete destruction of Spanish power in South America and the establishment of an English empire in its place." [1] If Raleigh's effort

[1] *Raleigh's Last Voyage* (London: Argonaut Press, 1932), with an introduction by Dr. V. T. Harlow. In Sir Walter's day, the spelling of English words and names had not yet been crystallized as it has today; it proceeded in haphazard fashion, even within any one document by a single writer. Dr. Harlow and the editors of the magnificent series of Argonaut books, spell his name "Ralegh" throughout. It is every bit as legitimate and acceptable as the more common "Raleigh," which is used in the present volume.

to colonize Virginia, begun in 1585, does not belong in the present volume on the exploration of South America, it was nevertheless significant as a challenge to Spain's conception of her role in the Americas. It was a direct challenge to the concepts arising from the papal line of demarcation under which all of the Americas—with the exception of the Brazilian bulge, which went to Portugal—were to be Spanish property. The Virginia adventure, to which Raleigh devoted a fortune and which paved the way for the later and more successful colonization venture in Plymouth, was one of the most dramatic of many proofs that Spain's exclusive sovereignty, granted by Pope Alexander VI, was clearly unenforceable, Spain lacking the men and means for defending and policing so vast a territory. If he could successfully challenge Spain's claims in Virginia, then why not in South America, which was producing tales of gold and precious stones in almost unimaginable quantities, fertile lands with Indians to work them, rich resources of all kinds, to inflame the imagination, envy, as well as cupidity of England and the rest of northwestern Europe?

In his lifetime, which ended tragically October 29, 1618, when King James I had his head chopped off to appease the king of Spain, Raleigh failed to induce his sovereigns to act on his bold dream of challenging Spanish domination and exclusivism in South America. Nevertheless, more than any other one man, he inspired his nation with dreams of imperialism which were to bear fruit in succeeding centuries. Harlow's chapter, quoted above, ends as follows:

> His was not the death of an unfortunate, and occasionally unscrupulous adventurer: it was the loss of a patriot and an idealist, who had toiled and suffered terribly in order to inspire the nation with his own great vision of imperial destiny. He pointed in the wrong direction; but he pointed outward. His call was answered, not upon the Orinoco, but upon the St. Lawrence and the Darling, the Zambezi and the Niger. When all has been said, and every fault and weakness candidly examined, the student closes the record of his life with a sense of personal affection and with veneration for the greatness of his spirit.

Two observations may here be added to Harlow's. The fact that the king of Spain demanded Raleigh's head, a demand which was finally granted by King James, indicated that the English poet-dreamer-adventurer had made a profound impression on the Spanish, who came to fear him on the Atlantic side of their South American holdings virtually as much as they feared Sir Francis Drake in the Caribbean and the Pacific. Moreover, when England did bestir herself to take imperial action in South America, it was Raleigh's concepts of strategic geography which led Sir Ralph Abercromby to take Trinidad from Spain in 1796, as it led to the establishment of British Guiana in 1834, and to England's later (unsuccessful) attempts to establish the mouth of Orinoco as that territory's northern boundary (Chapter XXI).

If Raleigh did not succeed in altering or filling in the maps drawn by the cartographers of his day, he did succeed in altering and expanding immeasurably the dream map of England's potential empire, slowly beginning to take shape in the minds of millions of Englishmen. In that sense, as a typical man of the Renaissance, he was one of the truly great explorers of modern history.

In his classic work *The Discovery of Guiana,* from which the following passages are taken,[2] Raleigh translated, for the benefit of his queen and countrymen, the great Spanish dream which led to so much exploration and heroic, if inhumanly brutal, conquest. Faithfully reporting the things which had been told him by his prisoner, Berrio, Raleigh used the El Dorado—Manoa account as a lure to tempt his queen into conquering Spanish America by way of Trinidad and the Orinoco River. By no means, however, was the postulated existence of Manoa, so convenient as bait, Raleigh's only motivation for invading South America. Like every modern advertising man, he knew how to use the dramatic and sensational for the purpose of capturing his readers' imagination; his real interest, as noted, lay in empire-building in a land rich in a variety of natural resources.

An important part of Raleigh's plan for England's conquest of Spain's American empire was the idea of cashing in on Spain's brutal treatment of the Indians. Treat them well, he reasoned,

[2] Published by Gressner and Schramm, Leipzig; date of publication is not indicated. This work, in which the spelling of words has been modernized, is here used instead of the Argonaut Press volume cited above, whose archaic spelling, just as Raleigh wrote it, is at times difficult to follow.

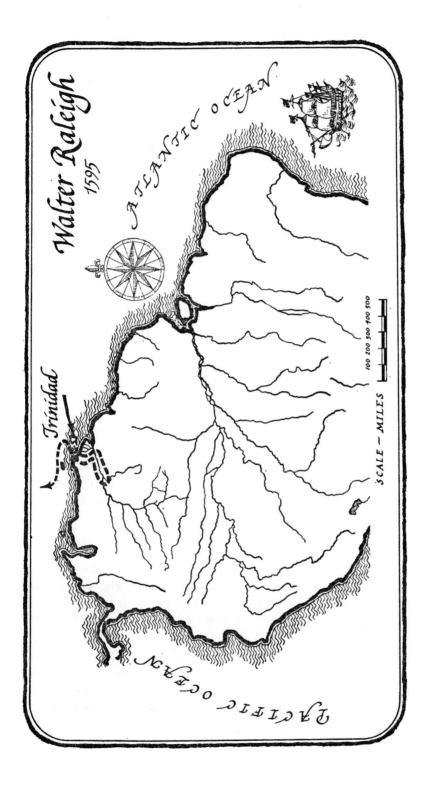

Walter Raleigh
1595

ATLANTIC OCEAN

Trinidad

PACIFIC OCEAN

SCALE ~ MILES

100 200 300 400 500

convince them that we English want to liberate them from their
Spanish oppressors, convince them that our Queen is a great,
humane monarch and a friend of the oppressed and downtrod-
den, and they will become our allies. It will be seen from the
passages quoted below that he carried out that policy in the
course of his brief travels on the Orinoco. After his return to
England from his first voyage, he sent occasional ships to the
Guianas, to trade with the Indians and keep alive their faith and
interest in the England which let Raleigh himself down so
shabbily. Later English and Dutch explorers reported that the
name of Raleigh was so revered even by Indians who had no
direct contact with him that it opened virtually all doors to
native homes and hearts.

Between 1585 and 1602, Raleigh sent no fewer than six expeditions in his dogged but unsuccessful attempts to found an
English colony in Virginia, while also dispatching a number of
privateers to harass the Spanish on the high seas, steal their
wealth, and bring it to England. Until 1592 he was in high favor
with Queen Elizabeth, who in that year became displeased with
him over his marriage to, preceded by the seduction of, one
of her maids of honor, Elizabeth Throgmorton. It was then,
and perhaps in part to regain his queen's favor, that he began
to plan his first expedition to Guiana, setting sail in February,
1595, and publishing his famous account of the voyage after his
return to England. He commanded a flotilla of five ships of
various kinds and sizes. His account begins as follows:

> On Thursday, the 6th of February, in the year 1595, we de-
> parted England, and the Sunday following had sight of the
> North Cape of Spain, the wind for the most part continuing
> prosperous; we passed in sight of the Burlings and the rock, and
> so onward for the Canaries, and fell in with Fuerte Ventura the
> 17th of the same month, where we spent two or three days, and
> relieved our company with some fresh meat. . . . We arrived
> at Trinidad the 22nd of March.

They saw fires on land, but Raleigh stated that the Indians,
fearing Spanish reprisals, were afraid to come out to their ships.
He set out to explore the Trinidad shore, and to make contact
with the Indians, in a small boat which he called his "barge."

> I rowed to another port, called by the naturals Piche, and by
> the Spaniards Tierra de Brea. At this point . . . there is that

abundance of stone pitch, that all the ships of the world may therewith be laden from thence, and we made trial of it in trimming our ships most excellent good, and melteth not with the sun as the pitch of Norway, and therefore, for ships trading the south parts, very profitable.

Having discovered the Asphalt Lake, which was centuries later to play so important a role in the economy of England's colony of Trinidad, Raleigh rejoined his ships near the river "Carone, on which the Spanish city was seated." He now goes on to describe Trinidad in terms of terrain and natural resources:

> The north part is very mountainous; the soil is very excellent, and will bear sugar, ginger, or any other commodity that the Indies yield. It hath store of deer, wild porks, fish, and fowl. It hath also for bread sufficient maize, cassavi, and of those roots and fruits which are common everywhere in the West Indies. It hath divers beasts, which the Indies have not; the Spaniards confessed that they found grains of gold in some of the rivers, but they, having a purpose to enter Guiana (the magazine of all rich metals), cared not to spend time in the search thereof any farther.

At a place called "Puerto de los Hispanioles [Port of Spain]," Raleigh tarried some time, making friendly trading contacts with a few Spaniards and persuading some Indians to inform him of the city's Spanish strength. He invited several Spanish soldiers to visit him on his ship, got them drunk, plied them with questions about Guiana and Manoa, and convinced them that his mission was peaceful, "that I was bound only for the relief of those English which I had planted in Virginia." He was especially interested in the governor, whose name he spelled "Berreo," claiming that the latter needed to be punished for having, the year before, betrayed and killed eight men from an English ship which Raleigh had sent to that part of South America to scout the country. In line with his strategy of trying to turn the Indians against the Spaniards, he grew eloquent about Berreo's [3] maltreatment of the natives.

> For although he [Berreo] had given order through all the island that no Indian should come aboard to trade with me

[3] For convenience, Raleigh's spelling of the name will hereafter be used.

upon pain of hanging and quartering . . ., yet every night
there came some with the most lamentable complaints of his
cruelty; how he had divided the island, and given to every soldier a part; that he made the ancient Caziqui, which were lords
of the country, to be their slaves, that he kept them in chains,
and dropped their naked bodies with burning bacon, which I
found afterwards to be true.

After describing in detail the evidences of atrocities which he
later uncovered in the Spanish city, Raleigh went on to the sack-
ing of the city and his capture of Berreo.

So as both to be avenged of the former wrong, as also considering that to enter Guiana by small boats, to depart 400 or
500 miles from my ships, and to leave a garrison in my back
interested in the same enterprise, who also daily expected supplies out of Spain, I should have savoured very much of the ass;
and therefore, taking a time of most advantage, I set upon the
Corp du guard in the evening, and having put them to the
sword, sent Captain Calfield onwards with sixty soldiers, and
myself followed with forty more, and so took their new city,
which they called St. Joseph, by break of day; they abode not
any fight after a few shot, and all being dismissed but only
Berreo and his companions, I brought them with me aboard,
and at the instance of the Indians I set their new city of St.
Joseph on fire.

We then hastened away towards our purposed discovery, and
first I called all the captains of the island together that we were
enemies to the Spaniards, . . . and by my Indian interpreter,
which I carried out of England, I made them to understand that
I was the servant of a queen, who was the great Cazique of the
north, and a virgin, and had more Caziqui under her than
there were trees in their island; that she was the enemy of the
Castellani in respect to their tyranny and oppression, and that
she delivered all such nations about her as were by them oppressed, and having freed all the coast of the northern world
from their servitude, had sent me to free them also, and withal
to defend the country of Guiana from their invasion and conquest. I showed them her Majesty's picture, which they so ad-
mired and honored as it had been easy to have thought them
idolatrous thereof.

Raleigh now goes on to discuss Berreo and to say that "having
[him] . . . as my prisoner, I gathered from him as much of

Guiana as he knew." Eventually he set out for the South American mainland, leaving his ships anchored near Trinidad and traveling in small craft.

> In the bottom of an old gallego which I caused to be fashioned like a galley, and in one barge, two wherries, and a ship's boat of the *Lion's Whelp*, we carried one hundred persons and their victuals for a month in the same, being all driven to lie in the rain and weather in the open air, in the burning sun, and upon the hard boards, and to dress our meat and to carry all manner of furniture in them, wherewith they were so pestered and unsavoury, that what with victuals being most fish, with the wet clothes of so many men thrust together, and the heat of the sun, I will undertake there was never any prison in England that could be found more unsavoury and loathsome, especially to myself, who had for many years before been dieted and cared for in a sort far differing.

He laments the circumstances of small force and delay which on that occasion prevented him "either to have gone to the great city of Manoa, or at least to have taken so many of the other cities and towns near at hand as would have made a royal return." However, he assures his readers of the staggering wealth of Guiana, of which he had heard from Berreo. He writes of the manner in which the civilized empire of Guiana had been founded by Incas, fleeing the wrath of the Spaniards in Peru, and assures his readers that "it hath more abundance of gold than any part of Peru, and as many or more great cities than ever Peru had when it flourished most." Of Manoa, Guiana's capital city, he writes "that for the greatness, for the riches, and for the excellent seat, it far exceedeth any of the world, at least of so much of the world as is known to the Spanish nation; it is founded upon a lake of salt water of two hundred leagues long." He quotes Spanish chroniclers on the wealth which Pizarro and his *conquistadores* had found in Peru, and assures his readers that the empire of Guiana is far richer.

After discussing the failure of Orellana and other Spaniards to discover Manoa everywhere else, he quotes a man named Martínez, who was said actually to have spent seven months in the mighty capital of Guiana, as a prisoner-guest of the ruling Inca, having been brought there, and taken out again, blindfolded to prevent his observing the route to the city. Naturally, the account of the mythical Martínez, possibly invented by an imaginative Spaniard for the purpose of revitalizing the immensely valuable El Dorado legend, served to buttress Raleigh's wildest dreams about the city's size and wealth. After giving accounts of a number of Spanish El Dorado searches, with the then standard account of the Amazons thrown in for good measure, Raleigh gives a faithful recital of Berreo's travels in search of the fabled city. He also tells of the encouraging results he had had from his own indefatigable questioning of the Indians.

For some weeks the Englishmen bumbled about in the maze of rivers, creeks, and islands of various sizes which comprise the Orinoco's delta. Their Indian guide whom they had brought from Trinidad was virtually as lost as they; Raleigh replaced him with another, an old man whom he captured from a group of Indians. Their supplies ran dangerously low and they had difficulties in living by foraging. The morale of the men sank daily.

> Our old pilot of the Ciawani . . . told us that if we would enter a branch of a river on the right hand with our barge and wherries, and leave the galley at anchor the while in the great river, he would bring us to a town of the Arwacas where we should find a store of bread, hens, fish and of the country wine, and persuaded us that departing from the galley at noon, we might return ere night.

Happily, Raleigh set out with three boats, two captains, and sixteen soldiers, taking no provisions with him because he had been asssured that the town was quite near. But they labored upstream all afternoon and far into the night without seeing any settlement.

> We saw no sign, and our poor watermen, even heartbroken and tired, were ready to give up the ghost; for we had now come from the galley near forty miles.
> At the last we determined to hang the pilot, and if we had well known the way back again by night, he had surely gone, but our own necessities pleaded sufficiently for his safety; . . . at last, about one o'clock after midnight we saw a light and rowing towards it, we heard the dogs of the village. When we landed we found few people, for the lord of that place was gone with divers canoes above 400 miles off, upon a journey towards the head of the Orinoco to trade for gold, and to buy women

of the cannibals. . . . In his house we had good store of bread, fish, hens, and Indian drink, and so rested that night; and in the morning, after we had traded with such of his people as came down, we returned towards our galley, and brought with us some quantity of bread, fish, and hens.

Proceeding upstream, the reunited company was soon out of food again. They met four canoes, two large and two small, and managed to capture the larger ones, loaded with food. They were happy to have the victuals, "but in the lesser there were three Spaniards, who, having heard of the defeat of their governor in Trinidad, came away in those canoes: one of them was a cavallero, as the captain of the Arwacas after told us, another a soldier, and the third a refiner."

Evidently the three decamped. The Englishmen spread out, searching the country for those Spaniards.

I then landed more men, and offered £500 to what soldier soever could take one of those three Spaniards that we thought were landed. But our labors were in vain in that behalf, . . . but seeking after the Spaniards, we found the Arwacas hidden in the woods which were pilots for the Spaniards and rowed their canoes; of which I kept the chiefest for a pilot and carried him with me to Guiana. . . .

This Arwacan pilot with the rest, feared that we would have eaten them, or otherwise have put them to some cruel death, for the Spaniards, to the end that none of the people in the passage towards Guiana or in Guiana itself might come to speech with us, persuaded all the nations that we were men eaters and cannibals; but when the poor men and women had seen us, and that we gave them meat, and to everyone something or other, which was rare and strange to them, they began to conceive the deceit and purpose of the Spaniards, who indeed (as they confessed) took from them both their wives and daughters daily, by strength. But I protest before the majesty of the living God, that I neither know nor believe that any of our company one or other, by violence or otherwise, ever took any of their women, and yet we saw many hundreds, and had many in our power, and of those very young and excellently favored which came among us without deceit.

It took them some time to work their way out of the delta country, but on "the fifteenth day we discovered far off the mountains of Guiana to our great joy, and towards the evening had a slant of a northerly wind that blew very strong, which brought us in sight of the great river of the Orinoco, out of which this river descended where we were."

> In the morning there came down according to promise the lord of that border called Toparicama, with some thirty or forty followers, and brought us divers sorts of fruits, and of his wine, bread and fish, and flesh, whom we also feasted as we could; at least he drank good Spanish wine, whereof we had a small quantity in bottles, which above all things they love. I conferred with this Toparicama of the next way to Guiana, who conducted our galley and boats to his own port, and carried us from thence some mile and a half to his town, where some of our captains caroused of his wine till they were reasonably pleasant, for it is very strong with pepper, and the juice of divers herbs, and fruits digested and purged; they keep it in great earthen pots of ten or twelve gallons very clean and sweet, and are themselves at their meetings and feasts the greatest carousers and drunkards of the world. . . .
>
> The lord of this place gave me an old man for a pilot, who was of great experience and travel, and knew the river most perfectly both by day and night, and it shall be requisite for any man that passeth it to have such a pilot, for it is four, five, and six miles over in many places and twenty miles in other places, with wonderful eddies and strong currents, many great islands and divers shoals, and many dangerous rocks, and besides upon an increase of wind so great a billow, as we were sometimes in great peril of drowning in the galley, for the small boats durst not come from the shore but when it was very fair.

The Englishmen spent several days ascending the Orinoco, and at one point a reconnaissance party, scouting the north bank, became what were probably the first non-Spanish Europeans to see the vast, level plains of today's state of Monagas, which were before long to become important for cattle breeding. Raleigh deals briefly with the Indians inhabiting the plains, and, as almost everyone else who wrote of travel in those lands, he digresses into the subject of their arrow poisons.

> There was nothing whereof I was more curious than to find out the true remedies of these poisoned arrows, for beside the mortality of the wound they make, the party shot endureth the

most insufferable torment in the world, and abideth a most ugly and lamentable death, sometimes dying stark mad, sometimes their bowels breaking out of their bellies, and are presently discoloured, as black as pitch, and so unsavoury, as no man can endure to cure or to attend them.

In that matter, Raleigh was obviously drawing a very long bow. No such evil effects of curare poisoning have ever been noted or reported. While the nature of South American curare varies over a wide range, from place to place and tribe to tribe, the substance actually results in as humane a death as one can imagine. In strong doses it "relaxes" its victims to death; weaker, controlled doses are used in modern medicine to relax patients suffering from tetanus and spastic paralysis. Raleigh's listed "cures" for arrow poisoning include the admonition that victims of curare must refrain from drinking alcohol, which leads to certain death, plus several remedies which sound as folkloric as does his description of the poison's effects. He omits the one standard remedy, namely a strong solution of salt in water, taken internally.

Early on the fourth day of their ascent of the Orinoco's mainstream,

> we arrived at the port of Morequito, and anchored there, sending away one of our pilots to seek the king of Aromaia, uncle to Morequita, slain by Berreo as aforesaid. The next day following before noon he came to us on foot from his house which was fourteen English miles (himself being 110 years old), and returned on foot the same day, and with him many women and children, that came to wonder at our nation, and to bring us down victual, which they did in great plenty.

Raleigh talked to the old king about Berreo and the bad Spaniards, leading naturally to Queen Elizabeth and the fine English who had come to liberate the Indians from Spanish tyranny. He also asked innumerable questions about Guiana and the way thither, getting (unless he invented them later) fine descriptions of the richness of the Guiana interior, its fine cities, great rulers, and ruthless, marauding fighters. The next morning the Englishmen made their way upriver to the mouth of the Caroní, which Raleigh spelled "Caroli" and which Berreo had assumed to be the best southward entrance to El Dorado. From a Cazique named Wanuretona, who had on request come from inland to meet him with many people and fine provisions, Raleigh heard apparent confirmation of Berreo's belief.

> And as I had before made my coming known to Topiawari, so did I acquaint this Cazique therewith, and how I was sent by her Majesty for the purpose aforesaid, and gathered also what I could of him touching the estate of Guiana, and I found that those also of Caroli were not only enemies to the Spaniards but most of all to the Epuremei, which abound in gold; and by this Wanuretona I had knowledge that on the head of this river were three mighty nations, which are seated on a great lake, from whence this river descended, and were called Cassipagotos, Esparagotos, and Arawagotos, and that all those either against the Spaniards or the Epuremei would join with us, and that if we entered the land over the mountains of Curaa, we should satisfy ourselves with gold and all other good things. He told us further of a nation called Iwarawaqueri . . ., that held daily war with the Epumerei that inhabited Macureguarai, the first civil town of Guiana, of the subjects of the Inga the Emperor.

Not only the swiftness of the Caroní itself, but also the fact that all the rivers were rising, due to the advent of the rainy season, prevented Raleigh and his men from ascending the river. He did, however, send men overland to scout out the country, and these returned with fine tales and many samples which they took to be gold ore and precious stones. Raleigh himself, "being a very ill footman," did not go inland very far, but he did reach the famous falls of the Caroní which President Betancourt's Venezuelan government recently harnessed for a mighty hydroelectric project. In the course of his ecstatic description of the country ("I never saw a more beautiful country, nor more lively prospects"), Raleigh digresses on men without heads, which had long intrigued medieval Europe. The ancient Greeks had placed such men in India and Ethiopia; it was not difficult for America's explorers, in all credulity, to transfer them, together with other ancient marvels, to the New World.

> Next unto Arui there are two rivers, Atoica and Caora, and on that branch which is called Caora are a nation of people whose heads appear not above their shoulders, which though it may be thought a mere fable, yet for mine own part I am resolved it is true, because every child in the provinces of

Arromaia and Caruni affirms the same. They are called Ewai-panoma. They are reported to have their eyes in their shoulders, and their mouths in the middle of their breasts, and that a long train of hair groweth backward between their shoulders. The son of Toiawari, which I brought with me into England, told me that they are the most mighty men of all the land, and use bows, arrows, and clubs thrice as big as any of Guiana.

Raleigh cites several people from whom he had heard about the men without heads, and laments: "It was not my chance to hear of them until I was come away, and if they had but spoken one word of it while I was there, I might have brought one of them with me to put the matter out of doubt."

The Englishman now digresses into a long description of the Orinoco River above the Caroní, and its many tributaries, all of it pieced together from what various Indians and some Spaniards told him, plus a certain amount of information which he had gleaned from reading Spanish travel accounts, plus undoubtedly a certain amount of invention. The picture, naturally, was complimentary to the country, though Raleigh laments that he could not go farther than the Caroní to examine things for himself.

But we had no time, means, nor season of the year to search those rivers for the causes aforesaid, the winter being come upon us, although the winter and summer as touching cold and heat differ not, neither do the trees ever sensibly lose their leaves, but have always fruit either ripe or green, and most of them both blossoms, leaves, ripe fruit, and green at one time; but their winter only consisteth of terrible rains and overflowings of the rivers, with many great storms and gusts, thunder and lightnings, of which we had our fill ere we returned.

He hints at the Cassiquiare Canal (see Chapter XVII), and claims that Peru, Colombia, and El Dorado itself could be invaded from the Orinoco.

Turning back, downriver, he stopped again at the port of Morequito and had another long talk with his old friend Chief Topiawari, in part "to deal with him for someone of his country to bring with us into England, as well to learn the language as to confer withal by the way, the time being now spent of any longer stay there." As usual, the two grew lyrical over the wicked

Spaniards, as well as over the wealth and power of the Guiana which beckoned Raleigh so maddeningly. Topiawari thought that Raleigh's force was far too small for an attempted invasion of Guiana, but agreed to give his aid whenever the English might return with sufficient force. On parting, Raleigh took Topiawari's son with him for the voyage back to England.

Raleigh spoke to several other caciques before finally negotiating the delta and reaching the sea, always in the same vein, asking innumerable questions about El Dorado and striving to create allies for England against Spain. After a certain amount of trouble in negotiating the Orinoco delta, they finally reached the sea and made their way to Trinidad, "where we found our ships at anchor, than which there was never to us a more joyful sight."

> Now that it hath pleased God to send us safe to our ships, it is time to leave Guiana to the sun whom they worship, and steer away towards the north. I will, therefore, in a few words, finish the discovery thereof.

But Raleigh was too full of enthusiasm, ideas, gossip, hearsay information, and wishful guesses to say *anything* in a few words. There follows a long recapitulation of his fanciful description of the Orinoco and Guiana, leading up to a passionate plea to England's government to send forces adequate for dislodging the Spaniards from that part of the world and conquering "the Inga" who ruled Manoa as emperor.

> For the rest, which I myself have seen, I will promise these things that follow and know to be true. Those that are desirous to discover and to see many nations, may be satisfied within this river, which brings forth so many arms and branches leading to several countries and provinces, above 2,000 miles east and west, and 800 miles south and north; and of these the most either rich in gold or in other merchandises. The common soldier shall here fight for gold, and pay himself instead of pence with plates half a foot broad, whereas he breaketh his bones in other wars for provant penury. Those commanders and chieftains, that shoot at honor and abundance, shall find there more rich and beautiful cities, more temples adorned with golden images, more sepulchres filled with treasure, than either Cortes found in Mexico, or Pizarro in Peru; and the shining glory of this con-

quest will eclipse all those so far extended beams of the Spanish nation.

It was probably fortunate for Raleigh that Queen Elizabeth did not send the desired expedition. He did, however, fall into her good graces again by participating brilliantly in England's 1596 attack on the Spanish city of Cádiz. Meanwhile, his faithful lieutenant Keymis set out on another search for El Dorado, thinking to reach it by ascending the Essequibo River in today's Guyana. Failing to find Manoa and Lake Parima by that route, he made another trip up the Orinoco as far as the Caroní River, only to find that Berrios—still insisting that the Caroní was the correct entrance to Guiana—had thought to guard the river's mouth by establishing there a small settlement.[4] Now it was obvious that a military force would be needed to dislodge the Spaniards from the supposed gateway to El Dorado.

On Queen Elizabeth's death, in 1603, Raleigh fell into disfavor with her successor, James I, and spent the better part of his life thereafter as a prisoner in the Tower of London. In 1616, however, he obtained his release—though not a royal pardon—by promising King James a rich gold mine in Guiana. That expedition, too, failed, though Raleigh's men did storm and burn San Tomé and proceeded some 300 miles farther up the Orinoco on an exploring expedition. Raleigh lost his son in the assault on San Tomé.

Things went badly with him after his return to England in 1618. Charges were cooked up to the effect that his promised gold mine, in which Raleigh had undoubtedly believed, had been a mere invention, designed to buy his way out of prison. On October 29th of that year King James obliged the king of Spain by having a death sentence of 15 years' standing carried out. Raleigh died on the chopping block at the age of sixty-six.

[4] The settlement was called "San Tomé" (or St. Thomas by the English). After a number of vicissitudes, including being burned by the English in 1616, it was moved several times until it came to rest on the narrow part of the Orinoco, under the name of "Angostura," which for some time produced the bitters of the same name, and then changed its name to "Ciudad Bolívar," which still exists as an important Orinoco River city. During the 1960s, however, the old San Tomé was rebuilt at its old location, first by a private concern as a port for shipping iron ore and later by the Venezuelan government as a well-planned, thriving industrial city called "Ciudad Guayana."

❧ XV ❧

THE MISSIONARIES

A S POINTED out in Chapter I, the Pope's division of the non-Christian world between Spain and Portugal could not be implemented, and resulted in many territorial disputes between the two powers. Not until January 13, 1750, did the Iberian nations sign a treaty, in Madrid, setting aside the earlier Treaty of Tordesillas, which had been based on the papal line, and establishing South American boundaries corresponding roughly to those which today separate Brazil from her Spanish-speaking neighbors. Throughout most of the preceding 150 years the question of territorial sovereignty in South America had been constantly disputed, especially along the Amazon River and several of its tributaries. When the treaty of 1750 was signed, Portugal acquired the lion's share of the basin. The present boundary between Brazil and Peru, on the Amazon, is some 1,800 miles upstream, and at least a thousand miles west of the most westerly possible location of the Pope's line.

Controlling the river's mouth, the Portuguese had the advantage of accessibility, being able to ascend the Amazon and its tributaries with relative ease. From the Spanish territories of Peru and Ecuador, the way led first over the Andes and then to the turbulent headwaters of the various rivers. In part for that reason, the Amazon system was commercially more valuable to the Portuguese than to the Spaniards on the Pacific coast. Heading upriver from their main Amazonian base at Pará, the city on the southernmost of the 84 mouths through which the Amazon pours its waters into the Atlantic, Portuguese traders went in search of sarsaparilla, cacao, and similar goods, while slavers, in search of labor for Brazil's growing plantations, had commercial relations with several powerful tribes of Indians, who made incessant war on their neighbors and sold the captives to the white men. Similarly, military expeditions to keep the Indians in line and patrol the rivers against white rivals, were far more easily sent to various parts of the basin from the Portuguese lower end than from the Spanish upper. Spain, on the other hand, had relatively little use for the river system. For the plantations and mines in the uplands there were enough Indians left over from the Inca empire to serve as slaves. For the tropical lowlands in some Pacific and Caribbean regions it was in any event more advisable and profitable to import African Negroes.

Like Portugal, Spain was not interested in true colonization by white overlords in the forested Amazonian lands. Feudalism was there a costly proposition, not only because of the need for clearing lands, but also because it was too easy for the serfs to escape from plantations into the dense forests. Policing them toward the end of keeping them at their jobs was too difficult and expensive.

At the onset of the seventeenth century, Brazil's need for slaves became increasingly pressing. The resulting growth in the commercial value of the Amazon basin led to increasing Portuguese commercial activity there and to correspondingly increasing friction between the two countries. The first attempt to mark a definite boundary between the two, disregarding the papal line of demarcation, was made by the Portuguese Pedro Teixeira, who, in 1637–39, made a remarkable round-trip transcontinental journey from Pará to Quito and back again. According to the Rev. Dr. George Edmunson: [1]

> The cause, which led to the despatch from Pará of the expedition under the command of Teixeira, was as follows: In 1636 a body of soldiers, under the command of Captain Juan de Palacios, accompanied by five Franciscan missionaries, left Quito to found a settlement on the River Napo. . . . The settlement was made at a spot about twenty leagues lower than the mouth of the Aguarico, an affluent of the Napo. In an attack made upon the settlement by the natives, Palacios was killed. The

[1] This account, like the others in the present chapter, is taken from *Journal of the Travels and Labours of Father Samuel Fritz in the River of the Amazons between 1686 and 1723* (translated from the Evora MS and edited by the Rev. Dr. George Edmundson; London: Hakluyt Society, 1922).

bulk of his followers thereupon resolved to return to Quito; but five soldiers with two of the Franciscans, allured by the report of gold mines farther down the river, set off in a large boat, descended the Napo, entered the Amazon, and after four months' voyaging arrived at Pará, February 1637.

This extraordinary feat on the part of these Spanish Franciscans stirred the Portuguese to emulation, and a great expedition started upstream from Pará for Quito in July, 1637, under the experienced Pedro Teixeira as captain-major. Having reached the abandoned settlement on the river Napo, where Palacios had been killed, Teixeira left his fleet under the command of Pedro da Costa Favella and Pedro Bayan; and himself with a number of chosen followers made his way to Quito. The Spanish authorities gave him a friendly reception; but the presence of this Portuguese in the heart of the Castilian dominion, aroused jealousy; and instructions came from Lima that Teixeira and his fleet must return; and two Spanish Jesuits were ordered to accompany Teixeira and to make a careful report of all that they observed upon the voyage, for the information of the Council of the Indies. Cristóbal de Acuña, one of the Jesuit Fathers, was the actual historiographer of the return journey, and his report [2] contains the first detailed account of the Amazon, its affluents and its inhabitants, that we possess. Teixeira arrived at Pará, December 1639.

It was in the course of this return voyage that Pedro Teixeira solemnly took possession of a certain site in the name of Philip IV, as King of Portugal, and set up a memorial as a mark of delimitation between the Portuguese and Spanish dominions on the river Amazon.

There follows, in Dr. Edmundson's account, a translation of the formal "Act of Possession" drawn up by Teixeira, which is solemn enough, though weak in that it fails to locate the spot. The actual mark of delimitation, a carved log, was soon washed away, and Teixeira's document gives its location only as being "before the mouths of the Rio do Ouro" (River of Gold). But several Amazonian streams were called the "River of Gold." Many Portuguese insisted that Teixeira had referred to the same Aguarico, the tributary of the Napo, *below* which the Spaniards had earlier established their ill-fated settlement. That location would place the boundary on the present border be-

[2]*Nuevo descubrimiento del gran río de las Amazonas* (New Discovery of the Great River of the Amazons), published in Madrid, 1641.

tween northern Peru and Ecuador. The location claimed by the Spaniards would place it some 600 miles east of the Portuguese spot, far in today's Brazil, near the mouth of the River Teffé. Dr. Edmundson develops some very convincing arguments that it had been actually at the latter point, almost 400 miles east of today's Amazonian border between Brazil and Peru, that Teixeira had erected his boundary post.

Spanish efforts to oppose the Portuguese encroachments on the Amazon consisted primarily of the work of Jesuit missionaries, working out of their order's college in Quito. Starting in 1658 with a mission at Borja, immediately below the Pongo de Manseriche (see Chapter XVI), they worked eastward, gathering the Indians around them in mission stations and at times persuading them to move upstream in order to escape from the slavers. In 1759, they were expelled from all the Amazonian territories which had been granted to Portugal by the treaty of nine years earlier, probably because, in combatting the enslavement of the natives, they had interfered with free enterprise.

Among the most important of the Indians reached by the Jesuits were the Omaguas, whose territory extended along the Amazon's north bank from the mouth of the River Napo for some 300 miles to that of the Japurá. Orellana had first encountered them in 1541 (see Chapter X), apparently on the main stream's south bank and largely below the Japurá. There is some evidence, however, that they had subsequently moved to the location where the Jesuits were to find them, undoubtedly in a futile effort to evade the Portuguese slavers. In 1681 a delegation of their headmen arrived at the mission at Pueblo de la Laguna, upstream, at the mouth of the Huallaga, to beg that a missionary be sent to them. According to Dr. Edmundson, "the Jesuit Superior at that place . . . undertook to grant their request, but was unable to do so until 1686. It was in that year that Samuel Fritz arrived from Spain at the Jesuit College of Quito, and was sent by his Superiors to the Marañón to be the missionary of the Omaguas."

Born in Bohemia in 1654, a brilliant scholar, Father Fritz was admitted into the Society of Jesus in 1673 and was sent to Quito in 1686, after having decided to become a missionary. His 37 years as such, along the Amazon, were interrupted for 22 months of imprisonment by the Portuguese in Pará, in 1689–91. The first missionary to preach the gospel in the land of the Omaguas and their downstream neighbors, nearly always working alone, he achieved brilliant success and came to be regarded by the Indians with almost supernatural awe.

Father Fritz was the first to compile a reliable map of the Amazon's entire course. In fact, he drew two maps, the first in 1691 and the second in 1707. The latter was published in Quito in reduced form and both were published in England early in the twentieth century, in documents pertaining to disputes over the boundary between British Guiana and Brazil. The Hakluyt volume from which the present material was taken reproduces the 1707 map. Evidently compiled with great care, it is crammed with an astonishing amount of detail and is remarkably accurate in the areas which had been personally visited by Father Fritz. Beyond the mainstream of the Amazon, however, the tributaries go wandering off into cartographic errors. As was customary in those days, the map shows Lake Parima, the fabled site of El Dorado, in approximately the location where Raleigh had placed it (see Chapter XIV). It shows the Orinoco River and the Río Negro (inaccurately), but omits the Cassiquiare, which connects the two (see Chapter XVII).

Large portions of Father Fritz's journals and letters were included in the so-called "Evora Manuscript," a Spanish document which was found, and translated by Dr. Edmundson in 1902, in the Portuguese town of Evora. While the author's name is unknown, he was evidently a contemporary and close associate of Father Fritz. The document begins as follows:

> The most glorious Mission, which has left a memorial on the banks of the Marañón of the zeal of the members of the Company [of Jesus], and almost entirely destroyed the grasping cupidity of the Portuguese of Gran Pará, is that of the Omaguas, Jurimaguas, Aysuares, Ybanomas and other tribes, who inhabited the isles of the above-named river from the mouth of the Napo to the mouth of the Río Negro, a distance of more than five hundred leagues.

After a long and fascinating account of the Omaguas and their customs, the document tells of the arrival of Father Fritz at La Laguna, en route to the land of the Omaguas, and of the latter's reception of the news of his coming.

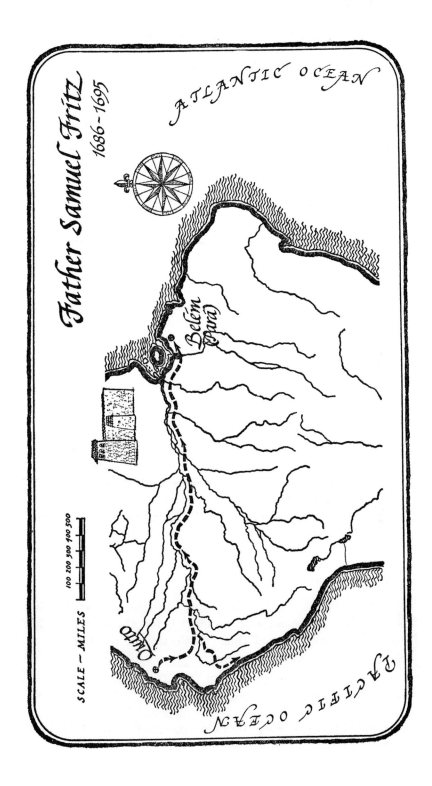

Father Samuel Fritz
1686-1695

ATLANTIC OCEAN

PACIFIC OCEAN

Belém
(Pará)

Quito

SCALE — MILES

100 200 300 400 500

These barbarians, on being informed that new Missionaries had arrived from Quito to the Laguna, and that one of them was preparing to descend to their lands, with great eagerness—convoyed in more than thirty canoes—set out upstream to meet him, and brought him with much rejoicing to their first village-settlement. On arrival at the port, not content that he should go up from the canoe on his feet, they insisted on carrying him in their arms, and, amidst dances and music of flutes, fifes and other instruments, brought him to the abode that they had provided for him. They did the same in many other village-settlements in more than thirty islands, so that the Father took steps as quickly as possible to make himself known, and to communicate to them the first elements of the Christian religion. In every part the inhabitants showed themselves ready to receive the Faith. They received it as the preacher set it forth; notwithstanding that he had no apparatus with him save a wooden cross, nor was he accompanied by any ministering-assistants, save one or two boys of this same Omagua nation, as his servers.

The Father was thus journeying all the year round from island to island, with exceeding discomfort and danger, navigating in that little sea, for such is the Marañón below the junction of the Napo, guided frequently by some lads, without stopping longer than was necessary in each settlement; baptizing the little ones; instructing, exhorting and preaching to the adults; with this result that the whole nation in less than three years was found capable of baptism. Many churches or chapels were built, and in every part divine worship and teaching, for the use of the Christian settlements, was established. The principal village-settlement in which the Father at times resided for some considerable periods, because it was the most populous and near the missions upstream, was called San Joaquim, this being the Saint that Father Samuel [Fritz] chose as patron of his apostolical conquest.

As shown on the Fritz map of 1707, San Joaquim was on the main river's north bank, some 25 miles below the mouth of the Napo. The Omaguas told their missionary of a neighboring downstream tribe, the Jurimaguas.

They told him much of their skill and dexterity, and how they painted their womenfolk with much art, and spoke of their customs as being less barbarous than those of the rest, and of a kind of police by which they were governed, living all of them in subjection to the will of a Principal Chief of whom the

Father learnt that they were very well disposed to submit themselves to the yoke of the Gospel. With this news he conceived a great desire to convert them and resolved to go down-stream, and visit them in their settlements.

The Jurimaguas had already heard of the Father, and had so high an opinion of his way of life and wondrous work that they were in doubt whether he were a mortal man or a spirit from the other world. An evil spirit was exercising such despotic dominion over them, that from time to time he suddenly fell upon them and beat them cruelly, and when he went away, embarking himself in a canoe, he was lost to the sight of all by submerging in the depths of the Marañón. Some were afraid lest the Father should prove to be a similar spirit, but when he arrived at their lands and they saw his different method of treating them with kindness and affection, they all returned from their hiding-places, from whence they had been watching for some time in much fear and caution. All unanimously received him with great demonstrations of gladness and rejoicing.

After taking care of the evil spirit by making, blessing, and erecting a great wooden cross which proved adequate in that it discouraged the Devil (as Fritz called him) from further visiting and whipping the Jurimaguas, the missionary proceeded to instruct and convert the latter, as well as neighboring tribes, as far as the Río Negro.

In the midst of these continuous journeyings and labours for the welfare of so many souls, while the Father was in the principal village of the Jurimaguas, by the special ordering of God a dangerous illness attacked him with inflammation of the whole body, that compelled him for fear of perishing in this abandonment to descend [the river] to Gran Pará in search of some remedy. This was that celebrated descent full of wonderful happenings, which may be reckoned as among the chief discoveries of the River Marañón, since the Father, particularly on his return journey, noted attentively and with greater exactness than any other, everything that pertains to a general notice and geographical description of the said river, and the more principal nations that inhabit its banks.

The Evora manuscript now reproduces Father Fritz's own account of his journey to the mouth of the Amazon and his return after being held prisoner by the Portuguese in Pará for nearly two years. Of the Jurimaguas, the Father wrote:

In former days the Jurimaguas had been very warlike and masters of almost the whole River of the Amazons; and their women (as I have heard) fought with arrows, as valiantly as the Indians. Such an encounter, it seems to me, was that which Orellana had, which led to his giving to this great river the name of the Amazons; but now they are much intimidated and wasted by the wars and enslavements that they have suffered and suffer from their neighbors of Pará. Their villages and homesteads were a league and more in extent; but since they saw themselves persecuted many of them have withdrawn to other lands and rivers, so as to be somewhat more secure.

While Father Fritz was bedridden with his illness, the river rose in flood.

Meanwhile, as I was staying in this Jurimagua village, already almost wholly inundated, . . . I fell sick of most violent attacks of fever and dropsy that began in the feet with other complaints principally caused by worms. I was obliged to remain day and night for the space of well-nigh three months shut up in [my] shelter without being able to stir. In the daytime I felt somewhat easier, but the nights in unutterable burnings, as the river, though it was passing but a hairbreath from . . . [my] bed, was out of reach of my mouth, and in sleeplessness, caused not only by my infirmities, but also from the grunting of the crocodiles or lizards that all night long were roving around the village, beasts of horrible deformity. . . .

Besides the lizards so many rats made their way into my dwelling place, and so hungry, that they gnawed even my spoon and my plate and the haft of my knife, and ate up the little food that I had for my sustenance. Almost all the people of the village began to take themselves off in search of dry ground and forest fruits to escape starvation, since their store of food, that is the mandioca, was buried beneath the water, and I for my sustenance was reduced to obtaining at times by fishing a few little fish, and to begging for some plantains, which it was necessary to send for lower down, and to fetch from the Aysuares.

Father Fritz tells of a visit from the Manoa (or Manáo) Indians, whom he calls the "Manaves." Because they dealt in gold, their name was given by the Spaniards to the principal city of El Dorado, the city of Manoa on Lake Parima. It was also after them that the modern city of Manaus was named, near the mouth of the Río Negro. The Manáos were a numerous tribe on the Río Negro, itinerant traders who, among many other things, captured Indian slaves for the Portuguese. Some years after Father Fritz's contact with them, they came under the leadership of a powerful chief named Ajuricaba, slaver and raider, who flew the Dutch flag on his canoe and raised havoc up and down the Río Negro and neighboring streams. He was beaten and killed in 1727 by a formidable Portuguese military expedition. Dr. Edmundson writes: "For many years after Ajuricaba's overthrow the river [Negro] remained depopulated and deserted by its native inhabitants.

While in my hut I was wrestling with my attacks of sickness there came to trade with the Jurimaguas a troop of Manaves [Manáos], a tribe of unconverted Indians. On their arrival . . . , [they] passed my dwelling at full speed. On the next day having sent an invitation to them, they came and were very friendly . . . , calling me in their language, Abba, Abba, that means Father, the same as in Hebrew. These Manaves Indians are very brave and feared by neighboring tribes, and offered resistance for years to a Portuguese troop. . . . Their lands lie in a northerly direction upon a stream called Jurubetts, to which one arrives by the River Japurá. . . .

The trade that these Manaves have with the Aysuares, Ybanomas and Jurimaguas consists of small plates of gold, vermilion, yuca graters, hammocks of *cachivance,* and various kinds of clubs and shields which they work very curiously. They do not themselves extract the gold, but they go to the river Jurubetts . . . , where they obtain it by barter, and this is the river much famed for its gold amongst these tribes.

There also arrived at this same time, when the village was inundated, eight Indians, Ybanomas, from below the mouth of the River Japurá to see me, and they invited me to descend to their settlement. These Ybanomas likewise brought me news of some Portuguese who had come up from Pará as far as the Cuchivaras to obtain sarsaparilla, eight days lower down than the Jurimaguas. Wherefore I resolved to descend in search of the Portuguese in hopes of getting some remedy in my sufferings, since it was an impossibility for me to go upstream, and manifestly dangerous, seeing that I was so weakened and beset with infirmities. I should have to spend more than two months on my journey before meeting the first Father of the Castilian missionaries.

After the river began to fall, I made a move on my journey downstream, in charge of the chief Mativa and ten Indians. I set out from the settlement . . . on the third of July, 1689. . . .

On the 6th at dawn I passed the mouth of the river Japurá, and visited the settlement of the Ybanomas, called Juaboni, whose chief is Arimavana, with whom I stayed four days, teaching and collecting stores for my further journey. . . . The 15th I arrived at some deserted houses which the Portuguese had built on some high banks, they had already gone away some days before my descent. . . . Directly I arrived at that place many Indians and Indian women, Cuchivaras, with their children, came from their settlements, and were occupying those houses while I was there—that was for eight days. They assisted me with great readiness and affection, more than if they had been Christians, bringing me a quantity of fish, turtle, and plantains. . . .

On the 24th I departed, being convoyed downstream by Cuchivaras Indians. The 26th on the approach of night I arrived at the mouth of the Río Negro. The 28th we met with a chief of the Portuguese native tribe, the Tupinambaranas, . . . who had been accompanying the slave-raiding troops. My Cuchivara Indians, judging them to be Taromas, their enemies of the Río Negro, immediately got their arrows ready. I planted my cross in the prow, until, on the arrival of the canoes, they were recognized as friends, and the Chief, Cumuaru, gave me an Indian guide to the village of Ibuivua.

On July 30th I arrived at the settlement of Urubú where Father Theodosio Vegas, a Mercenarian, was serving as missionary. He was absent on my arrival. After he came back to the settlement he treated me with great kindliness. On August 1st the Portuguese troop of slave-raiders returned from the Río Negro to this settlement of Urubú. . . .

It should be observed that in this voyage of mine a great stir arose about me, not only among the surrounding natives, but it made its way as far as Pará and San Luis de Marañón. Some said that I was a saint and a son of God, others a Devil. Some, because I carried a cross, said that a Patriarch or Prophet had come; others an envoy from Persia. Even the Negroes of Pará said that their liberator had come from the way of Angola to free them. Others retreated from fear, saying that I carried fire with me and came along burning as many settlements and people as I met.

They had published many other and greater fictions about

me, so that Father Theodosio Vegas, to whom I immediately sent a notice of my arrival, wrote me a note, as to a dubious person, concluding it by saying that they had told him so many strange things concerning me that he was in doubt whether some thing or portent from the other world had arrived at his settlement. The head of the troop [of slavers], Piñero, when he arrived from the Río Negro at Urubú, said the same concerning me afterwards in Pará, that he did not dare, on the night that he came, to enter into conversation with me, because of the great absurdities that they had told him, but through a small opening he stood watching whether I were a man, or something from the other life.

In this settlement of Urubú they detained me for fifteen days, taking care of me with much kindness. . . . But not only was I not benefited, but made worse than ever before. Up till then I had been able to stand on my feet, henceforth I was obliged to allow myself to be carried in a hammock without being able to walk a step, because the dropsy made progress, spreading over the whole body and causing me much anguish and fatigue.

On the fifteenth of August the said head of the troop, seeing that my symptoms were every day becoming increasingly bad, and that a more prolonged method of cure was required, sent me in one of his own canoes to Pará. . . .

On the 3d of September I arrived at Guaricurú, a settlement of the Engaibes and a mission of the Father Antonio de Silva of the Company [of Jesuits], with whom I met the troop of war that was on its way to chastise some Indians, for what insolence I know not, consisting of eighty Portuguese soldiers and two hundred Indians. . . . On the 11th I arrived by night at the city of Gran Pará, more dead than alive. The Fathers of the College belonging to the Company received me with much kindliness, and sought all possible means for the recovery of my health. . . . At last, at the end of two months, in which different medical remedies were applied to me, God deigned to restore my health and to grant me restoration of strength, wherewith to bear with patience other hardships that were awaiting me, and that were more painful than any illness.

The authorities at Pará suspected Father Fritz of being a spy sent by the Spaniards to observe and report on Portuguese encroachments on territories claimed by Spain. They also asserted that his missions were located in areas belonging to Portugal. For both reasons they sent word to the city's Jesuit College to treat him well but under no circumstances to permit him to leave the institution. The authorities sent a message to Lisbon, to ask their king what to do with him, holding him prisoner while awaiting an answer.

> I, seeing that I was kept in ward without power to return to my mission, sought to embark for Lisbon, appealing to both their Castilian and Portuguese Majesties, that I might answer for myself, so that the Gospel of Christ might be left in immunity and liberty. All my endeavors however were disappointed. I was retained there in that city eighteen months to the bitter affliction of my heart for the abandonment in which meanwhile my neophytes remained, and many unbelievers that had been left with good inclinations towards conversion.

While in Pará, Father Fritz seems to have engaged in many arguments over the boundary between Spanish and Portuguese possessions.

> The ground on which the Portuguese of Pará base their claim is found in a Cedula of the Royal Audiencia of Quito, brought by the expedition of Teixeira when returning to Pará with Father Acuña in 1639, in which leave was given to them to take possession of a village, where in their voyage up the Marañón they had come across some ear-rings of gold in the hands of the heathen, and for this reason had named it the Village of Gold. The position was on the southern bank on elevated ground somewhat higher than the river Cuchivara, where they rightly say that they took possession and left there, as a memorial, a great trunk of a tree.
>
> This memorial then is the cause now of the whole dispute; and as already there is no one who has an exact remembrance of the spot where the said memorial was placed, it is now pretended that it was farther up than the province of the Omaguas, and accordingly they had informed the King of Portugal that I have been conducting a mission in lands belonging to him.

Father Fritz wrote to the Spanish ambassador in Lisbon and to the "Procurator-General of the Indies" in Madrid, advancing his claim that he had scrupulously conducted his activities above the location of the lost Teixeira memorial mark, but it seems to have done little good except, perhaps, to win him leniency from the Portuguese king. After 18 months of waiting, a royal message arrived in Pará, ordering that the father be freed.

In consequence of the good relations that his Catholic Majesty was professing, whose vassal I was, and being moreover a Father of the Company of Jesus, he [the king] commanded that I should be sent back, at the charges of his Royal Treasury, to my mission, and even to Quito should it be necessary. The . . . Governor having received this order from the King immediately sent me on the spot his congratulations, offering to carry out at once whatever I should direct.

In order not to frighten the Indians along the way, Father Fritz wanted to take with him only Indian boatmen, but the governor insisted on sending an officer and some soldiers with him. Three more months were spent on preparations for the journey, bringing the father's stay in Pará to a total of 22 months.

The party left Pará July 6, 1691. The next few pages of Father Fritz's journal are filled with a pedestrian account of his upstream journey, meticulously listing all the places, rivers, and Indian tribes which were later to appear on his celebrated map.

On September 2nd we arrived at night at a sandbank that is some two leagues below the mouth of the Urubú. Here the Father . . . Theodosio Vegas, a Mercenarian and Missionary of Urubú, awaited us with a large number of his people. He gave me a kind welcome as he had done on my voyage downstream. His Indians were very anxious to see me, for some of them, while I was kept prisoner in Pará, frightened all the natives around, saying that an earthquake and horrible parting-asunder of the ground which had occurred some eight leagues higher up, on the same northern shore, had happened because of me, and that they would all perish if the Portuguese did not restore me to my mission. . . . Another fictitious story, while I was kept in Pará, was bruited among these natives, that they had cut me in pieces, but that I was immortal, and that my soul caused the pieces immediately to unite and to enter a second time into the body.

After a procession of notes on where he had been from day to day, the father arrived at the scene of the earthquake about which he had heard.

On the 6th in the morning, on the north bank, we came upon the lands where in the month of June in the past year, 1690, there was a very great earthquake. Ruins of large villages were visible, fallen rocks, huge plantations uprooted and thrown into the river, very high ground with the scrub on the top fallen, and white, red, and yellow earth, stones and trees hurled from the height and piled up above the river. In another part lagoons drained, woods destroyed, and everything mixed together in disorder. Where the soil had been of sand or clay, there had not been any havoc. Fr. Theodosio said that at the same time there were terrible tides in the river and an immense quantity of fish had died, and this the natives were attributing to my detention, saying that Pará and all of them were doomed to perish. They were declaring further that for some four hundred leagues of the river there had been even greater havoc inland, and that the earthquake had travelled for some three hundred leagues upstream as far as the islands of the Omaguas, whose houses . . . had been much shaken. . . .

On the 7th of September we encountered a strong current against which the two canoes could make no headway. By night we arrived at the mouth of the Río Negro. . . . Here we celebrated on the following day the festival of the Nativity of our Lady. This day there came to see me more than eighty Indian natives, Taromas, . . . bringing many gifts of food. All were much afraid of me because of the earthquake referred to. They promised me that they would not from that day forward wage war any more with the Cuchivaras, Ybanomas, and Jurimaguas.

After leaving the mouth of the Río Negro, they "journeyed for nine days without seeing a settlement." On arriving at the territory of the Cuchivaras, who had treated Father Fritz well on his downstream journey, they found the settlement burned as a result of a war against the Urubú Indians. The Cuchivaras themselves had abandoned the land in search of safer regions. Reaching a former settlement of the Ybanomas on September 19th, they found that it, too, had been deserted and burned. "From here we traveled thirteen days without meeting people. On the 22nd the Taromas went away, and so we were left without a guide."

On the 2nd of October, at the opening of night, we obtained a view of the village, Juaboni, of the Ybanomas. We did not enter so as not to disturb them at night time. On the 3d at dawn I went forward in a canoe with four Indians, and on arriving at the port I caused the big drum to be struck. The people of the village, as soon as they saw me, . . . received me

with great gladness. I conferred with them so that they should
not be disturbed by the coming of the Portuguese, who accompanied me, and I at once said the votive mass of the Holy
Trinity as an act of thanksgiving.

The travelers, proceeding upstream through the territory of
the Aysuares, found village after village abandoned. "On the
thirteenth we meet two Jurimaguas, that were fleeing. They said
that all in the neighbouring settlements had fled because an
Ybanoma Indian called Manoto, a one-eyed cripple, had alarmed
them by saying that the Father was coming no more, but only
the Portuguese, burning, enslaving, and killing." Even the
father's principal Mission station among the Jurimaguas was
found "entirely uninhabited, and the church burnt through the
carelessness of a lad, except the painting-on-canvas of our Lady,
which was most marvellously preserved."

> We took up our abode on a neighboring sandbank and des-
> patched two canoes in search of people. I sent my cross that
> they might be assured of my arrival. On the 16th the chief
> Mativa came with some of his men. As I saw that all the people
> were alarmed by the coming of the Portuguese in my company,
> I begged the Captain to return with his soldiers downstream,
> since we were already within my mission, but he pressed me to
> take him with me at any rate to the first settlement of the
> Omaguas, as the Governor had charged him to accompany me
> as far as the Omaguas.

They reached the easternmost village of the Omaguas October 18, but found it deserted. The Portuguese soldiers then
agreed to return downstream and Father Fritz accompanied
them "to the village of the Jurimaguas." But his troubles were
not over.

> On the 20th, the troop being on the point of starting on their
> downward journey, the captain explained to me that the motive
> for seeking to pass to the Omaguas had been to take possession
> of those lands according to the secret order he received from
> his governor, and intimated to me that I should immediately
> withdraw from these lands, I should say provinces, since they
> belong to the Crown of Portugal. I was much surprised at the
> novelty of this proposal, as being so little in agreement with the
> map, and the intention of his own King.

The good father explained that he was a missionary, that there could be no doubt that the disputed territories belonged to Spain, and that he intended to stay among his people. "On this the Captain and soldiers embarked and with firing of guns set off down the river."

> The Portuguese, after they had departed, went to Guapapate a day downstream, and stayed there in front of the village ten days, gathering . . . sarsaparilla. They also made there on the south bank a clearing . . ., leaving for a land-mark a large tree, . . . saying that they had come there to settle. I doubt not that they would do so because of their craving to make slaves of the Indians from here upward, in addition to which they imagine that from here they can find a gate of entrance to El Dorado. . . . That which I verified from the Omaguas—I mean the Jurimaguas—is that at those gold mines of which I made mention above, when speaking of the Manaves Indians, there existed in visible form a man, like a Spaniard, that according to the signs can be no other than the Infernal Dragon that in that shape stands guard over those golden apples.

After the departure of the Portuguese, Father Fritz labored some months, persuading his people to return to their abandoned settlements, pursuing his mission work, and slowly making his way upstream. Near the end of February he arrived at the principal mission station of La Laguna, whence he had departed for the land of the Omaguas three years earlier. He was happy to be reunited with his fellow Jesuits. After a brief rest, he made his way to Lima to report to the "Lord Viceroy" on the activities and aspirations of the Portuguese along the Amazon. He ascended the Huallaga River, crossed the Andes via Moyobamba, Chachapoyas, Cajamarca, and Trujillo, and at last arrived in Lima on the second of July, 1692. In the course of that journey, he made the observations and measurements he needed for completing his map of the upper Amazon.

In his introduction, Dr. Edmundson presents a short biography of Father Fritz. Parts of it read as follows:

> 1693. Fritz remained at Lima till the end of May, 1693, when he departed with many presents and promises of help in his work and in the defence of his missions. He returned by way of Jaen and the defile of the Pongo, taking as he went careful measure-

ments and levels for the perfecting of his map. He reached San Joaquim in August of this year.

1694. The Father was engaged in moving a large number of the Omaguas higher up the river to be out of reach of the Portuguese, and he founded two new mission villages. . . .

1695. Hearing that a Portuguese troop had ascended as far as the Jurimaguas, the Father on February the 24th started downstream and travelling by night as well as by day arrived at the Jurimaguas mission-station, Nuestra Señora de las Niebes, on March 14th. Here the chiefs of the Aysuares and Ybanomas came up to consult the Father. In consequence of the threats of the Portuguese to return in force, he tries to persuade these Indians to move higher up the river.

1697. Disturbances among the Omaguas. The Father having obtained an officer and some soldiers from Borja visited San Joaquim, San Pablo, and Guadeloupe and restored order.

Starting from San Joaquim, April 9th, the Father went downstream to visit Nuestra Señora de las Niebes and his Jurimagua mission. Hearing of the approach of a Portuguese troop accompanied by the Provincial of the Shod-Carmelites and another religious, Fritz went to meet them. He was informed that, by orders of the Governor and on petition of the chiefs of the Jurimaguas, Aysuares and Ybanomas, the troop was coming up to take possession of these lands. After a strong protest from Fritz, and much argument, it was agreed that the boundary question should be left to the decision of the home authorities; meanwhile both the Father and the Portuguese should depart simultaneously from the Jurimaguas; he upstream; they downstream. . . . The Father again arrived at San Joaquim on June 13th. He resided at San Joaquim till the end of the year, when two new fellow workers joined him, both like himself from Bohemia, Fathers Wenceslas Breyer and Francisco Vidra.

1698. The Father remained at San Joaquim until August. In compliance with the orders of the Superior he left on August 6th for Laguna. . . .

1699. Fathers Breyer and Vidra having come up from San Joaquim in fear of their lives, owing to disturbances among the Omaguas, Father Samuel [Felix] went down with them to that mission-station, appeased the disturbances, and remained at San Joaquim for the rest of the year.

1700. The Father anxiously awaited for some months the arrival of the Father Superior . . . with an escort for the purpose of visiting the Jurimaguas and Aysuares and assisting them to ascend higher up out of reach of the Portuguese, but . . . on August 21st he received a letter from the Superior requesting him to go up at once to La Laguna, and from there to Quito to bring down fresh misisonaries. He arrived at La Laguna September 9th, but on hearing that a number of Jurimaguas had reached San Joaquim, flying from the Portuguese, he obtained leave to go and meet them, and assist them to find a settlement near the mouth of the Napo. Having accomplished this task, he then set out by the river Napo for Quito on December 22nd.

1701. The Father reached Quito January 22nd, and was attacked with serious illness March 29th. On recovery left Quito, May 18th, accompanied by Father Juan Baptista Sanna, as new missionary at San Joaquim. Toilsome journey of nearly three months. Found it necessary to send to Borja for troops to quell disturbances among the Omaguas. The force arrived August 25th; the offenders were punished; and their leader, Payoreva, carried off as a prisoner. The escort remained until November 5th, having restored quiet throughout the mission.

1702. Payoreva escaped, and again caused trouble. Father Samuel [Fritz] finding the outbreak serious with much sadness abandoned San Joaquim, taking the church ornaments to the new settlement of the Jurimaguas. In April hearing of a Portuguese raiding force having ascended as far as San Joaquim, the Father set out at once down the river to visit the Omaguas, Jurimaguas and Aysuares, and persuade these Indians to come up out of reach of these raids. He spent three months on this journey.

1703–7 . . . In 1704 he was appointed Superior of the whole mission. . . . As Superior during these years Father Samuel made repeated visits to these extended missions, where he found Father Sanna doing excellent work. He made many quests to the various authorities for further help in these extended missions, and finally determined to pay in person a second visit to Quito, starting from La Laguna early in November, 1706.

1707. He reached Quito, January 21st, 1707, quite prostrate and broken in health. . . . A violent attack of fever kept him at Quito till the end of May, but when half convalescent, and though the floods were at their height, he set out with six companions. . . .

1708. News reaches the Superior at La Laguna of serious acts of violence committed by a Portuguese troop among the Omaguas. He sent to Borja, and also Quito, for help. His messenger . . . left for Quito January 24th and returned November 24th with the message that the Royal Audiencia would despatch 100 men to expel the Portuguese.

1709. On receiving news that the Portuguese had advanced as far as the new settlement of the Jurimaguas and had carried away a large number of prisoners, Father Samuel determined to descend with a large force of soldiers and Indians from Borja, and of others that had come down to Napo from Quito. He started on July 8th and went down visiting all the settlements of the Omaguas, Jurimaguas and Aysuares, taking several Portuguese prisoners. On August 14th he began his return journey. A large number of his native converts left their homes and accompanied him higher up the river. He did not return to La Laguna till November 28th, having to arrange for the fugitive Jurimaguas and Aysuares to make a new settlement at Guallaga.

1710. News came on June 8th that the Portuguese had again attacked the mission-station at San Joaquim and had carried off many Omaguas, and Father Juan Baptista Sanna himself, to Pará. He makes preparations for the defence of La Laguna should the Portuguese attack it.

1711. The Father Provincial at Quito informs Father Samuel that owing to lack of funds the Royal Audiencia can take no serious steps for defending the Marañón missions.

1712. In January, and again in October, the Father Superior sends down messengers with an escort to enquire about the state of things at San Joaquim. The report is that the Omaguas have been entirely dispersed. The fugitives were collected to form a settlement on the Ucayali. . . .

1713. Father Samuel, though at the end of the previous year he had been relieved of his charge as Superior of the Marañón missions, continues to reside and work at La Laguna.

1724. Samuel Fritz died on March 18th. On the following April 9th he would have completed his 70th year.

⚛ XVI ⚛

LA CONDAMINE

THE first non-Iberian scientist-explorer to work in South America was the Frenchman Charles Marie de La Condamine. In April, 1735, he left France for Peru, which was in those days still a colony of Spain and included today's Ecuador. With him were two other French scientists, M. Godin and M. Bouguer, as well as a physician, a surgeon, an engineer from the French Navy, a draftsman, and a watch- and instrument-maker. In South America that rather cumbersome expedition was joined by two Spanish naval officers. The expedition's principal aim was to measure the precise length of a degree of latitude at the equator,[1] while another French group did the same in the arctic. By means of astronomical measurements as well as work with the pendulum, they were also to test what Newton had already surmised: that the earth is not a perfect sphere, being flattened at the poles. Eventually the work of La Condamine and other Frenchmen led to the establishment of the meter as the world's most widely used unit of length measurement; a meter was orig-

---

[1] Near Quito, the scientists measured the length of a north-south line which straddled the equator and spanned a little more than three degrees of arc. The two ends of the line were marked by pyramids, precisely located, the bricks made in a special shape to discourage people from removing them and using them for the construction of their houses. The pyramid marking the northern end of the line was to suffer an interesting fate. More than a century after its erection, when Ecuador had become an independent republic, one of the country's presidents saw the structure and became deeply interested in the scientific labors which had produced it. As a patron of science, he was proud to have the pyramid in his country, but regretted that it stood in a location where few people saw it. In order to make the monument more effective, he had it moved to the top of a mountain, where it could be seen from far away and many angles.

inally defined as being one ten-millionth of the distance from the equator to the pole.

Outhwaite has the following to say about the venture [2]:

> The undertaking was a lengthy one and was carried out with all the precautions for scientific accuracy that were known at the time. Owing to supplementary scientific labors the expedition remained in this region for some seven years. The party was not a very harmonious one, and it finally broke up, the various members of the expedition passing to diverse and mostly tragic fates. One of the younger members of the expedition died only three days after arriving in Quito; the surgeon was killed in a local riot; the draftsman had fallen from a scaffold while carrying out architectural work on a church, and there were many deaths and accidents among the lesser personnel of the expedition. La Condamine's scientific associate Godin, and Madame Godin, later went through a series of travels so delayed and so difficult that they constitute a fantastic record of adventure.

On May 11, 1743, La Condamine left the party to return to France, choosing to cross South America via the Amazon River. All chroniclers of South American exploration credit him with having "explored" the Amazon. His observations as a scientist and the mapping he did en route do lend a certain flavor of exploration to his voyage. Primarily, however, that voyage, and more particularly the classic later one made by the wife of his associate, M. Godin, are of interest in illustrating the difficulties, frustrations, and almost unbelievable delays encountered in eighteenth-century Amazonian travel, through sparsely settled country, by primitive transportation, and in the face of bureaucratic obstacles arising from the territorial disputes between Spain and Portugal.

An abridged account of La Condamine's travels was presented by him at the meeting of April 28, 1745, of the Academy of Sciences in Paris. An English translation of the paper was published in 1813, in *John Pinkerton's Collection of . . . Voyages and Travels in All Parts of the World,* Volume 14. The following material was taken from that source.

> In order to multiply our opportunities for making observations, M. Godin, M. Bouguer, and myself planned different

[2] Leonard Outhwaite, *Unrolling the Map; The Story of Exploration* (New York, 1935), p. 173.

routes for our return. For my part I resolved on selecting one, almost unknown, and such as I felt persuaded no one would envy me, that of the river of Amazons, a river which crosses the whole continent of South America, from west to east, and which justly passes for the largest in the world. I proposed to render a voyage on this river of utility, by forming a chart of its course, and by remarks on such objects as a country so little known might afford.

La Condamine was an avid collector and reporter on everything that might be of interest to France's science. During his stay in Peru, he had sent samples and seeds of rubber to his home country, and is credited with being the first scientist to have rendered a reliable account of the uses of rubber. While crossing the Andes, he continued to collect. His narrative reads:

> The 3d of June, I spent the whole day on one of these mountains; though assisted by two Americans [3] of the neighborhood, whom I took with me for guides, I was able to collect no more than eight or nine young plants of Quinquina [Cinchona?] in a proper state for transportation. These I caused to be planted, in earth taken from the spot, in a case of suitable size, and had them carried on the shoulders of a man constantly in my sight, to the place at which I embarked, hoping to preserve at least some of the plants, to leave under charge at Cayenne, if they should not, on my arrival there, be in fit condition for transporting to France for the King's garden.

After crossing the crests of the Andes, La Condamine had a raft built, on which, and in dugout canoes, he descended various rivers until he came to the Marañón, as the upper stretch of the Amazon is called. On July 10, he arrived at the Pongo de Manseriche, the famous gorge through which the Marañón finally leaves the Andean mountains in a boiling rush to flow with greater tranquility another 2,500 or so miles over its alluvial plain to the Atlantic. He spent several days waiting for the river to subside, but:

> the 12th of July, at noon, I caused the raft to be unmoored, and pushed from shore; soon I found myself carried along by the

[3] Almost always, La Condamine referred to the native inhabitants as "Americans," only rarely—and then apparently through carelessness—using the term "Indians."

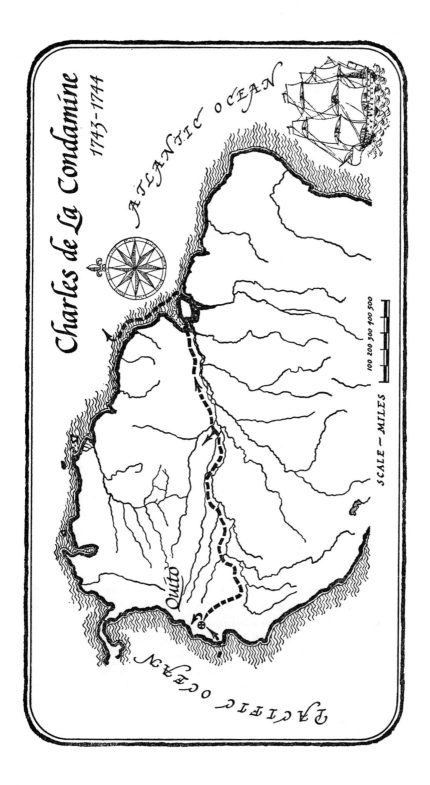

Charles de La Condamine

1743–1744

ATLANTIC OCEAN

PACIFIC OCEAN

Quito

SCALE — MILES

100 200 300 400 500

stream in a deep and narrow gallery, formed by two walls of rock, in some parts slanting, but in others perpendicular; in less than an hour, I was transported to Borja, three leagues, according to common computation, from Sant Yago. . . .

I struck twice or thrice with violence against the rocks in course of the different windings, an accident calculated, but for being forewarned of the little danger there to be apprehended, to create no small portion of alarm. A canoe on such an occasion would be dashed into a thousand pieces; and the spot was pointed out to me, as I passed along, where a governor of the Maynas thus met destruction: but the beams of the raft being neither nailed nor dovetailed together, the flexibility of the lianas, by which they are fastened, have the effect of a spring, and deaden the shock so, that when the strait is passed in a raft, these percussions occur unheeded. The greatest danger for these is, their being liable to be driven out of the stream into eddies. . . . Not a year had elapsed since a missionary, drawn thus into a vortex, was kept in it for two days destitute of provisions; and but for a sudden swell of the river, which brought him again into the current, he might there have perished of hunger.

Below the Pongo, La Condamine was happy, at last, to find himself in the lowland forest regions of the Amazon basin, where "new plants, new animals, and new races of men, were exhibited to view."

Obviously a scientist of the most pedestrian type, whose travel account is even more lacking in humor than it is in color, La Condamine liked to unburden himself of *ex cathedra* discussions of the things he observed. After telling about his descent of the Pongo, he has the following to say about the South American Indians:

Before I proceed farther, I deem it right to say a word of the genius and character of the primitive inhabitants of South America, improperly called Indians. . . .

All the old natives of the country are of a tawny color, inclining to a red of different shades of brightness; the difference in shading arising probably in a great degree from the varying temperature of the climate they inhabit, which embraces the intense heat of the torrid zone with the cold of the vicinage of snow.

This variety of climates; the wooded countries, plains, mountains, and rivers, which different sites afford; a difference of aliment; the little intercourse subsisting between neighboring nations, and numerous other causes, must necessarily have introduced a variety of occupations, as in the customs of these people.

However, after pointing out that no two South American Indian groups are alike, he nevertheless finds certain traits common to all of them.

Insensibility among these people is generally prevalent, which, whether to be dignified by the name of apathy, or sunk in that of stupidity, I leave to the devision [devising] of others. Undoubtedly it is caused by the paucity of their ideas, which extend no farther than their wants. [Such is the manner in which La Condamine leaves the causes of the Indian insensibility "to others."] Voracious gluttons, where means of satiety exist; when want enforces sobriety they patiently bear with abstinence, and seem to be void of care. Pusillanimous and timid in extreme, unless transported by drunkenness; inimical to toil; indifferent to every impulse of glory, honor, or gratitude; wholly engrossed and determined by the object of the moment, without concern for the future; destitute of foresight and reflection; and giving themselves up, when nothing prevents them, to a childish joy, which they manifest by leaping, and loud bursts of laughter, with no apparent object; they pass their lives without thought, and see old age advance, yet unremoved from childhood, and preserving all its faults. . . .

All the languages of South America with which I am acquainted, are very poor; . . . they are universally barren of terms for the expression of abstract or universal ideas, an evident proof of the slight progress of intellect among these people. Time, duration, space, entity, substance, matter, corporeity; these are words which, with many others, have no equivalent in their languages. . . . They have no words that correspond exactly with virtue, justice, liberty, gratitude, ingratitude; a fact with which it seems difficult to reconcile what Garcilasso [4] relates of the policy, industry, arts, government and genius of the ancient Peruvians. Unless the love he bore his country induced him to exaggerate, we must need allow that these people have generally degenerated from their ancestors. As for the other

[4] Garcilaso de la Vega, born in Cuzco, *ca.* 1539; died in Spain, 1616. His father was a Spaniard, his mother an Inca princess. His book *The Royal Commentaries of the Incas*, while undoubtedly inaccurate, has long been an important source of information on the Inca civilization.

nations in South America, they are not known to have ever emerged from their pristine barbarism.

In Borja, immediately below the Pongo de Manseriche, the French scientist came into contact with the Jesuit missionaries who passed him downriver from mission to mission. In his pedestrian fashion, he expressed gratitude to the missionaries and government officials who helped him descend the Amazon but has little to say about the country traversed except to throw in a number of such items as: "I found the latitude of Borja 4° 28′ S."

On July 19, he arrived at a place called Laguna, where he picked up a government official he had known in Ecuador and who was also headed for Europe. They embarked on July 23, after La Condamine had spent some days on astronomical observations in Laguna.

> Mr. Maldonado and myself left Laguna in two canoes from forty-two to forty-four feet long, by only three in breadth, each formed [of] the trunk of a single tree. . . .
>
> We resolved on continuing our voyage by night as well as by day, in order to overtake, if possible, the brigantines or large canoes dispatched annually by the Portuguese missionaries to Pará in quest of necessaries. During the day our Americans paddled along; only two of their number kept watch during the night, the one at the prow, the other at the stern, to preserve the boat in the current.

To relieve the tedium of the voyage, "in which the continued sameness of objects, however novel in themselves, tended to fatigue rather than please the eye," La Condamine kept his compass and watch out at all times and mapped the river as he proceeded downstream—a laudable effort which must have been interrupted for those stretches of river which were traveled at night. He describes the Indians, and their languages, encountered at various mission stations, and at one point he writes about the *"sarbacanas"* (blowguns, commonly called *"cerbatanas"*), and the arrow poisons which in those days intrigued virtually all scientific visitors to the Amazonian regions.

> The points of these diminutive [*cerbatana*] arrows, as well as those they shoot from their bows, are steeped in a poison of such activity, that when recent [fresh] it kills any animal from which

the instrument dipped in it may chance to draw blood. . . .
The antidote is salt, but of safer dependence sugar. In their
proper place, I shall notice the experiments I made to ascertain
the truth of this opinion, as well at Cayenne as at Leyden.

Diligently making astronomical observations and mapping
the river, La Condamine passed the mouth of the Napo and arrived, on August 1st, at a place called Pevas, which was the last
of the Spanish mission stations. (After his passage, the Spaniards
established a new station, Loreto, below Pevas, where Madame
Godin, more than 26 years later, was to be picked up by a boat,
specially sent by the king of Portugal to fetch her.)

> The name of Pevas, given to the town at which we landed, is
> that of an American nation, many individuals of which are
> inhabitants; but here are collected Americans of divers nations,
> each of which has a language peculiarly its own, as is common
> over the whole continent. It sometimes happens that a language
> is known to no more than two or three families, the wretched
> vestige of a tribe destroyed and devoured by some other: for
> notwithstanding there are at present no man-eaters along the
> banks of the Marañón, there yet exist inland, particularly
> towards the north, and along the Yapura, tribes of Americans
> who eat their prisoners. The majority of the new inhabitants of
> Pevas are savages, newly enticed from their woods, and yet un-
> converted to Christianity; the necessary preliminary to debrutal-
> izing them, a task of no small difficulty, not having yet been
> completed.

The travelers had now come very close to the present border
between Peru and Brazil, which was in those days the still
vaguely defined boundary between Spanish and Portuguese
possessions.

> From Pevas, the last of the missionary settlements belonging
> to the Spaniards, to St. Pablo, the first descending the river per-
> taining to the Portuguese, and in which a deputation from the
> order of Mount Carmel officiates, the distance is reckoned six or
> seven days' journey; this distance we travelled in three days and
> nights. In this interval no dwelling is found on the banks of
> the river. . . .
> On the immediate banks of the Marañón there is now no
> warlike tribe inimical to Europeans, all having either submitted
> or withdrawn themselves to the interior; still, in some places,

it would be hazardous to sleep on shore. But a few years back the son of a Spanish governor, whose father we knew at Quito, on descending this river, having ventured to land, was surprised in the woods, and massacred by savages from the interior, who by unlucky chance had stolen as far as the banks of the river.

The missionary at St. Pablo, apprised beforehand of our coming, had prepared for us a large canoe, with fourteen rowers and a master. He moreover afforded us, in another canoe, a Portuguese guide.

La Condamine now comments on the difference in standards of living between the Portuguese and Spanish regions. This difference stemmed from the fact that the Amazon had not yet been internationalized (see Chapter XX). The Portuguese, along the lower river, had direct water access to the Atlantic coast and thence to Europe. The Spaniards, not being permitted to travel freely through the Portuguese sections, had the infinitely more difficult task of transporting their goods over the Andes, from and to the Pacific coast.

At St. Pablo we began to notice, in lieu of rustic chapels, and bowers for dwellings made of reeds, houses and churches of stone, brick, and plaster, neatly whitened. We were likewise agreeably surprised at meeting here and there amid the deserts with native women all clad in Brittany linen, coffers with locks and keys, iron utensils, needles, knives, scissors, combs, and a variety of little European articles imported hither annually by the natives, who purchase them in a barter for the wild cocoa they gather on the banks of the river, and which they transport to Pará.

In five days' hard voyaging, they traversed the territories held by the Portuguese Carmelite missionaries, dotted by six mission stations which had first been established by Father Samuel Fritz but had later been taken from the Spaniards by the Portuguese. All the way, while speculating somewhat vaguely on reports of gold and the El Dorado legend, La Condamine was also busily asking questions about the Amazons.

In the course of our navigation, we inquired of the people of various nations, if they had any knowledge of those warlike women which Orellana pretended to have encountered; and if it were true they lived apart from men, receiving them but once a year, as is related by Father Acuña, in whose narrative this forms a part singularly curious, and well worthy of attention. We uniformly were answered that they had heard their fathers speak of such things, and repeated many particulars which it were tedious to detail, but which tended to confirm the fact that in this continent did exist a republic of women, who lived entirely separate from the men, and who withdrew towards the north into the interior, either by the Black River or some other which flows on the same side into the Marañón.

After citing a number of picturesque reports, oral as well as written, and stating his conviction that "if not all, yet the majority of the natives of South America are liars, credulous, and prone to the marvellous," La Condamine carefully states that there must be *something* to all that talk about South American Amazons. Mentioning Amazons who had been reported in Asia and Africa as well as in America, he concludes:

It must have been in America, where the frequent wanderings of the women, who often accompany their husbands to war, and the hardships of their domestic life, might not only originate such an idea, but likewise furnish them with numberless opportunities for shaking off the yoke of their tyrants, of forming an independent establishment, and of avoiding that vilifying condition of slavery, so little removed from that of beasts of burden, in which they had previously lived. Such a resolution once formed, it would neither be more extraordinary, nor more difficult to put into execution than similar plans, in the European colonies of America; whence slaves, who weary of ill-treatment, or disgusted with their condition, so frequently fly to the woods, either in bands, or where no associates are found, alone; thus passing years, and oftentimes their whole lives, in the solitude of the unbounded wilderness.

On arriving at the Río Negro, the territory of the Manáos Indians, La Condamine speculates at some length on the existence of the Cassiquiare River (see Chapter XVII) and El Dorado, concluding that the first was real and the second an invention.

On August 28, they landed at the "Portuguese fort Pauxis," today's Obidos, where the Amazon River narrows down to "135 toises," [5,631 feet—a little more than a mile]. Here, still more than 600 miles from the sea, La Condamine observed the tides for the first time, the water level rising and falling "visibly every twelve hours." The travelers stayed at Pauxis four days as guests of the commandante.

> The positive orders of His Portuguese Majesty, favorable in the extreme to my safety and comfort, were known at every station before I arrived, and insured the most obliging treatment, not to myself alone, but to all who accompanied me; a treatment continued through the whole of my journey to Pará, for which I am under the highest obligation to a minister who loves the sciences, who duly values their utility, and whose careful vigilance was ever on the alert to provide, during our long sojourn at Quito, for all the wants of our numerous companions.

About 16 hours after leaving the fort:

> We arrived opposite the fortress of Topayos [today's Santarém at the mouth of the Tapajoz River], at the entrance of the river of similar name; this again is a river of the first order; it descends from the mines of Brazil, crossing unexplored countries inhabited by wild and warlike nations, whom the missionary Jesuits are employed in civilizing. . . .
>
> Among the Topayos those green stones are more common than with other people, known by the name of Amazonian, of unknown origin, and which formerly were in high request for their supposed efficacy in curing the stone, nephritic colic, and epilepsy, and on which a treatise, under the title of *Pierre Divine,* or the Divine Stone, has been published. The stones differ nothing in colour and in hardness from oriental jade; and as they resist the file, it is unconceivable how the ancient Americans were enabled to fashion them as they did into the shape of various animals.[5]

September 4th:

> Began to distinguish the mountains in the north, ten or twelve leagues inland. . . . To these mountains it was, according to tradition in the country, that the Amazons withdrew. Another tradition, no less general, but of the truth of which less contestible evidence is said to be afforded, reputes these mountains to abound in mines of various metals. This last statement, however, though of a nature to excite the attention of

[5] See also Chapter XVII.

a greater number of inquisitive persons, is, nevertheless, no better substantiated than the other.[6]

On September 6th they reached the mouth of the Xingu, below which "the breadth of this [the Amazon] is so considerable, that . . . the spectator on the one bank would be unable to descry that opposite to him." On September 9th they arrived at the fortress of Curupa, where they were held up for three days of gala entertainment.

After leaving Curupa, La Condamine describes the famous Amazonian electric eel.

> In the neighborhood of Pará I saw a kind of lamprey, the body of which, like that of the common species, is pierced by many openings, but, at the same time, it possesses the same faculty with the torpido; whoever presumes to touch it with the hand, or even with the end of a stick, experiences a painful numbness in the arm, and a shock, which is said at times to be so powerful, as to lay one prostrate. Of this last asserted fact I had no ocular proof.

The following several pages of his account are given to discussions of the country's numerous turtles; barbasco, the poisonous plant with which the Indians stun fish to catch them; crocodiles and the dangers from them; Amazonian "tigers" of which he had heard vague rumors; the "elk," which is La Condamine's odd name for the tapir; the many monkeys; snakes, of which he erroneously reported that no poisonous species existed in the Amazonian regions, but among which the anaconda (boa constrictor) impressed him greatly; worms which infest human beings; vampire bats; and numerous birds.

> On reaching Pará on the 27th, we found in readiness for us a very commodious and richly furnished house, with a garden commanding the sea, and precisely situate as I wished, for the observations I had to make.

The scientist left Pará (today's Belém) on December 29, headed for Cayenne, whence he planned to take a ship for his native France. He arrived in Cayenne on February 26, 1744, after a sea-land voyage which offered certain misadventures and aggravating delays. Since his young cinchona trees had died dur-

[6] The Guiana mountains are now known to be highly mineralized, yielding gold and diamonds, as well as rich iron ores in their Venezuelan north.

ing the voyage, he distributed seeds of the cinchona in Cayenne, but discovered that they did not germinate. He spent some five months in French Guiana, waiting for a ship, and finally landed at Amsterdam on November 30th, where he was delayed two months, waiting "for the passports requisite to cross the low countries. . . . On the 23rd of February 1745, I arrived in Paris, after a lapse of ten years from my departure thence."

M. and Mme. Godin

If La Condamine's account of his journey across the continent is on the whole a rather pedestrian tale of travel through country which, while it had by that time become quite thoroughly familiar to the Spaniards and the Portuguese, was still so strange to northwestern Europe as to be virtually "unexplored," the ensuing voyage of his colleague's wife, Madame Godin, ranks among the epics of Amazonian travel.

The famous "Letter to M. de la Condamine from M. Godin des Odonais," giving details of those travels, was dated July 28, 1773, and begins as follows:

> Sir, You require of me a narrative of the travels of my spouse along the Amazons river, the same route I followed after you. The rumours which have reached your ears of the dangers to which she was exposed, and which she alone of eight persons surmounted, augment your curiosity. I had resolved never to speak of them again, so painful to me was the recollection of them; but, as an old companion in your travels, a distinction which I prize, I cannot refuse in turn for the interest you take in our welfare, and the marks of friendship you have shown me, to give you the satisfaction you require.
>
> We landed at Rochelle on the 26th of June last, after a passage from Cayenne, effected in sixty-five days.
>
> You will recall that the last time I had the honour of seeing you in 1742, previous to your leaving Quito, I told you that I reckoned on taking the same road that you were about to do, along the river of the Amazons, as much owing to the wish I had of knowing this way as to insure for my wife the most commodious mode of travelling, by saving her a long journey overland, through a mountainous country, in which the only conveyance

is on mules. . . . My wife was exceedingly solicitous of seeing France, but her repeated pregnancies, for several years after your departure, prevented my consent to her being exposed to the fatigues incident on so long a voyage.

Near the end of 1748, Godin had word that his father had died, apparently in French Guiana. He therefore, and in order to set his family affairs in order, left Quito in March, 1749, "leaving Mad. Godin at that time pregnant." Arriving in Cayenne after some six weeks of travel, he "immediately wrote to M. Rouillé, then minister of the navy, entreating him to procure me passports and recommendations to the court of Portugal, to enable me to ascend the Amazons, for the purpose of proceeding to my family, and bringing it back with me by the same channel." M. Godin, however, had to wait considerable time in Guiana, writing letters constantly, before the required permits and means of transportation arrived. Not until November, 1765, sixteen and a half years after he had parted from his wife and children in Riobamba, an Ecuadorean town south of Quito, did "a decked galliot arrive at Cayenne, equipped at Pará by order of the King of Portugal, . . . instructed to bring me to Pará, thence transport me up the river as high as the first Spanish settlement, to wait there till I returned with my family, and ultimately re-conduct me to Cayenne." He boarded the ship and they proceeded to the French port of Oyapoc to pick up some property which Godin had left there. But there the Frenchman "fell sick and even dangerously so." The captain waited six weeks for him, but Godin was still too sick to travel. He therefore sent a trusted friend, one Tristan D'Oreasaval, in his place, with a packet of letters, one to his wife, informing her that a Portuguese vessel would be waiting for her at the border between Portuguese and Spanish territories, and several to the authorities and Jesuits in Quito, asking them to provide Madame Godin with the transportation required to reach the Portuguese ship.

He was to wait until 1770, five years after he had dispatched his friend Tristan to fetch her, and more than twenty since their parting in Riobamba, before he saw his wife again. By then she was alone. In the course of her epic voyage down the Amazon, all of her travel companions had died under terrible circumstances. Curiously, M. Godin's letter made no mention of any

children that might have resulted from his wife's many pregnancies. Whether their mother had left them behind, or they,
too, had died in the course of the voyage, is not known.

Disobeying his instructions, Tristan, on arriving upriver at
the first Spanish mission, gave the packet of letters to the wrong
Jesuit; they traveled from hand to hand, from priest to priest,
but never did reach their proper destinations. Nobody ever discovered what became of them. Meanwhile, however, rumors
began to circulate in Quito and Riobamba of the arrival of a
Portuguese ship for Madame Godin. She sent a trusted Negro
slave over the Andes and downriver to check on them. He returned after considerable difficulty, mission unaccomplished.
She sent him again, and this time he returned after talking to
Tristan in the Spanish river mission of Loreto, informing her
that her transportation was indeed waiting near the Spanish-
Portuguese border. All that, of course, took time, while settling
her affairs, selling the Godin properties in Riobamba, and getting under way took more time. Not until October 1st, 1769,
did she finally set out on her tragic journey, having sent her
father ahead to make arrangements for her.

> M. de Grandmaison, my father-in-law, went on before to
> obtain every possible accommodation for his daughter on the
> road, to the point of embarkation beyond the great Cordillera.
> He at first met with obstacles from the president and captain-
> general of the province of Quito; for you, Sir, are aware that
> the passage by the Amazons is forbidden by the Spanish court;
> but these difficulties were soon overcome.

The official papers with which M. de Grandmaison had been
provided were too powerful to be overlooked.

> M. de Grandmaison, who preceded [his daughter and her
> companions] a month on the way, found the village of Canelos
> well inhabited, and immediately embarked, continuing his
> journey, to prepare everything necessary for the transport of
> his daughter at each stage of her way.

Canelos was the point at which Madame Godin was to change
from land travel to river travel; her father had there made provisions for canoes to pick up her and her companions.

When she left her home in Riobamba, the Frenchwoman was

accompanied by her two brothers, who were headed for Europe, one of whom took with him "a son about nine or ten years of age, whom he wished to educate in Europe." They were joined by a "M.R.," whose full name Godin never mentioned, "who reported himself to be a French physician, coming from Upper Peru, and on his way to Panama and Porto Bello, in view of passing thence to Santo Domingo." He changed his mind when he learned "that a lady of Riobamba was on the point of setting out for the Amazon River, and embarking thence in a vessel equipped by the order of his Portuguese Majesty." On the urging of her brothers, who saw advantage in having a physician in the party, Madame Godin agreed to take him with her. Later in his letter, her husband mentions "another Frenchman of the party," without saying who he was and where she had picked him up. Beside these, Madame Godin was accompanied by her faithful Negro "and three female mulattos or Americans."

The journey over the mountains to the river settlement of Canelos was sufficiently difficult.

> On her departure my wife was escorted by thirty-one American natives to carry herself and baggage. You know, Sir, that this road, the same pursued by M. de Maldonado, is impractical even for mules; that those capable effect the passage on foot, but that others are carried. The Americans who escorted Madame Godin . . . scarcely reached Canelos before they retraced their steps, either from dread of the air being infected, or from apprehension of being obliged to embark, a matter obnoxious in the extreme to individuals who had perhaps never seen a canoe in their lives but at a distance.

The Indians' fear of "the air being infected" stemmed from the fact that, between the time of M. de Grandmaison's passage and his daughter's arrival, the settlement of Canelos had been almost entirely deserted because of a sudden epidemic of smallpox.

> What under such circumstances was to be done? Had my wife been able to return, yet the desire of reaching the vessel waiting her,[7] together with her anxiety to rejoin a husband from whom she had been parted twenty years, were incentives powerful

[7] By this time, the Portuguese vessel, of the existence of which Madame Godin had never had sure confirmation, would have been waiting for its passenger well over three years.

enough to make her, in the peculiar circumstances in which she was placed, brave even greater obstacles.

In the village only two Indians remained free from contagion; these had no boat, but they engaged to construct one and pilot it to the mission of Andoas, about twelve days' journey below. . . . She paid them beforehand; the canoe being finished, they all departed from Canelos. After navigating the river two days, on the succeeding morning the pilots absconded; the unfortunate party embarked without anyone to steer the boat, and passed the day without accident.

The next day, at noon, they discovered a canoe in a small port adjoining a leaf-built hut, in which was a native recovering from illness, who consented to pilot them. On the third day of his voyage, while stooping over to recover the hat of Mr. K., which had fallen into the water, the poor man fell overboard, and, not having sufficient strength to reach the shore, was drowned. Behold the canoe, again without a steersman, abandoned to individuals perfectly ignorant of managing it; in consequence it was shortly overset, which obliged the party to land, and build themselves a hut.

The French "physician," Mr. K., now took the canoe and "set off with another Frenchman of the party, and the faithful Negro belonging to Madame Godin, taking special care to carry his effects with him." They proposed to proceed to the mission at Andoas, "now but from five to six days' journey" away, promising that

within a fortnight a canoe should be forwarded [to the stranded party] with a proper complement of natives. . . . [But] the fortnight expired, and even five and twenty days, when, giving over all hopes, they constructed a raft on which they ventured themselves, with their provisions and property. The raft, badly framed, struck against the branch of a sunken tree, and overset, all their effects perishing into the water. Thanks to the little breadth of the river in this place,[8] no one was drowned, Madame Godin being happily saved, after twice sinking, by her brothers.

Now the gallant Frenchwoman and her companions were in a truly difficult position, in apparently uninhabited country. They decided to proceed overland, along the river's banks.

[8] They had not yet reached the mainstream of the Amazon, being still on the Bobonasa, a small tributary of the Pastaza.

How difficult of effect this enterprise, you, Sir, are well aware, who know how thickly the banks of the rivers are beset with trees, underwood, herbage and lianas, and that it is often necessary to cut one's way. They returned to their hut, took what provisions they had left behind, and began their journey.

They grew tired of following the banks of the twisting river and foolishly struck inland, into the dense forest. They were not woodsmen and tried to make their way through country where even the greatest experts find it difficult to keep a course. "In a few days they lost themselves."

That was the end of all members of the party except Madame Godin.

Wearied with so many days' march in midst of woods, incommodious even for those accustomed to them, their feet torn by thorns and brambles, their provisions exhausted, and dying with thirst, they were fain to subsist on a few seed, wild fruit, and the palm cabbage. At length, oppressed with hunger and thirst, with lassitude and loss of strength, they seated themselves on the ground without the power of rising, and, waiting thus the approach of death, in three or four days expired one after the other.

Madame Godin, stretched on the ground by the side of the corpses of her brothers and other companions, stupefied, delirious, and tormented with choaking [sic] thirst, at length assumed resolution and strength enough to drag herself along in search of the salvation which providentially awaited her. Such was her deplorable condition she was without shoes, and her clothes all torn to rags: she cut the shoes off her brothers' feet, and fastened the soles on her own. It was about the period between the 25th and 30th of December 1769 that this unfortunate party (at least seven of the number of them) perished in this miserable manner.

Madame Godin was "ten days alone in the wood, two, awaiting death by the side of her brothers, the other eight wandering at random. . . . On the second day's march, . . . she found water, and the succeeding day some wild fruit and fresh eggs, of what bird she knew not, but which, by her description, I conjecture to have been a species of partridge."

(There speaks the true scientist. His wife had barely managed to save her life by devouring a few eggs, which "with the greatest of difficulty was she able to swallow, the aesophagus, owing to the want of aliment, having become so much parched and strait-ened," and he wants to know what kind of a bird had laid them.)

It was on the eighth or ninth day, according to Madame Godin, after leaving the dreadful scene of the death of her companions, that she found herself on the banks of the Bobonasa. At daybreak she heard a noise at about two hundred paces from her.

Badly frightened, she was on the point of fleeing back into the jungle, but she changed her mind on realizing that "nothing worse could possibly befall her, than to continue in her present state and that alarm was therefore childish." On proceeding to the river, she "perceived two native Americans launching a boat into the stream." They were Indians who had fled from Canelos and were now en route to Andoas.

They received my wife on board with kindness truly affec-tionate, shewed every attention to her wants, and conducted her to that village. Here she might have stopped some days to rest herself and recruit her strength, but, indignant at the conduct of the missionary at whose mercy she was left, she resolved on making no stay at Andoas, nor would even have stopped a single night had it been possible to be avoided.

The Jesuits had recently been evicted from the country, and replaced by "secular clergy, . . . of which class was the individ-ual who officiated as missionary at Andoas."

Madame Godin, stripped of almost everything, not knowing otherwise how to testify her gratitude to the two Americans who had saved her life, took from her neck two chains of gold, such as are usually worn in this country, of about four ounces weight, and gave one to each of them, whose admiration at the richness of the present equalled that they would have experienced had the heavens opened before them; but the missionary, in her very presence, took possession of the chains, and gave the poor Americans in lieu about three or four yards of coarse cotton cloth. . . . Conduct thus infamous exasperated my wife to such a degree that she instantly demanded a canoe and men, and the next day set out for Laguna. A female American at Andoas made a cotton petticoat for her, which she sent to pay for immediately on reaching Laguna, and which she preserves with care, with the soles of the shoes of her brothers, converted by her into sandals;—mournful tokens, rendered dear to me as they are to her herself.

Madame Godin stayed at Laguna six weeks, recovering her strength. She was joined there by the Frenchman, Mr. R., who had earlier caused all the tragic trouble by his failure to send a canoe back from Andoas. Her "faithful Negro," who had made a search for her and had actually found the putrefying corpses of her companions, had decided that she was dead and returned to Quito. The Frenchwoman and Mr. R., who returned to her some minor items of her property which had been entrusted to the Negro, had a stormy session. She blamed all her losses on him, but the head of the Laguna mission, M. Romero, who treated her with extreme kindness and "to whom she could refuse nothing," interceded for him. After he "represented to her that, if she abandoned Mr. R., his condition would be deplorable," she relented and agreed to let him accompany her to Cayenne, where the man was to have several more stormy sessions with her husband.

M. Romero dispatched Madame Godin downstream in a canoe. Various missionaries, hearing of her imminent arrival, sent her canoes loaded with the best available foods and other things. It appears that the Portuguese "galliot" which had been sent for her three years earlier, was still on the river, together with M. Tristan, who had so dismally botched the matter of the dispatches to her and the Quito authorities. The commander worked his vessel upriver to the Spanish mission at Loreto, "where he received her on board."

> I learn from her, that from that instant till she reached Oyapok, throughout a course of nearly a thousand leagues, she wanted for nothing to render her comfortable, not even the nicest delicacies, and such as could not be expected in the country; wine and liquors which she never uses, fish, game, etc., were supplied by two canoes which preceded the galliot. The governor of Pará, moreover, had sent orders to the chief part of the stages at which they had to halt, with additional refreshments.

In French Guiana, M. Godin felt that he had to settle accounts with Tristan.

Here I was engaged in a law-suit. Tristan demanded of me the wages I had promised him of sixty livres per month. I offered to pay him for eighteen months, the utmost time the voyage could have required, had he strictly followed his instructions. The sentence pronounced by the superior council of Cayenne condemned him to render me an account of from seven to eight thousand francs, the value of the effects I had committed to his care, deducting one thousand and eighty for the eighteen months' salary I had offered him; but the wretch, after dealing treacherously with me as he had done; after causing the death of eight persons, including the American who was drowned, and all the misfortunes which befell my wife; in short, after dissipating the whole of the effects I had entrusted him with, proved insolvent; and, for my part, I judged it unnecessary to augment the losses I had already sustained by having to support him in prison.

In the last paragraph of M. Godin's letter, it appears that his wife's father had come down the Amazon with her and proceeded with them to France, where they finally arrived in 1773, after 38 years' absence.

M. de Grandmaison had originally no intention of proceeding to France, but merely meant, by his voyage, to see his daughter safe on board the Portuguese vessel; but finding old age creep on apace, and penetrated with the most lively grief at the intelligence of the sad death of his children, he abandoned all and embarked with her. . . . For my wife, however, solicitous all about to enliven her spirits, she is constantly subject to melancholy, her horrible misfortunes being ever present to her imagination. How much did it cost me to obtain from her the relations requisite for the judges in the course of my lawsuit! I can even readily conceive that, from delicacy, she has abstained from entering into many details, the remembrance of which she is anxious to lose, and which, known, could but add to the pain I feel. Nay, she was even anxious that I should not prosecute Tristan, compassionating even that wretch; thus following the gentle impulse of a heart inspired with the purest benevolence, and the genuine principles of religion!

Determining the length of the meter, a little longer than the English yard, was a costly matter for some of the people involved.

BARON VON HUMBOLDT

L A CONDAMINE was the first Amazonian explorer to travel primarily in quest of detailed knowledge of the regions traversed. Of the scientists who followed him, Baron Alexander von Humboldt was by far the greatest. Indeed, his descriptive discourses on the regions in which he traveled, illuminating those regions from dozens of points of view, plus speculative departures into the meanings of history from the viewpoint of the "natural philosopher," have never been equaled, before or since his day, in the history of Latin-American exploration. The restless, all-encompassing mind with which he carried out his work as a traveler resulted in so much knowledge which was "new," especially in non-Iberian Europe, that he ranks as one of the greatest tropical explorers of all time. Even today the conscientious observer, traveling in country where Humboldt had worked more than 16 decades earlier, can hardly hope to attain optimum understanding of his field of operations without first reading the great German's many-sided treatises on it.

Baron Friedrich Heinrich Alexander von Humboldt—scholar, naturalist, scientist, and diplomat—was born in Berlin, Germany, in 1769, in an age when North European science was going through one of its great eras of "awakening." Very early he demonstrated a remarkable aptitude for science—not any one branch of that specialized approach to knowledge, but all branches, within the framework of a point of view in which all science, being closely interrelated, is philosophically the sphere of every scientist. His early scientific work in Germany included investigations in chemistry, physics, botany, as well as in geology, which he related specifically to mining. Indeed, he never considered himself as a "pure" scientist who regarded the quest for knowledge sufficient unto itself. Behind all of his investigations was always the question of how human societies might, immediately or eventually, profit from them in "practical" ways.

The account of his travels cited below was published in London in 1852, under the title *Personal Narrative of Travels to the Equinoctial Regions of America, during the years 1799–1804, by Alexander von Humboldt and Aimé Bonpland; Written in French by Alexander von Humboldt; Translated and edited by Thomasina Ross.* In his introduction, Humboldt said:

> I had in view a two-fold purpose in the travels of which I now publish the historical narrative. I wished to make known the countries I had visited; and to collect such facts as are fitted to elucidate a science of which we as yet possess scarcely the outline, and which has been vaguely denominated Natural History of the World, Theory of the Earth, or Physical Geography. The last of these two objects seemed to me to be the most important. I was passionately devoted to botany and certain parts of zoology, and I flattered myself that our investigations might add some new species to those already known, both in the animal and vegetable kingdoms; but preferring the connection of facts which have been long observed, to the knowledge of insulated facts, although new, the discovery of an unknown genus seemed to me far less interesting than an observation on the geographical relations of the vegetable world, on the migrations of the social plants, and the limits of the height which their different tribes attain on the flanks of the Cordilleras.

Because of his widely ranging interests and his encompassing philosophy, which included both skills and interests in such widely varied subjects as geology, meteorology, astronomy, botany, zoology, and terrestrial magnetism, Humboldt has come to be regarded as the "Father of Physical Geography and Meteorology." The present editor, himself an adherent of the view that there is only one geography, namely "human geography expressed in terms of regionalism," considers the term too narrow. With all his interests and in all his descriptions, Humboldt was first and foremost concerned with people, with their histories, ethnology, nature, and problems within the environment where he found them. He deserves to be known, simply but far more broadly, as the "Father of Modern Geography."

With help from Spain, Humboldt and Bonpland undertook their American travels in 1799, returning to Europe in 1804 after working in Tenerife, Venezuela, Cuba, Colombia, Ecuador, Peru, and Mexico, Humboldt ending his American work with a brief visit to the United States. Later scientific voyages, interspersed with diplomatic missions and periods in Paris devoted to writing popular and scientific reports on his fieldwork, took him to Italy and large parts of the Russian Empire, including Siberia.

His voluminous writings included 30 magnificent volumes plus a great body of other scientific contributions, and made him "the most famous man in Europe after Napoleon Bonaparte." He died in 1859. The present account deals with his famous travels along the Cassiquiare, his description of which is still standard. Humboldt is widely credited with being the "discoverer" of that river, though he was far too good a historian ever personally to lay claim to that distinction.

The Cassiquiare

The work of that indefatigable El Dorado seeker, Antonio de Berrios, as presented in English by that indefatigable pirate of ships and ideas, Sir Walter Raleigh, had given to all of western Europe (and not merely to Spain) a clear idea of the lower Orinoco River, its nature, its course to the Atlantic Ocean, and its strategic importance. However, in the course of centuries one report after another reached Europe to the effect that the upper Orinoco behaved in a strange and unprecedented manner. Reports began to filter out that the great river flows not only directly into the Atlantic, but indirectly into the Amazon as well. Insistent "rumors," known today to be true, had it that after rising somewhere in the Parima Mountains in one of South America's least accessible regions, and after flowing about 150 miles in a general northwesterly direction, the river bifurcated itself, one part flowing approximately southwest into the upper Río Negro and thence eventually into the Amazon, while the mainstream continued northwest and later, in a great sweep, north and then east to the Atlantic. The branch connecting the Orinoco with the Río Negro was called the Cassiquiare. Some called it a "river" and others a "canal," though many others doubted that it existed at all. While Indians, missionaries, Portuguese slavers, soldiers, and many others traversed the Cassiquiare for centuries, without knowing that they were making exploration history, educated men, especially in England and France, found it difficult to believe in so strange a phenomenon.

Baron von Humboldt settled the controversy once and for all by traveling through the Cassiquiare from the Río Negro to the Orinoco, determining the astronomical coordinates of its two ends and several interior points, and describing it to the world in his inimitable, all-encompassing manner. From the beginning, he was not among the European scientists whose skepticism about the Cassiquiare's very existence stemmed from the fact that they knew of no similar phenomenon anywhere on earth. On the matter of possibility, he wrote as follows:

> When immense rivers may be considered as composed of several parallel furrows of unequal depth; when these rivers are not enclosed in valleys; and when the interior of a great continent is as flat as the shores of the sea with us; the ramifications, the bifurcations, the inter-lacings in the form of network, must be infinitely multiplied.

Humboldt himself made no claim of "discovery." In dealing with the controversy in his book, he cited pros and cons as advanced by a number of authorities, and mentioned Father Fritz and Padre Gumilla—the outstanding chronicler of the Orinoco who spent years on the lower river, as far up as the Maipure rapids—as being firmly convinced that the Cassiquiare did not exist. Near the end of his life, however, Gumilla changed his mind, as a result of meeting Father Manuel Roman, who had actually traversed the route and of whom Humboldt wrote:

> He was the first white man who went from the Río Negro, consequently from the basin of the Amazon, without passing his boats over any portage, to the basin of the Lower Orinoco.

Roman made his voyage in 1744. Humboldt's error in calling him the "first white man" to have made it, is revealed by Humboldt himself, when he describes the activities of Portuguese slavers and says:

> The incursions undertaken from the middle of the seventeenth century, to procure slaves, had gradually led the Portuguese from the Río Negro, by the Cassiquiare, to the bed of a great river, which they did not know to be the Upper Orinoco. . . . From the year 1737 these visits of the Portuguese to the Upper Orinoco became very frequent.

La Condamine, working along the Amazon in 1743, was greatly interested in the question of whether or not the Cassiquiare existed, and tireless in his efforts to throw light on the problem by asking innumerable questions. His mounting conviction that the Cassiquiare was a geographic fact was clinched by news of Father Roman's voyage.

> The tidings of this extraordinary passage spread with such rapidity that La Condamine was able to announce it at a public sitting of the Academy, seven months after the return of Father Roman to Pararruma. "The communication between the Orinoco and the Amazon," said he, "recently averred, may pass so much more for a discovery in geography, as, although the junction of these two rivers is marked on the old maps . . ., it had been suppressed by all the modern geographers in their new maps, as if in concert. This is not the first time that what is positive fact has been thought fabulous, that the spirit of criticism has been pushed too far, and that this communication has been treated as chimerical by those who ought to have been better informed."

Humboldt goes on to say:

> Since the voyage of Father Roman in 1774,[1] no person in Spanish Guiana, or on the coasts of Cumana and Caracas, has admitted a doubt of the existence of the Cassiquiare and the bifurcation of the Orinoco.

Fascinated by the controversy, Humboldt planned his Orinoco River trip of 1800 in such a manner as to include a voyage from the Río Negro to the Orinoco via the Cassiquiare. Ascending the Orinoco, he and Bonpland picked up a priest, Father

---

[1] Obviously a misprint for 1744.

Bernardo Zea, at Atures, on the middle stretch, and proceeded to San Fernando de Atabapo. They ascended the Atabapo River and crossed over to the Río Negro via the famous Yavita-Pimichin portage, descending the Negro through the settlement of Maroa as far as San Carlos.

The Amazons

In writing of his work on the upper Río Negro, and in line with his habit of repeatedly moving from observed facts to historic accounts, and thence into speculations of his own, Humboldt had the following to say about the Amazons who had agitated European scholarship since being first reported by Orellana:

> We found in the possession of the Indians of the Río Negro some of those green stones, known by the name of "Amazon stones," because the natives pretend, according to an ancient tradition, that they come from the country "of the women without husbands, . . . or women living alone."

He discussed at great length the fame of the green stones, their possible geologic origins, and their value in trade because of their reputed medicinal powers.

> In the midst of enlightened Europe, on occasion of a warm contest respecting native bark, a few years ago, the green stones of the Orinoco were gravely proposed as a powerful febrifuge. After this appeal to the credulity of Europeans, we cannot be surprised to learn that the Spanish planters share the predilection of the Indians for these amulets, and that they are sold at a very considerable price.

Discussion of the green stones led Humboldt into discussion of the Amazons from whom the stones were supposed to have come. At the start he makes clear his own conviction that many of the marvels reported by early explorers in the Amazon basin were simply marvels which had been reported much earlier by the ancient Greeks. Believing the Greeks implicitly, medieval Europe had—after Columbus' epoch-making voyages—transplanted those marvels to the New World.

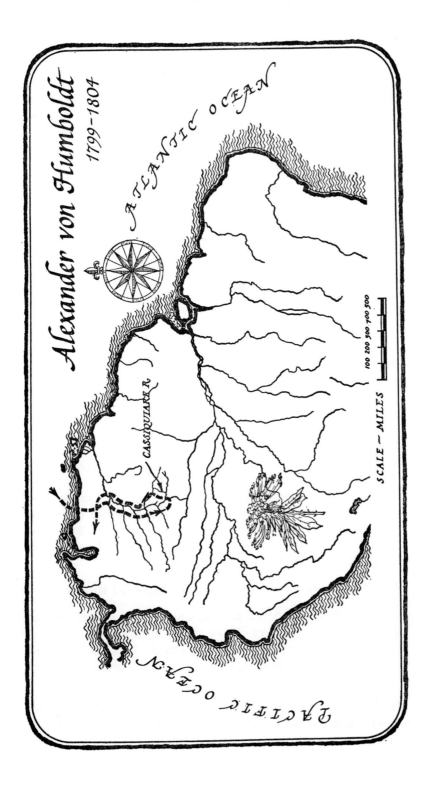

Alexander von Humboldt
1799-1804

ATLANTIC OCEAN

CASSIQUIARE R.

SCALE ~ MILES
100 200 300 400 500

PACIFIC OCEAN

In perusing the works of Vespucci, Fernando Columbus, Geraldini, Oviedo, and Pietro Martyr, we recognize this tendency of the writers of the sixteenth century to find among the newly discovered nations all that the Greeks have related to us of the first age of the world, and of the manners of the barbarous Scythians and Africans. But if Oviedo, in addressing his letters to Cardinal Bembo, thought fit to flatter the taste of a man so familiar with the study of antiquity, Sir Walter Raleigh had a less poetic aim. He sought to fix the attention of Queen Elizabeth on the great empire of Guiana, the conquest of which he proposed. . . . Nothing could be better adapted to strike the imagination of Queen Elizabeth, than the warlike republic of women without husbands, who resisted the Castilian heroes. Such were the motives which prompted exaggeration on the part of those writers who have given most reputation to the Amazons of America; but these motives do not, I think, suffice for entirely rejecting a tradition which is spread among various nations having no communication one with another.

In his account of his travels, after mentioning La Condamine's preoccupation with the legend of the Amazons, together with a somewhat plausible account of their actual existence, which came to light 30 years after La Condamine's voyage, Humboldt goes on:

What must we conclude from this narration . . . ? Not that there are Amazons on the banks of the Cuchivero, but that women in different parts of America, wearied of the state of slavery in which they were held by the men, united themselves together; that the desire of preserving the independence rendered them warriors; and that they received visits from a neighboring and friendly horde.

Humboldt passed three nights at San Carlos del Río Negro.

I count the nights because I watched during the greater part of them in the hope of seizing the moment of the passage of some star over the meridian. That I might have nothing to reproach myself with, I kept the instruments always ready for an observation.

In the course of his voyage of 1932, for the study of the earth's magnetism, the editor of this volume had the same trouble at San Carlos. The sky was so overcast, day and night, that astronomical observations could be made only by accident and after long waiting.

San Carlos, a little below the confluence of the Negro and the Cassiquiare, was Humboldt's point of departure for the latter river. If he was in no way the river's "discoverer," he was the first to ascertain its precise location in terms of latitudes and longitudes and to substitute meticulous, far-ranging observations, descriptions, and speculative discussions for mere bald announcements. However, at the start he had grave misgivings as to the wisdom of making the Cassiquiare voyage at all.

On the 10th of May, our canoe being ready before sunrise, we embarked to go up the Río Negro as far as the mouth of the Cassiquiare, and to devote ourselves to researches on the real course of that river. . . . The morning was fine; but, in proportion as the heat augmented, the sky became obscured. . . . We were every day more grieved at the aspect of the cloudy sky. M. Bonpland was losing by this excessive humidity the plants he had collected; and I, for my part, was afraid lest I should again find the fogs of the Río Negro in the valley of the Cassiquiare. . . . The important point of our voyage was confined . . . to fixing by astronomical observations the course of the Cassiquiare, and particularly the point of its entrance into the Río Negro, and that of the bifurcation of the Orinoco. Without a sight of the sun and the stars this object would be frustrated, and we should have exposed ourselves in vain to long and painful privations.

We passed between the islands of Zaruma and Mini, or Mibita . . . : and, after having ascended the rapids of the Piedra de Uinumane, we entered the Río Cassiquiare at the distance of eight miles from the small fort of San Carlos. . . . It much resembles the Río Negro in the general aspects of its landscape. The trees of the forest, as in the basin of the latter river, advance as far as the beach, and there form a thick coppice; but the Cassiquiare has white waters,[2] and more frequently changes its direction. Its breadth, near the rapids of Uinumane, almost surpasses that of the Río Negro. I found it everywhere from two

[2] Amazonian rivers are generally divided into "white water" and "black water" rivers. The former arise in mountains and carry loads of silt which give them a light, brownish color. The latter arise in lowlands and carry no silt. The vegetable matters suspended in their otherwise clear waters give them a somber, dark-brown color which on cloudy days appears to be a shining black. The Orinoco is a white-water river, the Río Negro, as its name indicates, is black.

hundred and fifty to two hundred and eighty toises [1,500 to 1,781 feet], as far as above Vasiva. . . .

The mission of San Francisco Solano, situated on the left bank of the Cassiquiare, was founded, as were most of the Christian settlements south of the Great Cataracts of the Orinoco, not by monks, but by military authority.

Here Humboldt gives a detailed and lively account of the history of the region's early settlement. Elsewhere, on several occasions, he deals with the encroachments of the Portuguese slavers up the Río Negro, of the resulting boundary disputes, and of the efforts made by the Spanish to stop their Portuguese enemies by establishing fortified military points here and there, which also served as mission stations and the nuclei of settlements.[3]

At this point Humboldt indulges in an account of the many live birds, monkeys, and other animals which M. Bonpland had acquired, and which made of their large boat a veritable floating zoo.

Most of our animals were confined in small wicker cages; others ran at full liberty in all parts of the boat. At the approach of rain the macaws sent forth noisy cries, the toucan wanted to reach the shore to fish, and the little monkeys (the titis) went in search of Father Zea, to take shelter in the large sleeves of his Franciscan habit. These incidents sometimes amused us so much that we forgot the torments of the mosquitos. At night we placed a leather case (petaca), containing our provisions, in the centre; then our instruments and the cages of our animals; our hammocks were suspended around the cages, and beyond were those of the Indians. The exterior circle was formed by fires which are lighted to keep off the jaguars. Such was the order of our encampment on the banks of the Cassiquiare.

On the night of May 11th, a little above San Francisco Solano, Humboldt did manage an astronomical observation.

This observation made known to us at the same time, with sufficient precision for the purposes of geography, the positions of the mouth of the Pacimoni, of the fortress of San Carlos, and

---

[3] In 1932, the editor saw a number of old cannon, relics of the days of boundary conflicts, scattered at such points as San Fernando de Atabapo and San Carlos.

of the junction of the Cassiquiare with the Río Negro. The rock of Culimacari is precisely in latitude 2° 0' 42", and probably in longitude 69° 33' 50".

Mentioning the discovery by M. Bonpland of a majestic *almendrón* (Jamaica tree), Humboldt now goes off into a discussion of the manner in which various trees often become scattered over large areas of land. This is followed by detailed descriptions of the flora found on the banks of that part of the river, in turn followed by speculations on the region's general abandonment by settlers.

> We left the rock of Culimacari at half past one on the morning of the 12th. . . . We passed some turbulent rapids before we reached the mission of Mandavaca. The village . . . contains only sixty natives. The state of the Christian settlements is in general so miserable, that, in the whole course of the Cassiquiare, on a length of fifty leagues, not two hundred inhabitants are found. The banks of this river were indeed more peopled before the arrival of the missionaries; the Indians have withdrawn into the woods, toward the east; for the western plains are almost deserted. The natives subsist during a part of the year on those large ants of which I have spoken above. These insects are much esteemed here, as spiders are in the southern hemisphere, where the savages of Australia deem them delicious.

Cannibalism

A conversation with the mission's priest leads Humboldt into a long discussion of cannibalism, a part of which is given below:

> We found at Mandavaca the good old missionary, who had already spent "twenty years of mosquitos in the *bosques* [forests] *del Cassiquiare*," and whose legs were so spotted by the stings of insects, that the color of his skin could scarcely be perceived. He talked to us of his solitude, and of the sad necessity which often compelled him to leave the most atrocious crimes unpunished in the two missions of Mandavaca and Vasiva. In the latter place, an Indian alcalde had, a few years before, eaten one of his wives, after having taken her to his *canuco*,[4] and fattened her

---

[4] A hut surrounded with cultivated ground; a sort of country house, which the natives prefer to residing in the missions.

by good feeding. The cannibalism of the nations of Guiana is never caused by the want of subsistence, or by the superstitions of their religion, as in the islands of the South Sea; but is generally the effect of the vengeance of a conqueror, and (as the missionaries say) "of a vitiated appetite." Victory over a hostile tribe is celebrated by a repast, in which some parts of the body of a prisoner are devoured. . . . It is civilization only, that has made man feel the unity of the human race. . . . Savages know only their own family; and a tribe appears to them but a more numerous assemblage of relations. . . . These . . . savages detest all who are not of their family, or their tribe; and hunt the Indians of a neighboring tribe as we hunt game. They know the duties of family ties and relationship, but not those of humanity, which require the feeling of a common tie with beings framed like ourselves. No emotion of pity prompts them to spare the wives or children of a hostile race; and the latter are devoured in preference, at the repast given at the conclusion of a battle or warlike incursion.

Indians as Linguists

After some pages on cannibalism in general, Humboldt goes off on the linguistic ability of the Indians. Many missionaries and travellers in the Amazonian regions, the present editor included, have remarked on the Indians' remarkable musical taste and ability, as well as on the ease with which they learn languages.

Although the Indians of the Cassiquiare readily return to their barbarous habits, they evince, while in the missions, intelligence, some love of labour, and, in particular, a great facility in learning the Spanish language. The villages being, for the most part, inhabited by three or four tribes, who do not understand each other, a foreign idiom, which is at the same time that of the civil power, the language of the missionary, affords the advantage of a more general means of communication. I heard a Poiñave Indian conversing in Spanish with a Guahibo, though both had come from their forests within three months.

Agriculture

As a man who held great hopes and visions on the Amazon basin's future colonization and development, Humboldt is again and again drawn into speculations on the possibilities for agriculture.

> We were told that the Indians of the Cassiquiare and the Río Negro are preferred on the Lower Orinoco . . . to the inhabitants of the other missions, on account of their intelligence and activity. Those of Mandavaca are celebrated among the tribes of their own race for the preparation of *curare* poison, which does not yield in strength to the *curare* of Esmeralda. Unhappily the natives devote themselves to this employment more than to agriculture. Yet the soil on the banks of the Cassiquiare is excellent.

However, after discussing the soil's geological composition and painting a glowing picture of its agricultural yields, he does arrive at some drawbacks.

> Here, as at the Río Negro, the humidity of the air, and the consequent abundance of insects, are obstacles almost invincible to new cultivation. Everywhere you meet with those large ants that march in close bands, and direct their attacks the more readily on cultivated plants, because they are herbaceous and succulent, whilst the forests of those countries afford only plants with woody stalks. If a missionary wishes to cultivate salad, or any culinary plant of Europe, he is compelled as it were to suspend his garden in the air. He fills an old boat with good mould, and, having sown the seed, suspends it four feet above the ground with the cords of the chiquichiqui palm tree; but most frequently places it on a slight scaffolding. This protects the young plants from weeds, worms, and those ants which pursue their migration in a right line, and, not knowing what vegetates above them, seldom turn from their course to climb up stakes that are stripped of their bark. I mention this circumstance to prove how difficult, within the tropics, on the banks of great rivers, are the first attempts of man to appropriate to himself a little spot of earth in that vast domain of nature, invaded by animals, and covered by spontaneous plants.

The travelers left Mandavaca Mission at half past two in the morning, May 13th, after obtaining the last astronomical observations they were able to make along the Cassiquiare.

> On the 14th, the mosquitos, and especially the ants, drove us from the shore before two in the morning. We had hitherto been of the opinion that the ants did not crawl along the cords by which the hammocks are usually suspended; whether we were correct in this supposition,[5] or whether the ants fell on us from the tops of the trees, I cannot say; but certain it is that we had great difficulty to keep ourselves free from these troublesome insects.

The travelers passed the little mission of Vasiva, located on an island, on the fourteenth, but apparently did not stop there. From there, Humboldt's account of the remainder of his voyage on the Cassiquiare consists of the naturalist's description of flora and fauna plus the geographer's general descriptions of the river itself and its several tributaries, alternating with accounts, rare in Humboldt's writings, of the hardships endured.

> From the 14th to the 21st of May we slept constantly in the open air; but I cannot indicate the spots where we halted. The regions are so wild, and so little frequented, that with the exception of a few rivers, the Indians were ignorant of the names of all the objects which I set by the compass. . . . During the five following nights our passage was the more troublesome in proportion as we approached the bifurcation of the Orinoco. The luxuriance of the vegetation increases in a manner of which it is difficult even for those acquainted with the aspect of the forests between the tropics [of Cancer and Capricorn] to form an idea. There is no longer a bank: a palisade of tufted trees forms the margin of the river. You see a canal two hundred toises broad [about 1,100 feet], bordered by two enormous walls, clothed with lianas and foliage. We often tried to land, but without success. Towards sunset we sailed along for an hour seeking to discover, not an opening (since none exists), but a spot less wooded, where our Indians by means of the hatchet and manual labour, could clear space enough for a resting-place for twelve or thirteen persons.[6] It was impossible to pass the

[5] They were incorrect, as attested by a disagreeable experience suffered by the editor on the Orinoco in 1932.
[6] This indicates one of Humboldt's writing idiosyncrasies: he knew precisely how many persons there were.

night in the canoe; the mosquitos, which tormented us during the day, accumulated toward evening beneath the toldo covered with palm leaves [7] which served to shelter us from the rain. Our hands and faces had never before been so much swelled. . . . We experienced great difficulty, amid a thick forest, in finding wood to make a fire, the branches of the trees in those equatorial regions where it always rains, being so full of sap, that they will scarcely burn. . . . However, fire was necessary to us only as a defense against the beasts of the forest; for we had such scarcity of provisions that we had little need of fuel for the purpose of preparing our food. . . .

The most depressing of all physical sufferings are those which are uniform in their duration and can be combated only by long patience. . . . The ants and the mosquitos troubled us more than the humidity and the want of food. . . . The navigation from Mandavaca to Esmeralda has always appeared to us the most painful part of our travels in America. I advise those who are not very desirous of seeing the great bifurcation of the Orinoco, to take the way of the Atabapo in preference to that of the Cassiquiare.

Emerging from the Cassiquiare into the Orinoco, the travelers ascended the latter river a short distance, to the mission hamlet of Esmeralda, on the Orinoco's right bank, near the celebrated Mount Duida.

A mineralogical error gave celebrity to Esmeralda. The granites of Duida and Maraguaca contain in open veins fine rock-crystals, some of them of great transparency, others colored by chlorite or blended with actonite; these were mistaken for diamonds and emeralds.

Esmeralda had originally been founded as a prison colony, a place of exile for criminals.

We were surprised to find . . . many zambos,[8] mulattos, and copper-colored people, who called themselves Spaniards . . . and who fancy they are white, because they are not so red as the Indians. These people live in the most absolute misery; they have for the most part been sent hither in banishment. . . . Solano, in his haste to found colonies in the interior of the country, in order to guard its entrance against the Portuguese,

[7] Arched roof, covering about half of the canoe.
[8] Half-breeds, a mixture of Indian and Negro.

assembled in the llanos, and as far as the island of Margareta, vagabonds and malefactors, whom justice had vainly pursued, and made them go up the Orinoco to join the unhappy Indians who had been carried off from the woods.

After roving in his inimitable fashion over the fine pineapples growing near Esmeralda, over the settlement's administration, and many other things, Humboldt has this to say about El Dorado:

> So near the sources of the Orinoco we heard of nothing in these mountains but the proximity of El Dorado, the lake Parima, and the ruins of the great city of Manoa.

Curare

In Humboldt's time Northeastern Europe's scientific world was greatly interested in curare, the poison which the Amazonian Indians still use on their arrows and the darts of their blowguns. With a few relatively short side excursions into such matters as the long, smooth reeds from which blowguns are made (incidentally, the vicinity of Mount Duida is still famous as the best source of those reeds) and Brazil nuts, Humboldt gives some 15 pages to a thorough discussion of that interesting substance.

> Esmeralda is the most celebrated spot on the Orinoco for the preparation of that active poison, which is employed in war, in the chase, and, singularly enough, as a remedy for gastric derangements.

Citing Raleigh, Gumilla, and others to the effect that the preparation of curare was a closely guarded secret, and going on from there to discussing preparations for a drunken feast, he writes:

> We were fortunate enough to find an old Indian more temperate than the rest, who was employed in preparing the *curare* poison from freshly-gathered plants. He was the chemist of the place. We found at his dwelling large earthen pots for boiling the vegetable juice, shallower vessels to favour the evaporation by a larger surface, and leaves of the plantain-tree rolled up in the shape of our filters, and used to filtrate the liquids, more

or less loaded with fibrous matter. The greatest order and neat-
ness prevailed in this hut, which was transformed into a chemical laboratory. The old Indian was known throughout the
mission by the name of the poison-master (*amo del curare*). He
had the self-sufficient air and tone of pedantry of which the
pharmacopolists of Europe were formerly accused. "I know,"
said he, "that the whites have the secret of making soap, and
manufacturing that black powder which has the defect of
making a noise when used in killing animals. The *curare,* which
we prepare from father to son, is superior to anything you can
make down yonder [beyond the sea]. It is the juice of an herb
which kills silently, without any one knowing whence the stroke
comes.

Because of its silence and lack of flash or smoke, and because
the question of range is of minor importance in forest country
where visibility is always circumscribed, the blowgun with its
poisoned darts is still preferred to firearms as a hunting weapon
by Orinoco Indians. During World War II, when the desirability of a silent, flashless, smokeless weapon with limited range
became apparent for use in combatting Japanese snipers in the
forested Southwest Pacific, the editor secured for the U.S. Armed
Forces a supply of curare made by the Piaroa Indians along the
middle Orinoco, downstream from Esmeralda. This stirred interest in the Army Medical Corps, but was never seriously considered for active warfare, probably because, once a "poison"
was employed, the enemy could be expected to unleash greater
terrors in "chemical warfare." Actually, today's use of weak
curare in medicine, for relaxing patients, shows the substance
to be an extremely humane means of causing death, "relaxing"
its victims to the ultimate limits.

After describing the manner in which the old man made the
poison, as well as the liana from the bark of which it was made,
Humboldt goes on to say:

A yellowish water filters during several hours, drop by drop,
through the leafy funnel. This filtered water is the poisonous
liquor, but it acquires strength only when concentrated by
evaporation. . . . The Indian from time to time invited us to
taste the liquid; its taste, more or less bitter, decides when the
concentration by fire has been carried sufficiently far. There is
no danger in tasting it, the *curare* being deleterious only when
it comes into immediate contact with the blood.

After three days at Esmeralda, during which Humboldt asked innumerable questions about subjects ranging from physical geography and botany through the El Dorado legend to the sources of the Orinoco River and the nature of the Indians living farther up, the travelers were ready to depart for their long downstream journey.

> We left the mission of Esmeralda on the 23d of May. . . . Our canoe was not ready to receive us till near three o'clock in the afternoon. It had been filled with innumerable swarms of ants during the navigation of the Cassiquiare; and the toldo, or roof of palm leaves, beneath which we are again doomed to remain stretched out during twenty-two days, was with difficulty cleared of these insects. We employed part of the morning in repeating to the inhabitants of Esmeralda the questions we had already put to them.

Thus, through his published accounts, the indefatigable intellectual adventurer, the scientist who had trained himself in virtually all conceivable (at that time) fields, illuminated all areas and regions which he visited. Regardless of the hardships endured, like all men of spirit and imagination, Humboldt remained throughout the man of vision who saw a bright future, developed and "civilized," for the lands which he had investigated.

After completing the account of his voyage along the Cassiquiare, Humboldt delved into details of his day's great "bifurcation controversy," and proceeded to speculate on the Cassiquiare's future:

> The bifurcations of the Orinoco . . . will ere long fix the attention of commercial Europe. The Cassiquiare, as broad as the Rhine and the course of which is one hundred and eighty miles in length, will no longer form uselessly a navigable canal between two basins of rivers which have a surface of one hundred and ninety thousand square leagues. The grain of New Granada will be carried to the banks of the Río Negro; boats will descend from the sources of the Napo and the Ucuyabe, from the Andes of Quito and of Upper Peru, to the mouths of the Orinoco, a distance which equals that from Timbuctoo to Marseilles. A country nine or ten times larger than Spain, and enriched with the most varied productions, is navigable in every direction by the medium of the natural canal of the Cassi-

quiare, and the bifurcation of the rivers. This phenomenon, which will one day be so important for the political connections of nations, unquestionably deserves to be carefully examined.

While the great Baron von Humboldt was not necessarily wrong in his rosy views on the future of the Amazonian regions, he was certainly premature. Only today, pressed by mounting populations and the desperate need for revolutionary social and economic reform, are the various Amazonian nations beginning to view the imminent possibility of Amazonian settlement and development with realistic interest, though Venezuela, within whose boundaries the Cassiquiare flows, is far less concerned with the possible development of its Amazonian forest regions than in that of Northern Guiana, rich in water power, iron, and other resources.

❧ XVIII ❧

CHARLES DARWIN

THE latest edition, and one of the best, of Charles Darwin's classic book *The Voyage of the Beagle,* edited and annotated by Leonard Engel, was published in paperback form in 1962 by Doubleday & Company in cooperation with the American Museum of Natural History. Mr. Engel's introduction begins:

> In its influence on modern man's outlook upon the world, no voyage since Columbus matches the voyage described in this book. The *Beagle* was a ten-gun brig, a class of small warships used by the British Navy for a wide variety of duties a century and a third ago. In 1831, the *Beagle*—refitted for the occasion as a three-masted bark—was sent to complete a survey of the South American coast and to carry out a chain of longitude measurements around the world. There were many similar survey voyages during the nineteenth century. The *Beagle's* stands out for a single reason. A remarkable young man who was "extremely fond of geology and indeed all branches of natural history" accompanied her as the ship's naturalist to take advantage of the opportunity for "collecting, observing and noting anything worthy to be noted in natural history." The youthful naturalist was Charles Darwin. It was the vast and changing panorama of life, both living and extinct, observed by Darwin during the *Beagle's* cruise that set him on the road to *The Origin of Species. . . . The Voyage of the Beagle*—which is also one of the greatest scientific travel-adventure tales ever written—plainly foreshadows the revolutionary line along which Darwin's thought was to develop.[1]

[1] Charles Darwin, *The Voyage of the Beagle.* Introduction by Leonard Engel (Garden City, N.Y.: Doubleday & Co., 1962). Reprinted by permission of the publisher.

Darwin was born February 12, 1809, at Shrewsbury in western England. His father was a well-known physician; his mother was a daughter of Josiah Wedgwood, founder of the Wedgwood pottery works. In his autobiography (as quoted by Engel) he was to write: "By the time I was eight, my taste for natural history, and more especially for collecting, was well-developed. I tried to make out the names of plants, and collected all sorts of things, shells, seals, franks, coins, and minerals." He was relatively uninterested in his schooling, getting little out of it. Successive exposures to the study of medicine and theology brought barren results and failed to deflect him from his abiding interest in natural history.

In 1831, on returning from a geological fieldtrip to Wales in the company of Adam Sedgwick, Cambridge's professor of geology, he was asked to join the *Beagle* as a naturalist, for a cruise around the world. After some vicissitudes, when it looked several times that he would not be able to make the voyage after all, Darwin joined the ship at her London dock and was appalled at her small size—carrying capacity of only 242 tons—and cramped quarters for the accommodation of no fewer than 74 persons. Near the end of 1831, she managed to get away and head for South America by way of the Cape Verde Islands. Darwin's narrative begins:

> After having been twice driven back by heavy south-western gales, Her Majesty's ship *Beagle,* a ten-gun brig, under the command of Captain Fitz Roy, R.N., sailed from Devonport on the 27th of December, 1831. The object of the expedition was to complete the survey of Patagonia and Tierra del Fuego, commenced under Captain King in 1826 to 1830—to survey the shores of Chile, Peru, and some of the islands in the Pacific—and to carry a chain of chronometrical measurements around the world. On the 6th of January we reached Teneriffe, but were prevented landing, by fears of our bringing the cholera: the next morning we saw the sun rise behind the rugged outline of the Grand Canary island, and suddenly illumine the Peak of Teneriffe, whilst the lower parts were veiled in fleecy clouds. This was the first of many delightful days never to be forgotten. On the 16th of January, 1832, we anchored at Porto Praya, in St. Jago, the chief island of the Cap de Verd archipelago.

Between Rio de Janeiro
and Bahía Blanca

The *Beagle* headed for South America, via Bahía, and Darwin spent three months, April 4 to July 5, in and around Rio de Janeiro, while his ship returned to Bahía to check longitude determinations. The naturalist's accounts of his excursions from the city are delightful, his descriptions of nature (birds, clouds, rains, musical frogs, phosphorescent insects, noises made by butterflies, ants, spiders, and the like) are far-ranging, clear, and thoughtful. His one comment on slavery runs as follows:

> We passed under one of the massive, bare, and steep hills of granite which are so common in this country. This spot is notorious from having been, for a long time, the residence of some runaway slaves, who by cultivating a little ground near the top, contrived to eke out a subsistence. At length they were discovered and a party of soldiers being sent, the whole were seized with the exception of one old woman, who, sooner than again be led into slavery, dashed herself to pieces from the summit of the mountain. In a Roman matron this would have been called a noble love of freedom: in a poor negress it is mere brutal obstinacy.[2]

The *Beagle* picked up Darwin July 5, 1832, and headed south for the Plate estuary, doing scientific work in and around Montevideo while Darwin "staid ten weeks" at a "most quiet, forlorn little town" named Maldonado.

> *July 24th, 1833.*[3] The *Beagle* sailed from Maldonado, and on August the 3d she arrived off the mouth of the Río Negro.[4] This is the principal river on the whole line of coast between the Strait of Magellan and the Plata. It enters the sea about three hundred miles south of the estuary of the Plata. About fifty

---

[2] At the end of his book, in a section entitled "Retrospect," Darwin lashes out emotionally against slavery, giving many instances of brutal maltreatment of slaves which he had witnessed personally.

[3] Darwin's book is not arranged in strict chronological order, and it is often difficult to guess what year he is dealing with. His first reference to Maldonado, some twenty-five pages before the one here cited, was dated July 5, 1832. Between those two dates, more than a year apart, the *Beagle*, with Darwin on board, sailed south to Patagonia and Tierra del Fuego.

[4] This Río Negro is in south-central Argentina, not the one in the Amazon basin.

years ago, under the Spanish government, a small colony was established here; and it is still the most southern position (lat. 41°) on this eastern coast of America, inhabited by civilized man.

The settlement was located 18 miles up the river. On the road there, Darwin "passed the ruins of some fine *'estancias,'* which a few years since had been destroyed by the Indians." Surprisingly enough, these had been the fierce Araucanos who had given the early conquerors and governors of Chile so much trouble and who now made long raiding voyages all the way to the Atlantic coast.

They [the *estancias*] withstood several attacks. A man present at one gave me a very lively description of what took place. The inhabitants had sufficient notice to drive all the cattle and horses into the "corral" which surrounded the house, and likewise to mount some small cannon. The Indians were Araucanians from the south of Chile; several hundred in number, and highly disciplined. They first appeared in two bodies on a neighboring hill; having there dismounted, and taken off their fur mantles, they advanced naked to the charge. The only weapon of an Indian is a very long bamboo or chuzo, ornamented with ostrich feathers, and pointed by a sharp spear-head. My informer seemed to remember with the greatest horror the quivering of these chuzos as they approached near. When close, the cacique Pincheira hailed the besieged to give up their arms, or he would cut all their throats. As this would probably have been the result of their entrance under any circumstances, the answer was given by a volley of musketry. The Indians, with great steadiness, came to the very fence of the corral: but to their surprise they found the posts fastened together by iron nails instead of leather thongs, and, of course, in vain attempted to cut them with their knives. This saved the lives of the Christians; many of the wounded Indians were carried away by their companions; and at least one of the under caciques being wounded, the bugle sounded a retreat. They retired to their horses, and seemed to hold a council of war. This was an awful pause for the Spaniards, as all their ammunition, with the exception of a few cartridges, was expended. In an instant the Indians mounted their horses, and galloped out of sight. Another attack was still more quickly repulsed. A cool Frenchman managed the gun; he stopped till the Indians approached close, and then raked their line with grape-shot; he thus laid thirty-nine of them on the ground; and, of course, such a blow immediately routed the whole party.

The *Beagle* was to return to Buenos Aires, some 600 miles north of the Argentine Río Negro, but Darwin decided to make the trip overland by primitive travel.

> To the northward of the Río Negro, between it and the inhabited country of Buenos Ayres, the Spaniards have only one small settlement, recently established at Bahía Blanca. The distance in a straight line to Buenos Ayres is very nearly five hundred British miles. The wandering tribes of horse Indians, which have always occupied the greater part of this country, having of late much harassed the outlying *estancias,* the government at Buenos Ayres equipped some time since an army under the command of General Rosas [5] for the purpose of exterminating them. The troops were now encamped on the banks of the Colorado, a river lying about eighty miles northward of the Río Negro.

Having a letter of introduction from the Buenos Aires government to the general, Darwin called on him in his camp and was received hospitably. "We took up our residence in the *rancho,* or hovel, of a curious old Spaniard, who had served with Napoleon in the expedition against Russia."

Darwin devotes considerable space to the General, his ruthless warfare against the Indians, his iron discipline among his men, his popularity with the gauchos, all of whom he could outride and outfight. At one point he said: "He is a man of an extraordinary character, and has a most predominant influence in the country, which it seems probable he will use to its prosperity and advancement." (In 1845 he was to add a footnote to that remark, saying: "This prophecy has turned out entirely and miserably wrong.")

Darwin spent nearly two weeks, from September 8 to September 20, riding from Bahía Blanca to Buenos Aires. As always,

[5] Footnote by Mr. Engel: Juan Manuel de Rosas, born in Buenos Aires in 1793 and died in England in 1877, began his life as a gaucho . . . and ended it in exile. In between, Rosas became a well-known Indian fighter, a wealthy landowner, governor of the province of Buenos Aires . . . and dictator of all Argentina (1835–52). Argentines concede that he held Argentina together, but he was an oppressive tyrant who was finally overthrown by a revolt aided by Uruguay and Brazil.

Callao

Iquique

Valparaíso

Concepción

PACIFIC OCEAN

ATLANTIC OCEAN

Charles Darwin

1832 - 1833

SCALE — MILES

0   500

he missed little or nothing along the way; everything was grist for his inquiring intellect, his diary, and his charming pen. His chapter on the trip ranges in content from travel accounts, through habits and customs of the people encountered, landscapes, weather, birds, to the effects of cattle on vegetation. Foreshadowing some modern trends in nutrition are his remarks on the meat diet. Arriving at an *estancia* on September 17th, he was happy to be able to buy "some biscuit."

> I had now been several days without tasting any thing besides meat: I did not at all dislike this new regimen; but I felt as if it would only have agreed with me with hard exercise. I have heard that patients in England, when desired to confine themselves exclusively to an animal diet, even with the hope of life before their eyes, hardly have been able to endure it. Yet the Gaucho in the Pampas, for months together, touches nothing but beef. But they eat, I observe, a very large proportion of fat, which is of a less animalized nature; and they particularly dislike dry meat, such as that of the Agouti. Dr. Richardson also has remarked "that when people have fed for a long time solely upon lean animal food, the desire for fat becomes so insatiable, that they can consume a large quantity of unmixed and even oily fat without nausea": this appears to me a curious physiological fact. It is perhaps from their meat regimen that the Gauchos, like other carniverous animals, can abstain long from food. I was told that at Tandeel [Tandil], some troops voluntarily pursued a party of Indians for three days without eating or drinking.[6]

Darwin spent until December 6 in and around Buenos Aires and Montevideo, visiting the surrounding countryside, naturalizing, collecting, and observing the people's customs. Among many other things, his account of those days deals with geological formations, a "singular breed of oxen," manners of breaking in horses, flocks of butterflies, the phosphorescence of the sea,

[6] The arctic explorer Vilhjalmur Stefansson observed and reported in the course of his second expedition that meat without fat, eaten exclusively, is virtually a poison, an observation which was verified by medical research (on Stefansson himself) in 1929. Modern medical practitioners, such as Dr. Blake Donaldson of New York, who prescribe the all-meat diet for a large variety of ailments in some manner connected with obesity, also know that lean meat without a "protein sparer" is extremely harmful. All they do when putting their patients on the all-meat diet is to take them off starches and sugar as protein sparers and switch them to animal fats in the general proportion of about 25 percent fat by volume, or 80 percent fat by calorie count.

and gigantic fossils. He was interested in the relations between sheep dogs and the sheep they were guarding:

> While staying at this *estancia,* I was amused with what I saw and heard of the shepherd-dogs of the country. When riding, it is a common thing to meet a large flock of sheep guarded by one or two dogs, at a distance of some miles from any house or man. I often wondered how so firm a friendship had been established. The method of education consists of separating the puppy, while very young, from the bitch, and in accustoming it to its future companions. An ewe is held three or four times a day for the little thing to suck, and a nest of wool is made for it in the sheep-pen. The puppy is, moreover, generally castrated; so that, when grown up, it can scarcely have any feelings in common with the rest of its kind. From this education it has no wish to leave the flock, and just as another dog will defend its master, man, so will these the sheep. It is amusing to observe, when approaching a flock, how the dog immediately advances barking, and the sheep all close in his rear, as if round the oldest ram. These dogs are also easily taught to bring home the flock at a certain hour in the evening. Their most troublesome fault, when young, is their desire of playing with the sheep; for in their sport they sometimes gallop their poor subjects most unmercifully.

Patagonia and Tierra del Fuego

Rejoining the *Beagle* on December 6, Darwin sailed southward toward Patagonia, arriving at Port Desire (Puerto Deseado) on December 23. His description of the country, its geology, fauna, and flora, includes the following notes on the guanaco:

> The guanaco, or wild llama, is the characteristic quadruped of the plains of Patagonia; it is the South American representative of the camel of the East. It is an elegant animal in a state of nature, with a long, slender neck and fine legs. It is very common over the whole of the temperate parts of the continent, as far south as the islands near Cape Horn. It generally lives in herds of from half a dozen to thirty in each; but on the banks of the St. Cruz we saw one herd which must have contained at least five hundred.
> They are generally wild and extremely wary. . . . [There fol-

lows a description of their shyness and nervousness.] That they
are curious [however] is certain; for if a person lies on the
ground, and plays strange antics, such as throwing up his feet
in the air, they will almost always approach by degrees to reconnoitre him. . . . These animals are very easily domesticated,
and I have seen some thus kept in northern Patagonia near a
house, though not under any restraint. . . . The wild guanacos,
however, have no idea of defence; even a single dog will secure
one of these large animals, till the huntsman can come up.
Thus when they see men approaching in several directions on
horseback, they soon become bewildered, and know not which
way to run. This greatly facilitates the Indian method of hunting, for they are thus easily driven to a central point, and are
encompassed.

Of the famous "giant" Patagonians (see Chapter VI) he was
to write in a later chapter:

We had an interview at Cape Gregory with the famous so-
called gigantic Patagonians who gave us a cordial reception.
Their height appears greater than it really is, from their large
guanaco mantles, their long flowing hair, and general figure: on
an average their height is about six feet. . . . Altogether they
are certainly the tallest race which we anywhere saw. In features
they strikingly resemble the more northern Indians whom I
saw with Rosas, but they have a wilder and more formidable
appearance; their faces were much painted with red and black,
and one man was ringed and dotted with white like a Fuegian.
Captain Fitz Roy offered to take any three of them on board,
and all seemed determined to be of the three. It was long before
we could clear the boat; at last we got on board with our three
giants, who dined with the Captain, and behaved quite like
gentlemen, helping themselves with knives, forks, and spoons:
nothing was so much relished as sugar. This tribe has had so
much communication with sealers and whalers, that most of the
men can speak a little English and Spanish; and they are half
civilized and proportionally demoralized.

On December 17, 1832, the *Beagle,* with Darwin on board
paid her first visit to Tierra del Fuego.

A little after noon we doubled Cape St. Diego, and entered
the famous strait of Le Maire. We kept close to the Fuegian
shore, but the outline of the rugged, inhospitable Staten-land

was visible amidst the clouds. In the afternoon we anchored in the Bay of Good Success. While entering we were saluted in a manner becoming the inhabitants of this savage land. A group of Fuegians partly concealed by the entangled forest, were perched on a wild point overhanging the sea; and as we passed by, they sprang up, and waving their tattered cloaks sent forth a loud and sonorous shout. The savages followed the ship, and just before dark we saw their fire and again heard their wild cry. . . .

In the morning the Captain sent a party to communicate with the Fuegians. When we came within hail, one of the four natives who were present advanced to receive us, and began to shout most vehemently, wishing to direct us where to land. When we were on shore the party looked rather alarmed, but continued talking and making gestures with great rapidity. It was without exception the most curious and interesting spectacle I ever beheld: I could not have believed how wide was the difference between savage and civilized man: it is greater than between a wild and domesticated animal, inasmuch as in man there is a greater power of improvement. The chief spokesman was old, and appeared to be the head of the family; the three others were powerful young men, about six feet high. The women and children had been sent away. . . .

The party altogether closely resembled the devils which come on the stage in plays like *Der Freischütz*.

Their very attitudes were abject, and the expression of their countenances distrustful, surprised, and startled. After we had presented them with some scarlet cloth, which they immediately tied around their necks, they became good friends. . . .

They are excellent mimics: as often as we coughed or yawned, or made any odd motion, they immediately imitated us. Some of our party began to squint and look awry; but one of the young Fuegians (whose whole face was painted black, excepting a white band across the eyes) succeeded in making far more hideous grimaces. They could repeat with perfect correctness each word in any sentence we addressed them, and they remembered such words for some time. Yet we Europeans all know how difficult it is to distinguish apart the sounds in a foreign language. . . .

I have not as yet noticed the Fuegians whom we had on board. During a former voyage of the *Adventure* and *Beagle* in 1826 to 1830, Captain Fitz Roy seized on a party of natives, as hostages for the loss of a boat, which had been stolen, to the

great jeopardy of a party employed in the survey; and some of
these natives, as well as a child whom he bought for a pearl-
button, he took with him to England, determined to educate
them and instruct them in religion at his own expense. To settle
these natives in their own country was one chief inducement of
Captain Fitz Roy to undertake our present voyage. . . . The
natives were accompanied by a missionary, R. Matthews. . . .
Two men, one of whom died in England of smallpox, a boy and
a litle girl were originally taken; and we had now on board,
York Minster, Jemmy Button (whose name expressed his pur-
chase-money), and Fuegia Basket. . . . York Minster was a full-
grown, short, thick, powerful man. . . . Jemmy Button was
a universal favorite . . .; the expression of his face at once
showed his nice disposition. . . . Fuegia Basket was a nice,
modest reserved young girl . . . very quick in learning anything, especially languages. . . . York Minster was very jealous
of any attention paid to her; for it was clear he determined to
marry her as soon as they were settled on shore. . . .

It was interesting to watch the conduct of the savages, when
we landed, towards Jemmy Button; they immediately perceived
the difference between him and ourselves, and held much conversation one with another on the subject. The old man addressed a long harangue to Jemmy, which it seems was to invite
him to stay with them. But Jemmy understood very little of
their language, and was, moreover, thoroughly ashamed of his
countrymen.

On December 21, the *Beagle* got under weigh and rounded
Cape Horn, but was driven out to sea by sudden gales, and,
after several days, sought shelter in "a snug little harbor" called
Wigwam Cove.

The cove takes its name of "Wigwam" from some of the
Fuegian habitations; but every bay in the neighborhood might
be so called with equal propriety. The inhabitants, living chiefly
upon shell-fish, are obliged constantly to change their place of
residence; but they return at intervals to the same spots, as is
evident from the piles of old shells, which must often amount
to many tons in weight. . . .

The Fuegian wigwam resembles, in size and dimensions, a
haycock. It merely consists of a few broken branches stuck in
the ground, and very imperfectly thatched on one side with a
few tufts of grass and rushes. . . . At Goeree Roads I saw a

place where one of these naked men had slept, which absolutely offered no more cover than the form of a hare. The man was evidently living by himself, and York Minster said he was "very bad man," and that probably he had stolen something. On the west coast, however, the wigwams are rather better, for they are covered with seal-skins. . . .

While going one day on shore near Wollaston Island, we pulled alongside a canoe with six Fuegians. These were the most abject and miserable creatures I anywhere beheld. . . . [They] were quite naked, and even one full-grown woman was absolutely so. It was raining heavily, and the fresh water, together with the spray, trickled down her body. . . .[7]

These poor wretches were stunted in their growth, their hideous faces bedaubed with white paint, their skins filthy and greasy, their hair entangled, their voices discordant, and their gestures violent. . . . At night five or six human beings, naked and scarcely protected from the wind and rain of this tempestuous climate, sleep on the wet ground coiled up like animals. Whenever it is low water, winter or summer, night or day, they must rise to pick shellfish from the rocks; and the women either dive to collect sea-eggs, or sit patiently in their canoes, and with a baited hairline without any hook, jerk out little fish. If a seal is killed, or the floating carcass of a putrid whale discovered, it is a feast.

Darwin now goes on to speculate whether the Fuegians have any religious beliefs, and decides that they have virtually none. He also states: "The different tribes have no government or chief; yet each is surrounded by other hostile tribes, speaking different dialects, and separated from each other by a deserted border or neutral territory: the cause of their warfare appears to be the means of subsistence."

After six days in Wigwam Cove, on December 30th, they put to sea again, only to run into more bad weather.

When at sea we had a constant succession of gales, and the current was against us: we drifted to 57° 23' south. On the 11th of January, 1833, by carrying a press of sail, we fetched within a few miles of the great rugged mountain of York Minster (so called by Captain Cook, and the origin of the name of the elder

[7] Elsewhere, Darwin had written that "the climate is certainly wretched; the summer solstice was now passed, yet every day snow fell on the hills, and in the valleys there was rain, accompanied by sleet. The thermometer generally stood about 45°, but in the night fell to 38° or 40°."

Fuegian), when a violent squall compelled us to shorten sail and stand out to sea. The surf was breaking fearfully on the coast, and the spray was carried over a cliff estimated at 200 feet in height. On the 12th the gale was very heavy and we did not know exactly where we were. . . . On the 13th the storm raged with its full fury: our horizon was narrowly limited by the sheets of spray borne by the wind. . . . At noon a great sea broke over us, and filled one of the whale-boats, which was obliged to be instantly cut away. The poor *Beagle* trembled at the shock, and for a few minutes would not obey her helm; but soon, like a good ship that she was, she righted and came up to the wind again. Had another sea followed the first, our fate would have been decided soon, and forever.

On January 15th, they anchored in Goeree Roads. "Captain Fitz Roy having resolved to settle the Fuegians, according to their wishes, in Ponsonby Sound."

19th. Three whale boats and the yawl, with a party of twenty-eight, started under the command of Captain Fitz Roy. In the afternoon we entered the eastern mouth of Beagle Channel. . . . The next day (20th) we smoothly glided onwards in our little fleet, and came to a more inhabited district. Few if any of these natives could ever have seen a white man; certainly nothing could exceed their astonishment at the apparition of the four boats. Fires were lighted on every point (hence the name of Tierra del Fuego, or the land of fire), both to attract our attention and to spread far and wide the news.

They were now in contact with the tribe adjoining that of their own Fuegians and were badgered at every turn with insatiable demands for presents. "Jemmy was thoroughly ashamed of his countrymen, and declared his own tribe were quite different, in which he was woefully mistaken."

22nd. After having passed an unmolested night, in what would appear to be neutral territory between Jemmy's tribe and the people whom we saw yesterday, we sailed pleasantly along. . . . At night we slept close to the junction of Ponsonby Sound with the Beagle Channel. A small family of Fuegians, who were living in the cove, were quiet and inoffensive, and soon joined our party round a blazing fire. We were well clothed, and though sitting close to the fire were far from too warm; yet these naked savages, though further off, were observed, to our great surprise, to be streaming with perspiration at undergoing such a roasting. They seemed, however, very well pleased, and all joined in the chorus of the seamen's songs: but the manner in which they were invariably a little behindhand was quite ludicrous. . . .

Jemmy was now in a district well known to him, and guided the boats to a quiet pretty cove named Woollya, surrounded by islands. . . . We found here a family of Jemmy's tribe, but not his relations: we made friends with them; and in the evening they sent a canoe to inform Jemmy's mother and brothers. The cove was bordered by some acres of good sloping land, [and] . . . Captain Fitz Roy determined to settle here the whole party, including Matthews, the missionary. Five days were spent in building for them three large wigwams, in landing their goods, in digging two gardens, and sowing seeds.

The next morning after our arrival (the 24th) the Fuegians began to pour in, and Jemmy's mother and brothers arrived.[8] Jemmy recognized the stentorian voice of one of his brothers at a prodigious distance. The meeting was less interesting than that of a horse, turned out into a field, when he joins an old companion. There was no demonstration of affection; they simply stared for a short time at each other; and the mother immediately went to look after her canoe. . . .

Everything went on peacefully during the next three days, whilst the gardens were digging and wigwams building. We estimated the number of natives at about one hundred and twenty. The women worked hard, whilst the men lounged about all day long, watching us. They asked for everything they saw, and stole what they could. They were delighted at our singing and dancing, and were particularly interested at seeing us wash in a neighboring brook; they did not pay much attention to anything else, not even to our boats.

Some of the boats were now sent back to the *Beagle* while Darwin, Fitz Roy, and a group of men spent some days surveying Beagle Channel. They returned to the Woollya camp on February 6th.

Matthews gave so bad an account of the conduct of the Fuegians, that Captain Fitz Roy determined to take him back to the *Beagle;* and ultimately he was left at New Zealand, where his brother was a missionary. From the time of our leaving, a regular system of plunder commenced; fresh parties of the

[8] His father had died during Jemmy's stay in England.

natives kept arriving: York and Jemmy lost many things, and Matthews almost everything which had not been concealed underground. Every article seemed to have been torn up and divided by the natives. Matthews described the watch he was obliged always to keep as most harassing; night and day he was surrounded by the natives, who tried to tire him out by making an incessant noise close to his head. One day an old man, whom Matthews had asked to leave his wigwam, immediately returned with a large stone in his hand; another day a whole party came armed with stones and stakes, and some of the younger men and Jemmy's brother were crying; Matthews met them with presents. Another party showed by signs that they wished to strip him naked and pluck all the hairs out of his face and body. I think we arrived just in time to save his life.

The three Fuegians whom Fitz Roy had resettled in their own country seemed also to have been mistreated by their relatives and fellow tribesmen. Darwin writes that they, "though they had been only three years with civilized men, would, I am sure, have been glad to have retained their new habits; but this was obviously impossible."

A year later, after a cruise up South America's east coast, the *Beagle* returned to Tierra del Fuego.

On the 5th of March, we anchored in the cove at Woollya, but we saw not a soul there. We were alarmed at this, for the natives in Ponsonby Sound showed by gestures, that there had been fighting; and we afterwards heard that the dreaded Oens men had made a descent. Soon a canoe, with a little flag flying, was seen approaching, with one of the men in it washing the paint off his face. This man was poor Jemmy,—now a thin haggard savage, with long, disordered hair, and naked, except for a bit of blanket round his waist. . . . We had left him plump, fat, clean, and well dressed;—I never saw so complete and grievous a change. As soon however as he was clothed, and the first flurry was over, things wore a good appearance. He dined with Captain Fitz Roy, and ate his dinner as tidily as formerly. He told us . . . that he was not cold, that his relations were very good people, and that he did not wish to go back to England; in the evening we found out the cause of this great change in Jemmy's feelings, in the arrival of his young and nice-looking wife. . . . Jemmy had lost all his property. He told us that York Minster had built a large canoe, and with his wife Fuegia, had several months since gone to his own country, and had taken farewell by an act of consummate villainy; he persuaded Jemmy and his mother to come with him, and then on the way deserted them by night, stealing every article of their property.[9]

Darwin summarizes as follows his observations on the Fuegians:

> I believe, in this extreme part of South America, man exists on a lower state of improvement than in any other part of the world. The South Sea Islanders of the two races inhabiting the Pacific, are comparatively civilized. The Esquimaux, in his subterranean hut, enjoys some of the comforts of life, and in his canoe, when fully equipped, manifests much skill. Some of the tribes of Southern Africa, prowling about in search of roots, and living concealed in the wide and arid plains, are sufficiently wretched. The Australian, in the simplicity of the arts of life, comes nearest to the Fuegian: he can, however, boast of his boomerang, his spear and throwing stick, his method of climbing trees, of tracking animals, and of hunting.

The West Coast of South America

After passing through the Strait of Magellan, the *Beagle* sailed north to Valparaiso and then doubled back to the large island of Chiloé and the nearby Chonos Archipelago. While surveying among the Chonos islands, they encountered bad weather and anchored in a safe harbor which they had discovered. On that wild and presumably uninhabited coast, they were astonished to find five American seamen.

> *December 28th.* Directly [after anchoring] a man was seen waving his shirt, and a boat was sent which brought back two seamen. A party of six had run away from an American whaling vessel, and had landed a little to the southward in a boat, which

[9] According to Mr. Engel, quoting a book published late in the century, "Jemmy Button . . . organized the massacre of a party of six missionaries who attempted to found a settlement at Woollya in 1859. . . . York Minster was killed in retaliation for killing another Fuegian. Fuegia Basket, his wife, remarried and was last seen, ill and near her end, by the Rev. Thomas Bridges . . . in 1883, at which time she was about 62 years old."

was shortly afterward knocked to pieces by the surf. They had now been wandering up and down the coast for fifteen months, without knowing which way to go or where they were. What a singular piece of good fortune it was that this harbor was now discovered! Had it not been for this one chance, they might have wandered till they had grown old men, and at last have perished on this wild coast. Their sufferings had been very great, and one of their party had lost his life by falling from the cliffs. . . . Considering what they had undergone, I think they had kept a very good reckoning of time, for they had lost only four days.

In his own journal, Captain Fitz Roy had entered a somewhat more detailed, and slightly different, version of the incident, which is quoted by Mr. Engel in a footnote. The end of the Fitz Roy account is of interest in connection with the "meat diet" discussion raised earlier by Darwin:

Their permanent abode was then taken up at the point which shelters Port San Estevan, now called Rescue Point, where they passed a year in anxious hope. Of course the few provisions which their boat had carried ashore were soon exhausted, and for thirteen months they had lived only upon seals' flesh, shellfish, and wild celery; yet those five men, when received on board the *Beagle,* were in better condition, as to healthy fleshiness, colour, and actual health, than any five individuals belonging to our ship.

Throughout his travels on the west coast, Darwin was greatly interested in earthquakes and in the restless manner in which those lands had risen from the sea in comparatively recent times. After leaving Chiloé and proceeding to the city of Valdivia, he experienced his first quake.

February 20th. This day has been memorable in the annals of Valdivia, for the most severe earthquake experienced by the oldest inhabitant. I happened to be on shore, and was lying down in the wood to rest myself. It came on suddenly, and lasted two minutes, but the time appeared much longer. The rocking of the ground was very sensible. The undulations appeared to my companion and myself to come from due east, whilst others thought that they proceeded from south-west: this shows how difficult it sometimes is to perceive the direction of the vibrations. There was no difficulty in standing upright, but the motion made me almost giddy: it was something like the movement of a vessel in a little cross-ripple, or still more like that felt by a person skating over thin ice, which bends under the weight of his body.

A bad earthquake at once destroys our oldest associations; the earth, the very emblem of solidity, has moved beneath our feet like a thin crust over a fluid;—one second of time has created in the mind a strange idea of insecurity, which hours of reflection would not have produced.

On March 4th, Darwin landed at the city of Concepción, where he heard the terrible news of the great earthquake of February 20th. The major-domo of an estate on Quiriquina Island told him "that not a house in Concepción or Talcahuano [the port] was standing; that seventy villages were destroyed; and that a great wave had almost washed away the ruins of Talcahuano." Darwin then goes on to give graphic, detailed, and bloodcurdling descriptions of the havoc he had seen at Talcahuano and Concepción. "Both towns," he writes, "presented the most awful yet interesting spectacle I ever beheld." After devoting the better part of six pages to these descriptions, he goes on to say:

> I have not attempted to give any detailed description of the appearance of Concepción, for I feel that it is quite impossible to convey the mingled feeling which I experienced. Several of the officers visited it before me, but their strongest language failed to give a just idea of the scene of desolation. It is a bitter and humiliating thing to see works, which have cost man so much time and labour, overthrown in one minute; yet compassion for the inhabitants was almost instantly banished by the surprise of seeing a state of things produced in a moment of time, which one was accustomed to attribute to a succession of ages. In my opinion, we have scarcely beheld, since leaving England, any sight so deeply interesting.

The *Beagle* stayed three days at Concepción, and then sailed for Valparaiso. While the ship returned to Concepción, to continue its survey, the indefatigable Darwin went to Santiago, Chile's inland capital, obtained the needed horses and mules, and set out on a trip of almost a month in the saddle, crossing the Andes by Uspallata Pass into Argentina's province of Mendoza.

Our manner of traveling was delightfully independent. In the inhabited parts we bought a little firewood, hired pasture for the animals, and bivouacked in the corner of the same field with them. Carrying an iron pot, we cooked and ate our supper under a cloudless sky, and knew no trouble. My companions were Mariano Gonzalez . . . and an *"arriero"* [muleteer], with his ten mules and a *"madrina."* The *madrina* (or god-mother) is a most important personage: she is an old steady mare, with a little bell round her neck; and wherever she goes, the mules, like good children, follow her. The affection of these animals for their *madrinas* saves infinite trouble. If several large troops are turned into one field to graze, in the morning the muleteers have only to lead the *madrinas* a little apart, and tinkle their bells; and although there may be two or three hundred together, each mule immediately knows the bell of its own *madrina* and comes to her. . . . The mule always appears to me a most surprising animal. That a hybrid should possess more reason, memory, obstinacy, social affection, powers of muscular endurance, and length of life, than either of its parents, seems to indicate that art has here outdone nature.

The trip's prime purpose had been for the study of the region's geology, and Darwin, as always, was fascinated by the upheavals which had once raised the Andes from the sea. "In these upper beds," he writes, "shells are tolerably frequent; and they belong to about the period of the lower chalk [Cretaceous period] of Europe. It is an old story, but not the less wonderful, to hear of shells which were once crawling on the bottom of the sea, now standing at nearly 14,000 feet above its level."

Like every traveler in the high mountains, Darwin was interested in the phenomenon of mountain sickness.

About noon we began the tedious ascent of the Peuquenes ridge, and then for the first time experienced some little difficulty in our respiration. The mules would halt every fifty yards, and after resting for a few seconds the poor willing animals started of their own accord again. The short breathing from the rarified atmosphere is called by the Chilenos *"puna";* and they have the most ridiculous notions concerning its origin. Some say "all the waters here have *puna*"; others that "where there is snow there is *puna*";—and this no doubt is true. The only sensation I experienced was a slight tightness across the head and chest, like that felt on leaving a warm room and running quickly in frosty weather. There is some imagination even in this; for upon finding fossil shells on the highest ridge, I entirely forgot my *puna* in my delight. Certainly the exertion of walking was extremely great, and the respiration became deep and laborious. . . . The inhabitants all recommend onions for the *puna*.[10] . . . For my part I found nothing so good as the fossil shells!

After returning to Valparaiso, Darwin set out on a ride to Coquimbo and thence to Copiapó, a straight-line distance of "only" 420 miles, "but my mode of travel made it a very long journey." He had made arrangements for the *Beagle* to pick him up at Copiapó.

His descriptions of the routes taken, of mining activities, geology, rains and earthquakes, the incidence and distribution of hydrophobia, Indian ruins, possible climatic changes, and the like, are, as always, fascinating and indicate again Darwin's far-roaming interests. Little by little, as he moved northward, the climate became more arid.

> The valley of Copiapó, forming a mere ribbon of green in a desert, runs in a very southerly direction; so that it is of considerable length to its source in the Cordillera. The valleys of Guasco and Copiapó may both be considered as long, narrow islands, separated from the rest of Chile by deserts of rock instead of by salt water. Northward of these, there is one other very miserable valley, called Paposo, which contains about two hundred souls; and then there extends the real desert of Atacama—a barrier far worse than the most turbulent ocean.

After leaving Copiapó, the *Beagle* put in at Iquique, a nitrate port which in those days belonged to Peru but came later to be taken over by Chile as a consequence of the "War of the Pacific" (1879–82). It was here that Darwin had his opportunity to study the Atacama Desert at first hand. (In a technical report he was to call it the world's driest desert.)

> *July 12th.* We anchored in the port of Iquique . . . on the coast of Peru. The town contains about a thousand inhabitants, and stands on a little plain of sand at the foot of a great wall of rock, 2,000 feet high, here forming the coast. The whole is

[10] During his own wanderings in the Chilean Andes, the editor found that garlic was highly recommended, to be rubbed into the mules' noses while pieces were inserted into the nostrils of the humans.

utterly desert. A light shower of rain falls only once in very many years; and the ravines are consequently filled with detritus, and the mountainsides covered by piles of fine white sand, even to a height of a thousand feet. . . .

The inhabitants live like persons on board a ship: every necessary comes from a distance: water is brought in boats from Pisagua, about forty miles northward, and is sold at the rate of nine reals (4s. 6d.) an eighteen gallon cask; I bought a wine-bottle full for threepence. . . . Very few animals can be maintained in such a place; on the ensuing morning I hired with difficulty at the price of four pounds sterling, two mules and a guide to take me to the nitrate of soda works. These are at present the support of Iquique. . . .

In the morning I started for the saltpetre works, a distance of fourteen leagues. Having ascended the steep coast-mountains by a zigzag sandy track, we soon came in view of the the mines of Guantajaya and St. Rosa. These two small villages are placed at the very mouths of the mines; and being perched up on hills, they had a still more unnatural and desolate appearance than the town of Iquique. We did not reach the saltpetre works till after sunset, having ridden all day across an undulating country, a complete and utter desert. The road was strewed with the bones and dried skins of the many beasts of burden which had perished on it from fatigue. . . . The appearance of the country was remarkable, from being covered by a thick crust of common salt, and of a stratified saliferous alluvium, which seems to have been deposited as the land slowly rose from the sea. . . . The appearance of this superficial mass very closely resembled that of a country after a snow, before the last dirty patches are thawed. The existence of this crust of a soluble substance over the whole face of the country, shows how extraordinarily dry the climate must have been for a long period.

From Iquique, the *Beagle* sailed north to Callao, the seaport of Lima, Peru's capital. Thence she proceeded for the Galapagos Islands, to New Zealand and Australia, around the Cape of Good Hope, across the Atlantic back to the South American east coast, and then home to England, having spent five years on the round-the-world voyage. On his return, Darwin went on to win world fame, and much abuse, for his theory of the origin of species.

XIX

HENRY WALTER BATES

IN 1836, after returning to England from the voyage of the *Beagle*, Charles Darwin set patiently to work, developing his general theory of the origin of species. But he was not the only Englishman to think along those lines; the fact that others were speculating and working on the same subject indicated England's general excitement over biology during the mid-nineteenth century. In fact, in 1858, when Darwin was at last ready to announce his findings to London's Linnaean Society, he received a manuscript from his friend Alfred Russel Wallace, setting forth substantially the same theory. Darwin was at first disposed to withhold his own paper and give precedence to Wallace's, who was then in the East Indies, but on the advice of friends, both papers were read at the same meeting and published together in the Linnaean Society's *Annals*. The following year, 1859, Darwin published his *On the Origin of Species*, followed in 1871 by *Descent of Man*.[1] The abusive controversy stirred up by those works has not yet abated in certain dark corners of religious fundamentalism; as recently as 1925 it flared into screaming public notice in the famous "monkey trial" in Dayton, Tennessee, in which William Jennings Bryan prosecuted the teacher John T. Scopes for illegally teaching Darwinian evolution to his pupils. In effect he defended the Scriptures against the naturalists, while his opponent Clarence Darrow rushed valiantly to the defense of both Scopes and Darwin.

[1] The full titles of these works are *On the Origin of Species by Means of Natural Selection, or the Preservation of Favoured Races in the Struggle for Life,* and *Descent of Man and Selection in Relation to Sex.*

While Darwin was formulating and developing his ideas, another naturalist, a young man named Henry Walter Bates, was indefatigably doing the work along the Amazon River which was to place him "among the foremost scientific explorers of all time." [2] Bates had been an apprentice to a hosiery manufacturer in Leicester, but his health was poor, his interests lay in the classics and natural history, and he was badly suited for the business of making stockings. He spent all of his spare time in catching and studying butterflies and beetles, and published his first article in the *Zoologist* at the age of eighteen.

One of Bates' friends was Alfred Russel Wallace, an English master in the Collegiate School in Leicester and a fellow aficionado of natural history. In 1847, when Bates was twenty-two, Wallace proposed a joint expedition to the River Amazon to gather facts "toward solving the problem of the origin of species." The two friends traveled together for two years but they parted company in March, 1850, a thousand miles up the Amazon at Barra (today's Manaus) "finding it more convenient to explore separate districts and collect independently." Wallace followed the Río Negro for two years and then returned to England, where he wrote his classic *Travels on the Amazon and Río Negro*. Later he explored the Malay Archipelago and the East Indian islands, whence he sent Darwin his own theory of evolution by means of natural selection.

Bates remained on the main Amazon until 1859, collecting, studying, working ceaselessly, often beset by poverty when his remittances failed to arrive from England, at times plagued by bad health and despondency, but amassing a collection of 14,712 species of animals, of which no fewer than 8,000 proved to be new to science. In England he immediately came under the influence of Darwin and Sir Joseph Hooker, and it was Darwin who persuaded him to write a book on his South American work, which was published in two volumes in 1863. It was an immediate success, the first edition being exhausted in a few months. A somewhat abridged edition was published a few years later and became one of the great classics on the Amazon River as well as in the literature of natural history.

---

[2] The material here given on Bates' life is taken from Robert Usinger's foreword to Bates' book *The Naturalist on the River Amazon* (University of California Press, 1962). The excerpts from Bates' writings are from the same book.

Perhaps Bates' great value as an interpreter stems from the fact that he never once seems to have regarded himself as an explorer. To him, the Amazonian countryside and its people were always interesting and sometimes rather odd, but never menacing, challenging, or even unpleasant. What is a compiler of exploration accounts to do with a man like that? A keen observer who was interested in all things living—including human beings—Bates spent his eleven years of fieldwork as a laboratory worker whose notes were perhaps more charmingly objective than were those of any other Amazonian traveler. He seems never once to have had a future audience in mind. By simply recording facts as he observed them, together with interpretations of such facts as they occurred to his questing, scientific mind, he was to win, on his return to England, a scientific and popular acclaim which has throughout more than a century kept him solidly in the forefront of exploring naturalists.

Leaving Liverpool on April 26, 1848, Bates and Wallace arrived a month later at Salinas, the pilot station for the city of Pará (today's Belém) near the Amazon's mouth and the only port of entry for the river.

On the following day and night we sailed, with a light wind, partly aided by the tides, up the Pará River [the southernmost of the many channels into which the Amazon divides itself at its enormously complex mouth; before its confluence with the Atlantic, the Pará turns northward]. . . . The immensity of the river struck us greatly, for although sailing sometimes at a distance of eight or nine miles from the eastern bank, the opposite shore was at no time visible. Indeed, the Pará River is 36 miles in breadth at its mouth; and at the city of Pará, nearly 70 miles from the sea, it is 20 miles wide; but at that point a series of islands commences which contracts the river view in front of the port.

On the morning of the 28th of May we arrived at our destination. The appearance of the city at sunrise was pleasing in the highest degree. It is built on a low tract of land, having only one small rocky elevation at its southern extremity; it therefore affords no amphitheatral view from the river; but the white buildings roofed with red tiles, the numerous towers and cupolas of churches and convents, the crowns of palm trees reared above the buildings, all sharply defined against the clear blue sky, give an appearance of lightness and cheerfulness which is most exhilarating. The perpetual forest hems the city in on all sides landwards; and towards the suburbs, picturesque country houses are seen scattered about, half buried in luxuriant foliage. The port was full of native canoes and other vessels, large and small; and the ringing of bells and firing of rockets, announcing the dawn of some Roman Catholic festival day, showed that the population was astir at that early hour.

Having found lodgings and installed themselves, Bates and Wallace lost no time in observing nature in the city's environs. After some pages devoted largely to birds, lizards, and miscellaneous insects, Bates comes to his classic description of ants.

> I will pass over the many other orders and families of insects, and proceed at once to the ants. These were in great numbers everywhere, but I will mention here only two kinds. We were amazed at seeing ants an inch and a quarter in length, and stout in proportion, marching in single file through the thickets. These belonged to the species called *Dinoponera-grandis*. Its colonies consist of a small number of individuals, and are established about the roots of slender trees. It is a stinging species, but the sting is not so severe as in many of the smaller kinds. There was nothing peculiar or attractive in the habits of this giant among the ants. Another far more interesting species was the Sauba (*Ecodoma cephalotes*). This ant is seen everywhere about the suburbs, marching to and from in broad columns. From its habit of despoiling the most valuable cultivated trees of their foliage, it is a great scourge to the Brazilians. In some districts it is so abundant that agriculture is almost impossible, and everywhere complaints are heard of the terrible pest.

He devotes nearly eight pages to a fascinating account of the life and habits of the sauba ant, resembling other ants in that its colonies

> consist . . . of three sets of individuals, or, as some express it, of three sexes—namely, males, females, and workers; the last-mentioned being undeveloped females. The perfect sexes are winged on their first attaining the adult state; they alone propagate their kind, flying away, previous to the act of reproduction, from the nest in which they have been reared. This winged state of the perfect males and females, and the habit of flying abroad before pairing, are very important points in the economy of

ants; for they are thus enabled to intercross with members of distant colonies which swarm at the same time, and thereby increase the vigor of the race, a proceeding essential to the prosperity of any species.

His ensuing description of Pará, including the city's history, the life and nature of its people, and the like, includes some salient points of general interest to students of the tropics.

TEMPERATURE: The temperature during three years only once reached 95° of Fahrenheit. The greatest heat of the day, about 2:00 P.M., ranges generally between 89° and 94°; but on the other hand, the air is never cooler than 73°, so that a uniformly high temperature exists, and the mean of the year is 81°. North American residents say that the heat is not so oppressive as it is in summer in New York and Philadelphia.

Health. After stating that "the country had for a long time a reputation for extreme salubrity," Bates goes on to recount the several epidemics of smallpox, yellow fever, and cholera which, after 1819, marred that reputation, but says of his own day:

Since then, the healthfulness of the climate has been gradually restored, and it is now fast recovering its former good reputation. Pará is free from serious endemic disorders, and was once a resort of invalids from New York and Massachusetts.

Bates stayed in Pará one and a half years, though making numerous excursions from the city during that time. In chapter II, describing his observations in the course of a walk in the surrounding forest, he explains why, as observed by so many travelers, the ground seemed peculiarly void of animal life. Everything goes up into the air. The larger trees shoot up and form canopies with their foliage, which tend to exclude sunlight from the ground. Lianas climb up the trees to struggle toward the sun at the tops.

There is no distinct group of plants whose special habit it is to climb, but species of many and the most diverse families the bulk of whose members are not climbers, seem to have been driven by circumstances to adopt this habit. . . . The number and variety of climbing trees in the Amazon forests are interesting, taken in connection with the fact of the very general tendency of the animals, also, to become climbers.

All the Amazonian, and in fact all South American, monkeys are climbers. There is no group answering to the baboons of the Old World, which live on the ground. The Gallinaceous birds of the country, the representatives of the fowls and pheasants of Asia and Africa, are all adapted by the position of the toes to perch on trees, and it is only on trees, at a great height, that they are to be seen. A genus of *Plantigrade Carnivora,* allied to the bears (*Cercoleptes*), found only in the Amazonian forests, is entirely arboreal, and has a long flexible tail like that of certain monkeys. Many other similar instances could be enumerated, but I will mention only the *Geodephaga,* or carnivorous ground beetles, a great proportion of whose genera and species in these forest regions are, by the structure of their feet, fitted to live exclusively on the branches and leaves of trees.

Bates' accounts of excursions and short voyages from Pará are interspersed, as always, with descriptions of, and observations on, flora and fauna: trees, lianas, ferns, and flowers; birds, mammals, snakes, and insects; everything he saw was grist for his mill. At one point he was able to confirm earlier reports which a number of European scientists had dismissed as improbable invention: those of the bird-catching spiders.

At Cametá I chanced to verify a fact relating to the habits of a large hairy spider of the genus *Mygale,* in a manner worth recording. The species was *M. avicularia,* or one very closely allied to it; the individual was nearly two inches in length of body, but the legs expanded seven inches, and the entire body and legs were covered with coarse grey and reddish hairs. I was attracted by a movement of the monster on a tree-trunk; it was close beneath a deep crevice in the tree, across which was stretched a dense white web. The lower part of the web was broken, and two small birds, finches, were entangled in the pieces; they were about the size of the English siskin, and I judged the two to be male and female. One of them was quite dead, the other lay under the body of the spider not quite dead, and was smeared with the filthy liquor or saliva exuded by the monster. I drove away the spider and took the birds, but the second one soon died.

Having been told of a place called Caripí, some 23 miles from Pará, which had "quite a reputation for the number and beauty

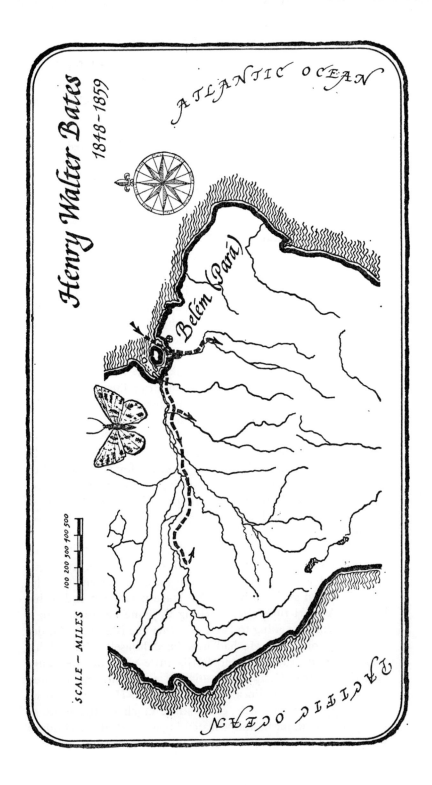

Henry Walter Bates
1848-1859

ATLANTIC OCEAN

Belém (Pará)

PACIFIC OCEAN

SCALE – MILES
100 200 300 400 500

of the birds and insects found there," Bates sailed for it on December 7, 1848, spending nine weeks on the spot, engaged in his studies and collecting. Of one of his neighbors and aides at Caripí, he wrote as follows:

The next day after I arrived, two blue-eyed and red-haired boys came up and spoke to me in English, and presently their father made his appearance. They proved to be a German family named Petzell, who were living in the woods, Indian fashion, about a mile from Caripí. Petzell explained to me how he came here. He said that thirteen years ago he came to Brazil with a number of other Germans under engagement to serve in the Brazilian army. When his time had expired he came to Pará to see the country, but after a few months' rambling left the place to establish himself in the United States. There he married, went to Illinois, and settled as farmer near St. Louis. He remained on his farm seven or eight years, and had a family of five children. He could never forget, however, the free river-life and perpetual summer of the banks of the Amazons; so he persuaded his wife to consent to break up their home in North America, and migrate to Pará. No one can imagine the difficulties the poor fellow had to go through before reaching the land of his choice. He first descended the Mississippi, feeling sure that a passage to Pará could be got at New Orleans. He was there told that the only port in North America he could start from was New York, so away he sailed for New York; but there was no chance of a vessel sailing thence to Pará, so he took a passage to Demerara, as bringing him, at any rate, near to the desired land. There is no communication whatever between Demerara and Pará, and he was forced to remain here with his family four or five months, during which they all caught the yellow fever, and one of his children died. At length he heard of a small coasting vessel going to Cayenne, so he embarked, and got thereby another stage nearer the end of his journey. A short time after reaching Cayenne he shipped in a schooner that was going to Pará, or rather the island of Marajó, for a cargo of cattle. He had now fixed himself, after all his wanderings, in a healthy and fertile little nook on the banks of a rivulet near Caripí, built himself a log-hut, and planted a large patch of mandioca and Indian corn. He seemed to be quite happy, but his wife complained much of the want of wholesome food, meat, and wheaten bread. I asked the children whether they liked the country; they shook their heads, and said they would rather be in Illinois. Petzell told me that his Indian neighbours treated him very kindly; one or other of them called almost every day to see how he was getting on, and they had helped him in many ways. He had a high opinion of the the Tapuyos, and said, "If you treat them well, they will go through fire to serve you."

Petzell and his family were expert insect-collectors, so I employed them at this work during my stay at Caripí. The daily occurrences here were after a uniform fashion. I rose with the dawn, took a cup of coffee, and then sallied forth after birds. At ten I breakfasted, and devoted the hours from ten until three to entomology. The evening was occupied in preserving and storing my captures. Petzell and I sometimes undertook long excursions, occupying the whole day. Our neighbours used to bring me all the quadrupeds, birds, reptiles, and shells they met with, and so altogether I was enabled to acquire a good collection of the productions of the district.

After nine weeks at Caripí, Bates returned to Pará, to spend another three months there before departing on an upriver trip on the main Amazon.

At the time of my first voyage up the Amazons—namely in 1849—nearly all communication with the interior was by means of sailing-vessels, owned by traders residing in the remote towns and villages, who seldom came to Pará themselves, but entrusted vessels and cargoes to the care of half-breeds or Portuguese *cabos* (foremen). . . . In the dry season, from August to December, when the trade-wind is strong and the currents slack, a schooner could reach the mouth of the Río Negro, a thousand miles from Pará, in about forty days; but in the wet season, from January to July, when the east-wind no longer blows and the Amazon pours forth its full volume of water, flooding the banks and producing a tearing current, it took three months to travel the same distance. It was a great blessing to the inhabitants when, in 1853, a line of steamers was established, and this same journey could be accomplished with ease and comfort, at all seasons, in eight days!

On the morning of October 3, Bates reached the town of Santarém, on the Amazon's south bank by the mouth of the Tapajoz River and some four hundred miles inland.

The town has a clean and cheerful appearance from the river. . . . At the first sight of Santarém, one cannot help being struck with the advantages of its situation. Although 400 miles from the sea, it is accessible to vessels of heavy tonnage coming straight from the Atlantic. The river has only two slight bends between this port and the sea, and for five or six months in the year the Amazonian trade wind blows with very little interruption, so that sailing ships coming from foreign countries could reach the place with little difficulty. We ourselves had accomplished 200 miles, or about half the distance from the sea, in an ill-rigged vessel, in three days and a half. Although the land in the immediate neighbourhood is perhaps ill adapted for agriculture, an immense tract of rich soil, with forest and meadow land, lies on the opposite banks of the river, and the Tapajoz leads into the heart of the mining provinces of interior Brazil. But where is the population to come from to develop the resources of this fine country? At present the district within a radius of twenty-five miles contains barely 6,500 inhabitants; behind the town, towards the interior, the country is uninhabited, and jaguars roam nightly, at least in the rainy season, close up to the ends of the suburban streets.

Less than two decades after Bates' visit, Santarém was to see the influx of a large group of settlers with their wives and children from the United States South, who, after the Civil War, chose not to live in the same country with the victorious North. During the 1920's the town was to become the bustling commercial center for the several rubber plantations established by the Ford Motor Company on the Tapajoz River. Only today, however, when the general, integrated development of the Amazon basin is getting under way, is Santarém beginning to attain some of the importance envisioned for it by Bates.

From Santarém Bates had a day's sail to Obydos (now Obidos), on the north shore and fifty miles upstream, "one of the pleasantest towns on the river."

Obydos and Santarém have received, during the last eighty years, considerable importations of Negro slaves; before that time a cruel traffic was carried on in Indians for the same purpose of forced servitude, but their numbers have now gradually dwindled away, and Indians now form an insignificant element in the population of the district. Most of the Obydos townsfolk are owners of cacao plantations, which are situated on the low lands in the vicinity. Some are large cattle proprietors, and possess estates of many square leagues in extent in the *campo*, or grass-land districts, which border the Lago Grande, and other similar inland lakes, near the villages of Faro and Alemque.

After some weeks of naturalizing and collecting in the forests near Obydos, observing and describing its monkeys and insects—especially the numerous butterflies (Obydos is still a favorite locale for professional butterfly hunters, who sell their catches to collectors in Europe and North America) Bates obtained passage upriver to Barra with a sailing trader named Penna. As always, his travel account of scenes and people encountered is meticulous and charming. A number of settlements, free Negro traders paddling along the river, captive Indian children, semi-civilized Indians engaging in religious festivals—such and many other matters he carefully noted.

> I was much annoyed, and at the same time amused, with the Urubú vultures. The Portuguese call them *corvos* or crows; in colour and general appearance they somewhat resemble rooks, but they are much larger, and have naked, black, wrinkled skin about their face and throat. They assemble in great numbers in the villages about the end of the wet season, and are then ravenous with hunger. My cook could not leave the open kitchen at the back of the house for a moment, whilst the dinner was cooking, on account of their thievish propensities. Some of them were always loitering about, watching their opportunity; and the instant the kitchen was left unguarded, the bold marauders marched in and lifted the lids of the saucepans with their beaks to rob them of their contents.

Sixty-four days after leaving Obydos, Bates was "comfortably settled" in new quarters in the town of Barra, today's Manaus, on the Río Negro, near the river's mouth.

> The town of Barra is built on a tract of elevated, but very uneven land, on the left bank of the Río Negro, and contained, in 1850, about 3,000 inhabitants. There was originally a small fort here, erected by the Portuguese to protect their slave-hunting expeditions amongst the numerous tribes of Indians which peopled the banks of the river. The most distinguished and warlike of these were the Manáos, who were continually at war with the neighbouring tribes, and had the custom of en-slaving the prisoners made during their predatory expeditions. The Portuguese disguised their slave-dealing motives under the pretext of ransoming (*resgatando*) these captives; indeed, the

term *resgatar* (to ransom) is still applied by the traders on the Upper Amazons to the very general, but illegal, practice of purchasing Indian children of the wild tribes. The older inhabitants of the place remember the time when many hundreds of these captives were brought down by a single expedition.

At Barra, Bates encountered his companion Wallace, with whom he roamed the surrounding forests for some weeks. When they finally parted again, Wallace undertook to explore the Río Negro while Bates took the Solimões, as the Amazon is called above the confluence of the Negro. On March 26, 1850, he ascended that river for Ega, 400 miles upstream, in whose vicinity he spent a year before ill-health, discouragement, and the failure of news and money to arrive from England, caused him to return to Pará. From that city he ascended the river again to Santarém, where he spent the years 1851–54, in 1852 making a memorable excursion up the Tapajoz River. As always, his description of that journey's adventures, his troubles with drunken members of his crew, the hospitality of the river's inhabitants, is interspersed with detailed accounts of fauna and flora.

[FIRE-ANTS:] Aveyros may be called the head-quarters of the fire-ant, which might be fittingly termed the scourge of this fine river. The Tapajoz is nearly free from the insect pests of other parts, mosquitos, sand-flies, *Motúcas* and piums; but the *formiga de fogo* is perhaps a greater plague than all the others put together. It is a small species, of a shining reddish colour, not greatly differing from the common red stinging ant of our own country (*Myrmica rubra*), except that the pain and irritation caused by its sting are much greater. The soil of the whole village is undermined by it: the ground is perforated with the entrances to their subterranean galleries, and a little sandy dome occurs here and there, where the insects bring their young to receive warmth near the surface. The houses are overrun with them; they dispute every fragment of food with the inhabitants, and destroy clothing for the sake of the starch. All eatables are obliged to be suspended in baskets from the rafters, and the cords well soaked with copauba balsam, which is the only means known of preventing them from climbing. They seem to attack persons out of sheer malice: if we stood for a few moments in the street, even at a distance from their nests, we were sure to be overrun and severely punished, for the moment an ant touched the flesh, he secured himself with his jaws, doubled in his tail, and stung with all his might. When we were seated on chairs in the evenings in front of the house to enjoy a chat with our neighbours, we had stools to support our feet, the legs of which as well as those of the chairs, were well anointed with the balsam. The cords of hammocks are obliged to be smeared in the same way to prevent the ants from paying sleepers a visit.[3]

[ANACONDAS:] We had an unwelcome visitor whilst at anchor in the port of Antonio Malagueita. I was awoke a little after midnight, as I lay in my little cabin, by a heavy blow struck at the sides of the canoe close to my head, which was succeeded by the sound of a weighty body plunging in the water. I got up; but all was again quiet, except the cackle of fowls in our hen-coop, which hung over the side of the vessel about three feet from the cabin door. I could find no explanation of the circumstance, and, my men being all ashore, I turned in again and slept till morning. I then found my poultry loose about the canoe, and a large rent in the bottom of the hen-coop, which was about two feet from the surface of the water; a couple of fowls were missing. Senhor Antonio said the depredator was a *Sucurujú* (the Indian name for the Anaconda, or great water serpent—*Eunectes murinus*), which had for months past been haunting this part of the river, and had carried off many ducks and fowls from the ports of various houses. I was inclined to doubt the fact of a serpent striking at its prey from the water, and thought an alligator more likely to be the culprit, although we had not yet met with alligators in the river. Some days afterwards the young men belonging to the different *sitios* [farmsteads] agreed together to go in search of the serpent. They began in a systematic manner, forming two parties, each embarked in three or four canoes, and starting from points several miles apart, whence they gradually approximated, searching all the little inlets on both sides of the river. The reptile was found at last, sunning itself on a log at the mouth of a muddy rivulet, and despatched with harpoons. I saw it the day after it was killed: it was not a very large specimen, measuring only eighteen feet nine inches in length, and sixteen inches in circumference at the widest part of the body. I measured skins of the Anaconda afterwards, twenty-one feet in length and two feet in girth. The reptile has a most hideous appearance, owing to its being very broad in the middle and

---

[3] From the editor's experience, "Flit," at least as it was made in 1932, not only kept the fire-ants away but was also an excellent balm for their sting.

tapering abruptly at both ends. It is very abundant in some parts of the country; nowhere more so than in the Lago Grande, near Santarém, where it is often seen coiled up in the corners of farm-yards, and is detested for its habit of carrying off poultry, young calves, or whatever animal it can get within reach of.

In the course of his Tapajoz voyage, Bates visited a settlement of Mundurucús, "perhaps the most numerous and formidable tribe of Indians now surviving in the Amazons region."

> At the first house we learnt that all the fighting men had this morning returned from a two days' pursuit of a wandering horde of savages of the Parárauáte tribe, who had strayed this way from the interior lands and robbed the plantations. A little further on we came to the house of the Tushaúa, or chief, situated on the top of a high bank, which we had to ascend by wooden steps. Our entrance aroused the Tushaúa from a nap; after rubbing his eyes he came forward and bade us welcome with the most formal politeness, and in very good Portuguese. He was a tall, broad-shouldered, well-made man, apparently about thirty years of age, with handsome regular features, not tattooed, and a quiet good-humoured expression of countenance. He had been several times to Santarém and once to Pará, learning the Portuguese language during these journeys. He was dressed in shirt and trousers made of blue-checked cotton cloth, and there was not the slightest trace of the savage in his appearance or demeanour.

Bates describes the recent expedition of the Mundurucús against their enemies:

> It would be a misnomer to call the Mundurucús of the Cuparí and many other parts of the Tapajoz, savages; their regular mode of life, agricultural habits, loyalty to their chiefs, fidelity to treaties, and gentleness of demeanor, give them a right to a better title. Yet they show no aptitude for the civilized life of towns, and, like the rest of the Brazilian tribes, seem incapable of any further advance in culture.
>
> Each horde of Mundurucús has its *pajé* or medicine man, who is the priest and doctor; fixes upon the time most propitious for attacking the enemy; exorcises evil spirits, and professes to cure the sick. All illness whose origin is not very apparent is supposed to be caused by a worm in the part affected. This the *pajé* pretends to extract; he blows on the seat of pain the smoke

from a large cigar, made with an air of great mystery by rolling tobacco in folds of Tauarí, and then sucks the place, drawing from his mouth, when he has finished, what he pretends to be the worm. It is a piece of very clumsy conjuring.

Ega, nearly 400 miles upstream from Barra, where Bates spent a total of nearly five years, interrupted by a three-year stay at Pará and Santarém, was situated on the Lake of Ega, "a magnificent sheet of water, five miles broad—the expanded portion of the [River] Teffé." The settlement was

> a cluster of a hundred or so palm-thatched cottages and white-washed red-tiled houses, each with its neatly-enclosed orchard of orange, lemon, banana, and guava trees. . . . Cattle were grazing before the houses, and a number of dark-skinned natives were taking their morning bath among the canoes of various sizes which were anchored or moored to stakes in the port. . . . A few days' experience of the people and the forests of the vicinity showed me that I might lay myself out for a long, pleasant, and busy residence in the place.

Just before arrival at Ega he had written:

> I reflected on my own wandering life: I had now reached the end of the third stage of my journey, and was now more than half way across the continent. It was necessary for me, on many accounts, to find a rich locality for Natural History explorations and settle myself in it for some months or years. Would the neighborhood of Ega turn out to be suitable, and should I, a solitary stranger on a strange errand, find a welcome amongst its people?

Ega did not disappoint him. With the exception of the Santarém interval of 1851–54, it was to be his headquarters until his departure for England in 1859.

> There were, of course, many drawbacks to the amenities of the place as a residence for a European; but these were not of a nature that my readers would perhaps imagine. There was scarcely any danger from wild animals; it seems almost ridiculous to refute the idea of danger from the natives in a country where even incivility to an unoffending stranger is a rarity. A Jaguar, however, paid us a visit one night. It was considered an extraordinary event, and so much uproar was made by the men who turned out with guns and bows and arrows that the animal scampered off and was heard of no more. Alligators were

rather troublesome in the dry season. During these months there was almost always one or two lying in wait near the bathing place for anything that might turn up at the edge of the water: dog, sheep, pig, child, or drunken Indian. When this visitor was about every one took extra care whilst bathing. I used to imitate the natives in not advancing far from the bank, and in keeping my eye fixed on that of the monster, which stares with a disgusting leer along the surface of the water; the body being submerged to the level of the eyes, and the top of the head, with part of the dorsal crest, the only portions visible. When a little motion was perceived in the water behind the reptile's tail, bathers were obliged to beat a quick retreat. I was never threatened myself, but I often saw the crowds of women and children scared, whilst bathing, by the beast making a movement towards them; a general scamper to the shore and peals of laughter were always the result in these cases. The men can always destroy these alligators when they like to take the trouble to set out with *montarias* and harpoons for the purpose; but they never do it unless one of the monsters, bolder than usual, puts some one's life in danger. This arouses them, and they then track the enemy with the greatest pertinacity; when half killed they drag it ashore and dispatch it amid loud execrations. Another, however, is sure to appear some days or weeks afterwards, and take the vacant place on the station. Besides alligators, the only animals to be feared are the poisonous serpents. These are certainly common enough in the forest, but no fatal accident happened during the whole time of my residence.

[CAPTIVE INDIANS:] Many of the Ega Indians, including all the domestic servants, are savages who have been brought from the neighbouring rivers; the Japurá, the Issá, and the Solimões. I saw here individuals of at least sixteen different tribes; most of whom had been bought, when children, of the native chiefs. This species of slave-dealing, although forbidden by the laws of Brazil, is winked at by the authorities, because, without it, there would be no means of obtaining servants. They all become their own masters when they grow up, and never show the slightest inclination to return to utter savage life. But the boys generally run away and embark on the canoes of traders and the girls are often badly treated by their mistresses, the jealous, passionate, and ill-educated Brazilian women. Nearly all the enmities which arise amongst residents at Ega and other places, are caused by disputes about Indian servants. No one who has lived only in old settled countries, where service can be readily bought, can imagine the difficulties and annoyances of a land where the servant class are ignorant of the value of money, and hands cannot be obtained except by coaxing them from the employ of other masters.

[FOODS:] We lived at Ega, during most part of the year, on turtle. The great fresh-water turtle of the Amazons grows on the upper river to an immense size, a full-grown one measuring nearly three feet in length by two in breadth, and is a load for the strongest Indian. Every house has a little pond, called a *curral* (pen), in the back-yard to hold a stock of the animals through the season of dearth—the wet months; those who have a number of Indians in their employ send them out for a month when the waters are low, to collect a stock, and those who have not, purchasing their supply; with some difficulty, however, as they are rarely offered for sale.

In commenting on the settlement's reliance on meats from the land and river, Bates said that "those who cannot hunt and fish for themselves, and whose stomachs refuse turtle, are in a poor way at Ega."

We sometimes had fresh bread at Ega made from American flour brought from Pará, but it was sold at ninepence a pound. I was once two years without tasting wheaten bread, and attribute partly to this the gradual deterioration of health which I suffered on the Upper Amazons. Mandioca meal is a poor, weak substitute for bread; it is deficient in gluten, and consequently cannot be formed into a leavened mass or loaf, but is obliged to be roasted in hard grains in order to keep any length of time.

There follow detailed descriptions of many other native foods, fruits and nuts, available at Ega, all of them interspersed with description of the palms, etc., which yielded them.

Visit to an Indian Chief. On May 23, 1850, Bates, accompanied by a Brazilian friend, visited a family of the Passé tribe who lived some hours' canoe trip from Ega. "The family we intended to visit on this trip was that of Pero-uassú (Peter the Great, or Tall Peter), an old chieftain or Tushaúa of the Passés."

As we landed, Pero-uassú himself came down to the port to receive us; our arrival having been announced by the barking of dogs. He was a tall and thin old man, with a serious, but benignant expression of countenance, and a manner much freer from shyness and distrust than is usual with Indians. He was clad in a shirt of coarse cotton cloth, dyed with *murishi,* and trowsers of the same material turned up to the knee. His features were sharply delineated—more so than in any Indian face I had yet seen; the lips thin and the nose rather high and compressed. A large, square, blue-black tattooed patch occupied the middle of his face, which, as well as the other exposed parts of his body, was of a light reddish-tan colour, instead of the usual coppery-brown hue. He walked with an upright, slow gait, and on reaching us saluted Cardozo (my Brazilian friend) with the air of a man who wished it to be understood that he was dealing with an equal. Arrived at the house, we were welcomed by Pedro's wife, a thin, wrinkled, active old squaw, tattooed in precisely the same way as her husband. She had also sharp features, but her manner was more cordial and quicker than that of her husband; she talked much, and with great inflection of voice; whilst the tones of the old man were rather drawling and querulous. Her clothing was a long petticoat of thick cotton cloth, and a very short chemise, not reaching to her waist. I was rather surprised to find the grounds around the establishment in neater order than in any *sitio,* even of civilised people, I had yet seen on the Upper Amazons; the stock of utensils and household goods of all sorts was larger, and the evidences of regular industry and plenty more numerous than one usually perceives in the farms of civilised Indians and whites.

After the preliminary greetings, Bates went for "a long ramble into the forest, Pedro sending his grandson, a smiling well-behaved lad of about fourteen years of age, to show me the paths, my companion taking with him his *Zarabatana,* or blowgun."

[THE BLOWGUN:] This instrument is used by all the Indian tribes on the Upper Amazons. It is generally nine or ten feet long, and is made of two separate lengths of wood, each scooped out so as to form one-half of the tube. To do this with the necessary accuracy requires an enormous amount of patient labour, and considerable mechanical ability, the tools used being simply the incisor teeth of the *Páca* and *Cutía.* The two half tubes, when finished, are secured together by a very close and tight spirally-wound strapping, consisting of long flat strips of *Jacitára,* or the wood of the climbing palm-tree; and the whole is smeared afterwards with black wax, the production of a *Malipona* bee. The pipe tapers towards the muzzle, and a cup-shaped mouth-piece, made of wood, is fitted in the broad end. The arrows are made from the hard rind of the leaf-stalks of certain palms, thin strips being cut, and rendered as sharp as needles by scraping the ends with a knife or the tooth of an animal. They are winged with a little oval mass of *samauma,* cotton being too heavy. The ball of *samauma* should fit to a nicety the bore of the blowgun; when it does so, the arrow can be propelled with such force by the breath that it makes a noise almost as loud as a pop-gun on flying from the muzzle. My little companion was armed with a quiver full of these little missiles, a small number of which, sufficient for the day's sport, were tipped with the fatal *Urari* poison.

On returning to the house, Bates and his companion, together with several Indians who had gathered, were served dinner, consisting of "boiled fowls and rice, seasoned with green peppers and lemon juice, and piles of new, fragrant farinha and raw bananas. It was served on plates of English manufacture on a *tupé,* or large plaited rush mat, such as is made by the natives pretty generally on the Amazons."

With his friend Cardozo and his men, Bates made many ex-cursions from Ega and up the Solimões River, hunting turtle eggs and camping nights on the beaches. During these trips he had many encounters with the Amazonian alligators and natu-rally devotes many pages to describing them and their habits. After recounting a number of incidents to show that "the na-tives at once despise and fear the great cayman," Bates writes:

These little incidents show the timidity or cowardice of the alligator. He never attacks man when his intended victim is on his guard: but he is cunning enough to know when this may be done with impunity: of this we had proof at Caicara, a few days afterwards. The river had sunk to a very low point, so that the port and bathing-place of the village now lay at the foot of a long sloping bank, and a large cayman made his appearance in the shallow and muddy water. We were all obliged to be very careful in taking our bath; most of the people simply using a calabash, pouring the water over themselves while standing on the brink. A large trading canoe, belonging to a Barra merchant named Soares, arrived at this time, and the Indian crew, as usual, spent the first day or two after their coming into port, in drunkenness and debauchery ashore. One of the men, during the greatest heat of the day, when almost every one was enjoying his afternoon's nap, took it into his head whilst in a tipsy state to go down alone to bathe. He was seen only by the Juez de Paz [Justice of the Peace], a feeble old man who was lying in his hammock, in the open verandah at the rear of his house on the top of the bank, and who shouted to the besotted Indian to beware of the alligator. Before he could repeat his warning, the man stumbled, and a pair of gaping jaws, appearing suddenly above the surface, seized him round the waist and drew him under the water. A cry of agony "Ai Jesús!" was the last sign made by the wretched victim. The village was aroused; the young men with praise-worthy readiness seized their harpoons and hurried down to the bank; but of course it was too late, a winding track of blood on the surface of the water, was all that could be seen. They embarked, however, in *montarias,* determined on vengeance; the monster was traced, and when, after a short lapse of time, he came up to breathe—one leg of the man sticking out from his jaws—was dispatched with bitter curses.

A fascinating chapter is devoted to the animals in the neighborhood of Ega, including several kinds of monkeys, bats, birds, cocoons, foraging ants, and blind ants. Five species of the large-billed toucans inhabited the vicinity of Ega. During the moulting season, when flight was difficult, large flocks gathered together from the neighboring forests, which are then in flood.

> The birds have now become exceedingly tame, and the troops travel with heavy laborious flight from bough to bough amongst the lower trees. They thus become an easy prey to hunters, and every one at Ega, who can get a gun of any sort and a few charges of powder and shot, or a blow-pipe, goes daily to the woods to kill a few brace for dinner; for, as already observed, the people of Ega live almost exclusively on stewed and roasted Toucans during the months of June and July; the birds being then very fat, and the meat exceedingly sweet and tender.

After observing the toucan's weight and clumsiness, and speculating on the function of its great bill, Bates says:

> The purpose of the enormous bill here becomes evident. It is to enable the Toucan to reach and devour fruit whilst remaining seated, and thus to counterbalance the disadvantage which its heavy body and gluttonous appetite would otherwise give it in the competition with allied groups of birds.

During 1856 and '57 he made several upriver excursions by steamer on the Solimões and some of its tributaries. At one point he attended and described a masked dance held by the Tucuná Indians at a place called São Paulo, near the Peruvian border, where he spent five months. Speculating at length on the primitive religious concepts of those people, he decided that they had no concept of "a spirit of a beneficient God or Creator."

The Jurupari or Demon is the only superior being they have any conception of, and his name is mixed up with all their ceremonies, but it is difficult to ascertain what they consider to be his attributes. He seems to be believed in simply as a mischievous imp, who is at the bottom of all those mishaps of their daily life, the causes of which are not very immediate or obvious to their dull understandings.

The only other tribe of this neighbourhood concerning which I obtained any information were the Majerónas, whose territory embraces several hundred miles of the western bank of the river Jauarí, an affluent of the Solimões, 120 miles beyond St. Paulo [Bates' anglicized spelling]. These are a fierce, indomitable, and hostile people, like the Aráras of the river Madeira; they are also cannibals. The navigation of the Jauarí is rendered impossible on account of the Majerónas lying in wait on its banks to intercept and murder all travellers, especially whites.

Bates had planned to cross into Peru and continue his studies in that country to the foot of the Andes. However, at São Paulo he came down with a violent attack of chills and fevers, undoubtedly malaria.

Every morning I shouldered my gun or insect-net, and went on my usual walk in the forest. The fit of shivering very often seized me before I got home, and I then used to stand still and brave it out. When the steamer ascended in January, 1858, Lieutenant Nunes was shocked to see me so much shattered, and recommended me strongly to return at once to Ega. I took his advice, and embarked with him, when he touched at St. Paulo on his downward voyage, on the 2nd of February. I still hoped to be able to turn my face westward again, to gather the yet unseen treasures of the marvellous countries lying between Tabatinga and the slopes of the Andes; but although, after a short rest in Ega, the ague left me, my general health remained in a state too weak to justify the undertaking of further journeys. At length I left Ega, on the 3rd of February,—1859, en route for England.

He descended to Pará and found the city greatly improved, though the cost of living had quadrupled since his last stay there.

> *June 2, 1859*—At length, on the second of June, I left Pará, probably forever; embarking in a North American trading-vessel, the *Frederick Demming,* for New York, the United States route being the quickest as well as the pleasantest way of reaching England. My extensive private collections were divided into three portions and sent by three separate ships, to lessen the risk of loss of the whole.

According to Dr. Usinger's introduction to the book here quoted, Bates' observations on mimicry were "of even greater significance than the discovery of new species." The marked protective ressemblance of certain insects to birds and leaves came to be ascribed by Bates to "natural selection, the selecting agents being insectiverous animals which gradually destroy those sports or varieties that are not sufficiently like *Ithomiae* to deceive them." Darwin, in commenting on the paper which Bates worked up on the subject for the Linnaean Society, said, "In my opinion it is one of the most remarkable and admirable papers I ever read in my life."

Of Bates' years in England after his return from the Amazons, Usinger says:

> Bates was married in 1861 while still in the midst of the laborious task of condensing his notes of eleven years into book form. Despite ill-health Darwin generously read the final manuscript; the two-volume first edition appeared in January, 1863. The book was a great success, the first edition being exhausted in a few months. Later the present abridged edition was prepared.

> In 1864 Bates was appointed Assistant Secretary of the Royal Geographical Society, his first and lifetime post where he gave devoted and inspired service. For nearly thirty years Bates played a modest but effective role in the scientific life of London, twice serving as president of the Entomological Society and in 1881 being elected a fellow of the Royal Society. Before his death in 1892 he was decorated by the Emperor of Brazil.

XX

THE UNITED STATES
DISCOVERS THE
AMAZON

NEAR the middle of the nineteenth century the United States became officially interested in the vast and reputedly wealthy Amazon basin, nearly three million square miles in area, virtually undeveloped, a social-economic vacuum in the heart of South America. The interest grew out of the interaction of a number of trends and factors, of which the following were the most important:

1. The burgeoning commerce and industrial plant of the United States had begun to demand increasing quantities of tropical raw materials.

2. The development of steam navigation was rapidly changing world patterns of, and prospects for, trade. The idea that United States steamships might "open" the Amazonian regions for American trade had a strong appeal.

3. In addition to promising trade possibilities of its own, the Amazon River system began to be regarded as a potential gateway to South America's west coast, where, as with such countries as Chile and Peru, North American trade was already flourishing. Moreover, Amazonian navigation might facilitate trade with several South American centers, west of the basin, which were relatively inaccessible by other routes. In his report, cited below, for instance, Lieutenant Gibbon pointed out that the construction of a portage road of less than 200 miles, around the rapids of the Madeira-Mamoré River, would permit a passage of "fifty-one days . . . from Baltimore to Cochabamba, or fifty-

nine days to La Paz, the commercial emporium of Bolivia, where cargoes arrive generally from Baltimore in one hundred and eighteen days, by Cape Horn."

4. The notion that our mounting tensions over the slavery issue might be relieved through the simple expedient of having the Southern planters move to the Amazon, slaves and all, there to expedite the North's trade with South America's tropical interior, began to be taken quite seriously by a number of people who were not Southern planters. It was believed that an official report, praising the Amazon country, might cause the South to be more kindly disposed toward the idea than it was.

5. Evidence of growing interest in the Amazonian regions on the part of European nations gave the Washington government food for thought. In 1827 Lieutenant Maw of the British Navy had descended the Huallaga and the Amazon to the latter's mouth. In 1835 Maw had been followed by another British naval officer, Lieutenant Smyth, who descended the Ucayali and then followed his predecessor down the Amazon. Between 1843 and 1847 Count Castelnau had explored South America's interior with the French Government's support.

For such and other reasons it behooved the United States to show an interest in the Amazon basin. It was therefore decided, apparently during President Zachary Taylor's brief term in office (1849 until his death in July, 1850), to send an official United States expedition to Amazonia to study possibilities for, and problems of, power navigation in various parts of the river system, the extent of existing development, resources available, possibilities for further settlement, health problems, and the like.

However, the President's death delayed the project somewhat. Final orders for the expedition to get under way, signed by the Secretary of the Navy William A. Graham, were issued February 15, 1851, during Millard Fillmore's administration.

The man selected to head the venture was Lieutenant William Lewis Herndon of the U.S. Navy. Born in 1813, in Fredericksburg, Virginia, he was related to Meriwether Lewis of Lewis and Clark fame. Commissioned a naval lieutenant in 1841, he served in the Mexican War and then spent three years in the U.S. Naval Observatory, whose superintendent, Matthew Fontaine Maury, was his brother-in-law. Maury was an ardent advocate of American exploration and development of the Amazon valley, especially as an outlet for United States slave labor, which was multiplying alarmingly. In 1855, after completing his Amazonian work and submitting his report, Herndon returned to sea duty and was lost in a marine disaster on September 12, 1857. His daughter, Ellen Lewis, later married Chester A. Arthur, who was to become President of the United States.

Less information is available on his partner and subordinate, the Philadelphian Lardner Gibbon, except that he was sent south to join Herndon directly from service in the National Observatory. The two must have known each other well before undertaking their South American venture. At the time of joining Herndon, Gibbon held the rank of "Passed Midshipman," meaning that he had fulfilled the requirements for winning the lieutenant's commission which was granted to him before the publication of his report.

Several months before receiving his final orders, Herndon had advance notice that he would soon be entrusted with an interesting mission. His report [1] begins: "Attached to the U.S. ship *Vandalia*, of the Pacific squadron, lying at anchor in the harbor of Valparaiso, in the month of August, 1850, I received a communication from the Superintendent of the National Observatory, informing me that orders to explore the Valley of the Amazon would be sent me by the next mail steamer." He thereupon left his ship and spent some months in Valparaiso and Santiago, waiting for further orders and gathering all the information on the Amazon that he could. On January 20th, 1851, he received orders from the Secretary of the Navy, dated October 30th, 1850, telling him to proceed to Lima, Peru, and to Bolivia, for the purpose of visiting monasteries and other institutions, toward the end of gathering all available pertinent information "concerning the headwaters of the Amazon and the regions of country drained by its Peruvian [and Bolivian] tributaries." His final orders, dated February 15, were delivered to him in Lima on April 4th by "Passed Midshipman" Lardner Gibbon.

Bidding him proceed over the Andes and down the Amazon

---

[1] *Exploration of the Valley of the Amazon,* by William Lewis Herndon and Lardner Gibbon, Lieutenants, U.S.N. (Washington: Robert Armstrong, Public Printer, 1854).

system by a route which was left to his discretion, the Secretary
of the Navy wrote Herndon:

> The Government desires to be put in possession of certain
> information relating to the valley of the river Amazon, in which
> term is included the entire basin, or watershed, drained by that
> river and its tributaries.
>
> This desire extends not only to the present condition of that
> valley, with regard to the navigability of its streams; to the num-
> ber and condition, both industrial and social, of its inhabitants,
> their trade and products; its climate, soil and productions; but
> also to its capacities for cultivation, and to the character and
> extent of its undeveloped commercial resources, whether of the
> field, the forest, the river, or the mine.

Secretary Graham instructed Herndon to avoid "any route
by which you and your party would be exposed to savage hostility, beyond your means of defense and protection." He was
explicit in his recurring requests for information on navigability. He asked for a report on "the present condition of the silver
mines of Peru and Bolivia—their yield; how and by whom are
they principally wrought?" Undoubtedly smelling possible new
outlets for American machinery, he asked for information on
the machinery used in those mines, where it had been obtained,
and how it had been transported, as well as advice on whether
the Peruvian and Bolivian silver might, in the event of free
navigation of the Amazon, be transported down that river to the
Atlantic instead of via the toilsome route to the Pacific on muleback and thence over the Isthmus of Panama to the Atlantic.
With regard to scientific investigations, he wrote:

> You will make such geographical and scientific observations
> by the way as may be consistent with the main object of the ex-
> pedition, always bearing in mind that these are merely inci-
> dental, and that no part of the main objects of the expedition
> is to be interfered with by them.

For all that and much more, having moreover been asked to
keep his party small in order not "to excite the suspicion of the
people, or give offense to the authorities, of the country through
which you may pass," Herndon was provided with equipment
(to be issued to him by the Navy Agent at Lima), and a sum "not

exceeding five thousand dollars," to be used "only for the *necessary* expenses of the party."

Chapter I of Herndon's report summarizes the information he had been able to find in his researches in Peru and Bolivia. He tells of the early days of conquest and of the search for El Dorado, but finds the pickings slim with regard to dependable geographic and other information. "It is not to be expected," he writes, "that information of an exact and scientific character could be had from the voyages of adventurers like these. They were mere soldiers, and too much occupied in difficulties of travel, conflicts with Indians, ambitious designs, and internal dissentions, to make any notes of the topography or productions of the countries they passed through." From later accounts, however, reports of special missions sent out from Peru and Bolivia, he did manage to glean enough specific information to permit him to formulate a plan of action. Under that plan, he and Gibbon traveled together from Lima to Tarma, a mountain town roughly a hundred miles inland from the capital, where they separated, Herndon to descend the Huallaga to the Amazon and then follow the main river to its mouth, while Gibbon was instructed to push southward to Cuzco. From that city he was to cross to the headwaters of the Madre de Dios with the aim of descending and exploring that little-known river to determine whether it was the same as the Purus, which was known to flow into the Amazon. Gibbon was given instructions for alternate action in the event that the Madre de Dios exploration proved inadvisable, but it was clear that Herndon's heart was set on Gibbon discovering whether the known headwaters of the one river connected in navigable fashion with the known mouth of the other.

After several interviews with the President of Peru, General Castilla, "who exhibited much interest in my mission," Herndon arranged for transportation to Tarma.

> On the 15th of May, I engaged the services of an *arriero*, or muleteer. He engaged to furnish beasts to carry the party and its baggage from Lima to Tarma at ten dollars the head, stopping on the road wherever I pleased and as long as I pleased, for that sum. An ordinary train of baggage mules may be had on the same route for about seven dollars the head. The *arrieros* of Peru, as a class, have a very indifferent reputation for faith-

fulness and honesty, and those on that route, (that from Lima
to Cerro de Pasco), to which my friend particularly belonged,
are said to be the worst of their class. He was a thin, spare, dark
Indian of the *Sierra*, or mountain land, about forty-five years of
age, with keen, black eyes, thin mustache, and deliberate in his
speech and gesture. I thought I had never seen a worse face; but
Mr. McCall said that he was rather better-looking than the
generality of them. He managed to cheat me very soon after
our acquaintance.

They obtained the services of a "Mr. Richards," a young master mate from a U.S. frigate, as well as those of a Peruvian interpreter. They bought four saddle mules, cloth, and a variety of
other items to be used as trade goods, saddles, clothing, camping
equipment, and the like. They left Lima on Wednesday, the
21st of May,

> though I had to cajole, and finally to bribe the old fellow, to
> take on all the baggage, which he represented to be too much
> for his beasts. . . . After a hard morning's work in drumming
> up the Peruvian part of the expedition, (these people have not
> the slightest idea that a man will start on a journey on the day
> he proposes), the party, consisting of myself, Mr. Gibbon, Mr.
> Richards, Mr. Ijurra (the interpreter), Mauricio, an Indian of
> Chamicuros (a village on the Huallaga), and the *arriero*, Pablo
> Luis Arredondo, with seven burden-mules, defiled out by the
> Gate of Marvels . . . , and took the broad and beaten road that
> ascends the left bank of the Rimac.

The travelers headed eastward and up into the mountains,
from town to town, making between ten and fifteen miles per
day, noting down the products, customs and ailments of the
countryside, Gibbon busily sketching scenery and people. On
May 29th they visited some silver mines near the town of San
Mateo. Herndon's account describes the technical process of
mining and reducing silver from the ore, beside dealing with
the economics of mining and the debt-slavery in which the Indian workers were kept. On a number of occasions they had
trouble in obtaining fresh food for themselves or alfalfa for the
mules.

> *June 2.* Got off at half past ten. Road tolerably good, and not
> very precipitous. At twelve we arrived on a level with the lowest
> line of snow. We were marking the barometer, when a traveler

rode up, who proved to be an old schoolmate of mine, whom I had not seen, or even heard of, since we were boys. The meeting at this place was an extraordinary and very agreeable occurrence. It was also fortunate for me, for my friend was head-machinist at the mines of Morococha, and gave us a note to the administrator, which secured us a hospitable reception and an interesting day or two. . . . At 2 P.M. we arrived at the highest point [about 16,044 feet above sea level], called the pass of Antarangra, or copper rock. . . .

Gibbon, with the camera lucida, sketched the cordillera. I expended a box of matches in boiling the snow for the atmospheric pressure; and poor Richards lay shivering on the ground, enveloped in our *pillons,* a martyr to the *veta.*

Veta is the sickness caused by the rarity of the atmosphere at these great elevations. The Indians call it *veta,* or vein, because they believe it is caused by veins of metal diffusing around a poisonous infection. . . . The affection displays itself in a violent headache, with the veins of the head swollen and turgid, a difficulty of respiration and cold extremities. The smell of garlic is said to alleviate the symptoms; and the *arrieros* generally anoint their cattle over the eyes, and on the forehead, with an unguent made of tallow, garlic, and wild marjoram.

Though not yet sixty miles from the sea, we had crossed the great "divide" which separates the waters of the Atlantic from those of the Pacific. . . .

I was now, for the first time, fairly in the field of my operations. I had been sent to explore the Valley of the Amazon, to sound its streams, and to report on their navigability. I was commanded to examine its fields, its forests, and its rivers, that I might gauge their capabilities, active and dormant, for trade and commerce with the states of Christendom, and make known to the spirit and enterprise of the age the resources which lie concealed there, waiting for the touch of civilization and the breath of the steam engine to give them animation, life, and palpable existence. . . .

Though the waters where I stood were bound on their way to meet the streams of our Northern Hemisphere, and to bring, for all the practical purposes of commerce and navigation, the mouth of the Amazon and the mouth of the Mississippi into one, and place it before our own doors, yet, from the head of navigation on one stream to the head of navigation on the other, the distance to be sailed could not be less than ten thousand miles. . . . The importance to the world of settlement, cultivation, and commerce in the Valley of the Amazon cannot be over-estimated. With the climates of India, and of all the habitable portions of the earth, piled one above the other in quick succession, tillage and good husbandry here would transfer the productions of the East to this magnificent river basin and place them within a few days' easy sail of Europe and the United States.

Only a few miles back we had first entered the famous mining district of Peru. A large portion of the silver which constitutes the circulation of the world was dug from the range of mountains upon which we are standing; and most of it came from that slope of them which is drained off into the Amazon. Is it possible for commerce and navigation up and down this majestic water-course and its beautiful tributaries to turn the flow of this silver stream from its western course to the Pacific, and conduct it with steamers down the Amazon to the United States, there to balance the stream of gold with which we are likely to be flooded from California and Australia?

Descending, they reached Morococha at five in the afternoon. Herndon describes the region's activities in mining copper and coal. About four P.M., on the 6th of June, "the pretty little city of Tarma, embosomed among the hills, and enveloped in its covering of willows and fruit trees, with its long lawns of alfalfa stretching out in front, broke upon our view."

After a rest at Tarma, the explorers spent some days descending the Chanchamayo River, and on June 19 they reached the wilderness fort of San Ramón.

The fort was constructed in 1847, under the direction of President Castilla, for the purpose of affording protection to the cultivators of the farms in its rear. It doubtless does this against the unwarlike Indians of this country; but I imagine that North American Indians, actuated by the feelings of hostility which these people constantly evince, would cross the river above the fort and sweep the plantations before the soldiers could reach them. The Indians have abandoned all idea of reconquering the territory they have lost, but are determined to dispute the passage of the rivers and any attempt at further conquest. They never show themselves now in person, but make their presence evident by occasionally setting fire to the woods and grass on the hill-sides, and discharging their arrows at any incautious person who may wander too near the banks of the rivers.

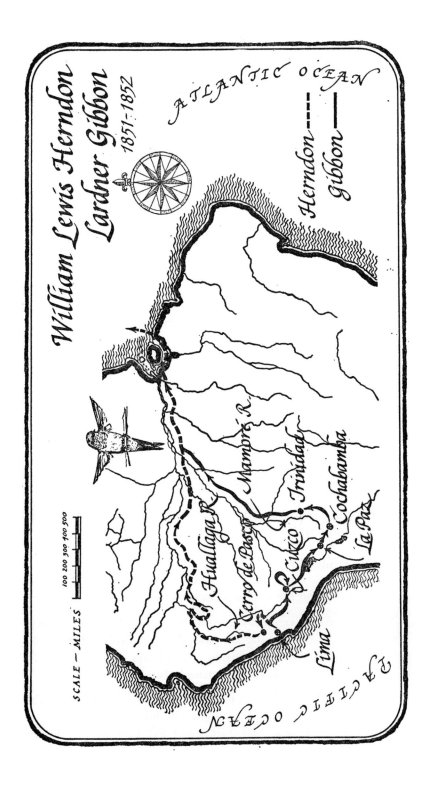

William Lewis Herndon
Lardner Gibbon
1851-1852

ATLANTIC OCEAN

Herndon ------
Gibbon ———

SCALE — MILES
100 200 300 400 500

Huallaga R.
Cerro de Pasco
Mamore R.
Cuzco
Trinidad
Cochabamba
La Paz
Lima

PACIFIC OCEAN

Herndon gives the altitude of Fort San Ramón as 2,605 feet; that of Tarma as 9,738 feet. After spending a few days visiting the several farms near the fort and making detailed notes on their products (sugar cane, coca, coffee, tree-cotton, yucca, corn, plantains, pineapples and other tropical fruits), they set out on June 23 to return to Tarma, reaching the town three days later.

> We delighted the Tarma people with our favorable reports of the Chanchamayo, and they loaded us with civilities and kindness. They did not like the idea of my visiting the Montaña of Pozuzu and Mayro; and seemed to fear that I might find there a better communication with the Amazon. . . .[2]
>
> Gibbon and I had a long and earnest consultation about the propriety of dividing the party; and I now determined to do so, giving to him the task of exploring the Bolivian tributaries, while I took the headwaters and the main trunk of the Amazon. It was a bold, almost a rash determination, for the party seemed small enough as it was; and we might readily encounter difficulties on our route which would require our united exertions to overcome. I had many misgivings . . . ; but the prospect of covering countries and rivers so little known; and the reflection that I need not abandon routes that I had looked upon with a longing eye, were so tempting that they overcame all objections; and we set about making our preparations for the separation. . . .
>
> *July 1.* Started at noon with Ijurra and Mauricio, accompanied by Gibbon. . . . Soon after, Gibbon and I lingered behind the company; and at the entrance of the valley of the Acobamba, which route I was to take, we shook hands and parted. . . .
>
> He returned to make the necessary arrangements for his expedition. We crossed the Chanchamayo by a stone bridge, and passed through the village of Acobamba.

The next day Herndon came to the plain of Junín, "where Bolívar, on the 6th of August, gave the Spaniards a heavy and very nearly conclusive overthrow." As always, he goes into details on the people's foods and eating habits.

> *July 3.* The inhabitants of Junín, and the other towns of this plain, are herdsmen. They raise cattle for the supply of Cerro

[2] The Tarmians wanted to see a waterway opened down their own Chanchamayo to the Amazon.

[de] Pasco and Tarma, and mules for beasts of burden. Their houses are built of mud and straw; and they eat mutton and *macas,* (a root of the potato kind but looking, and when boiled tasting, more like a turnip). The people of these regions find it very difficult to procure vegetables, as quinua and barley will not grain, nor potatoes grow, in the wet soil and cold atmosphere of the plain. They therefore have to resort to means for preserving the potato and its varieties, which are got from the valleys of the Andes. These means are, generally, drying and freezing; and they make a number of preparations from the potato in this way. The *macas* are simply exposed to the frost and sun for a number of days, and then put away in a dry room. The inhabitants make a sort of soup or syrup of them, the smell of which, Rivero says, "is a little disagreeable to people unaccustomed to it," (it is really very offensive); and it is the general opinion that it is a stimulant to reproduction.

The next day, the fourth of July, they arrived at the mining district of Cerro de Pasco, where today's mines, operated by the U.S. Cerro de Pasco Copper Corporation, are among South America's most important producers of copper, though the terrain is also rich in gold, silver, vanadium, and other metals. In honor of the day, Herndon donned his uniform

and went out to see Mr. Jump, director of the machinery, and Mr. Fletcher, an employee of the *Gremio,* (Board of Miners), to whom I brought letters of introduction from Lima. These gentlemen received me with great cordiality. Mr. Jump offered me a room in his house, and Mr. Fletcher handed me a number of letters from friends at home, at Lima, and at Santiago. These letters were cordial medicines to me; I had arrived cold, sick, and dispirited, and but for them should have passed the first night of mental and physical suffering that I had been called upon to endure since leaving Lima.

I went out with Mr. Jump to look at the town. It was a most curious looking place, entirely honey-combed, and having the mouths of mines (some two or three yards in diameter) gaping everywhere. . . . We visited a machine-shop, and the hacienda for grinding ores by steam, that Mr. Jump is erecting near the city. . . . The cost of the machinery, which is cast in England, in parts equal to a mule-load, and transported from Lima on the backs of these animals; the pay of machine and engine drivers; the digging of ditches for the supply of water; fuel; and all such expenses to which the other haciendas are not subject, I could not well calculate.

Nevertheless, Herndon made a good, rough analysis of the economics and mechanics of working the region's mines, whose silver had been discovered in 1630, and concluded that, even with the primitive transportation on muleback, it was a profitable business. He stayed in the vicinity until July 13, inspecting mines and reduction works, while also determining that Cerro de Pasco's altitude was 13,800 feet, and concluding that the climate was "exceedingly uncomfortable, and I should suppose unhealthy." However, several people talked to him enthusiastically about the manner in which the region would boom once commercial transportation had been opened to navigable Amazonian waterways.

> This is the day-dream of the Peruvians of that district. They know the difficulties of the Cordillera passage, and look earnestly to the eastward for communication with the world. . . . They say it will be a great day for them when the Americans get near them with a steamer.

He left Cerro de Pasco on July 13, making his way from town to town, diligently making notes on the mining industry. On July 15 he wrote:

> A few miles further on we crossed the boundary-line between the provinces of Pasco and Huánuco. The transition is agreeable, and I was glad to exchange the mining for the agricultural country. At half-past four we arrived at the town of Ambo, a village of one thousand inhabitants, situated at the junction of the rivers Huacar and Huallaga. The former stream comes down a ravine to the westward; each is about thirty-five yards broad, and, uniting, they pour their waters by the town with great velocity.

A little beyond Ambo, Herndon came to "the hospitable . . . hacienda Quicacan," which strongly reminded him "of the large farm-houses in some parts of Virginia: the same number of servants bustling about in each other's way; the children of the master and the servant all mixed up together; the same in the hospitable welcome to all comers; the same careless profusion."

The owner was an Englishman named Dyer. Of the conversation which followed dinner, Herndon writes:

> I conversed with an intelligent and manly Frenchman named Escudero. His account of the seeking and gathering of Peruvian bark [3] was exceedingly interesting; and I should judge that it is an occupation which involves much fatigue and exposure. He spoke very highly of the mechanical abilities of my countryman, Miguel Hacket, and gave me a letter to deliver to him wherever I might find him.

After describing the hacienda's profitable business of producing sugar, Herndon goes on to the town of Huánuco. There, ever mindful that one of his expedition's aims was to interest Southern planters in the idea of easing the slavery issue in the United States as well as helping the industrial North, by moving to South America, he describes the town's richest and most influential man, Colonel Lucar.

> He seems to have been the father of husbandry in these parts, and is the very type of the old landed proprietor of Virginia, who has always lived upon his estates, and attended personally to their cultivation. Seated at the head of his table . . . , his chair surrounded by two or three little Negro children, whom he fed with bits from his plate; and attending with patience and kindness to the clamorous wants of a pair of splendid peacocks, a couple of small parrots of brilliant and variegated plumage, and a beautiful and delicate monkey—I thought I had rarely seen a more perfect pattern of the patriarch. His kind and affectionate manner to his domestics (all slaves), and to his little grandchildren, a pair of sprightly boys, who came in in the evening from the college, was also very pleasing. There are thirty servants attached to the house, large and small.

After describing the farm's products and management, Herndon writes:

> People in Huánuco are fully alive to the importance of opening the navigation of the Huallaga to their city.[4] They speak of it as a thing that would be of incalculable advantage to them;

[3] Cinchona bark, the source of quinine, first discovered by the Amazonian Indians, later gathered wild on the slopes of the eastern Andes, now produced primarily in Asian plantations.
[4] The city is on the Huallaga, but the river is not navigable that far up, even by canoe.

and their leaders and influential men have often urged them to be up and doing. But, although they cannot be stirred up to the undertaking themselves, they are jealous of the attempt by any other route.

From Huánuco, Herndon made his way overland another ninety miles, along the Huallaga River, to Tingo María, which he reached August 2, and describes as "a prettily-situated village of forty-eight able-bodied men, and an entire population of one hundred and eighty-eight."

> The productions of the plain are sugar-cane, rice, cotton, to-bacco, indigo, maize, sweet potatoes, yuccas. . . . The woods are stocked with game—such as *pumas,* or American tigers; deer, pecarri, or wild hog; *ronsoco,* or river hog; monkeys, etc. . . . There are also rattlesnakes and vipers. But even with all these, I would advise no traveler to trust to his gun for support. The woods are so thick and tangled with undergrowth that no one but an Indian can penetrate them, and no eyes but those of an Indian could see the game. Even he only hunts from necessity, and will rarely venture into the thick forest alone, for fear of the tiger or the viper.[5]

At Tingo María, Herndon resorted to river transportation.

> *August 4:* I waked up with pain in the legs and headache . . . and found our men and canoes ready for embarkation. . . . We had two canoes; the largest about forty feet long, by two and a half broad; hollowed out from a single log, and manned each by five men and a boy. . . . When the river was smooth and free from obstructions, we drifted with the current; the men sitting on the trunks and boxes, chatting and laughing; but, as we approached a *mal-paso* [rapid], their serious looks, and the firm position in which each one planted himself at his post showed that work was to be done. I felt a little nervous at first;

---

[5] During the 1930's a Peruvian-built highway, from Lima through Cerro de Pasco and Huánuco, reached Tingo María and was later extended to Pucallpa on the Ucayali River. *The New World Guides to the Latin American Republics,* 1950 edition, besides describing modern Tingo María as a tourist center, has this to say of the place: "The road from Huánuco to Tingo María climbs over the Carpish mountains at 9,165 feet and follows along the right bank of the river. Tingo María is set in a tropical jungle containing the typical fauna and flora of the Peruvian hinterland. Since 1938 it has been a colonization center. Vast areas of the region have been divided into tracts both large and small for tillage, experimental farming and cattle-raising. The tropical agriculture stations are experimenting with tea, rubber, quinine, food crops, and cattle; health centers have been opened to combat the tropical handicaps of malaria and yaws."

but when we had fairly entered the pass, the rapid gesture of the *puntero* [bowman], indicating the channel; the elegant and graceful position of the *popero* [sternman], giving the boat a broad sheer with the sweep of his long paddle; the desperate exertions of the *bogas* [paddlers]; the railroad rush of the canoe; and the wild, triumphant, screaming laugh of the Indians, as we shot past the danger, made a scene that was much too exciting to admit of any other emotion than that of admiration.

We passed many of these to-day, and were well soaked by the canoes taking in water on each side.

Herndon's entry for August 6 consists largely of descriptions of the plentiful game seen on the riverbanks, chiefly deer, many howling monkeys, river hogs (*capibaras*), parrots, and many other birds.

> *August 7:* We got off at half-past eight; at a quarter to ten passed the port of Uchiza. This is a village nine miles from the river. The port itself, like that of Tingo María, is a shed for the accommodation of canoes and passengers. Nearly all the towns on the river are built six or eight miles from the banks, on account of the overflow of the country when the river is full. . . .
>
> It was a day of work; the men paddled well, and we must have made seventy miles. On approaching Tocache, which was their last stage, the Indians almost deafened me with the noise of their horns. These horns are generally made of pieces of wood hollowed out thin, joined together, wrapped with twine, and coated with wax. They are shaped like a blunderbuss, and are about four feet long; the mouth-piece is of reed, and the sound deep and mellow. The Indians always make a great deal of noise on approaching any place, to indicate that they come as friends. They fancy that they might otherwise be attacked, as hostile parties always move silently.

They spent several days at the port of Tocache, paid off their boatmen and hired a new crew. Herndon describes a hunt in the forest with an Indian who killed a toucan with his blowgun and poisoned dart. He also saw a *"tigre"* (jaguar) swimming in the river, pursued by a dog.

> This animal was . . . an ounce, or tiger-cat. It is called *tigre* throughout all this country, but it is never so large or ferocious as the African tiger. They are rather spotted like the leopard

than striped like the tiger. They are said, when hungry, to be sufficiently dangerous, and no one cares to bring them to bay without good dogs and a good gun.

We talked so much about tigers and their carrying off people whilst asleep, that I, after going to bed, became nervous; and every sound near the shed made me grasp the handles of my pistols.

They resumed their downstream journey at noon, on August 11, with two canoes and twelve men. Herndon's last remark about the surrounding country is: "I should judge from the periodical overflow of the lands, the heat of the sun, and the lightness and richness of the soil, that this would be the finest rice country in the world."

> *August 13:* Last night Ijurra struck with a fire-brand one of the boatmen, who was drunk, and disposed to be insolent, and blackened and burned his face. The man—a powerful Indian, of full six feet in height—bore it like a corrected child in a blubbering and sulky sort of manner. This morning he has the paint washed off his face, and looks as humble as a dog; though I observed a few hours afterwards that he was painted up again, and had resumed the usual gay and good-tempered manner of his tribe.

On August 14 they arrived at the settlement of Sion, where they again changed men and canoes. Going on, they went through three more sets of rapids.

> About sunset we arrived at Challuayacu, a settlement of twenty houses. All the inhabitants, except those of one house, were absent. We were told that they had been disobedient in some manner to the governor of the district, and that he had come upon them with a force and carried them off prisoners to Juan Juy, a large town further down the river, where authority might be brought to bear upon them.

> *August 16:* Lovely morning. On stepping out of the house my attention was attracted by a spider's web covering the whole of a large lemon-tree nearby. The tree was oval and well-shaped; and the web was thrown over it in the most artistic manner, and with the finest effect. Broad flat cords were stretched out, like the cords of a tent, from its circumference to the neighboring bushes; and it looked as if some genius of the lamp, at the com-

mand of its master, had exhausted taste and skill to cover with this delicate drapery the rich-looking fruit beneath. I think the web would have measured full ten yards in diameter.

On August 18, Herndon writes about a type of slavery which is still (1963) widely practiced in the more remote regions of the Amazon basin.

> We passed the mouth of the river Hunanza, a small stream coming in on the Infidel side of the river. Our *popero* says that the Infidels dwell near here, and the people of Tarapoto go a short distance up this river to capture young Indians and take them home as slaves. I believe this story; for I found servants of this class in Tarapoto, who were bought and sold as slaves. Slavery is prohibited by the laws of Peru; but this system is tolerated on the plea that the Infidel is christianized and his condition bettered by it. . . .
>
> It is possible that the story of the *popero* is not true, and that the whites may buy the children of the Indians; but if so, I imagine that the advantages of the bargain are all on one side.

Herndon spent several days in the town of Tarapoto, "by far the largest town I have seen since leaving Huánuco," some 20 miles west of the Huallaga River.

> I met at this place my countryman Hacket, whom I had heard spoken so highly of in Cerro [de] Pasco and Huánuco. He is employed in making copper kettles . . . for distilling, and in all kinds of blacksmith and foundry work. . . . I am indebted to him for the following statistics concerning Tarapoto.

There follows a long description of the town and district, its industries (mainly cotton weaving), transportation (westward overland, on the backs of Indians), agriculture (about which Herndon was enthusiastic).

> An American circus company passed through Tarapoto a few months ago; they had come from the Pacific coast, and were bound down the Amazon. . . .
>
> I spoke with an active and intelligent young Spanish trader . . . about the feasibility of a steamboat enterprise upon these rivers, bringing American goods and taking return cargoes of coffee, tobacco, straw-hats, hammocks, and sarsaparilla to the ports of Brazil on the river. He thought that it could not fail to enrich any one who would attempt it; but that the difficulty lay

in the fact that my proposed steamer would never get as far as this, for that my goods would be bought and paid for in return cargoes long before she reached Peru. . . .

Were I to engage in any scheme of colonization for the purpose of evolving the resources of the Valley of the Amazon, I think I should direct the attention of settlers to this district of Tarapoto. It combines more advantages than any other I know; it is healthy, fertile, and free from the torment of mosquitoes and sand-flies. Wheat may be had from the high lands above it; cattle thrive well; and its coffee, tobacco, sugar-cane, rice, and maize are of fine quality. . . .

I saw here fine fields of Indian corn. The stalk grows quite as high as on our best bottom-lands in Virginia, and the ears were full and of good grain. It may be planted at any time, and it yields in three months, thus giving four crops a year.[6]

August 25 saw the travelers again on the Huallaga, leaving the village of Chasuta, and heading for the *"pongo"* bearing the same name, traveling in company with a Portuguese trader.

August 26: Being in company with Antonio, the Portuguese, who knows how to arrange matters, we got a cup of coffee at the peep of day and are off by half past 5 A.M. At five miles of distance we passed the lower extremity of the *pongo,* which commences at Shapaja. *"Pongo"* is an Indian word, and is applied to designate the place where a river breaks through a range of hills, and where navigation is of course obstructed by rocks and rapids. The place where the Marañón breaks its way through the last chain of hills that obstructs its course is called the Pongo de Manseriche. This is the Pongo de Chasuta.

They had now, once and for all, left the Andean highlands, with their many rapids and turbulent stretches of river, and entered the broad Amazonian alluvial plain. They were at last on waters where today are found hundreds of the steamers and other power boats, large and small, of which Herndon had been dreaming, churning up and down thousands of miles of water-

---

[6] The district around Tarapoto and its neighboring city, Moyobamba, has been famous since the earliest conquest for its wealth, fertility, beauty, and fine climate. It declined after Herndon's visit, largely because of its isolation and transportation difficulties. Today an energetic Peruvian program of road-building is connecting it toward the west with the Pacific coast, toward the east with steamer ports on the Huallaga, and toward the south with Tingo María. As in Tingo María, the Peruvian government is engaged in an intensive program of settlement, agricultural experimentation, health services, education, and the like.

ways, side by side with canoes (many of them now with outboard motors) and balsa rafts.

They passed a night in Yurimaguas, a "little village situated upon a hill immediately upon the banks, and numbering two hundred and fifty inhabitants," which is today a modern, bustling, thriving, growing industrial city at the head of the river's navigation, and the port for the large inland region around Tarapoto and Moyobamba. Below Yurimaguas:

> We are now getting into lake country; and hence to the mouth of the Amazon, lakes of various sizes, and at irregular distances, border the rivers. They all communicate with the rivers by channels, which are commonly dry in the dry season. They are the resort of immense numbers of water-fowl, particularly cranes and cormorants; and the Indians, at the proper season, take many fish and turtles from them.
>
> Many of these lakes are, according to the traditions of the Indians, guarded by an immense serpent, which is able to raise such a tempest in the lake as to swamp their canoes, when it immediately swallows the people. It is called *"Yacu Mama,"* or Mother of the Waters; and the Indians never enter a lake with which they are not familiar that they do not set up an obstreperous clamor with their horns, which the snake is said to answer; thus giving them warnings of its presence.[7]

Herndon's narrative retains its unvarying character of travel description, intermingled with detailed notes on the country, settlements, agriculture, trade, and the like. On September 1, he came to the mouth of the Huallaga.

> The river upon which we now entered is the main trunk of the Amazon, which carries its Peruvian name of Marañón as far as Tabatinga, at the Brazilian frontier; below which, and as far as the junction of the Río Negro, it takes the name of Solimões; and thence to the ocean is called Amazon. It is the same stream throughout, and to avoid confusion I shall call it Amazon from this point to the sea.
>
> The march of the great river in its silent grandeur was sub-

[7] In 1932 the editor found a similar belief in the same location. He was informed, moreover, that if anybody harmed the "mother of the waters," the lake in which that particular great snake lived would dry up. The shallowing of the Amazon at Nauta, at the mouth of the Ucayali, which had once been the head of Amazonian steam navigation, was ascribed to the fact that a white hunter had there killed the town's "guardian" snake.

lime; but in the untamed might of its turbid waters, as they cut away its banks, tore down the gigantic denizens of the forests, and built up islands, it was awful. . . .

I was reminded of the Mississippi at its topmost flood. . . .

Its capacities for trade and commerce are inconceivably great. Its industrial future is the most dazzling; and to the touch of steam, settlement, and cultivation, this rolling stream and its magnificent watershed would start up into a display of industrial results that would indicate the Valley of the Amazon as one of the most enchanting regions on the face of the earth.

There follow detailed analyses of the region's commerce, and long speculations on the advantages of steam navigation. Herndon even sets up a hypothetical scheme for such navigation, arriving at the conclusion that it would be fantastically profitable.

The time will come when the free navigation of the Amazon and other South American rivers will be regarded by the people of this country as second only in importance to the acquisition of Louisiana. . . .

Had I the honor to be mustered among the statesmen of my country, I would risk political fame and life in the attempt to have the commerce of this noble river thrown open to the world.

In the town of Nauta, where he spent some weeks, Herndon bought a boat "thirty feet long, seven wide in its widest part, and three deep," for sixty dollars, had it calked and decked, and finally set off up the Ucayali. His hope was to ascend that river and the Perene to the Chanchamayo, "for I thought it possible that I might gather great reputation with my Chanchamayo friends by joining them again from below, and showing them that their darling wish (a communication with the Atlantic by the Perene and Ucayali) might be accomplished." Carrying out that aim would have been "exploration" in the classic geographical sense: solving the "mystery" of the unknown middle section of a river whose mouth and headwaters are known. It was precisely the kind of thing which he had asked Gibbon to do when he instructed him, if possible, to descend the Madre de Dios for the purpose of determining whether or not it flowed into the Amazon as the Purús. However, after traveling some weeks on the Ucayali, Herndon found it impossible to obtain the help he needed for proceeding further, and reluctantly turned back. In his report he expressed mild disappointment over Gibbon's failure to carry out the Madre de Dios part of his mission, but even greater disappointment over his own on the Ucayali.

> I felt, in turning my boat's head downstream, that the pleasure and excitement of the expedition were passed; that I was done, and had done nothing. I became ill and dispirited, and never fairly recovered the gayety of temper and elasticity of spirit which had animated me at the start, until I received the congratulations of my friends at home.

The ascent of the Ucayali, from Nauta to the mission settlement of Sarayacu had taken 23 days. The return to Nauta and the Amazon required eight. On November 5, Herndon set out again, downriver on the Amazon. On the evening of November 6 he arrived at the city of Iquitos, which was then a fishing village with 227 inhabitants and is today a bustling city of some 70,000, one of the fastest-growing in South America. Virtually all of Herndon's glowing opinions of the Amazon basin's possibilities for development are today being confirmed by the six nations which own the territory. The basin's "backwardness" between Herndon's day and the present was caused far more by political than by natural conditions.

On November 9 Herndon passed the mouth of the Napo, which Orellana had descended in 1540, and the next day Herndon decided to stop some days for a rest at a new town which was in process of being built,

> for I was now getting so weak that I could scarcely climb the banks upon which the towns are situated. . . . The inhabitants (328, all of them busily chopping trees and building houses) are principally *Oregones,* or Big Ears, from the custom of introducing a bit of wood into a slit in the ear and gradually increasing the size of it until the lobe hangs upon the shoulder. They have, however, now discontinued the custom, and I saw only a few old people thus deformed.

For some two weeks, Herndon visited neighboring Indian settlements which were mission stations, run by priests. He laments the laziness and backwardness of the Indians, for which he is inclined to blame the priests. On November 24, he gave a detailed description of calking his boat, what materials were used, how much it cost, who gathered it, and the like. On November 26 they resumed their downstream journey.

> Father Valdivia, who is musical, but chanted the mass in a falsetto that would be very difficult to distinguish, at a little distance, from the rattling of a tin pan, commissioned me to bring him out (should I ever return) a small piano and a French horn, which he would pay for in salt fish and sarsaparilla.

There follows the usual procession of towns and settlements, with notes on populations, government, conditions of health, productivity and the like. November 29, at the Indian settlement of Moromoroté:

> After dark he [the local priest] proposed that we should go out and see some of the incantations of the Indians for the cure of the sick. We heard music at a distance, and approached a large house whence it proceeded, in which the padre said there was almost always someone sick. We listened at the door, which was closed. There seemed to be a number of persons singing inside. I was almost enchanted myself. I never heard such tones, and think that even instrumental music could not be made to equal them. I have frequently been astonished at the power of the Indians to mock animals; but I had heard nothing like this before. The tones were so low, so faint, so guttural, and at the same time so sweet and clear, that I could scarcely believe they came from human throats; and they seemed fitting sounds in which to address spirits of another world.

December 4 they left Peru and entered Brazil at the border-settlement of Tabatinga.

> Since I purchased the boat at Nauta I had worn an American flag over it. I had been told that I probably would not be allowed to wear it in the waters of Brazil. But when the boat was descried at Tabatinga, the Brazilian flag was hoisted at that place; and when I landed, which I did dressed in uniform, I was received by the commandant, also in uniform, to whom I immediately presented my Brazilian passport. . . .
> As soon as my rank was ascertained, (which appeared to be that of a captain in the Brazilian army), I was saluted with seven guns.

Herndon was charmed with Tabatinga and the attentions of the Brazilian commandant.

I did not hoist my flag again, and the commandant seemed pleased. . . . He also earnestly insisted that I should take his boat in lieu of my own, which he said was not large enough for the navigation of the lower part of the Amazon. I declined for a long time; but finding that he was very earnest about it, and embarrassed between his desire to comply with the request of the Brazilian minister at Washington, contained in my passport —"that Brazilian authorities should facilitate me in my voyage, and put no obstacle in my way"—and the requirements of the law of the empire forbidding foreign vessels to navigate its interior waters, I accepted his proposition, and exchanged boats; thus enabling him to say, in a frontier passport which he issued to me, that I was descending the river in Brazilian vessels.

The law stipulating that only Brazilian vessels could sail on Brazil's inland waters was, of course, an obstacle to the United States navigation scheme for which Herndon was the pioneering scout. Not until 1866, after considerable pressure from the United States, was the Amazon made a free highway to all nations.

The commandant at Tabatinga, I was told, compelled the circus company that preceded me to abandon their Peruvian-built raft and construct another of the wood of Brazilian forests.

Herndon left Tabatinga on December 6 and arrived on December 17 at Ega, a commercial town of some 800 inhabitants which Bates (Chapter XIX) was soon to make famous through his classic account of his many years of diligent work on the Amazon. Again Herndon gives detailed accounts of the trade at Ega, with cost figures to indicate its profits. He remarks on the laziness of the local inhabitants, but exempts foreigners.

Not so with the Italians, the French, the English, and the Americans, whom I have met in this country. I do not know more popular people than my friends Enrique Antonii, the Italian, and his associate, Marcus Williams, the Yankee, who are established at Barra. Everywhere on the river I heard sounded the praises of my countryman. At Sarayacu, at Nauta, at Pebas, and at Ega, men said that they wished to see him again and to trade with him. He himself told me that, though the trade on the river was attended with hardships, exposure, and privation, there was a certain charm attending the wild life, and its freedom from restraint, that would always prevent any desire on his part to return to his native country. I heard that he carried this feeling so far as to complain bitterly, when he visited Norris, the consul at Pará, of the restraints of society that compelled him to wear trousers at dinner.

He spent Christmas at Ega, attending parties and church services, and entering his invariable meticulous notes on trade and economic life, always bearing in mind future possibilities for North American enterprises.

> The higher classes are taking a little Champagne, Teneriffe wine, or English ale. Ginger beer is a favorite and wholesome drink in this climate. I was surprised to see no cider. I wonder some Yankee from below has not thought to send it up. Yankee clocks abound and are worth from ten to twenty dollars.

On January 1 they passed the several mouths of the Purús without hearing news of Gibbon. On January 5 they entered the Río Negro, which they ascended to Barra, today's Manaus. Here Herndon unleashes all of his salesmanship. He gives an enthusiastic account of the country's wealth, of the trade of Barra in a number of commodities, its exports and imports, and states at one point:

> I presume that the Brazilian government would impose no obstacles to the settlement of this country by any of the citizens of the United States who would choose to go there and carry their slaves; and I know that the thinking people of the Amazon would be glad to see them. The President [of the Province of Amazonas], who is laboring for the good of the province, and sending for the chiefs of the Indian tribes for the purpose of engaging them in settlement and systematic labor, said to me, at parting, "How I wish you could bring me a thousand of your active, industrious, and intelligent population, to set an example of labor to these people"; and others told me that they had no doubt that Brazil would give titles to vacant lands to as many as came.

There follows a long account of life in Barra, and of that of the foreigners (especially Americans) living in the town, as well as of the wealth of the wilderness regions in the north. Herndon left the town on February 18, taking with him the eastbound mails and a foreign resident (presumably English), "Mr. Potter, the daguerrotypist and watchmaker." The same evening they reached the mouth of the Madeira, the Amazon's largest tributary, flowing in from the south, which Lardner Gibbon was to reach eight months later after an important, adventurous northward descent of the river from Bolivia.

As Herndon went on toward the Amazon's mouth, he was glad to meet increasing evidences of "civilization." Again, at the town of Obidos, he stopped to gather detailed information on life, industry, and commerce. On March 2 he reached Santarém at the mouth of the Tapajoz River, on which, during the 1920's, Henry Ford was to establish extensive rubber plantations. Santarém at that time had a population of "four thousand nine hundred and seventy-seven free, (eighty-seven being foreigners), and one thousand five hundred and ninety-one slave inhabitants," an official figure which included "all the settlers on the cocoa plantations for miles around, and all the *tapuios* [Tapuyas, an Indian people] engaged in the navigation of the river." Being by this time undoubtedly tired, Herndon was somewhat less enthusiastic about life in Santarém than he had been about that in other centers on the Amazon. He did, however, engage in long speculations, quoting a number of others, on what might happen if the Tapajoz River were conditioned and opened for navigation, so giving access to the fabulously rich Brazilian fields of diamonds and gold, around Cuiabá, some 900 miles to the south. Indeed, the major part of his writings on Santarém consists of quotations from Castelnau about the wealth of the Brazilian diamond fields and how fine it would be if their produce, instead of being carried laboriously overland to the Atlantic, could be born downriver to Santarém.

Lieutenant Herndon reached the city of Pará "at half past 9 P.M. on the 11th of April. . . . I was so worn out when we arrived, that, although I had not heard from home, and knew that there must be letters here for me, I would not take the trouble to go to the consul's house to seek them; but sending Mr. Potter and the Frenchman ashore to their families, I anchored in the stream, and, wrapping myself in my blanket, went sullenly to sleep."

There follows a long account of Pará's agriculture, commerce, and life. Again undoubtedly as an appeal to his fellow Southerners, he describes the gay life of the city's slaves, and says that "the Negro slave seems very happy in Brazil."

His last chapter, called "Resumé," begins:

> My report would be incomplete were I to fail to bring to the notice of the department circumstances concerning the free navigation of the river that have occurred since my return from the valley of the Amazon.
>
> These circumstances are clearly the result of my mission, which appears to have opened the eyes of the nations who dwell upon the banks of the Amazon, and to have stirred into vigorous action interests which have hitherto laid dormant. They have an important and direct bearing upon the question, whether the United States may or may not enter into commercial relations, by way of the Amazon, with the Spanish American republics, who own the headwaters of that noble stream.

No sooner had the United States begun even to discuss the matter of Amazonian navigation and development, than Brazil had concluded a treaty with Peru (October 28, 1851), providing for joint efforts in development and the encouragement of steam navigation, and for government subsidies to stimulate such navigation. However, the benefits from those efforts were to be kept by the two nations concerned.

> By a decree of the Emperor, of date August 30th, 1852, Brazil gives to Ireneo Evangelista de Souza, one of her own citizens, the exclusive privilege of the navigation of the Amazon for thirty years.

The U.S. Civil War and the later construction of the Panama Canal came to divert attention from the grand geographical design which Herndon's voyage dramatized. Growing pessimistic over the Amazon basin's possibilities, geographers came to discount Herndon's enthusiasm on the ground that he was primarily a salesman, a publicist. Only now is he beginning to be reexamined because only now is the systematic development and settlement of the basin, which he visualized, beginning to get dramatically under way. That modern development, however, results from the same internal strains in South America which have also resulted, among other things, in the famous "Alliance for Progress." Mounting population pressures and popular restlessness, the urgent need for industrialization with its concurrent need for raw materials, the rapid breakdown of the medieval feudalism which has so long retarded the nations owning the Amazon basin, have all combined to set in motion the beginnings of the Amazonian pioneer and development movement of which William Lewis Herndon was so avid, if frustrated, an exponent.

Lardner Gibbon

Accompanied by "Henry C. Richards, a native of Virginia, in the United States, and José Casas, of Spanish descent, a native of Peru," Passed Midshipman Lardner Gibbon "turned southeast" from Tarma on July 9, 1851. Like Herndon on his northward route, he had a relatively pleasant trip, enjoying the people's hospitality, observing and recording their ways of life, customs, economic productions, sounding out people wherever he went on the benefits of Amazonian power shipping, which would shift the country's stream of commerce from westward to the Pacific to eastward, downstream to the Atlantic. On July 30 they reached Ayacucho, Peru, capital of the department of the same name, a city of 10,000, containing "many pleasant people" and two schools with a total of thirty pupils. On August 22 they arrived "at the ancient curiosity of the New World—the city of Cuzco, centuries ago the seat of the Incas." This was their point of departure for the Madre de Dios exploration.

> I found a very friendly disposition towards the expedition, with a desire to aid me. The prefect offered twenty soldiers as as escort in the low country, to the east of the Andes. A number of young men volunteered to accompany me. A meeting of the citizens was held for the purpose of forming a company to join me. At their suggestion, the President of Peru was applied to for the payment of twenty thousand dollars, appropriated by Congress, for the exploration of the Rio Madre de Dios, supposed to be the same with the river Purús, rising in the mountains to the eastward of Cuzco. I was very much pleased also to hear a spirited young officer had applied to command the soldiers. From investigation made, I learned that the head of the Madre de Dios was some distance *beyond* the line between civilization and the savages, the Chuncho Indians.

September 16: The day for my departure had arrived, but neither volunteers nor regulars were ready. Richards was sick, and left behind with the baggage. The party was reduced to José and an Indian boy, who drove an old horse, with a box of instruments, a little camp furniture, and biscuit as his load.

Traveling eastward, they were received everywhere in a friendly fashion. In the town of Paucartambo (written "Porcatambo" by Gibbon), 25 eager volunteers joined them, but grew visibly less eager as they approached the territory of the Chuncho Indians, who were at war with Peru and of whom the countryside was mortally afraid. The following day the volunteers deserted.

At Totora farm we halted for the night, and met a young Philadelphian, named Charles Leechler, engaged in collecting Peruvian bark for a number of years. At first, he spoke with difficulty in his native language, but with a true American spirit assured me I might depend on him as a companion. He knew parts of the country I was directed to explore; his services were the more acceptable. He joined me.

They ascended the easternmost range of the Andes on September 21; Gibbon reports a difficult descent of the eastern slope, over bad roads.

Monday, September 22: We are now on the eastern frontier settlement, where one hundred men are engaged cultivating the coca plant. . . . I had arrived at the *end* of the road for mules. The only way to shorten the distance between us and the Atlantic was to dismount and cut a way through the forest on foot. The undergrowth is so thick, that it is difficult to see where the tigers and other wild animals get through.

José was left behind, in charge of the mules. With Leechler, a padre who had joined them with his four dogs, and four Indians, Gibbon pushed through the woods. "After a most difficult struggle, twelve hours brought us to the bank of the Cosnipata River, in the territory of the Chuncho savages." They had advanced nine miles.

They constructed a bush house and set to work building a raft. "Cutting enough balsa wood early in the morning, the logs were fastened together, and the first North American-built raft launched upon this tributary of the Amazon."

I embarked with Leechler and one old Indian for the opposite shore. There were falls above and below us; the current was swift; we poled part of the way, but soon found the river too deep for that process. We landed on a rocky little island, after being nearly carried over the falls; Leechler lost the balsa on his return for the padre; the current was too swift for him, and he had to swim for his life, while our bark was swiftly carried down stream, and wrecked against the rocks. . . . In the evening Leechler had been working with the padre and the Indians, cutting more timber. He swam over, and spent the night on the island with me, in preference to sleeping in the woods; we lay down upon the rocks, under a heavy rain, with loud claps of thunder, which echoed up the Andes. At midnight, the old Indian called us from our bed of water; the river was rising; the night was dark, and rain poured down. A match was lit, when it was discovered that we could not escape; we saw the rushing waters between us and the shore; a sudden rise of three feet would carry us off. Leechler assured me we could not gain the shore by swimming.

At daybreak, however, the storm subsided, the waters quieted down, and while the island was greatly reduced in size, it was still there. Reunited, the party continued its eastward overland way.

After following the Tono all day, we came to the river Piñipiñi, a stream as large as the Tono, with an average width of forty yards. I saw at once we could get no further, but it was a satisfaction to behold these two rivers, the Tono and Piñipiñi, join and reform the head of the river called by the Quichua Indians *Amaru Mayu* (Serpent River), which Padre Revello had not long since named "Rio Madre de Dios," for the reason the Chunchos had killed a number of Creoles and Quichua Indians, and after destroying their little church, had thrown the Catholic image into a tributary stream, whence it had floated down, and was found on a rock in the centre of Amaru-Mayu.

Reluctantly, Gibbon gave up the idea of exploring the Madre de Dios to determine whether or not it eventually became the Purús. He might have been disappointed to find that it does not. Had he followed the river he would eventually have come out on the Beni, whose mouth he was to pass months later, while descending the rapids of the Madeira-Mamoré. From

Leechler, Gibbon obtained a good deal of information about the Madre de Dios, concluding that "the great river must be explored from its mouth up." Still believing that he was on one of the headwaters of the Purús, he calculated the probable head of steam navigation, an island of which he heard, as being about 18 days from the mouth of the Amazon.

> A ship, loaded with woollen and cotton goods, and with hardware ploughs, and farming utensils—of which there are none, except some miserable old *muskets*—with corn, rice, buckwheat, hemp, tobacco, all kinds of flower and garden seeds, plants, vines, and shoes, would require twenty-five days to the mouth of the Amazon, eighteen days to the island, and ten days to Cuzco: in all 53 days. On the route travelled at the present day, by Cape Horn to Yslay, on the Pacific—the nearest seaport to Cuzco—the passage would occupy 105 days, and 15 days from there to Cuzco: in all 120 days. *Time* with merchants is money.

They now turned back to Cuzco.

> We arrived in Cuzco after an absence of twenty-one days. Richards was still much reduced, but gaining health. The prefect expressed his regrets at not being authorized to send troops with me, and asked the favor of a written account of my visit to the east, in behalf of the Peruvian government.

Gibbon was fascinated by the churches, ancient Inca ruins, old pottery and other artifacts, of Cuzco and its environs, presenting many sketches and descriptions in his report, together with a summary of how civilization had first been brought to the land by two people arriving from the west, the original Inca, Manco Capac, and his sister-wife, Coya Mama. Expressing the firm personal conviction that "Manco Capac and his wife were realities," he indulges in long speculations as to their possible origins, concluding that they must have come from Asia and that they may well have been Polynesians.[8]

[8] The idea of culture contacts between the Incas and ancient Asian or South Sea Island civilizations has been around a long time and was not invented by Gibbon. More recently, the anthropologist H. S. Gladwin published a book *Men out of Asia* (N.Y.: McGraw-Hill Book Co., 1947), developing the thesis that Polynesian civilization had stemmed from the Greek and had possibly reached the South Seas via the fleet which Alexander the Great had assembled, and manned largely by Phoenicians, to explore the ocean's mysteries. Since the Polynesians were magnificent seafarers, Gladwin reasons, it was more likely than not that they

From Cuzco, Gibbon traveled southeast to Lake Titicaca and thence to La Paz. He made his way through the Bolivian Altiplano, making detailed notes on trade, agriculture and silver-mining, and reached the "garden-city" of Cochabamba on December 10, 1851. Disturbing news had reached him:

> A Brazilian minister had concluded a treaty of limits and navigation between his country and Peru. He was now awaiting the actions of this government in Sucre, the capital, for the purpose of securing the use of navigable rivers in Bolivia for the Brazils alone. I decided to ask the right and privilege to navigate the rivers flowing through the territory of Bolivia by steamboats or other vessels.

It happened that the President of Bolivia, "his Excellency Captain General Manuel Isidoro Belzu," was in Cochabamba at the time, and the American officer obtained an interview with him, informing him: "The President of the United States desiring a more active exchange of the productions between the two Americas, I had the hope that a more direct route between the United States and Bolivia might be found than by the way of Cape Horn." President Belzu expressed friendship for the United States and a personal interest in Gibbon's mission. The Bishop of Cochabamba, however, was firmly opposed to any idea of allowing the United States to navigate Bolivian waters, informing the people "that it would be the cause of declaring religious liberty."

After a rather long stay in Cochabamba, gathering information about the country, Gibbon set out on the overland journey down the eastern Andean slopes, past coca plantations and through cinchona forests, which his report describes. After a

---

had contact with South America's west coast and so had an effective hand in shaping the civilization of the Incas. Later, Thor Heyerdahl, having noted striking similarities between a number of words in Quechua, the language of the Incas, and words in Polynesian, set out to "prove," with his dramatic Kon-Tiki drift, on a raft identical with that which was first seen by Pizarro's men in 1527, that the ancient Polynesian civilization stemmed from South America. All he did prove, however, was that there could well have been, and probably was, contact of sorts between Polynesia and Peru. In view of the enormous skill of the Polynesians as seafarers and navigators, and of the fact that their splendid ships could tack into the wind, it is more probable that the main stream of such contacts came the other way, from the East across the Pacific to America. The thesis is strengthened by the discovery, some decades ago, that many of the ancient temple carvings in Mexico were unmistakable stylizations or duplications of similar carvings on Burmese temples.

ten days' ride, he reached Vincuta, a river port where he abandoned mules for canoes. He describes the town's trade, and
writes, characteristically:

> Vinchuta is the easternmost commercial emporium of Bolivia,
> but foreign manufactures come down from the mountains of
> the country instead of up the rivers from the sea. After the cot-
> ton goods, glass ware, and cutlery of Europe and North America
> are disembarked at Cobija, they traverse the Cordilleras over
> rocky roads, through the desert of Atacama, the barren plains
> of Oruro, over the Andes, and down these terrible roads we
> have just travelled. After worrying and tugging for more than
> eight hundred miles, all of that part of the cargo not ruined
> by such a journey on the backs of mules, arrives at the most
> important commercial port this country possesses.
>
> There is very little trading going on here, because the outlet
> on the one hand is such as we describe, and the people seem to
> be ignorant of the advantages offered to them from the Atlantic
> direct, instead of the round-about way of the Pacific.

Now Gibbon's river explorations were to begin. On Tuesday,
May 25, he and Richards, with a dog named Mamoré, "descended the steep bank of Coni creek, stepping into a canoe
made of a log forty feet long and four feet wide. The model of
this canoe appeared to us a beautiful one as she sat upon the
water. She was one of the largest used by the Bolivian Indians,
and the contour of the vessel resembled a modern frigate more
than any other." A fellow passenger of theirs was a young Creole
schoolmaster, "going down to one of the small towns in the
country to teach the Indians Spanish."

> Respectfully taking off our hats to the gigantic Andes, we
> push on in our little canoe. As the men dip their paddles in
> the water we glide rapidly along with the current of Coni
> creek. After being tossed up and down on the mountains for
> a year, the change is enlivening. . . .
>
> The Indians suddenly began to work hard at their paddles;
> the fine-looking old captain talked to the crew sharply, and we
> went dashing over rapids at a most furious rate. . . .
>
> Our cargo was bulky—cakes of salt brought her down so deep
> in the water that she moved sluggishly. . . .
>
> Coni creek is not navigable for a steamboat; the lands on
> both sides are flat and thickly wooded with a rich growth of

bamboo; these lands are all overflowed in the wet season, and therefore are uninhabitable.

The creek brought them into the River Chaparé. On May 30, after three adventurous days of travel through uninhabited country, they entered the Mamoré River, where Gibbon remarked the presence of freshwater seals and porpoises. Now they were in cattle country, and on June 2 they reached the city of Trinidad, where Gibbon acquired a new boat and made other preparations for the descent of the Mamoré and the negotiation of the notorious rapids of some 240 miles at the point where the Mamoré River becomes the Madeira. While Gibbon was far from being the first explorer to travel over those rapids, it was necessary for him to study their terrain. A portage around them, adequate for commercial purposes, could open the entire river for steam navigation, from the Amazon as far as Trinidad.

The American explorer spent some two and a half months in Trinidad and its vicinity, observing and noting the customs of the country, its trade, health problems (more than a hundred Indians died there of smallpox during his stay) and the like. On August 18 he was off again with two sturdy new boats, one of them carrying a Brazilian trader and his goods. There was a week's delay in the town of Exaltación, for the purpose of having farinha prepared as a travel ration which would not spoil in the heat. A few days brought them to country inhabited by hostile Indians.

> Our crew know tolerably well what parts of the country are populated, and when there is a probability of meeting the enemy. . . . The men tell me that the Chacobo savages inhabit the west bank of the river, and a tribe called "Houbarayos," the most unmerciful, live on the east bank; therefore, we are between two fires.

On September 4 they reached the Iténez [9] River, which flows into the Mamoré and forms the boundary between Bolivia and Brazil. To avoid the hostile savages on the Bolivian side, they hugged the uninhabited Brazilian shore, heading upstream a short distance for the Brazilian fort Do Principe da Beira, where Gibbon was to present his credentials.

[9] It is also called the Guaporé.

As we neared the fort our small American ensign was supported by a Cayavabo arrow in the stern. We saw soldier people
rushing about as though they had been suddenly awakened
from sleep or surprised. A canoe came down to meet us with
two armed Negro soldiers; one of them politely gave his commander's compliments to me, with the request that we would
keep off. As this appeared warlike, I sent my compliments to
the commander that we would remain by the rocky island in
the middle of the river until he read a letter from the Brazilian
minister plenipotentiary in Bolivia, which I sent him by the
Negro sergeant. Two old bald-headed Negroes came, by order
of the commander, to inquire if we had any cases of smallpox
on board, saying, if not, the commander invited us to land at
the fort.

Gibbon and Richards acquired a new boat at the fort, one
sturdy enough to navigate the rapids and be dragged over rocks,
together with a new crew of five Negro soldiers, assigned to them
by the commander. On September 14, they said goodbye to the
Brazilian trader with whom they had been traveling, and were
off again.

As our little boat passed swiftly down the current among the
rocks, the men paddled as though they feared being recalled.
They all sang as we bid farewell to the grim old fort. The commandante treated us with marked attention, and appeared sorry
to let us go so soon. . . . Officers generally shrunk from orders
here, for the place had the name of being unhealthy. . . .
There is a horrible disease among the soldiers, called the "Fort
fever," which, for the want of medicine, slowly destroys the
garrison.

They descended the Iténez some 35 miles, reaching its mouth,
and again entered the Mamoré, on September 17.

September 20: By daylight we were up and off, pulling across
to the Bolivian shore to the head of the falls. We were in
doubts how our boat would behave in the rapids. After taking
out part of the baggage, which was passed over the rocky shore
below, the boat was pulled through without any difficulty. . . .
We embarked, and found our little boat, which had been named
"Nannie," gliding beautifully over the short waves formed by
the rapid motion of the water. . . .

No sooner had we cleared these falls than we found ourselves

at the head of another rapid, more steep, called "Guajará-assu."
. . . Our cargo was landed, and while Richards, with one man,
was engaged carrying the baggage down, I took the boat over
on the Bolivian side, and we hauled her three hundred yards
over the rocks and through the small channels, down an inclined
shelf of about twelve feet fall. The main channel is in the
middle of the river, with waves rolled up five feet high by the
swiftness of the current, through which a steamboat could pass
neither up nor down.

The river cuts its way through an immense mass of rock,
stretching across the country east and west like a great bar of
iron. The navigation of the Mamoré is completely obstructed
here; the river's gate is closed, and we see no way to transport
the productions of Bolivia towards the Amazon, except by a
road through the Brazilian territory.

Laboriously they made their way down rapids after rapids,
portaging their baggage overland, always fearful of dividing
their party lest hostile Indians attack them, praying that their
sturdy little boat would stand the strain. "The long canoes of
Bolivia would have been broken to pieces in this first day's travel
among the rapids. There are no paths through the wilderness by
which we could travel in case of an accident, and rafts we had
seen enough of at the head of the Madre de Dios."

On September 22 they met some naked Jacare savages with
whom they traded and in general had good relations.

Three miles below Lajens we came to the mouth of the
Beni river. This stream resembles the Mamoré in color and
width. . . . The junction of these two streams forms the head
of the great Madeira, which is one mile wide.

September 23: The river was seven hundred yards wide, and
one hundred and five feet deep. . . . The channel was clear
of rocks, and we soon came to the "Ribeirao" falls, which are
two miles long. The baggage was carried five hundred yards
over a path on the east bank. . . .

Our boat was beginning to give way to the rough service,
and as she leaked, it became necessary to lighten her load; then,
too, the men began to fag. After they succeeded in getting the
boat safely over a dangerous place, the boxes had to be carried,
one by one. The heaviest box was that in which were planted
three specimens of Majos sugar-cane. I had just cut my first

crop, and found the plants were doing well, when it became necessary to relieve our little boat, and we were unwillingly obliged to leave behind what might have proved of importance to a Mississippi sugar-planter.

Day after day, falls after falls, rapids after rapids, and always they prayed fervently that the boat would hold out. At one point, while the boat was negotiating a bad stretch of water, Gibbon was alone on shore, when he suddenly found himself "surrounded by a party of savage women and children, who had come up behind me."

> There were eight women, ten children, and two unarmed men, all, from external appearances, savages of the purest water. . . . One of the men stepped before me, and putting his hand into my pocket, took all the fish-hooks out, and appropriated them to his own use, by handing them to a homely woman who bore a sucking baby, and then coolly inquired whether I had a knife to give him. . . . At my suggestion, they walked to the boat with me. . . . They were quite friendly with us. Some of the men who came afterwards, left their bows and arrows behind the rocks, and walked up unarmed. . . . The infants appeared terribly frightened at the sight of a white man; one of them screamed out when Pedro milked the mother into a tin pot, for the benefit of Richards' ear, which still troubled him. The woman evidently understood what was wanted with it, and stood still for Pedro to milk her as much as he chose.

They met more savage Indians in the days which followed but had no untoward or disagreeable experiences with them.

> *October 2:* Five miles below are "San Antonio" falls, which we passed by towlines without disembarking our baggage. The difference of level is very small; the bed of the river much choked with rocks. . . . We took breakfast on the west side, at the foot of these falls, with feelings of gratitude we had safely passed the perils of *seventeen* cataracts. . . . . We had been twelve days descending the falls, which is considered by Brazilian navigators fast traveling.
>
> Those parts of the rivers Madeira and Mamoré, between the foot of "San Antonio" and the head of "Guajará-merim" falls, are not navigable for any class of vessels whatever.

Gibbon advocated the cutting of a portage road, "straight through the territory of Brazil," not following the river's windings. Such a road, he stated "would not exceed one hundred and eighty miles." In part to justify the construction of such a road, he described the country's wealth in rubber and Brazil nuts.

> *October 6:* We landed on the west bank, at "Roscenia de Crato," which is a frontier post of the Brazilians, on the Madeira. The entire country between this settlement and the town of Exaltación, in Bolivia, is inhabited by savages. The Portuguese have ascended the Amazon and Madeira thus far on their southwestward emigrations. The Spaniards, who crossed the Isthmus of Panama and the mountains of Bolivia, are now on their northeast descent, to meet the Brazilians. The movement, on both sides, is slow, but the white man is crowding close upon each flank of the savage, who occupies but a narrow strip of land between the emigrants from Spain and Portugal— gradually working through the wilderness toward each other.

They proceeded down the Madeira, through a long stretch of uninhabited country, finding no obstacles whatever to steam navigation.

> During the 21st of October we lay all day by a sand island, unable to proceed until evening. When the wind died away, we paddled on by the light of the moon. As the Negroes lifted their paddles out of the water, we dipped the thermometer in the Madeira for the last time, 88° Fahrenheit. Suddenly, the bow of our little canoe touched the deep waters of the mighty Amazon.
>
> Now that we are at the mouth of this magnificent stream, we find no deeply loaded vessels enter it. The value of the present foreign trade of South Peru and Bolivia may be worth ten millions of dollars per annum.

The Amazon was Herndon's territory. Reaching it marked the completion of Gibbon's assignment. He closed his report by again pointing out how much time could be saved if goods from the United States to Bolivia and Peru could travel via the Madeira-Mamoré route, improved by the construction of the portage road, instead of going around Cape Horn.

Gibbon's report was studied carefully in many quarters and began to be acted upon before too long. In 1870, after some years of study and negotiations, the American engineer Colonel George Earl Church obtained a concession to navigate the Madeira-Mamoré, plus some 538 square miles of land, in return for which he was to build a railroad where Gibbon had proposed a road. An English company undertook to build the railroad, but repudiated its contract a year after its engineers had first landed at San Antonio, the construction town at the proposed railroad's northern terminus. The reasons it gave were "that the country was a charnel house, their men dying off like flies, that the road ran through an inhospitable wilderness of a swamp and porphyry ridges alternating, and that, with the command of all the capital in the world and half its population, it would be impossible to build the road." [10]

Colonel Church now sought a new contractor, and on October 25, 1877, the American firm of P. & T. Collins signed papers, agreeing to build the railroad within three years. The first American effort entailed enormous hardships and many deaths, and ended in disaster, largely because funds for the job were tied up in litigation in England, and the company could not meet its payrolls or even buy supplies. (Throughout the past century, and even into World War II, there have been repeated indications that England was against American penetration into the Amazon basin and did whatever could be done to prevent or at least hamper it.)

Thirty years after the Collins failure, "another attempt was made to build this road. This time, equipped with a better understanding of the health problems of this region and fully prepared to combat disease and death, another firm of American contractors finally brought the work to a successful conclusion on July 15, 1912, after great loss of life and a total expenditure of $30,000,000." [11] The cost may have been inordinately high because the American firm of May, Jeckyl and Randolph had a fine "cost-plus" contract under which the Brazilian government, which had agreed to build the road in return for the Acre Territory ceded to it by Bolivia, repaid every dollar spent, plus a good profit. The fact that the railroad ties were imported from

[10] From *Recollections of an Ill-Fated Expedition*, by Neville B. Craig (Philadelphia: J. B. Lippincott Company, 1907).
[11] From *The Jungle Route*, by Frank W. Kravigny (N.Y.: Orlin Tremaine Company, 1940).

Australia instead of being cut locally from the fine, hard Amazonian trees which had to be felled in any event to create the right of way, is one of many explanations for the road's enormous cost. Under that splendid system, too, every dollar stolen by a thieving petty clerk was graciously refunded to the contractors by the Brazilian government, with a handsome profit added. The railroad is still in operation, though the time of its completion coincided with the collapse of the Amazon rubber boom, so depriving the road of much of its anticipated revenue.

When Gibbon passed the mouth of the Beni, he wondered whether that river could serve to open its part of Bolivia's interior. However, in those days little was known about the Beni. It was first explored for its full length about 1880, by the American explorer Heath. Shortly after his voyage the Bolivian firm of Suarez Hermanos established itself at the rapids of Cachuela Esperanza, not far from the mouth, and founded the town of Riberalta, farther up. The firm, which managed an enormous rubber empire, was of course instrumental in having the portage railroad built. In 1932, at the worst time of the world depression, the editor visited the original firm's last survivor, Sr. Nicolas Suarez, at Cachuela Esperanza. He seemed sad over the depression. His warehouses were filled with rubber but he claimed that it no longer paid to ship it out, even over the railroad. Nevertheless, he spent thousands of dollars painting and repairing his small town and starting a new business. He had his fieldworkers gather Brazil nuts, imported machinery from the United States, and put a number of Indian women to work shelling and canning the nuts. Since there was a steady market for luxury goods, even during the depression, Suarez' shelled Brazil nuts, vacuum-packed in tins, found a ready sale in New York.

The lower Beni River, served by the Madeira-Mamoré Railroad, is today one of Bolivia's major sugar producers and is the scene of an energetic settlement and development program.

❦ XXI ❧

SCHOMBURGK IN
THE GUIANAS

THE English called Walter Raleigh "chivalric"; the Spanish called him a pirate and gained the satisfaction, as a result, of seeing King James I chop off his head in 1618. There can be no doubt, however, that his romantic account of the Guianas, with their postulated Lake Parima and El Dorado, did more than any other man's labors to focus English interest on the South American regions south of the lower Orinoco, whence Raleigh had failed so dismally to evict the Spaniards. Long after the search for Lake Parima and El Dorado had petered out, that interest was to lead to Britain's acquisition of Trinidad in 1802 and of today's Guayana a little later. The greatest of the naturalist-explorers in the Guianas, who was in no way interested in discovering golden cities and stealing them from the Indians, was a German named Robert Hermann Schomburgk, working for the English.

In his enthusiastic book *A Description of British Guiana*, published in 1840 after an interrupted five years of exploring the colony's interior, Schomburgk gives a brief history of the land. Between 1580, which saw the first arrival of Dutch settlers, and July 21, 1831, when "the colonies of Demerara, Essequibo, and Berbice were united into one colony, named British Guiana, and Sir Benjamin D'Urban was appointed governor and vice admiral over the same," the entire coast from the mouth of the Amazon to that of the Orinoco was under constant, turbulent dispute among England, the Netherlands, and France, with the Spanish and Carib Indians meddling occasionally in the fighting for their own ends, while imported Negro slaves added to the turmoil through bloody, periodic uprisings. The details of the constant squabbling do not belong in an account of this kind, though there is some interest in Schomburgk's account of English penetration of what is today the Dutch Surinam:

> The English returned in 1652 to Paramaribo, and the Caibi Indians having removed from Wanica to the Coponam, they were more successful in founding a settlement.
>
> In 1662 the whole colony was granted by Charles II to Lord Willoughby, the then governor of Barbados, who named the principal river, wherein Paramaribo is situated, Surryham, in honor of the earl of Surry; from which the whole colony took its name. The British Crown bought afterwards this colony from the heirs of Lord Willoughby, and exchanged it with the Dutch government in 1667 for New Holland, in North America, the present New York.

After 1831, the English were fairly sure of the boundary between their Guiana and that of the Dutch, especially on the Atlantic coast. However, they were not at all sure, since others than the Dutch were involved, of the demarcation between British Guiana and Venezuela in the north and west, as well as Brazil in the south and southwest, where most of the disputed boundary lines lay in wild and often unexplored territories. They studied the rather vague claims of the Dutch, from whom they had finally obtained their colony, and were inclined to establish those claims as their own. But neither the Spaniards nor the Portuguese, the Venezuelans nor the Brazilians who took over in those lands after the several revolutions, had ever acknowledged the ancient Dutch claims. In the interior of their Guiana domain, and along its northern fringe, the British had inherited an apparently endless series of territorial disputes, which, at least so far as Venezuela was concerned, were not "settled" until 1899, though they flare up from time to time to this day. Since too little of a definite nature was known about the interior border regions, the situation called for a considerable amount of geographic and other exploration in search of reliable factual data.

Robert Hermann Schomburgk began his work in the Guianas

—at first purely as a naturalist—in 1835, ending his field services in October, 1843, after his boundary survey to establish England's interior territorial claims along the famous "Schomburgk Line." On November 1, 1844, writing in London to Lord Stanley, Secretary of the Colonies, he appealed for adequate British recognition, which was soon granted to him in the form of a knighthood. In that letter he summarized his services to England as follows:

> My love for botany and natural history, and an ardent desire to travel, led me, in 1830, to the West Indies. In the course of my excursions I visited also, in 1831, Anegada, the most northern of the group of islands under Her Majesty's dominion, which are called the Virgin Isles, and of which Tortola is the seat of government. The low situation of Anegada, and a continuation of coral reefs which extend many miles in a south-easterly direction, have always rendered that island dangerous to navigation. During the short time I remained there I witnessed the total wreck of three vessels, and all the accompanying misery; but the most vivid and painful impression was left by the intense human suffering connected with the loss of the schooner *Restanadora,* a Spanish slaver, loaded with 135 Africans, the ablest of whom, chained in the hold when she struck and sunk, perished most miserably.

Schomburgk now obtained instruments and undertook, at his own expense, to survey the currents and waters around Anegeda in order to help mariners to avoid their dangers.

> The fatigues of this survey were much increased by the difficulties which some of the inhabitants of the island, who made their livelihood at the expense of the unfortunate vessels, and possessed all the bad propensities of wreckers, put in my way to prevent the survey, and one of them went so far as to attempt my life, and no doubt would have been successful had it not been for the interference of the bystanders.
>
> I forwarded the elements of this survey to the Hydrographical Office of the Admiralty, where it was published, and copies of it are now to be found on board every one of Her Majesty's vessels.

After his account of other services of a similar nature at Tortola, for which he had been promised a reimbursement which he never received, Schomburgk relates how, in 1835, he proceeded to British Guiana.

> The Royal Geographical Society resolved, in 1834, to send an expedition to the interior of Guiana for the twofold purpose of investigating thoroughly the physical and astronomical geography of that vast province and of connecting the line of positions which might be ascertained with those of the Baron de Humboldt at the Upper Orinoco.
>
> Her Majesty's Government, desirous that the resources of the colony, which so properly has been styled the "Magnificent," should be developed, on hearing of the enterprise, were pleased to stamp it with their approbation, and to extend to it their patronage and assistance. I received the appointment to command the expedition, with orders to proceed to Demerara.

In the course of that work, and in order to tie his astronomic and other observations in with those of Baron von Humboldt, Schomburgk did manage to cut a dramatic, almighty swath all the way across the Guianas, clear to Esmeralda on the Orinoco, an overland journey which it would be difficult to duplicate even today. He traversed the Cassiquiare to the Río Negro (see Chapter XVI), descended that river to the mouth of the Rio Branco, ascended the Branco to São Joaquim (near today's city of Boa Vista), and crossed back into British Guiana.

> These researches occupied me up to the month of June, 1839, when ill-health obliged me to retire to Europe, and they received the approbation of the Royal Geographical Society, in token of which they presented me with their gold medal in 1840.

It was in that year, too, that he published his famous description of British Guiana, though, after describing briefly the entire Guiana region between the lower Orinoco River in the north and "the confluence of the Río Negro and the Amazon in the south," he complained that it was difficult to ascertain precisely what part of it was "British."

> The following description is limited to those parts which comprehend British Guiana; but the exact knowledge of its area depends upon the determination of its boundaries; and in the uncertainty whether the pretensions of the Brazilian and Venezuelan governments will be attended to, it is impossible to come to a result.

His report is an enthusiastic account of British Guiana's nature, resources, and possibilities. His impassioned plea for adequate development and settlement ends as follows:

> The imports of British manufacturers would increase with the population and the prosperity of the colony. Thousands, who in Great Britain depend upon the poor funds for mere subsistence, would in so rich a colony as Guiana become independent, and appear in the list of those who contribute to the consumption of British manufactures, and thus add their share towards the increase of national prosperity.
>
> Guiana bids fair ere long to become a focus of colonization; and with her fertility, her facilities of water communication, she may yet vie with the favoured provinces of the eastern empire, and become, as Sir Walter Raleigh predicted, the El Dorado of Great Britain's possessions in the west.

The boundary which Schomburgk was sent to survey and mark in 1841 enclosed a British-claimed territory which, in general, included the entire drainage basin of the Essequibo River, the southern boundary being the height of land immediately south of the mainstream's farthest source, while the western boundaries, in general and with the exception of the mighty Cuyuni River, encompassed the entire lengths of all the tributaries flowing into the Essequibo from the west. The neighboring countries, on the other hand, Venezuela in the north and Brazil in the south, insisted that the Essequibo River itself must be the dividing line, and so the western limit of British Guiana, while the two agreed upon the eastward extension of the Pacaraima Mountains as the border between their respective sections. Schomburgk was sent not to arbitrate the dispute but to gather reliable geographic information which could later serve as a basis for arbitration, and to mark the British-claimed borders with appropriate, carved boundary posts which the Venezuelans and Brazilians naturally tore up after he had proceeded farther on his journey.

The following excerpts are from *Reports and Letters of Sir Robert Hermann Schomburgk with Reference to his Surveys of the Boundaries of British Guiana,* comprising Volume 5 of the series of official British government papers entitled *Further Documents Relating to the Question of Boundary between*

British Guiana and Venezuela, printed in 1896, when the boundary dispute between the two nations had begun to take on serious proportions.

Schomburgk's Report No. 1, dated June 22, 1841, and prepared "for transmission to the Right Honorable Her Majesty's Secretary of State for the Colonies" was written beside the River Manari, a tributary of the Barima, after the explorer had descended that river to its mouth on the Orinoco delta and had there "planted . . . in the presence of witnesses who have subscribed their names hereto, a post branded with Her Majesty's initials, as a testimonial of Her Majesty's right of possession to the River Barima and its tributaries, and all the land through which they flow. This post lies, according to my observations, in latitude 8° 36′ 9″ north, and longitude 60° 40′ 36″ west of Greenwich. . . . I have also branded three trees with Her Majesty's initials (situated . . . about 30 yards from the above post) as further proof thereof." That dispatch, like others until the British knighted him, he signed: "Robert H. Schomburgk, Knight of the Prussian Order of the Red Eagle, Third Class."

His instructions, in other words, had been to establish the Orinoco River delta as the northern end of British Guiana, permitting Britain to share control of the delta with Venezuela, and so also following Sir Walter Raleigh's admonition of centuries before, to the effect that control of Trinidad would assure control of the Orinoco River. In 1899, however, after the dispute with Venezuela had been adjudicated, the northern tip of British Guiana was to be settled at the mouth of the River Waini, some 75 miles southeast of Schomburgk's boundary post, which was not, in any event, to stay in position very long after the Venezuelans discovered it.

After a stormy passage from England, the explorer had arrived at the Waini's mouth on April 21, where he set up camp for himself and his 18 men—to whom was added, as the expedition's botanist, Schomburgk's brother Richard. After some men had been sent inland in search of fresh water, the party stayed at the mouth of the Waini long enough to make astronomical observations and explore the Waini's navigability. A visit from an Indian chief, on April 28, throws light on the apprehensions which were in those days and regions aroused by uncertainties as to sovereignty.

We received the visit of a Warrau chieftain from Canyballi, a tributary of the Waini, and about two days' journey from its mouth, who, having heard of our arrival, came with part of his men, and appeared rejoiced that at last it should be decided whether the Waini was in the British or in the Venezuelan territory, as at present they did not consider themselves secure against being carried away by the Venezuelans, and forced to work at low wages at Angostura, or in other parts of the Venezuelan territory.

In view of all the interest and scientific debate which had earlier been centered on the Cassiquiare as a stream connecting the Orinoco with the Río Negro, it is interesting to note that in British Guiana Schomburgk found a number of similar phenomena.

We ascended the Waini to the remarkable passage which connects that river with the Barima, and, although not navigable for sailing vessels, affords a ready communication in boats and canoes between the two rivers. This natural channel, which may be compared in some respects with the Cassiquiare, which connects the Upper Orinoco with the Río Negro, is known in the colony under the name of Mora Creek.

After some delay—caused by illness among his men—at an Indian village called Cumaka on the Aruka River (whose inhabitants assured him that they had long regarded themselves as British subjects), Schomburgk engaged more boats and men and set out for the mouth of the Barima, a journey of some 80 miles which he made in the remarkably short time of less than two days. Having planted his marking post, he immediately proceeded west to plant another at the mouth of the Amacuro River, the eastern bank of which was regarded by his employers as British Guiana's western boundary in those latitudes.

Having completed his work on the Orinoco delta, Schomburgk returned to Cumaka, and then, losing no time, ascended the rivers Aruka and Aruau, made a short portage, and finally arrived on the Amacuro some 60 miles above the point on the river's mouth where he had previously planted one of Her Majesty's boundary posts. He ascended a small tributary, the Otucamabo, flowing into the Acura from the right bank, claimed by Britain, visited a settlement of Arawak and Warrau

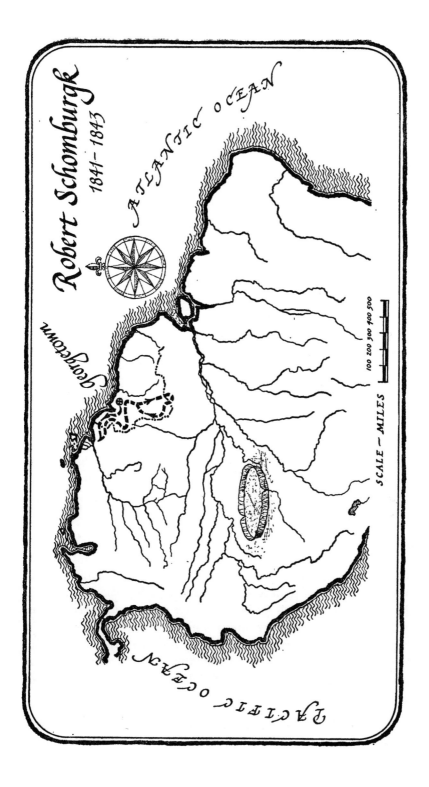

Robert Schomburgk
1841–1843

Indians under the chieftainship of an Arawak named Jan, who spoke Creole Dutch very well, and again gathered information on the region's turbulent conditions.

> The complaints of Captain Jan of the cruelties of the Vene-zuelans, or Spaniards as they are generally styled, were numer-ous. He related that they frequently came to his place and took from him and his people plantains, cassava, hammocks, paddles, etc., without paying for them at all, or at the very best very inadequate prices. . . . In the small River Otucamabo, which Jan inhabits, there was, at a short distance from the mouth, a settlement of Warrau Indians, called Awarra, who, a few months ago were surprised by a number of Venezuelans, led, as they told me, by the Commandant of the Lower Orinoco, and three of them were carried to the Venezuelan post, Coriabo. Sometime after, however they found means to get away at night, in a small canoe; and . . . (I conversed with them through our interpreter). . . . One of the Indians, who had been forced to work at an estate called Carussima, . . . said that those who, by age or infirmity, were not able to finish their tasks, were flogged with a four-tongued whip of ox-hide, or they were drawn up with their hands to a beam in the work-house, and, when thus hanging above the ground, were un-mercifully beaten. Their nourishment, during the period they were forced to work, was scanty and of the coarsest description; and, as to a reward for their labour, if they should be allowed to return to their homes, this was out of the question.

As late as the early nineteenth century, and in isolated locali-ties even today, South America's remotest interior was still re-garded by the nations which own or claim it primarily as a source of Indian slave labor, to be carried off for toil in the more developed parts of the continent. Again and again Schom-burgk was to cite the need for protecting such Indians as among the reasons for British Guiana's taking in as much territory as possible. He was, however, meticulous in respecting Venezuela's "rights" in territories not claimed by him for Queen Victoria. At one point in his descent of the Amacuro River he visited a scattered settlement off the river's left bank, which he regarded as Venezuelan territory.

> The whole population . . . amounts nearly to ninety per-sons, but as the natives are, according to the limit at present

claimed by Her Majesty, in the Venezuelan territory I did not consider myself authorized to hear or interfere in their complaints against Venezuelan oppression, nor would I give them any encouragement to settle in British Guiana, in order to prevent the Venezuelan Government from accusing me hereafter of having enticed inhabitants of their territory to settle in the British Colony.

After some difficulties imposed by a waterfall, Schomburgk managed to reach the mouth of the Amacuro, "where we were happy to observe that the boundary post which we had planted here on the 13th of May was still standing. The same refers to the post which we had planted at Point Barima, and which we visited the next morning on our ascent of the Barima." (Not many weeks later, he received word that both posts had been removed by the Venezuelans.)

Schomburgk's next dispatch, dated "Demerara, August, 1841," begins with an account of his ascent, from Cumaka, of the Barima River, in its great bend (when ascended) toward the south and eventually the west. The party left Cumaka on June 13, proceeding from one Indian settlement to another, in all of which the explorers seem to have found friendly and helpful receptions. They went as far as possible, upstream, in boats, and, when the going became too rough, Schomburgk sent most of his men back while he proceeded, thoroughly drenched and miserable from the season's torrential rains, as far as the River Mehokawaina, which he reached June 28, and where the numerous rapids made further ascent of the Barima too difficult to be worth the labor. On June 27, he wrote:

> It is not known to the Indians inhabiting these regions that white men had ever penetrated so far before. We might have stopped here, and commenced our return, the more especially since the weather was so unfavorable; but I found the course of the Barima so different from what it is laid down on maps that I considered it important to trace it higher up, as, by its western course on its ascent, every mile would add to the British territory. This course, differing so much from the Barima of theoretical geographers, will, I presume, be deemed sufficient evidence of the importance which Her Majesty's Government have resolved upon, namely, that an actual survey should prelude the definitive negotiations with the Governments interested in the determination of these boundaries.

All along the Barima River he assiduously carved Queen Victoria's initials on various trees, and all through his dispatch he comments on the natural resources which warranted Britain's settlement and development of the land. He comments, for instance, on "the most stately Mora trees" which at one point began to replace palms and "overshadowed the river."

> In all my travels in Guiana I have nowhere seen trees of this description so gigantic as on the land adjoining the Barima at its upper course. . . . The importance of the Mora in naval architecture is now fully recognized in Great Britain, and a new export trade has been opened to the Colony. At the Upper Barima this tree is so abundant, and grows to such a size, that the whole British Navy might be reconstructed merely from the trees which line its banks, a circumstance well worth consideration, especially as being near a river which is navigable to vessels of twelve feet draught, the craft intended for the transport of the timber might load up at the very spot where the trees are cut down.
>
> It is only lately that the timber of Guiana has come into notice in England; but so superior is the Mora and the Greenheart for objects of naval architecture that a higher price is given for them in seaport towns than for any other wood imported into England.
>
> It appears that, at the commencement of this century, a white man—very likely a Dutch settler—had advanced so far inland as the Herera River. The Indians showed us the place where he had cultivated sugar, and they told us that he had possessed a schooner and several punts, with which he had carried on a timber trade. The Indian, in his expressive language, called the former settlement "the last place of the white man."

On June 25, after passing the Indian village of Simuita, he writes:

> We were accompanied by a number of Indians from Simuita . . . who intended to ascend the river to the falls, to shoot the delicious fish called *maracotto* or *ossibu,* which, at the time these waters were full, migrate beyond the falls for the purpose of depositing their spawn. We formed a flotilla of small boats, our canoe being the leading frigate. Several fish were procured on the first day. In order to attract them to the shore, a number of the seeds of the *carapa,* or crab-nut, are pounded, and,

having been surrounded by a netting made of withes, they are put in the water and soon attract the greedy *maracotto;* an Indian stands ready with a light spear which he lances into them one after another with unerring skill. I have in my former report alluded to the importance of following up the fisheries as an additional resource of the colony. I here observed that the *maracotto* reaches frequently a length of 30 inches, and is 26 inches in girth, while its delicious flavor recommends it to attention as an article of trade.

After returning to the Indian village of Marani, he sent some of his men downstream in boats while "Mr. Echlin [the expedition's artist and medical officer] and the men best fitted for such an undertaking were to accompany me overland to the River Cuyuni." (Schomburgk was nearly always vague about how many men, and who, were included in his various parties.) They hired Indian porters, "and we commenced on the 8th July our march overland." After some six hours' walking, they reached the village of Paripu, a settlement of Waika Indians.

> We found the inhabitants in great tribulation: a messenger had arrived from the Cuyuni, informing them that some Spaniards had come across from Angostura, and were building corials [dugout canoes] at the banks of the Cuyuni for the purpose of surprising the Indians of that river; that they intended to kill the adults, and lead the young portion away into captivity. This messenger was sent to urge the Waikas of these regions to assist them in making war against the Spaniards. Not only here, but likewise in the sequel, where I found that this alarm had spread, I showed them the inutility of such a violent measure, as neither in numbers nor in the means could they cope with their assailants. But I advised them, provided the report were true, to be on the alert; and on the approach of their oppressors, to retire into the woods.

They arrived at the Barima River late that same afternoon and spent some days at the village of Cariacu, organizing a four-day ascent of that river in frail bark canoes. After reaching the great falls of the Barima they again struck overland in a general westerly direction to the River Acarabisi, which Britain claimed as a boundary line and which Schomburgk followed along its eastern bank to its confluence with the Cuyuni, carving Her Majesty's initials into a number of trees en route. Reporting with his usual enthusiasm on the rich soils and fine agricultural products observed along the way (sugar cane, cotton, plantains, and tobacco, grown by the Indians), Schomburgk made his way down the Cuyuni to its confluence with the Essequibo, which he reached on July 27th and where some of his men were waiting for him at a Protestant mission station. Like virtually all explorers of those regions, before and after him, he commented on the aptness of the Indians for languages and music.

> The school is attended by from 40 to 50 children, mostly Indians. Some of the latter (I think 24) are maintained by the mission and instructed in the normal school, that they may hereafter return among their tribes and relations and assist in working out the great objects of conversion and civilization. Their progress is indeed encouraging. Some of them, in the short space of four months, have learned to read and write; and the copybooks which I saw would not have dishonored an European school of even higher pretensions. One of the boys, an Arawak, had advanced to the Rule of Three in arithmetic. Their psalmody is sweet, and when, on the evening of our arrival, we attended prayers, we were much pleased with the attention they paid to the exhortation of their religious teacher.

He ends his second report with an account of the various Indian tribes inhabiting various regions, and pleads for better treatment of those people and their assimilation into the general economy.

After the completion of that journey, Schomburgk spent considerable time in Georgetown and Demerara, writing many respectful letters and reports. However, there seems to have been a bureaucratic change in his lines of communication. His letters are now no longer addressed to the "Right Honorable Her Majesty's Secretary of State for the Colonies"; they are henceforth addressed to "His Excellency, Governor Light," who seems to have been the Governor of British Guiana and may well have complained about an explorer's rummaging about in his territory without keeping the governor fully informed of what he was doing. Moreover, while the governor's letters and inquiries were not published by the Parliament together with Schomburgk's answers, it seems, from the latter, that the colony's chief executive may well have been apprehensive and inquisitive as to what Schomburgk had been up to, and why. The explorer's

letter of November 30, 1841, went into details on why he had
staked out the mouth of the Barima and the east shore of the
River Amacuro as British Guiana's boundaries (undoubtedly
the governor had by this time received complaints from the
Venezuelans over those actions of the boundary surveyor). One
of the several inclosures with that letter is a long, patient—as
though to a backward schoolboy—development of the entire
boundary thesis from both the historic and geographic points of
view. That memorandum ends on what sounds slightly like a
note of admonition to a high official who seems to have shown
slight signs of restiveness. (On reading between the lines, one
has the impression that the governor may have raised some such
natural question as this: "With everything peaceful, why rake
up all this trouble during *my* term of office?")

> Great Britain has not undertaken the question of determining
> the boundaries of British Guiana upon the principles of ag-
> grandizement. She does not wish more than belongs to her by
> justice, but with the example of the United States before her,
> where, if the question of the Canadian limits had been settled
> at the close of the last century, it would have met no difficulties,
> she is naturally anxious to settle the boundaries of a colony
> of such vast importance as Guiana promises to be (as well out
> of political and philanthropic motives), at a period when there
> are comparatively few difficulties.

On December 23, 1841, Schomburgk set out to ascend the
Essequibo River, near the headwaters of which a boundary conflict seemed to be brewing with Brazil. The British were sending
troops to the settlement of Pirara, near the upper Rupununi
River, which was claimed, and had been partly occupied, by
Brazilians. Schomburgk (whose original complement of men
was now greatly depleted by resignations, and who now de-
pended increasingly on Indians hired locally for specific limited
journeys) was entrusted with a note to the Brazilian commandant of that village, giving the latter official notice that the British troops were arriving. He reached the place on February 10 and
had peaceful relations with the Brazilians, who agreed to with-
draw to their Fort São Joaquim on the Rio Branco and leave
Pirara in British hands. British troops, and a missionary, arrived
at Pirara soon after Schomburgk did, and the latter, who had
found the settlement virtually deserted, had the satisfaction of

seeing a large number of Indians now returning to it, to seek protection under British rule. Shortly thereafter, however, as a result of some acidulous letters from the Brazilian authorities at Fort São Joaquim, Pirara was declared neutral territory by the British, who withdrew their troops.

Inclosed with his report from Pirara of May 30, 1842, giving an account of boundary explorations out of that settlement, was Schomburgk's formal declaration that on the 5th day of April he had "claimed . . . in the name of Her Majesty Victoria, Queen of Great Britain and Ireland, . . . the right bank of the River Takutú, to form the south-western boundary of Her Majesty's Colony of Guiana, preserving at the same time to Her Majesty and loyal subjects the right of navigation, fishing, and other uses of the said river as may seem proper." In witness of the claim he had again marked several trees with the Queen's initials and "three broad arrows." It is indicative to note that his similar proclamation of May 13, the previous year, attesting to his having claimed the mouth of the Barima River, had been witnessed by an official assistant surveyor, the colony's Superintendent of Rivers and Creeks; William L. Echlin, the expedition's then artist and medical officer; a man named Thomas Hancock; eleven English crew members, who signed their marks; and seven Indians, who did the same. The proclamation of April 5, 1842, was witnessed by a Mr. Edward Goodall, an artist whom Schomburgk had hired at his own expense to replace Echlin; the Commander's brother, Richard Schomburgk; a Mr. Nicolas Reiter; four English expedition members, only one of whom had appeared on the earlier proclamation; and thirteen Indians.

Schomburgk's report to the governor, dated Georgetown, October 13, 1843, gave an account of the "full success of the last expedition to survey the boundaries of British Guiana." It deals largely with explanations of the reasons that the explorer had not been able to complete the trip within the time limit which had evidently been set by the peremptory governor.

> Your Excellency will please to remember that, while I was yet traveling under the direction of the Royal Geographical Society, I visited already the sources of the Essequibo, and traced the rivers which flow southward into the Amazon to some distance. It remained now to search for the sources of

the first river of any consequence, which flows northeastwards of the Essequibo into the Amazon, and from thence to accomplish the line towards the headwaters of the River Corentyn [Courantyne], where the British, the Dutch, and the Brazilian boundaries were likely to concentrate.

The party under my command [which by now seems to have consisted of Mr. Goodall and assorted Indians] left a village of Taruma Indians at the Upper Essequibo (approximate latitude 1° 45′ N.) on the 8th of July, and tracing the River Onoro, or Onororo, a tributary to the Essequibo, to its sources, we traversed the ridge of mountains which divides the basin of the Amazon from that of the Essequibo, and stood, on the 13th of July, at the sources of the River Caphiwuim, or Apiniau, most likely the River Trombetas of the maps. We entered soon after a village of Maopityan, or Frog Indians, from whence, according to the information which I procured, we had to continue our journey by water upon the Caphiwuim as far as the junction of that river with the Wanamu, and to ascend the latter to the settlements of the Pianaghotto and Drio Indians, an undertaking, we were told, which it would occupy us eight days to execute. As the Maopityans did not possess any crafts, we had to prepare our canoes of the bark of trees, and we continued on the 19th of July our journey the Caphiwuim downwards.

Acquainted with the suspecting character of the uncivilized Indians, who fancy in every stranger an enemy, I dispatched several days previous to our departure, two Maopityans as messengers to inform the Pianaghottos of our intended visit, and to desire them to have a supply of provisions ready for us, as the Maopityans were so short that they were obliged to mix rotten wood with their cassava flour, to increase the quantity of bread prepared from it.

In lieu of eight days, as we had been told, it occupied us eighteen to reach the first Pianaghotto settlement, and after many deprivations and continued labor to descend a river studded with dangerous falls, we met with the cruel disappointment to see the inhabitants fly at our arrival, leaving their whole village with all that they possessed at our mercy, not even allowing themselves to carry their hammocks with them.

It became evident that the Maopityans had deceived us; the two messengers which I had sent had never proceeded on their journey, and they painted the journey so short in order to make me satisfied with a less quantity of provisions than otherwise I should have done had I known that it was such a distance, and for which provisions, after all, I had to pay exhorbitant prices.

Six Maopityan Indians had accompanied the expedition; I found, however, soon occasion to mistrust them, and I kept a watchful eye over their proceedings. Their bad character showed itself most glaringly the first night after our arrival at the Pianaghotto village, and obliged me to avail myself of the strongest measures at my command to prevent their pilfering the village, and to leave us at the mercy of savages, who, already mistrusting us, naturally would have laid the outrage at our charge.

While approaching the village, two canoes with Pianaghotto Indians came from the opposite direction, and scarcely had they observed our boats when, taking us for Brazilians, they turned their canoes and fled towards the shore. I urged the Maopityans, who were in my boat, and who spoke their language, to inform them of their mistake, but nothing could induce them to comply with my request, and although I hastened after the canoes, we came too late, and found the village, as already stated, deserted.

There were several axes, cutlasses, knives, etc., all of Dutch manufacture, lying about in the houses, and attracted immediately the attention of the Maopityans of our party. I gave strict orders that nothing should be touched. However, during the night, a Wapisiana of our party, who understood somewhat their language, informed me that he had overheard them planning to take all the valuable articles away, and to leave us during midnight.

My resolutions were soon formed. The six Maopityans were put in one of the huts, and taking sentry before it with some of our Indians whom I could trust, I threatened to use our firearms if they attempted to escape. Mr. Goodall shared the watch with me. With daylight I found that the information of their bad intentions had been too true; before nightfall they had already removed all the axes and cutlasses and every other valuable article they could lay their hands upon. Satisfying myself to keep the three chief men as hostages, I ordered the others to return every article they had stolen, and that besides I should keep the others as close prisoners until they had persuaded the Pianaghotto Indians that we had come as their friends, and brought them presents as knives, axes, beads, etc. Before many hours elapsed, I saw everything restored, and parties were sent out in search of the fugitive Indians.

Our situation was by no means enviable. We had been mistaken for Brazilians, and our apprehensions were increased by the information we had previously received that of a party of Brazilians who came up the River Dara every person, with the exception of an Indian boy, was murdered. Our scouts had traced the footsteps of many Indians departing in different directions, no doubt to give a general alarm, and the marks of footsteps which were shown to me close to our camp proved that we had been reconnoitred. Our party being so small, we had little chance of escaping if it came to the extreme. Anxiety of mind and the nightly watches were no doubt the cause of the indisposition which Mr. Goodall and myself were subjected to about this time; the first suffered more than myself.

After more than two weeks had elapsed in vain attempts to fall in with Indians who did not immediately fly at their appearance, our scouts succeeded to reassure a Zurumata family, and matters took now a better appearance. The reason of our coming was explained to them, and it spread soon among the other Indians, and we ultimately entered a village of the Drio Tribe, who received us friendly, and promised to return for our baggage, which for want of assistance we had been obliged to leave behind us.

The village was situated near the River Cutari, here a mere brook, but of importance, as it forms the western branch of the River Corentyne [Courantyne]. It was my intention to embark here, and we had again to prepare the necessary bark canoes, as our journey had led us for thirty miles over land and hills. The 6th of September approached before these frail crafts were finished, with which we intended to navigate a river perfectly unknown at its upper course. By that time nearly all the baggage had come up, with the exception of our tents, several objects of natural history, and, by some fatality, our stock of salt. I did not wish, however, to delay the expedition a single day for the sake of these comforts, and we descended the Cutari, which was so much impeded by trees fallen across it, and which we had to cut through to make a passage for our canoes, that our progress on the 11th of September, or the first six days, amounted to only 15 miles.

Their progress was somewhat more rapid after those first six days, but they had still to negotiate a series of dangerous falls, while the country traversed in the course of 26 days proved uninhabited.

I had to restrict our party from the 19th of September to a daily allowance of six ounces of farin [farina] to each man. Two to three days passed sometimes without our succeeding in procuring either fish or game as an addition to so small an allowance, while the unceasing labor rendered our wants more feeling. Several of the Indians suffered from fever, and our little company was so divided that we could scarcely spare the physical force of a single individual: it required, therefore, all persuasion to encourage the others, and to show them in perspective the plenty they would enjoy when we entered safely the Lower Corentyne. Our last farin was shared out in the morning of the 1st of October, amounting to about two ounces to each individual; but happily that evening, after having travelled 26 days without meeting a human being, we entered the Carib settlements, and our physical wants were provided for.

I continued my journey already next morning toward the Post to make arrangements to proceed without delay to the coast. Mr. Goodall followed the next day, after some rest to our worn-out crew, and we ultimately reached Berbice on the 9th of October.

These are the causes which unavoidably prolonged the conclusion of the survey, and I venture to hope that your Excellency will kindly consider them sufficient to exonerate me from any neglect or want of exertion to comply with the instructions which emanated from your Excellency.

Having tendered his apologies because his voyage required more time than a civil servant sitting in Georgetown had allotted for it, Schomburgk went into some technical details of the country traversed. Summing up his two years of strenuous fieldwork, he said:

The actual survey of the boundaries is now finished, and within the period I mentioned when it was first planned. It gives me uncommon satisfaction that I can state no human life has been lost in its execution. Those engaged in the survey have had to brave dangers of various kinds; thousands of miles, never before trodden by the foot of civilized man—nay, many not even by the savage Indian—have been traversed, now on foot, now in small canoes, but a kind Providence has everywhere protected us, and no sad remembrance of any individual being carried away by sickness or accident accompanies the retrospect in after years.

Professor Charles Edward Chapman makes brief mention of the boundary dispute between British Guiana and Venezuela, in his *Republican Hispanic America: A History* (N.Y.: The Macmillan Company, 1937). Discussing the period of around 1890, in Guzmán Blanco's *caudillo* rule in Venezuela he says:

> Once again there was revolutionary chaos. In the midst of it, a serious boundary question with Great Britain came to a head, about the limits of Venezuela and British Guiana. Succeeding Holland's rights in 1814, Great Britain had proceeded to advance westward into territory which had long been considered Venezuelan, through colonial grants of the Spanish kings. Great Britain paid no attention to the protests of Venezuela, and, eventually, relations between the two countries were severed. Matters came to a head in 1895, when President Crespo appealed to the United States for aid against British aggressions. Secretary of State Olney of the Cleveland administration, sent off a despatch to England in which he insisted that the Monroe Doctrine applied to the controversy and demanded arbitration. The British government, for a while, refused, denying the applicability of the Monroe Doctrine. When the United States threatened war, however, it decided to yield the point, being faced with difficulties in South Africa and in European opposition at the time, and not wishing to add the United States to its list of enemies. The British insisted, nevertheless, that a fifty-year occupation should carry title. On this basis, when the arbitration was held, Great Britain got most of the territory in controversy, but failed of what may well have been the main objective, in that the mouth of the Orinoco remained wholly in Venezuelan hands.

The final awards of the arbitration were not made until 1899. It was during the preceding few years that Great Britain, in preparing its case, added much to the literature of exploration and geography. For instance, Schomburgk's reports were published in 1896, while English research men, rummaging in old documents in Spain, unearthed the letters of Antonio de Berrio (see Chapter XIII).

The principle of arbitration having been established, British Guiana's boundary with Brazil was similarly fixed in 1904.

In 1960, however, Venezuela reopened its case in the United Nations, again claiming the main stream of the Essequibo as the boundary with British Guiana, now the Republic of Guyana.

The principal basis for the claim is that, in the U.S. tribunal which had considered the case and made the final decision and award, Venezuela had been represented, not directly, but by the Chief Justice of the U.S. Supreme Court. Negotiations toward arriving at a new award, or confirming the old one, are being carried out at the time of the present writing, January 1967.

PERCY HARRISON
FAWCETT

IN 1925, the English explorer Colonel Percy Harrison Faw-cett plunged into an unknown part of Brazil's state of Mato Grosso, near the Xingú River, accompanied by his son Jack and the latter's friend, Raleigh Rimell. Already well known to several South American governments and to scientific socie-ties in England and America for his many years of indefatigable exploration, devoted to the surveying and demarcation of inter-national boundaries in the relatively inaccessible parts of the Amazon basin, he was now to win world fame by failing to re-turn from his last expedition. The North American Newspaper Alliance, which had exclusive rights to that venture's story, kept the mystery of his disappearance alive for years. Several search expeditions, trekking into the interior for traces of him, failed to emerge with satisfactory indications of his fate. Now and then, here and there, men came out of the wilderness with reports that they had seen the colonel and talked to him, and that he was being held a prisoner by the Indians, but always some flaw in the story prevented its acceptance by Fawcett's family. The disappearance of the three men is at present rated as one of the most famous unsolved mysteries of South American exploration.

A first-class technician and an expert wilderness traveler, Faw-cett had come, by the time of his final entry into unexplored territory, to be regarded as a "mystic" with a special, personal mission in the continent's interior. Years of reading, pondering, and listening to strange old tales, had convinced him that a great civilization had at one time existed in the heart of Brazil, south of the Amazon. Every scrap of "evidence" which he had gathered in the course of his various expeditions, every romantic account of the "Lost Atlantis," the reports of several "psychometrists" whom he had at times hired to interpret the "vibrations" of an ancient stone idol which H. Rider Haggard had given him, plus an ancient document which he had examined in Rio de Janeiro, strengthened his firm conviction that such a civilization had once existed and had left behind the ruins of at least one ancient city, waiting to be discovered by Colonel Fawcett. The fact that the city and its surrounding countryside was more often than not supposed to be full of gold led to the facile assumption that the colonel was at heart a treasure seeker, the last of the El Dorado hunters. However, he was an extremely complex person who could not be classified in so facile a fashion.

Fawcett spent the years between 1921 and 1924 in England, writing up his previous labors and adventures in South America's interior, and chafing to return to Brazil for one last try at the postulated ancient city. After his disappearance in 1925, his family waited 25 years before consenting to the publication of his book. Edited by the younger of his two sons, Brian Fawcett, who had spent most of his adult life as a mechanical engineer on Peru's famous "Central Railway," where the editor knew him briefly in 1932, the volume was published in 1953 in England under the title *Exploration Fawcett,* and in the United States as *Lost Trails, Lost Cities.*[1] The excerpts given in the present chapter are taken from the American volume.

Well edited and engagingly illustrated by Brian Fawcett— who is known in Peru as an able artist as well as an expert engineer—the book consists of a preface by Brian, 22 chapters by his father, and two final chapters by the son, giving an account of the search for the colonel, the rumors concerning him and reported "sightings" of him by various travelers after 1925. Colonel Fawcett's personal account, written in 1924 when he was fifty-seven, ends as follows, with a summary of his life:

> If the journey is not successful my work in South America ends in failure, for I can never do any more. I must inevitably

[1] Col. P. H. Fawcett, *Lost Trails, Lost Cities,* selected and arranged by Brian Fawcett (New York: Funk & Wagnalls Company, 1953).

be discredited as a visionary, and branded as one who had only personal enrichment in view. Who will ever understand that I want no glory from it—no money for myself—that I am doing it unpaid in the hope that its ultimate benefit to mankind will justify the years spent in the quest? The last few years have been the most wretched and disillusioning in my life—full of anxieties, uncertainties, financial stringency, underhand dealing and outright treachery. My wife and children have been sacrificed for it, and denied many of the benefits that they would have enjoyed had I remained in the ordinary walks of life. Of our twenty-four years of married life only ten have been spent together. Apart from four years in the Great War, I have spent ten in the forests, yet my wife has never complained. On the contrary, her practical help and constant encouragement have been big factors in the successes so far gained, and if I win in the end the triumph will be largely due to her.

Then a major in the British Army, P. H. Fawcett was asked, in 1906, to request a leave of absence in order to undertake a boundary survey for the Bolivian government in the rubber country along the Abuna and Acre rivers where Peru, Brazil, and Bolivia meet. According to his account, the president of the Royal Geographical Society, asking him to undertake the task, said: "There is considerable argument about the frontier, and so fantastically high is the price of rubber now that a major conflagration could arise out of this question of what territory belongs to whom!"

After making his way to Bolivia's capital, La Paz, via New York, the Isthmus of Panama, Peru, and Lake Titicaca, and fretting in the city over inevitable delays, Fawcett and a young English assistant named Chalmers left the capital July 4, 1906, "bound for Sorata and the Beni." The assignment kept Fawcett in the field some 17 months, and when, on October 18, 1907, he handed his maps and reports to Bolivia's president, he was asked to return to South America the following year "to undertake the frontier delimitation with Brazil on the Rio Paraguay."

The Englishman's first task did not take him into "unknown" or "unexplored" country. It did take him into wild frontier regions which were being torn apart by the rubber boom, then at its height. Rubber was plentiful; its price on the world market was high; but labor was scarce. Wild Indians were therefore captured and enslaved. White men were forced into debt; they were sent to the rubber regions to work off their obligations; the bookkeeping was so stacked against them that their debts grew greater year by year; they faced lifetimes of slave labor, which eventually came to be ended only by the collapse of the rubber boom about 1911. Colonel Fawcett's observations on those conditions, made during his trip of 1906–7, bear out completely Sir Roger Casement's report on conditions on the Putumayo River which was to shock the world a few years later.

Held up by red tape and the nonarrival of some needed supplies, Fawcett spent considerable time in Riberalta, a town on the lower Beni River, opposite that stream's confluence with the Madre de Dios. In those days Riberalta was a rubber-gathering center, dominated by a few powerful firms; today it is the metropolis for a region devoted to cattle raising and the production of sugar, and one of the nuclei for the Bolivian government's labors to tame and settle its "Wild East"; when the present editor was there in 1932, it was a sleeping town, commercially almost dead since the collapse of the rubber boom, supported largely by the Bolivian government's payrolls for officials, the police, and a garrison of soldiers, anxiously awaiting the end of the world depression.

Of conditions in 1906, Fawcett writes:

> Two of the big firms in Riberalta kept forces of armed toughs for hunting Indians, and wholesale butchery went on. The wretched captives were taken to work so far away from their tribes that they lost all sense of direction, and so escape was all the more difficult. They were given a shirt, the necessary tools, and a portion of rice, and ordered to produce an annual total of about seven hundred pounds of rubber under threat of the whip. This may not seem a great deal, but rubber trees were scattered sparsely over a huge area, and unceasing toil was necessary to locate and work them. With rubber at the boom prices of those days the system brought immense profits to the firms.

Occasionally, of course, bands of wild Indians attacked white men, or seemed to threaten such attacks. In such cases they had to be punished.

> A Swiss and a German from a *barraca* [rubber-gathering station] below the confluence of the Madidi had recently raided

the savages with a sizable force. A village was destroyed, men and women butchered, and children killed by dashing their brains out against trees. The raiders returned proudly with a prize of eighty canoes! The only reason for it was that a few timid Indians had come into camp and an attack was feared. I was told that these warriors from the *barraca* considered it grand sport to throw Indian babies up in the air and catch them on the points of machetes. Decent people on the river were disgusted at the whole affair; and the Government were also indignant when they heard about it, but could do nothing.

From Riberalta, Fawcett made his way to the Acre Territory, which had long been the scene of armed conflicts over boundary disputes between Bolivians and Brazilians. His survey work completed there, he returned to Riberalta, whence he ascended the Madeira River to Rurrenabaque, from which frontier settlement he traveled overland, westward, to La Paz. His story of the trip is full of accounts of slavery, insect pests, savage Indians, snakes, and always slavery again. He has much to say of the debt-slavery in which white men were held.

Once in the hands of the big firms it was difficult for any man, black or white, to leave against the will of his employers. An Englishman in Riberalta told me a story to illustrate this.

"I travelled on the Orton with a man who had quit his job with a well-known firm and was clearing out with all his savings —about £350. He was a useful man, you understand, and they didn't want to lose him, so what did they do but decoy him ashore at one of the firm's *barracas,* where they soon made him drunk.

"They kept him like that for three days—so drunk that he didn't know what he was doing. At the end of that time they let him sober up, and then pushed a bill under his nose for £75 more than the whole of his savings. What could he do? No court would have upheld his case if he had made a claim against the swindlers. . . . He was forced to sell his wife and daughter to cancel the debt, and then get back up river to work, where he was before. It was on the way up river that I met him, and what made him mad when he told me the story was not so much the trick they played on him, but that his womenfolk had gone for too low a price!"

George Morgan, a Negro, was bought by one of the Riberalta Englishmen . . . for £30. Miserably treated, he had no prospect of any other fate but slavery, and possibly being sold up river to a *barraca* where his treatment would be worse than at the hands of the human devil who owned him. . . .

Besides spending twenty-four hours in the stocks at the police station, debtors had to work off what they owed to their creditors. A Peruvian employed at one *barraca* died, and his wife and six children in Riberalta were seized and sent into slavery at another *barraca* of the same firm. . . .

A German, in debt to a large firm, was sent off to one of the most isolated *barracas,* where all the other workers had died. There was no hope of his ever being able to escape from this place. An Englishman named Pae started a business in Riberalta and aroused the jealousy of the bigger houses. They undersold him, ruined him, ran him into debt, and he was taken for service at a nominal wage—not quite a slave, but hopelessly bound.

On March 6, 1908, Fawcett left Southampton for Buenos Aires, whence he proceeded inland to survey the Bolivia-Brazil boundary on the Paraguay River. His story of some two years of work, ending with a voyage through the Strait of Magellan and northward to Bolivia, is an engaging tale of adventures, hardships, a Paraguayan revolution, and a mounting preoccupation with all traces, reports, and rumors of the ancient Indian civilization which was to become a passion, dominating his life. Somehow, all savage Indians who were lighter in color than other Indians, or a little more civilized in their behavior, came in Fawcett's mind to trace their ancestry to that city-building ancient culture. In the town of Corumbá he heard one of many reports which were to attain increasing significance in his mind:

> There was talk of White Indians again.
>
> "I know a man here who has met one," said the British Consul. "They are very savage, and have the reputation of coming out only at night. They're known as 'bats' for that reason."
>
> "Where do they live?" I asked.
>
> "Oh, somewhere up in the region of the lost Martirios gold mines, north or northwest of Diamantino. Nobody knows quite where they are. Mato Grosso is almost unknown country. The hilly regions in the north have never been entered, to anyone's knowledge, though many expeditions have gone there, only to be lost. It's bad country all right. Mark my words—it'll never be

explored on foot, however big and well-equipped the expeditions. Possibly, in a hundred years' time, flying machines will do it—who knows?"

His words had a significance for me that made them unforgettable.

Very few years later, Fawcett himself was to penetrate that forbidding, "unexplored" land, where he was destined to disappear in 1925. During the period 1942–45, in connection with the World War II effort to procure Amazonian rubber, virtually every square foot of that land came to be surveyed from the air by U.S. "flying machines."

Except for brief returns to England, Colonel Fawcett spent virtually his entire time in the South American interior, running boundary lines and seeking lost cities, until the end of 1914, when World War I claimed his services. In 1914, accompanied by two young Englishmen named Manley and Costin, he worked for a time in totally unexplored country in today's Brazilian territory of Rondonia, formerly that of Guaporé, east of the famous Madeira-Mamoré Railway. They made their way up the Guaporé River, most of which forms the boundary between Brazil and Bolivia.

> Game is plentiful on the upper Guaporé, for there are few people to disturb it. Eleven days of hard paddling brought us to the Mequens River, where there was a German rubber *barraca,* and here we met Baron Erland Nordenskiöld, who with his plucky wife was engaged in investigating the more accessible Indian tribes of the Guaporé. . . .
>
> About twelve miles away to the east were hills, which the Baron considered it would be rash to visit.
>
> "There are sure to be large tribes of savages there," he observed, "and they are almost certain to be dangerous. I've heard something from the Indians we have visited. They all speak of cannibals somewhere in that direction."
>
> "They say the men are big and hairy," put in the Baron's wife.
>
> I laughed. "We'll know soon, for it's where we're going."
>
> "Most rash!" muttered the Baron. "Frankly, I won't expect to see you again. You're doing a most foolhardy thing."
>
> Weighed down by heavy packs, we left the Rio Mequens and for two days waded through the soft mud of extensive swamps

until we came to a sluggish river emptying into them. We followed up this river, and some days after reached grassy plains
forming the first hills of the Serra dos Parecis. . . .

Climbing the Serrania we came again to forest, where the undergrowth afforded little obstacle to our progress, and where
the huge rubber trees, . . . showed no signs of regular tapping.
True, some had been clumsily hacked, but we could see that it
was not the work of a company *seringuero* [rubber tapper]. It
looked as though white men had never been here before, but
the traces of Indians were obvious. . . .

It was three weeks after we entered the forest that we came
to a wide and well-used trail crossing our own at right angles.

The new trail looked well used, which meant that an Indian
settlement must be fairly near. After some debate as to which
trail to follow, they decided, through the toss of a coin, to take
the new one.

We followed it for two or three miles, passing several [Indian]
plantations, and suddenly daylight broke upon us in full force
at the edge of a large clearing. With great caution we peeped
out from the undergrowth, and there in front of us, on a wide
space of smoothly packed earth, were two large huts shaped
like beehives. They were quite forty feet high in the centre and
a hundred in diameter, but only one door could be seen in the
nearer one—perhaps thirty feet away.

As we watched, a naked copper-coloured child came out of
the hut, a nut in one hand and a little stone axe in the other.
He squatted down on his haunches before a flat stone, laid the
nut on it, and then started to hammer on the shell with the
side of the axe.

I forgot my companions and all else as I gazed on this scene.
The curtain of time was drawn aside to reveal a glimpse of the
distant past—a prehistoric peep—for just so would the neolithic
child have looked and acted when man was beginning his ascent
of the ladder of evolution. The primeval forest, the clearing,
the hut, all were exactly as they might have been countless
thousands of years ago! Then the nut broke, the child gave a
little grunt of satisfaction, and, laying down the stone axe,
popped the kernel into his mouth.

With a mental effort I brought my mind back to the present,
and gave a low whistle. The child looked up, his jaws ceased to
move and his eyes rolled; two arms came out of the darkness of

the hut's interior, grabbed him and pulled him inside. There was an excited jabbering, the rattle of bows and arrows, and smothered screams. It's no use lurking in the forest once your presence is known to the savages, so I came out of cover, swiftly crossed to the hut, and slipped through the low entrance to crouch down behind the darkness of the wall.

When my eyes had accustomed themselves to the gloom I saw that the hut was empty but for an old woman, who stood watching me from amongst a number of high earthenware urns under the centre pole. There were other doors on the far side, through which the occupants had fled. The explanation dawned on me —we had arrived when every man was away in the plantations, and the women and children but a moment ago in the hut were by now racing off to give the alarm, leaving only the ancient crone who was too old to escape.

The old woman muttered to herself, and then bent to continue the work she was doing when the excitement began—the brewing of maize beer over a fire. I signaled to her that I was hungry, and, obviously terrified, she took up a gourd and came hobbling over to me, still muttering. The gourd was filled with very tasty food, whatever it may have been, and I took it out to the others, who were still waiting in the scrub at the edge of the clearing.

The sky had clouded over, and with a thunder in the foliage above, torrential rain began to fall.

"Come on inside with me," I shouted. "We may as well be in there as out here."

Together we entered the hut, and when the gourd of food was empty I took it over to the old woman to be refilled. It was while we were eating the second helping that the men came in. They slipped in by various entrances not previously noticed, and through the doorway beside us we could see the shadows of more men outside, probably surrounding the hut. All the men carried bows and arrows. A man, whom I took to be the chief, stood beside the old woman listening to her excited tale of what had happened. I went over to him and tried to convey to him by signs that we were friendly and only wanted food, explaining that we had already had some. He stood perfectly still as I approached, and gave no indication of understanding what I was trying to tell him. I went back to the doorway, took some small gifts from the pack, and returned to hand these to him. He took them without any kind of acknowledgement, but the women came over to us with gourds full of peanuts. Our friendship was now accepted, and the chief himself sat down on a carved stool and shared the peanuts with us.

I found out later that these people were the Maxubis, that they had twenty-four villages and numbered over two thousand. They were not very dark, but of a bright copper colour; rather small, and with a tint of red in their hair. The men wore shells and sticks in their ears, pegs through their nostrils and lower lips, and armlets of seeds and carved chonta wood. On ankles and wrists they wore rubber bands tinted red with urucú, and in these were perceived the answer to the mystery of the tapped rubber trees. The women wore no ornaments, and their hair was short, while that of the men was long, a curious reversal of our own custom. I believe that these people, like many others in Brazil, are the descendants of a higher civilization. In one of the Maxubi villages was a red-headed boy with blue eyes—not an albino.

Our destination was yet much farther toward the east, and we stayed with the Maxubis only long enough to learn a little of their language and their ways. They are sun-worshippers, and one or two men in each village are on duty every morning to greet the sunrise with musical voices, chanting a weird and haunting song in what I should say was the pentatonic scale— similar to the *yaravi* of the mountain Indians in Peru. In the utter silence of the forest, when the first light of day had stilled the night-long uproar of insect life, these hymns impressed us greatly with their beauty. It was the music of developed people, not the mere rhythmic noise beloved of the true savage. They had names for all the planets, and called the stars *Vira Vira*— curiously suggestive of the name *Viracocha* by which the Incas knew the sun.

They had a gentle courtesy in their manner, and their morals were beyond reproach. Their feet and hands were small and well formed, their features delicate. They knew the art of making pottery; they grew tobacco, and smoked it in small-bowled pipes or in cigarettes rolled in maize leaves. In every way they indicated a fall from a high state in man's development rather than a people evolving from savagery.

Scattered over the vast expanse of unknown South America are tribes like this one—a few better organized, and some even clothed—utterly refuting the conclusions arrived at by ethnologists, who have only explored the rivers and know nothing of the less accessible places. At the same time there are real savages, ugly, dangerous, and treacherous.

Never had we seen peanuts such as those grown by the Maxubis. It was their staple diet, and the nuts in their pods were between three and four inches long. Their taste, as well as the nutritive value, was excellent, and it would be hard to find a more convenient food to carry on a journey—as we learned later. At meals, every man helped himself from a communal bowl filled with these huge peanuts, while the women ate apart and kept the men's bowl replenished.

In about ten days we could exchange ideas with the Maxubis in their own language, and it was then that they told us of a tribe of cannibals to the north—the Maricoxis. *"Vincha Maricoxi, chimbibi coco!"* they said—to give you a sample of their speech. "If you visit the Maricoxis you will be food for the pot!" A gruesome pantomime accompanied the warning.

The information obtained from the Maxubis was useful and interesting, and after visiting several of the nearer villages we took our farewell of them and set off toward the northeast where the Maricoxis were said to live. We entered entirely trackless forest—probably no man's land avoided by Maxubis and Maricoxis alike—and on the fifth day struck a trail which looked as if it were in regular use.

As we stood looking from right to left, trying to decide which direction was the more promising, two savages appeared about a hundred yards to the south, moving at a trot and talking rapidly. On catching sight of us they stopped dead and hurriedly fixed arrows to their bows, while I shouted to them in the Maxubi tongue. We could not see them clearly for the shadows dappling their bodies, but it seemed to me they were large, hairy men, with exceptionally long arms, and with foreheads sloping back from pronounced eye ridges—men of a very primitive kind, in fact, and stark naked. Suddenly they turned and made off into the undergrowth, and we, knowing it was useless to follow, started up the north leg of the trail.

It was not long before sundown, when, dim and muffled through the trees, came the unmistakable sound of a horn. We halted and listened intently. Again we heard the horn call, answered from other directions till several horns were braying at once. In the subdued light of evening, beneath the high vault of branches in this forest untrodden by civilized man, the sound was as eerie as the opening notes of some fantastic opera. We knew it was made by the savages, and that those savages were now on our trail. Soon we could hear shouts and jabbering to the accompaniment of the rough horn calls—a barbarous, merciless din, in marked contrast to the stealth of the ordinary savage. Darkness, still distant above the treetops, was settling rapidly down here in the depths of the wood, so we looked about us for a camping site which offered some measure of safety from attack, and finally took refuge in a tacuara thicket. Here the naked savages would not dare to follow on account of the wicked inch-long thorns. As we slung our hammocks inside the natural stockade we could hear the savages jabbering excitedly all around, but not daring to enter. Then, as the last light went, they left us, and we heard no more of them.

Next morning there were no savages in our vicinity, and we met with none when, after following another well-defined trail, we came to a clearing where there was a plantation of mandioca and papaws. Brilliantly coloured toucans croaked in the palms as they picked at the fruit, and as no danger threatened we helped ourselves freely. We camped here, and at dusk held a concert in our hammocks, Costin with a harmonica, Manley with a comb, and myself with a flageolet. Perhaps it was foolish of us to advertise our presence in this way; but we were not molested, and no savage appeared.

In the morning we went on, and within a quarter of a mile came to a sort of palm-leaf sentry-box—then another. Then all of a sudden we reached open forest. The undergrowth fell away, disclosing between the tree boles a village of primitive shelters, where squatted some of the most villainous savages I have ever seen. Some were engaged in making arrows, others just idled—great, apelike brutes who looked as if they had scarcely evolved beyond the level of beasts.

I whistled, and an enormous creature, hairy as a dog, leapt to his feet in the nearest shelter, fitted an arrow to his bow in a flash, and came up dancing from one leg to the other till he was only four yards away. Emitting grunts that sounded like "Eugh! Eugh! Eugh!" he remained there dancing, and suddenly the whole forest around us was alive with those hideous ape-men, all grunting "Eugh! Eugh! Eugh!" and dancing from leg to leg in the same way as they strung arrows to their bows. It looked like a very delicate situation for us, and I wondered if it was the end. I made friendly overtures in Maxubi, but they paid no attention. It was as though human speech were beyond their powers of comprehension.

The creature in front of me ceased his dance, stood for a moment perfectly still, and then drew his bowstring back till it was level with his ear, at the same time raising the barbed point

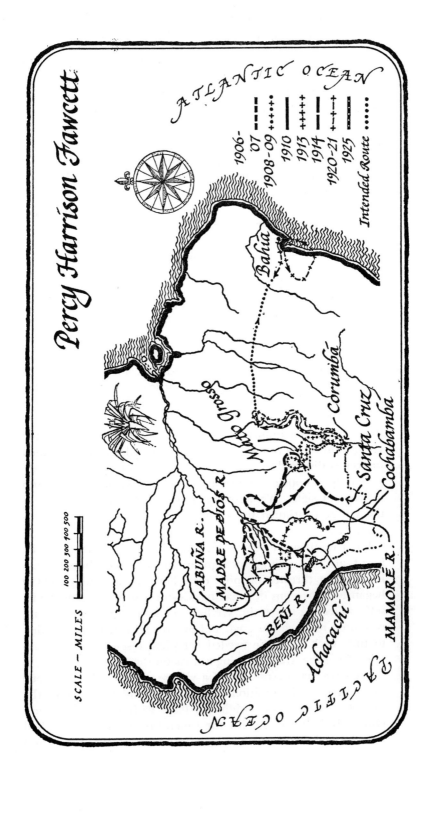

Percy Harrison Fawcett

ATLANTIC OCEAN

1906-07
1908-09
1910
1913
1914
1920-21
1925
Intended Route

Bahia

Corumba

Santa Cruz
Cochabamba

Mato Grosso

ABUÑA R.
MADRE DE DIÓS R.

BENI R.

Achacachi

MAMORÉ R.

PACIFIC OCEAN

SCALE — MILES
100 200 300 400 500

of the six-foot arrow to the height of my chest. I looked straight into the pig-like eyes half hidden under the overhanging brows, and knew that he was not going to loose that arrow—yet. As deliberately as he had raised it, he now lowered the bow, and commenced once more the slow dance, and the "Eugh! Eugh! Eugh!"

A second time he raised the arrow and drew the bow back, and again I knew he would not shoot. It was just as the Maxubis had told me it would be. Again he lowered the bow and continued his dance. Then for the third time he halted and began to bring up the arrow's point. I knew he meant business this time, and drew out a Mauser pistol I had on my hip. It was a big, clumsy thing, of a calibre unsuited to forest use, but I had brought it because by clipping the wooden holster to the pistol-butt it became a carbine, and was lighter to carry than a true rifle. It used .38 black powder shells which made a din out of all proportion to their size. I never raised it; I just pulled the trigger and banged it off into the ground at the ape-man's feet.

The effect was instantaneous. A look of complete amazement came into the hideous face, and the little eyes opened wide. He dropped his bow and sprang away as quickly as a cat to vanish behind a tree. Then the arrows began to fly. We shot off a few rounds into the branches, hoping the noise would scare the savages into a more receptive frame of mind, but they seemed in no way disposed to accept us, and before anyone was hurt we gave it up as hopeless and returned down the trail till the camp was out of sight. We were not followed, but the clamour in the village continued for a long time as we struck off northwards. . . .

Later we turned east, and for some days went on through the forest, always watching for signs of Indians, and always listening for the threatening note of a horn. . . . Manley's nerve began to show signs of breaking, Costin was jumpy, and I myself was feeling the strain. We had to admit that we were in no condition to reach our goal, and so with reluctance we decided to turn back. . . . We needed complete rest—complete relaxation from the strain of being always on the alert.

We gave that wasps' nest of a village as wide a berth as our calculations of its position would allow, and returned to the Maxubis, striking the original village with perfect accuracy. Our arrival coincided with the funeral of a warrior who had been hunted down and shot by a Maricoxi foraging party, and

I wondered if the two events might be thought by superstitious tribesmen to be connected. . . .

The dead man's entrails had been extracted and put in an urn for burial. The body was then cut up and distributed for consumption by the twenty-four families of the hut he had occupied, a religious ceremony not to be confused with cannibalism. Finally the hut was freed from the ghost of the deceased by the following elaborate ritual.

The chief, his second-in-command, and the medicine man sat down in a row on their little stools before the largest entrance of the hut, and performed movements like those of squeezing something down each limb, catching it as it emerged at fingers and toes, and throwing it at a palm leaf screen about three feet square. Beneath the screen was a half-gourd partly filled with water, with herbs of some sort floating on the surface, and every now and then all three of them would carefully examine the screen and the water under it. This was repeated many times, and then they went into a trance, and for about half an hour sat immobile on their stools, eyes rolled up into their heads. When they came to, they first rubbed their stomachs, and were then violently sick.

All night long they sat on their stools and chanted singly or in chorus a series of three notes, descending in octaves, with the words, repeated over and over again, *"Tawi-Tacni, tawi-tacni, tawi-tacni."* In response, the families inside the hut joined in a chorus of lamentations.

These ceremonies lasted for three days, and the chief solemnly assured me that the dead man's ghost was within the hut and visible to him. I could see nothing. On the third day the proceedings reached a climax; the screen was carried into the hut and placed where the light from the doorway fell on it; the people dropped to their knees and lowered their faces to the ground; the three headmen discarded their stools and crouched in great excitement before the entrance to the hut; and I knelt down beside them to watch the screen at which they were all gazing intently.

Inside the hut, to one side of the screen, was a closed cubicle where the dead man had slept, and the eyes of the headmen turned towards this cubicle. For a moment there was absolute silence, and in that moment I saw a dark shadow emerge from the cubicle, float towards the centre pole of the hut, and there fade from sight. Mass hypnotism, you say? Very well, let's leave it at that; all I know is that I saw it!

The two chiefs and the medicine man relaxed, broke out into a profuse sweat, and fell prone to the ground. I left them and returned to my companions, who had not been present at the ceremony.

In three villages which we visited after this event our arrival coincided with a *tapi,* or ghost-laying ceremony. There was the same singing, but I was not allowed to witness it, for there were growing suspicions that the deaths were due to the baneful influence of our presence. They construed my work with the theodolite in the environs of the villages as "talking with the stars," and were ill at ease about it. There were only three of us, and kindly though these people appeared to be there was the possibility that superstitious dread might turn to anger against us.

Before we departed I learned that the Maricoxis numbered about one thousand five hundred. To the east was another tribe of cannibals, the Arupi, and another and more distant tribe to the northeast—short black people covered with hair, who spitted their victims on a bamboo over a fire, and when cooked picked off pieces to eat—a human barbecue, in fact. I had heard rumors of these people before, and I know now that the stories were well founded. The Maxubis obviously considered themselves to be civilized, and spoke of the surrounding cannibals with great scorn. They had a careful system of guards on the borders of their territory where unfriendly tribes lived, and the "sentry-boxes" we saw—common to all these Indians—were screens from which arrows could be fired.

Loaded with string bags of peanuts, stone axes, and bows and arrows—the weapons were real works of art—we left the Maxubis and turned southwest towards Bolivia. Game was scarce; it was one of those periods when for some reason or other animal and bird life goes elsewhere. Once we managed to shoot three monkeys, but a roving jaguar walked off with two of them, and we kept going on a diet of eight peanuts a day each. Perhaps that saved us from excessive prostration, for it is a fact that while a vegetable diet, if sufficient, endows one with plenty of strength and energy, under conditions of semi-starvation meat induces a feeling of great lassitude.

At this point, the explorer's son and editor, Brian Fawcett, added the following footnote:

> The chief of the Maxubis, enchanted by the photographs my father showed him of the family in England, gave him a large string-bag of the giant peanuts for us children. This was brought

Pizarro's men. It seems that, during the reigns of the last four Incas, a number of Spaniards and mestizos, stragglers, ambassadors, and at least two friars were permitted to enter the Vilcabamba province. Only bodies of soldiers were not welcome.

Manco was succeeded by the eldest of his three sons, Sayri Tupac, who loved peace and luxury. After ruling without incident for ten years, he foolishly allowed the Spaniards to lure him out of Vilcabamba to settle in the beautiful Yucay Valley, near Cuzco. He died a few years later—of illness, according to the Spaniards; of poison, according to his own people.

In 1560, Manco's middle son, Titu Cusi, ascended the throne. He ruled eleven years and then died. His attending physician, the Spanish Friar Diego, ascribed the death to double pneumonia. The nobles and one of Titu's widows accused the friar of having poisoned him and therefore put him to death "with great cruelty."

The youngest son, Tupac Amaru, took over the government in 1571, but then, at long last, Spanish soldiers managed to invade Vilcabamba. They captured the last independent Inca, took him, his family, and a number of his captains to Cuzco and tortured them all publicly to death with fiendish brutality.

Shortly after Titu Cusi ascended the throne, he was visited in Vitcos by the Spaniard, Don Diego Rodriguez, who had been sent by the viceroy to try to convert the Inca to Christianity and lure him out of Vilcabamba as his brother had previously been lured. Titu Cusi received him well but largely, it seems, for the purpose of giving him a show of his military strength and expressing his defiance of the Spaniards. Rodriguez' mission failed, but his written account of it made mention of another city in the region besides Vitcos. In order to make his martial spectacles more impressive, the Inca had sent for 300 soldiers to march to Vitcos from a city called Vilcabamba, which was the region's real capital.

Two Augustinian friars now came to Vitcos from Cuzco. They were Marcos García and Diego Ortiz. The story of their experiences, as recorded by one Father Calancha, has come to be the principal guide for modern explorers, laboring to locate and identify ruins of the important ancient cities of Vitcos and Vilcabamba. With the Inca's permission, they established two mission stations, Father Marcos at Puquiura, near Vitcos, and Father

home intact—not even the pangs of starvation had induced my father to broach it—and I feel ashamed now to recall the nonchalant way in which we youngsters ate them. I still have the bag; and a few of the nuts were preserved as curios, but unfortunately the termites destroyed them later in Peru.

In his remarks on the effects of meat under conditions of semistarvation, Colonel Fawcett was correct only in relation to *lean* meat. As recorded by Darwin (Chapter XVIII), and confirmed by much modern medical experience, a straight diet of meat with the proper proportion of fat is virtually unbeatable as a source of energy.

> It was not easy going, and we were very hungry men when eventually we struck a rubber-gatherer's hut on the bank of a small stream. Here we stayed for two days, fattening up on rice and *charque* [dried meat].

The explorers now made their way overland, by ox cart, toward Santa Cruz, and eventually La Paz.

> At San Ignacio, which we reached at the beginning of September 1914, . . . we heard that war had broken out in Europe. A German told me; and in spite of our being officially enemies he lent me enough money to take us to Santa Cruz—for all I had left was £4—merely requesting that the loan be repaid to his representative there.

Finally:

> We passed through La Paz, crossed Lake Titicaca in the *Inca*, and arrived at the coast in time to see Admiral Craddock's ill-fated squadron steaming to its doom off Coronel. After that, Englishmen had a thin time in the Pacific ports, especially those in Chile where the German influence was strongest, till the tide turned with the Battle of the Falkland Islands. . . .
>
> By the beginning of January 1915 we were absorbed into the great armies to be.

❧ XXIII ❧

THE LAST REFUGE OF THE INCAS

THE country near Peru's city of Cuzco is dotted with impressive old Inca ruins, some of which have been known since the conquest while others were discovered only in recent decades, and still others undoubtedly exist largely as rumors, spread by rubber scouts and resident Indians. The most famous ruins which came to light in relatively recent times are those of Machu Picchu, a city about 80 miles northwest of the former capital of the Incas, located in surroundings of indescribable grandeur, on a mountain of the same name, at an altitude of about 7,500 feet. It was discovered in 1911 by the American, Hiram Bingham, cleared of vegetation and studied the following year with the help of the National Geographic Society, and amply publicized thereafter by that organization. Today, reached from Cuzco by rail and car, and provided with a government-managed inn, it is one of Peru's major tourist attractions.

The discovery of that monumental site was made in the course of a search which is still going on, namely the quest for "the last refuge of the Incas." In the last of his several books,[1] Bingham devotes a chapter to the lives and fates of the last four Incas whose collective rule lasted 35 years after Pizarro's conquest of Peru.

After conquering most of the Inca empire, Pizarro set up a young nobleman named Manco as puppet ruler. The latter

[1] Hiram Bingham, *Lost City of the Incas* (N.Y.: Duell, Sloan and Pearce, 1948).

was happy over being emperor but unhappy over being a pet. Soon after being installed, he organized an army and in revolt. But he could not prevail against the Spaniards their horses and guns and their own many Indian allies troops were routed in 1537 and he fled with them from vicinity of Cuzco down into the valley of the Urubamba taking with him his three sons and a quantity of "C Women." Contemporary chronicles state that he also carr a vast treasure but repeated subsequent efforts to find it r in failure.

The province into which Manco fled was that of Vilca north of the high and rugged Andean range of the same in the western watershed of the upper Urubamba Riv matically temperate only in its upper portions, the p extends eastward, northward, and downward into the tropical Amazonian rain-forest country. Well guarded b tains, canyons, and torrential rivers, in Manco's time a from the south only over two passes, both higher tha Blanc, the last of the Incas were there, for a time, fair against the Spaniards.

Bingham writes as follows about Manco, whom Manco II:

> Manco's army fled over the Pass of Paticalla, wen the Lucumayo River, crossed the Urubamba on an Ir sion bridge at a place called Chuquichaca. They w enter one of the affluents of the Urubamba which is t the Vilcabamba, and passing that valley established in a pleasant region where their favorite crops coul and their llamas and alpacas find adequate pastura
>
> Manco established himself on top of a mountai built a long "palace" and characteristic Inca stru place was called Vitcos or possibly Uiticos.[2] . . . He the armed forces of his enemy, he was able to enjoy of a dry climate in a well-watered region where co toes, as well as the fruits of the sub-tropical zones,

Piecing together his story from several old chror ham tells how Manco, after ruling ten years, was k of eight Spaniards, members of the Almagro facti he had given refuge after the final defeat of th

[2] Later, he also gives Pitcos and Viticos as alternate spellings.

home intact—not even the pangs of starvation had induced my father to broach it—and I feel ashamed now to recall the nonchalant way in which we youngsters ate them. I still have the bag; and a few of the nuts were preserved as curios, but unfortunately the termites destroyed them later in Peru.

In his remarks on the effects of meat under conditions of semistarvation, Colonel Fawcett was correct only in relation to *lean* meat. As recorded by Darwin (Chapter XVIII), and confirmed by much modern medical experience, a straight diet of meat with the proper proportion of fat is virtually unbeatable as a source of energy.

It was not easy going, and we were very hungry men when eventually we struck a rubber-gatherer's hut on the bank of a small stream. Here we stayed for two days, fattening up on rice and *charque* [dried meat].

The explorers now made their way overland, by ox cart, toward Santa Cruz, and eventually La Paz.

At San Ignacio, which we reached at the beginning of September 1914, . . . we heard that war had broken out in Europe. A German told me; and in spite of our being officially enemies he lent me enough money to take us to Santa Cruz—for all I had left was £4—merely requesting that the loan be repaid to his representative there.

Finally:

We passed through La Paz, crossed Lake Titicaca in the *Inca*, and arrived at the coast in time to see Admiral Craddock's ill-fated squadron steaming to its doom off Coronel. After that, Englishmen had a thin time in the Pacific ports, especially those in Chile where the German influence was strongest, till the tide turned with the Battle of the Falkland Islands. . . .

By the beginning of January 1915 we were absorbed into the great armies to be.

❦ XXIII ❧

THE LAST REFUGE OF
THE INCAS

THE country near Peru's city of Cuzco is dotted with impressive old Inca ruins, some of which have been known since the conquest while others were discovered only in recent decades, and still others undoubtedly exist largely as rumors, spread by rubber scouts and resident Indians. The most famous ruins which came to light in relatively recent times are those of Machu Picchu, a city about 80 miles northwest of the former capital of the Incas, located in surroundings of indescribable grandeur, on a mountain of the same name, at an altitude of about 7,500 feet. It was discovered in 1911 by the American, Hiram Bingham, cleared of vegetation and studied the following year with the help of the National Geographic Society, and amply publicized thereafter by that organization. Today, reached from Cuzco by rail and car, and provided with a government-managed inn, it is one of Peru's major tourist attractions.

The discovery of that monumental site was made in the course of a search which is still going on, namely the quest for "the last refuge of the Incas." In the last of his several books,[1] Bingham devotes a chapter to the lives and fates of the last four Incas whose collective rule lasted 35 years after Pizarro's conquest of Peru.

After conquering most of the Inca empire, Pizarro set up a young nobleman named Manco as puppet ruler. The latter

[1] Hiram Bingham, *Lost City of the Incas* (N.Y.: Duell, Sloan and Pearce, 1948).

was happy over being emperor but unhappy over being a puppet. Soon after being installed, he organized an army and rose in revolt. But he could not prevail against the Spaniards with their horses and guns and their own many Indian allies. His troops were routed in 1537 and he fled with them from the vicinity of Cuzco down into the valley of the Urubamba River, taking with him his three sons and a quantity of "Chosen Women." Contemporary chronicles state that he also carried off a vast treasure but repeated subsequent efforts to find it resulted in failure.

The province into which Manco fled was that of Vilcabamba, north of the high and rugged Andean range of the same name, in the western watershed of the upper Urubamba River. Climatically temperate only in its upper portions, the province extends eastward, northward, and downward into the humid tropical Amazonian rain-forest country. Well guarded by mountains, canyons, and torrential rivers, in Manco's time accessible from the south only over two passes, both higher than Mont Blanc, the last of the Incas were there, for a time, fairly secure against the Spaniards.

Bingham writes as follows about Manco, whom he calls Manco II:

> Manco's army fled over the Pass of Paticalla, went on down the Lucumayo River, crossed the Urubamba on an Inca suspension bridge at a place called Chuquichaca. They were able to enter one of the affluents of the Urubamba which is today called the Vilcabamba, and passing that valley established themselves in a pleasant region where their favorite crops could be grown and their llamas and alpacas find adequate pasturage.
>
> Manco established himself on top of a mountain where he built a long "palace" and characteristic Inca structures. The place was called Vitcos or possibly Uiticos.[2]. . . Here, safe from the armed forces of his enemy, he was able to enjoy the benefits of a dry climate in a well-watered region where corn and potatoes, as well as the fruits of the sub-tropical zones, grow rapidly.

Piecing together his story from several old chronicles, Bingham tells how Manco, after ruling ten years, was killed by one of eight Spaniards, members of the Almagro faction, to whom he had given refuge after the final defeat of the faction by

[2] Later, he also gives Pitcos and Viticos as alternate spellings.

Pizarro's men. It seems that, during the reigns of the last four Incas, a number of Spaniards and mestizos, stragglers, ambassadors, and at least two friars were permitted to enter the Vilcabamba province. Only bodies of soldiers were not welcome.

Manco was succeeded by the eldest of his three sons, Sayri Tupac, who loved peace and luxury. After ruling without incident for ten years, he foolishly allowed the Spaniards to lure him out of Vilcabamba to settle in the beautiful Yucay Valley, near Cuzco. He died a few years later—of illness, according to the Spaniards; of poison, according to his own people.

In 1560, Manco's middle son, Titu Cusi, ascended the throne. He ruled eleven years and then died. His attending physician, the Spanish Friar Diego, ascribed the death to double pneumonia. The nobles and one of Titu's widows accused the friar of having poisoned him and therefore put him to death "with great cruelty."

The youngest son, Tupac Amaru, took over the government in 1571, but then, at long last, Spanish soldiers managed to invade Vilcabamba. They captured the last independent Inca, took him, his family, and a number of his captains to Cuzco and tortured them all publicly to death with fiendish brutality.

Shortly after Titu Cusi ascended the throne, he was visited in Vitcos by the Spaniard, Don Diego Rodriguez, who had been sent by the viceroy to try to convert the Inca to Christianity and lure him out of Vilcabamba as his brother had previously been lured. Titu Cusi received him well but largely, it seems, for the purpose of giving him a show of his military strength and expressing his defiance of the Spaniards. Rodriguez' mission failed, but his written account of it made mention of another city in the region besides Vitcos. In order to make his martial spectacles more impressive, the Inca had sent for 300 soldiers to march to Vitcos from a city called Vilcabamba, which was the region's real capital.

Two Augustinian friars now came to Vitcos from Cuzco. They were Marcos García and Diego Ortiz. The story of their experiences, as recorded by one Father Calancha, has come to be the principal guide for modern explorers, laboring to locate and identify ruins of the important ancient cities of Vitcos and Vilcabamba. With the Inca's permission, they established two mission stations, Father Marcos at Puquiura, near Vitcos, and Father

Diego at a place called Guarancalla. Bingham writes, quoting Calancha:

> One day Friar Marcos and Friar Diego were with Titu Cusi when he said that he was willing to take them to the city of Vilcabamba, his "principal seat," which neither of them had yet seen. He said, "Come with me; I desire to entertain you." They left the next day with the Inca who was accompanied by a small party of his captains and caciques. . . . "The fathers desired and had often attempted to go to Vilcabamba to preach, because it was the chief town and the one in which was the University of Idolatry and the professors of witchcraft, teachers of the abominations."

The missionaries reported later that the journey from Puquiura to Vilcabamba took three days, during which, in an effort to discourage them and persuade them to return to Cuzco, Titu Cusi seems to have made life and travel as difficult for them as possible. Bingham, apparently in order to strengthen his claim that Machu Picchu was Vilcabamba, here adds an aside: "It is three days' journey from Puquiura to Machu Picchu."

But the Inca had no intention of admitting the two Christians into his capital. He kept them on the city's outskirts, where they spent three weeks, preaching against the Indians' heathen abominations. This annoyed Titu Cusi, who selected the choicest of his Chosen Women and sent them out to seduce the missionaries, thinking that a breach of their vows of chastity would surely shame them into returning to Cuzco. But all the sirens' tricks were of no avail against the friars' sterling characters. However, growing sick of the shabby treatment accorded to them, the two priests requested, and received, permission to return to Puquiura.

Once back there, they decided to make a strong demonstration because "they found that their chief opposition came from a very sacred shrine near Vitcos, where in a spring underneath a huge white rock there resided a devil who was chief of a legion of devils." [3] At the head of a number of their converts, each bearing a load of firewood, they marched to that site, erected a cross, laid wood around the "large white rock," set fire to it,

[3] Hiram Bingham, "A Search for the Last Inca Capital," *Harper's Magazine*, October, 1912.

and exorcised the devil, "calling him by all the vile names they could think of." Though risky, the effort seems to have been successful. According to Father Calancha, the devil fled, "roaring in a fury," and never again returned to the rock or to the district.

When Titu Cusi heard of that desecration of his sacred temple, he also roared in a fury. He hastened back from Vilcabamba to Vitcos and had Father Marcos stoned out of the province. Father Diego was permitted to stay on, and he and the Inca eventually became good friends. As stated earlier, he was finally killed after Titu Cusi's death had been blamed on him.

It was the memory of that "large white stone over a spring" which was to lead Bingham to discover the site of Vitcos a few weeks after he had discovered the ruins on Mount Machu Picchu.

During the period 1907–24, Hiram Bingham taught Latin-American history at Yale University. In connection with that work, he went to South America to follow the route of Simón Bolívar and his army from Venezuela into Colombia. As a result of that trip he was sent to Santiago de Chile in December, 1908, as a delegate to the First Pan-American Scientific Congress. After the congress, he and a friend went to Peru and "undertook to cross Inca Land on muleback." But the weather was execrable at that time of year, and in Cuzco the two allowed themselves to be sidetracked for the purpose of examining the ruins of an ancient city.

> The Prefect . . . of the Province of Apurímac, . . . had taken the trouble to come to Cuzco and urge me to visit his province, and particularly to explore the ruins of Choqquequirau. He said it had been the home of the last of the Incas. Since Choqquequirau means "Cradle of Gold," a number of attempts had been made in fairly recent times to explore the ruins in order to discover the treasure which it was believed the Incas had hidden there instead of allowing it to fall into the hands of the Spanish Conquerors.
>
> Owing to the very great difficulty of reaching the site, it had only been seen three times in a hundred years. . . . It was generally believed among the officials and sugar planters of the region that Choqquequirau had once been a great city, "con-

taining over 15,000 inhabitants" and that the buried treasure was well worth the expense of an adequate expedition.[4]

Shortly before Bingham's visit, a company had been formed to send men to the ruins and dig for gold. Their failure to find it had led the Prefect of Apurímac to beg the noted American scholar to look around and report where treasure might be found. Bingham's protests that he was no archeologist were waved aside. His standing as a doctor of philosophy assured his superior knowledge.

After four days' muleback travel from Cuzco, over tortuous mountain trails and uncertain, swaying bridges, Bingham and his companion reached Abancay, capital of the Province of Apurímac, whence, after being feted by all the best people, they set out for the ruined city.

> All day long through the rain and heavy mist that broke away occasionally to give us glimpses of wonderfully deep green valleys and hillsides covered with rare green flowers, we rode along a slippery path that grew every hour more treacherous and difficult. In order to reach a little camp on the bank of the Apurímac River that night, we hurried forward as fast as possible although frequently tempted to linger by the sight of acres of magnificent pink begonias and square miles of blue lupins. By five o'clock we began to hear the roar of the great river seven thousand feet below us in the canyon.
>
> We were about to be initiated into what it means to go exploring in the wild region where the Incas were able to hide away from the conquistadores in 1536.

The following day they crossed the river over a bridge "less than three feet wide but two hundred and seventy-three feet long . . . [which] swayed in the wind on its six strands of telegraph wire." The trip seemed to grow more difficult hourly, and the effects of an altitude of 10,000 feet added to the travelers' difficulties.

> At times the trail was so steep that it was easier to go on all fours than to attempt to walk erect. Occasionally we crossed

[4] The book from which these extracts are taken contains one map showing the topography around Machu Picchu and another showing its immediate environs. Without a map showing places like Choqquequirau, much of Bingham's account becomes a mystifying recital of old Indian place names. The map here given was adapted from one drawn by Mr. Gene Savoy, copyrighted by the Andean Explorers Club and published in the *Peruvian Times*, April 9, 1965.

streams in front of waterfalls on slippery logs or treacherous little foot-bridges. Roughly constructed ladders led us over steep cliffs. Although the hillside was too precipitous to allow much forest growth, no small part of the labor of making a path had been the work of cutting through dense underbrush and bamboo thickets.

Finally, with the help of Indian bearers and some soldiers furnished them by the prefect, the two explorers managed to reach the ruins from which much of the covering vegetation had been removed by the treasure hunters then working there. Bingham was impressed by the ruins, which he describes in his book.

> Apparently Choqquequirau was a frontier fortress that defended the upper valley of the Apurímac, one of the natural approaches to Cuzco, from the country occupied by the Chancas and the Amazonian Antis.
>
> The Prefect of Apurímac was much disappointed that I was unable to indicate the possible whereabouts of any buried treasure. The chief satisfaction derived by the local gentry who had invested several thousand dollars in the unsuccessful enterprise was due to the claim that they had laid bare the capital of the last of the Incas. For this they took considerable credit.

The idea that Choqquequirau was the Incas' last capital was widespread. It was not, however, shared by

> Don Carlos Romero, one of the chief historians of Lima, who assured me that the Spanish chronicles contained enough evidence to show that the last Inca capital was not at Choqquequirau but was probably over beyond the ranges in the region where I had seen snow-capped peaks. . . . He placed Vitcos "near a great white rock over a spring of fresh water." [5]

In 1911, Bingham returned to Peru at the head of the "Yale Peruvian Expedition," in which he was joined by several now famous men, including Dr. Isaiah Bowman (Chapter II). As soon as they reached Cuzco, he began diligently to ask everybody in sight about "the places mentioned in Calancha," without receiving reliable information. He writes:

[5] Bingham repeatedly calls Vitcos "the last capital." Not until he had failed to find the white rock and the spring at Machu Picchu did he advance the idea that that city had once been named Vilcabamba, and so had been the Incas' last capital.

It will be remembered that it was in July, 1911, that I began the search for the last Inca capital. Accompanied by a dear friend, Professor Harry Ward Foote, of Yale University, who was our Naturalist, and my classmate Dr. Wm. G. Erving, the Surgeon of the Expedition, I had entered the marvellous canyon of the Urubamba below the Inca fortress of Salapunco near Torontay.

. . . We passed an ill-kept grass-thatched hut, turned off the road through a tiny clearing, and made our camp at the edge of the river on a sandy beach. Opposite us, beyond the huge granite boulders which interfered with the progress of the surging stream, the steep mountain was clothed with thick jungle. Since we were near the road, yet protected from the curiosity of passers-by, it seemed to be an ideal spot for a camp. Our actions, however, aroused the suspicions of the owner of the hut, Melchor Arteaga, who leased the lands of Mandor Pampa. He was anxious to know why we did not stay at his "tavern" like other respectable travelers. Fortunately the Prefect of Cuzco . . . had given us an armed escort who spoke Quichua. Our *gendarme,* Sergeant Carrasco, was able to reassure the inn keeper. They had quite a long conversation. When Arteaga learned that we were interested in architectural ruins of the Incas, and were looking for the palace of the last Inca, he said there were some very good ruins in this vicinity—in fact, some excellent ones on top of the opposite mountain, called Huayna Picchu, and also on a ridge called Machu Picchu.

The morning of July 24th dawned in a cold drizzle. Arteaga shivered and seemed inclined to stay in his hut. I offered to pay him well if he would show me to the ruins. He demurred and said it was too hard a climb for such a wet day. But when he found I was willing to pay him a *sol* (a Peruvian silver dollar, fifty cents, gold), three or four times the ordinary daily wage in this vicinity, he finally agreed to go. When asked just where the ruins were, he pointed straight up to the top of the mountain. No one supposed that they would be particularly interesting. And no one cared to go with me. The Naturalist said there were "more butterflies near the river!" and he was reasonably certain he could collect some new varieties. The Surgeon said he had to wash his clothes and mend them. Anyhow it was my job to investigate all reports of ruins and try to find the Inca capital.

They climbed the better part of half a day, over wet, slippery, and difficult terrain. They ran into a pair of Indians who had established themselves on one of the ancient Inca agricultural terraces and were farming on the rich soil there, happy to be remote from tax collectors and officials looking for army "volunteers." They chatted a while about the ruins which they had not yet spotted, and then went on.

> Hardly had we left the hut and rounded the promontory than we were confronted with an unexpected sight, a great flight of beautifully constructed stone-faced terraces, perhaps a hundred of them, each hundreds of feet long and ten feet high. They had been recently rescued from the jungle by the Indians. A veritable forest of large trees which had been growing on them for centuries had been chopped down and partly burned to make a clearing for agricultural purposes. The task was too great for the two Indians so the trunks had been allowed to lie as they fell and only the smaller branches removed. But the ancient soil, carefully put in place by the Incas, was still capable of producing rich crops of maize and potatoes.
>
> . . . We patiently followed the . . . guide along one of the widest terraces . . . and made our way into an untouched forest beyond. Suddenly I found myself confronted with the walls of ruined houses built of the finest quality of Inca stone work. It was hard to see them for they were partly covered with trees and moss, . . . but in the dense shadow, hiding in bamboo thickets and tangled vines, appeared here and there the walls of white granite ashlars [rough-hewn stones] carefully cut and exquisitely fitted together.

Bingham's text now gives three pages of deservedly breathless description of the ruins of Machu Picchu, the fantastically beautiful and dramatic ancient city on a mountain whose picture today appears in every travel circular and airline advertisement dealing with Peru. "Dimly, I began to realize that this wall and its adjoining semicircular temple over the cave were as fine as the finest stonework in the world." Bingham's chapter on the discovery of the Machu Picchu ruins ends:

> Could this be the "principal city" of Manco and his sons, that Vilcabamba where was the "University of Idolatry" which Friar Marcos and Friar Diego had tried to reach? It behooved us to find out as much about it as we could.

The following year Bingham returned to Machu Picchu at the head of an expedition sponsored by Yale University and the

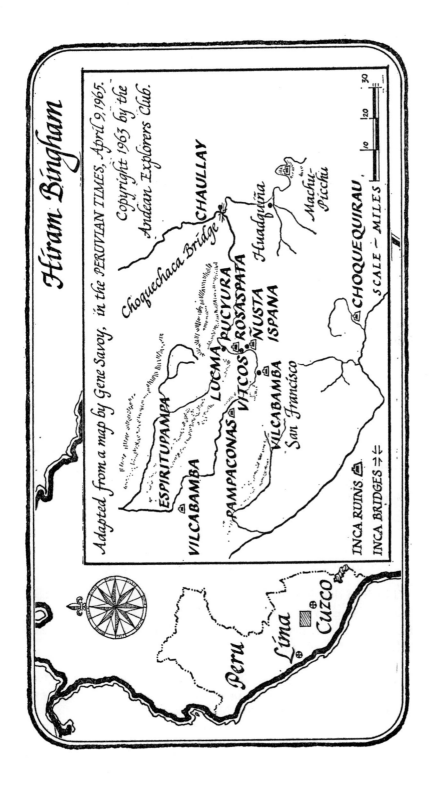

Hiram Bingham

Adapted from a map by Gene Savoy, in the PERUVIAN TIMES, April 9, 1965.
Copyright 1963 by the Andean Explorers Club.

CHAULLAY

Choquechaca Bridge

VILCABAMBA

ESPIRITUPAMPA

LUCMA

PUCYURA

VITCOS

ROSASPATA

ÑUSTA ISPANA

PAMPACONAS

VILCABAMBA
San Francisco

Huadquiña

Machu-Picchu

CHOQUEQUIRAU

SCALE ~ MILES

INCA RUINS ⌂

INCA BRIDGES ⇉⇇

Peru

Lima

CUZCO

SCALE ~ MILES
10   20   30

National Geographic Society, to clear the ruins of overgrowth, map them, photograph them, and study them scientifically. While at times wavering between belief and certainty, he repeatedly claims that the ruins are those of "Vilcabamba the Old," so called to distinguish that city from the modern town of Vilcabamba.

> The ruins of what we now believe was the lost city of Vilca-bamba the Old, perched on top of a narrow ridge lying below the peak of Machu Picchu, are called the ruins of Machu Picchu because when we found them no one knew what else to call them. And that name has been accepted and will continue to be used even though no one now disputes that this was the ancient Vilcabamba.

He was wrong in stating that "no one" disputed his claim. Writing in 1941, in the *New World Guides to the Latin-American Republics,* the historian and archeologist Philip Ainsworth Means said:

> The whole history of Machu Picchu cannot be deduced from the few remains that Bingham's painstaking expeditions unearthed. Since none of the bones found were those of robust adult males and since most of the artifacts were women's bracelets, rings, earrings, mirrors, brooches, and the like, it is assumed that the place was at the end a refuge for the Virgins of the Sun from the Spanish conquistadores. The Incas did not penetrate beyond Ollantaytambo until the 15th century, during the reign of Pachacutec. It is apparent that Machu Picchu was not a place of great importance when the Spaniards came, or they would have heard of it; its remarkable preservation is in large part due to the fact that they never did.

The idea that Machu Picchu was Vilcabamba, and so Manco's capital, seems to have occurred to Bingham as an afterthought. He did, however, realize that it was not Vitcos, which he repeatedly calls Manco's capital.

> Suffice it to say that the ruins . . . were not "near a great white rock near a spring of water" and that there was no evidence that this was Vitcos, Manco's capital for which we were looking. So a few days later we crossed the river on the fine new bridge of San Miguel and pushed on down the Urubamba ask-

ing for ruins, offering cash prizes for good ones—and a double bonus for any that would fit the description of the Temple of the Sun which Father Calancha had said was "near Vitcos."

Our first stop was the hospitable plantation of Huadquiña which once belonged to the Jesuits. . . .

Our hosts, Señora Carmen Vargas and her family, read with interest my copy of those paragraphs of Calancha's "Chronicle" which referred to the location of the last Inca capital. . . . They ordered the most intelligent tenants on the estate to come in and be questioned. The best informed . . . was a sturdy mestizo foreman . . . who said that a few hours down the Urubamba, there were "important ruins.". . . Even more interesting and thrilling was his statement that on a ridge up the Salcantay Valley was a place called Yurak Rumi (*yurak*—white; *rumi*—stone) where some very interesting ruins had been found by his workmen. . . . We all became excited over this, for among the paragraphs I had copied from Calancha's "Chronicle" was the statement that "close to Vitcos" is the "white stone of the aforesaid house of the Sun which is called Yurak Rumi."

Their hostess sent Indians ahead to clear the trail to the Yurak Rumi ruins, while the explorers examined ruins near the plantation, without finding anything to get excited about. When they reached the spot about which the foreman had told them, they were bitterly disappointed. There was no white stone and the ruins were too insignificant to have been Vitcos.

So . . . we . . . proceeded down the valley past the mouth of the Lucumayo . . . to the hamlet of Chauillay, where the Urubamba is joined by the Vilcabamba River. . . . A few rods from Chauillay was a fine bridge. The natives called it Chuquichaca. Steel and iron have superseded the old suspension bridge of huge cables made of vegetable fiber. . . . Yet here it was in 1572 the military force sent by the Viceroy . . . found the forces of the young Inca drawn up to defend Vitcos.

While still on the Urubamba, they asked diligently about the ruins of Vitcos, with no success until there arrived the Lieutenant Governor of the village of Lucma, some 30 miles up the Vilcabamba River, "a crusty old fellow named Evaristo Mogrovejo," who seemed to know something. They loaded up and went to Lucma with him. Bingham's account of who had preceded him in that country is somewhat conflicting.

So far as we have been able to learn, only one other explorer had preceded us—the distinguished cartographer, Raimondi. . . .

A new road had recently been built along the Vilcabamba River by the owner of the sugar estate at Paltaybamba to enable his pack animals to travel more rapidly.

Señor Mogrovejo tended to be uncooperative, despite the fact that his superior, the subprefect of the province, had ordered him to give all possible help to the explorers. But the Yale professor knew how to loosen the tongue of a lieutenant governor.

We offered him a *gratificación* of a *sol*, . . . for every ruin to which he would take us, and double that amount if the locality should prove particularly interesting. This aroused all his business instincts. . . . Now he saw a chance not only to make money out of the ancient sites, but also to gain official favor by carrying out with unexampled vigor the orders of his superior, the sub-prefect.

They rummaged about for some days, inspecting a number of ruins without finding any that fitted the ancient descriptions of Vitcos. But finally, among some ruins on top of a hill, they found a large building which caught their attention.

Ocampo [6] says of Pitcos, "There is an extensive level space with a very sumptuous and majestic building erected with great skill and art, all the lintels of the doors . . . being marble elaborately carved."

Most interesting of all is the structure which caught the attention of Ocampo. . . . Enough remains of this building to give a good idea of its former grandeur. It was indeed a residence fit for an Inca, an exile from Cuzco. It is 245 feet long by 43 feet wide. There were no windows, but it was lighted by thirty doorways, fifteen in front and the same in back. It contained ten large rooms, besides three hallways running from front to rear. . . . The doorways are better than any other ruins in the Vilcabamba valley thus justifying the mention made of them by Ocampo, who lived near here and had time to become thoroughly familiar with their appearance.

The view from here does command "a great part of the

---

[6] Captain Baltazar de Ocampo, a Spanish soldier who went to the Vilcabamba valley after gold in Titu Cusi's day and wrote an account of the province.

province of Vilcabamba." It is remarkably extensive on all sides;
to the north are snow-capped mountains, to the east and west,
deep verdure-clad hills.

Having satisfied himself that he had found ruins which fitted
the Ocampo description of the "fortress of Pitcos," [7] Bingham
still remembered that Calancha had written "close by Vitcos in
a village called Chuquipalpa, is a House of the Sun and in it a
white stone over a spring of water." In reply to his questions,
one Indian said that there was such a stone in a neighboring
valley.

> On the next day, I followed the impatient Mogrovejo—whose
> object was not to study ruins but to earn dollars for finding
> them—and went over the hill on its northeast side of the Valley
> of *Los Andenes* ("The Terraces"). Here, sure enough, was a
> large white granite boulder, flattened on top, which had a
> carved seat on its northern side.

That was exciting fare, but the stone was over a cave rather
than a spring. However:

> When we learned that the present name of the immediate
> vicinity is Chuquipalta we were excited. . . .
> Continuing, we followed a trickling stream through the thick
> woods until we suddenly arrived at an open place called Ñusta
> Isppana. Here before us was a great white rock . . . beneath
> the trees where the ruins of an Inca Temple, flanking and
> partly enclosing the giant granite boulder, one end of which
> overhung a small pool of running water.
> Since the surface of the little pool, as one gazes at it, does not
> reflect the sky, but only the overhanging rock, the water looks
> black and forbidding, . . . It is easy to understand that simple-
> minded Indian worshippers in this secluded spot could believe
> that they actually saw the Devil appearing . . . in the water,
> and that Indians came from the most sequestered villages of the
> dense forest to worship here and offer gifts and sacrifices.
> It was late on the afternoon of August 9, 1911, when I first
> saw this remarkable shrine. . . .
> With the contemporary accounts in our hands and the physi-
> cal evidence before our eyes we could be fairly sure that we

[7] From here on, "Vitcos" usually becomes "Pitcos" in Bingham's writing. In making a case for Machu Picchu, he repeatedly remarked on the similarity between
Pitcos and Picchu.

had located one of Manco's capitals and the residence known to the Spaniards, visited by the missionaries and ambassadors as well as by the refugees who had sought safety here from the followers of Pizarro and had unfortunately put Manco to death. While it was too near Puquiura to be his "principal capital," Vilcabamba, it certainly was Vitcos.

After an account of the excavations he carried on at the site for some days—with extremely interesting and significant results —Bingham writes, correctly:

> Our identification of these localities mentioned by Calancha and the other Spanish chroniclers has now been accepted by Peruvian archaeologists and historians.

Bingham's search for Vilcabamba first took him to a town of that name, "near the source of the Vilcabamba River, not more than three or four leagues from Puquiura." However, all its three score houses were of solid Spanish construction, and its full name proved to be "San Francisco de la Victoria de Vilcabamba."

> When Don Pedro Duque de Santa Ana was helping us to identify places mentioned in Calancha and Ocampo, the reference to "Vilcabamba Viejo," or Old Vilcabamba, was supposed by two of his informants to point to a place called Conservidayoc. Don Pedro told us that in 1902 López Torres, who had traveled much in the *montaña* [the forested eastern slopes of the Andes] looking for rubber trees, reported the discovery there of the ruins of an Inca city.

The explorers were warned against Conservidayoc, being told on the one hand that it was now an abandoned wilderness, and on the other that its owner was a typical rubber baron and sugar planter, who lived in luxury, slave-drove his Indians, and resented visitors. Fearlessly, however, they plunged westward from Vilcabamba San Francisco, in a series of marches through beautiful, dramatic, but difficult terrain to which Bingham does full justice in his graphic descriptions. They reached the village of Pampacona, at 10,000 feet altitude, and confirmed an old Spanish description of the site as a "high, cold place." The next day:

> leaving the village we climbed the mountain . . . and followed a faint trail by a dangerous route along the crest of the ridge.

The rains had not improved the path. Our saddle mules were of little use. We had to go nearly all the way on foot. Owing to the cold rain and mists we could see but little of the deep canyon which opened below us, and into which we now began to descend four thousand feet through the clouds by a very steep zigzag path, to a hot tropical valley.

They reached the plantation of Conservidayoc and found the owner, a Señor Saavedra, to be a most friendly, interested, and hospitable man, who told them that the ruins they sought were at a nearby place called Espiritu Pampa (Spirit Plain), which could be reached only over a very difficult trail. Saavedra sent his son, and Bingham his Indians, to clear the trail. Then they found the ruins without too much trouble, though the undergrowth was so thick that they saw relatively little and apparently failed even to suspect the rest. They found "eighteen or twenty" round huts, possibly the residences of Amazonian Indians serving the Inca, and the local Indians offered to guide them to other ruins.

It was very difficult for us to follow their rapid pace. Half an hour's scramble through the jungle brought us to a natural terrace on the bank of a little tributary of the Pampaconas. They called it Eromboni Pampa. Here we found several artificial terraces and the rough foundations of a rectangular building 192 feet long. . . . Nearby was a typical Inca fountain with three spouts. Two hundred yards beyond the water carriers' rendezvous, hidden behind a curtain of hanging vines so dense we could not see more than a few feet in any direction, the savages showed us the ruins of a group of Inca stone houses whose walls were still standing in fine condition. . . . In the buildings we picked up several fragments of Inca pottery.

They spent a day clearing away "as much as possible of the tangled growth at Eromboni Pampa," making a few more discoveries which did not excite Bingham greatly.

Nothing gives a better idea of the density of the jungle than the fact that the savages themselves have often been within five feet of these fine walls without being aware of their existence.

After giving detailed descriptions of the ruins, Bingham goes on:

There appears to me every reason to believe that the ruins here are those of one of the favorite residences of Titu Cusi. It may have been the place from which he journeyed to meet Rodriguez in 1565.

Who built the best buildings of Eromboni Pampa? Was this the "Vilcabamba Viejo" of Father Calancha, that "University of Idolatry where lived the teachers who were wizards and masters of abomination," the place to which Friar Marcos and Friar Diego went with so much suffering?

After posing such questions, Bingham reasons himself into the conclusion that the ruins could not, after all, have been those of Old Vilcabamba.

They (the monks) called it a "three days' journey over rough country" (from Puquiura). Calancha speaks of Puquiura as being "two long days from Vilcabamba." It was rough country all right, but it took us five days to go from Espiritu Pampa to Puquiura. It did not seem to be reasonable to suppose that the priests and the Virgins of the Sun (the personnel of the "University of Idolatry") who fled from Cuzco with Manco and were established by him somewhere in the fastnesses of Vilcabama would have cared to live in this hot valley. The difference in climate is as great as that between Scotland and Egypt. They would not have found in Espiritu Pampa the food which they liked. Furthermore, they could have found the seclusion and safety which they craved just as well in several other parts of the province, together with a cool, bracing climate and foodstuffs more nearly resembling those to which they were accustomed. Finally, Calancha says "Vilcabamba the Old" was "the largest city in the province, a term hardly applicable to anything here.

Obviously, Bingham was determined to establish Machu Picchu as the last capital of the Incas. Recently, however, he has been boldly challenged on the history of the Espiritu Pampa ruins.

During 1964 and 1965, the Lima weekly magazine *Peruvian Times* published a series of articles by an American explorer, Gene Savoy, who had led three expeditions into the Incas' Vilcabamba Province, after acquainting himself thoroughly with the old chronicles as well as with Hiram Bingham's writings. As a result of careful work, he concluded with excellent reason that the Espiritu Pampa ruins actually *are* those of Old Vilcabamba, the last refuge of the Incas. His article of December 4, 1964, reads in part as follows:

> The mystery of the location of Vilcabamba Grande or Vilcabamba Viejo, long known as the "last refuge of the Incas," has engaged the greater part of my attention over the past two years, in research in old libraries and monasteries and in the two expeditions this year to the Espiritupampa region.[8]

After listing his literary sources, Savoy goes on:

> Bingham had gone to Espiritupampa on the strength of a report made by a certain López Torres, a Peruvian rubber gatherer who had visited the site in 1902. As Bingham spent only two or three days in the area, his report published in his book *Inca Land,*[9] . . . failed to take into account the very considerable extent of the ruins. This was of course due to the fact that the ruins then, as they are now—except for the relatively limited extent of clearing that my expedition was able to carry out this year—were covered by a dense blanket of tall trees and thick undergrowth, which calls for the employment of experienced guides and also a numerous contingent of machete men.
>
> Also the local citizenry—few and far between—have a great fear of the unknown and believe the ruins are enchanted, the abode of the spirits of their ancient habitants—hence the name Espiritupampa. This belief is very strong and not only kept Bingham from exploring the general area but has also limited the findings of others who have followed him.
>
> I was able to overcome these obstacles because I had more time to explore and was able to engage the services of up to seventy part-time machete men to help clear the jungle growth.
>
> In *Inca Land* and elsewhere Bingham describes the scattered circular structures in the immediate Espiritupampa area, which have been cleared by local farmers for agricultural purposes

[8] In 1965, Savoy led a third expedition to the ruins, doing a considerable amount of clearing and preparing maps, not only of the ruins but also of the entire Vilcabamba province with its numerous other ruins. The difference between Savoy's and Bingham's spellings of place names is probably due to the fact that, since Bingham's day, the Peruvians have standardized their place names, and Savoy uses the official versions.

[9] Bingham's report in the book here cited is virtually the same as that in his earlier book, *Inca Land.* The "Spanish tiles" mentioned by Savoy are mentioned in the earlier volume but not in that of 1948, here used.

over the past fifty years or so. He reported eighteen or twenty such structures. I found a hundred or more but lack of time did not allow me to exhaust by any means the exploration possibilities of the area.

Unfortunately, neither Bingham nor Savoy mentions the diameter of the round structures, though Savoy's map, presumably drawn to scale, indicates it to be approximately forty feet. Circular structures of that size are not uncommon in Peru and were built by the Incas as granaries. If the hundred counted by Savoy actually *were* granaries, the ancient city was indeed far larger than Bingham supposed it to be.

> Bingham reports that he was led to artificial terraces called Eromboni—a Machiguenga Indian word for "ruins." He reported the existence of a structure 192 feet long with 24 doors. Actually the structure is 230 feet in length and, in addition to the doors, contains a stone altar. More important ruins lie in this vicinity which Bingham evidently did not visit as the area is unbelievably overgrown with centuries of vines and parasitic plants that cling to the towering trees, soaring up to 200 feet or more. Three stone fountains stand not far away and nearby is the stone bridge which Bingham also reported.
>
> From this area Bingham moved up to a group which, as noted in previous *Peruvian Times* articles (Aug. 14 & Sept. 18, 1964) I have named the Spanish Palace, owing to its Spanish-Inca influence and the abundance of Spanish-type tiles. Bingham reports the existence of a small amount of this Spanish-type tile (about 4 sq. feet) and expresses the opinion that the Inca tile makers may have been experimenting with this structural material which they had seen the Spaniards make in Cuzco. What he did not know was that this tile exists in abundance in the ruins, and that the principal structures were roofed with this material. It was no experiment as he suggests, but an integral part of the ruins, denoting a late Inca city.

Actually, it was naïve of Bingham to believe that the Incas had "seen" the Spaniards make tiles in Cuzco. Pizarro and his fellow *conquistadores* hadn't come to the New World for the purpose of doing their own work. Between the time of the conquest and that of Manco's withdrawal into Vilcabamba, they must have turned out many hundreds of expert Indian tile makers.

Bingham describes two groups of ruins, the bridge and the two fountains. These remains appear to be the exact sites to which local guides will take an explorer, such as "Pepe" Pancorvo of Quillabamba who visited the area in the late 1950's. He, like Bingham, was not greatly impressed. On the other hand, I conducted a more comprehensive exploration over a period of several weeks, as far as 50 kilometers, proving the existence of numerous groups comprising an extensive metropolitan layout.

Bingham's account and my own explorations serve to reaffirm the fact that no one really knows how extensive the ruins are. This cannot be determined until a more extensive exploration program is undertaken, followed by scientific archeological excavation and research. . . .

Summing up Bingham's work at Espiritupampa, it may be said that he got to the front door but failed to go in. This is understandable, owing to the diversion of his interest to Machu Picchu. He would certainly have been fascinated by the large *ñusta* or *huilca* stone which is almost an exact duplicate of the famous *yurakrumi* or white stone at Vitcos, some two days away by foot or mule. Had he been able to examine the large amounts of ceramic tile and studied the structures of finer stone he would never have turned back. . . .

As Geza de Rosner, noted motion picture cameraman, remarked during the second phase of this year's exploration, in which he participated: "Bingham discovered some of the ruins of Vilcabamba Grande, but he did not discover Vilcabamba Grande."

The maps drawn by Savoy after his 1965 expedition show that the known ruins—with large, overgrown areas in the center yet to be cleared and examined—cover an area approximately half a mile by half a mile, which is considerably larger than the area of the Machu Picchu ruins. The fact that at least one large building was roofed with clay tiles is, of course, proof enough that that building had been erected after the Spaniards had arrived in Peru.

The two explorers disagree on the travel time required between Vitcos and Espiritupampa. Bingham said it was five days; the old chroniclers said that it was a hard two or three days' trip; Savoy said it was two days "by foot or mule." But in his article of April 9, 1965, covering the work done by his third expedition, Savoy also wrote that *a stone-paved Inca road still leads from Vitcos to Vilcabamba,* another circumstance which helps to convince him that the Espiritupampa ruins are actually those of Old Vilcabamba. His photographs show that it was actually a trail, some three feet wide, but still paved and still in serviceable condition. The fact that Bingham failed to report that road can mean only that his guides took him over a different and possibly longer route.

Savoy's case is excellent, and the fact that Espiritupampa probably was the Incas' last capital detracts nothing from the importance of Machu Picchu and the value of Bingham's work in discovering it.

Postscript: As the writing of the present chapter neared completion, word came from Peru that Gene Savoy had made another major archeological discovery. A notice in the *Peruvian Times* of October 1, 1965, reads:

> Although extensive pre-Inca ruins have long been known to exist in the Pataz region, east of the Marañón River, Department of La Libertad, there has been no attempt until recently to carry out a survey of the same, although gold mining operations were conducted in the region for a number of years.
>
> A dispatch of September 27 from Trujillo to the newspaper *La Prensa,* Lima, states that Gene Savoy, indefatigable North American explorer, whose previous discoveries inland from the coast in north central Peru, and in the Vilcabamba region of southern Peru, have been recorded at length in the *Peruvian Times,* recently penetrated the forested area beyond Pataz with a party of 12 men, including his chief assistant, Douglas Sharon, and the Lt. Governor of Pataz, Humberto Aranda.
>
> The Savoy expedition reportedly found extensive ruins dispersed over an area of some 20 square kilometers. The culture or civilization to which they may belong has not been determined, but they are said to have similarities with the Chavin culture found east of the Cordillera Blanca in the Department of Ancash, south of La Libertad, and also certain similarities with Maya and Aztec remains in Mexico. An abundance of large carved stone heads and examples of zoomorphic sculpture, especially of serpents, was found.
>
> There are also said to be stone-paved roads four meters in width, numerous *andenes* [terraces for agriculture] and a huge

wall, erected presumably for defensive purposes, giving the ruins an impressive aspect. The area is known locally as the *Selva de Pajatén* (the Pajatén Forest) and is said to have abundant wild life, including the Andean puma or jaguar. The expedition was in the field 15 days. Mr. Savoy plans to continue exploration in this area.

The quest for precisely such a city, somewhere in the Amazonian forests, occupied Percy Harrison Fawcett many years and cost him his life in 1925 (Chapter XXII).

EPILOGUE

$\mathbb{S}$OUTH AMERICA and particularly the Amazon basin, has seen a great deal of exploration in the course of the twentieth century. Caryl P. Haskins writes: [1]

> The twentieth century has, too, been the period of well-equipped expeditions which have traversed the valley for a variety of purposes, chiefly connected with exploration, medicine, or science. Outstanding among the expeditions undertaken primarily for purposes of exploration and for natural-history studies was the famous Roosevelt-Rondon Expedition, with its consequent description and name of the Rio Teodoro, tributary of the Madeira. The party began its work immediately after the retirement of the President, and, under the leadership of Roosevelt and Colonel Rondon, famous in South American annals for his devoted public service, the expedition traversed the Amazon, the Tapajos, and the Madeira, in addition to visiting the Plata River and various points in Argentina and Brazil, and ended at Belém in May, 1914.

> The Rice expeditions, extending from 1910 to 1924, undertaken with the extensive facilities of Harvard's Institute of Geographical Exploration, carried on exploratory and scientific work of great note in the valley. . . . The Fleming Expedition in 1919, the Mulford Biological Expedition in 1921–22, the Ellsworth-Farabee-Fawcett Expedition in 1931 were noteworthy. The rubber interests have undertaken some expeditions of value in the course of investigation of and experimentation with *Hevea brasiliensis* [the rubber tree], outstanding among

[1] From *The Amazon, The Life History of a Mighty River,* by Caryl P. Haskins (Garden City, N.Y.: Doubleday & Company, Inc., 1943).

454

which was that sent out by the American Rubber Mission in 1923–24. The American Geographical Society has undertaken geographic explorations of importance. The American Museum of Natural History of New York and the Carnegie Museum, among others, have sent collecting trips into various parts of the valley at different times. These comprise but a small proportion of all the Amazonian expeditions that have been undertaken in the first forty-three years of this century.

To that list, compiled by the man who is today the head of the Carnegie Institution of Washington, the present editor modestly adds his own expedition of 1931–33, sent by Washington's Carnegie Institution for the prime purpose of studying the behavior of the earth's magnetic field over a territory straddling the "magnetic equator."

At the very time when Haskins was writing his book, one of the greatest coordinated exploratory efforts in all history was getting under way in the Amazon basin. The history leading up to that activity was as follows:

Among the many things which European man obtained from the South American Indians, rubber was outstanding. Late in the nineteenth century, when the substance began to acquire unprecedented industrial importance, the Amazon basin began to experience its world-famous "rubber-boom" (see Chapter XXII). But seeds of *Hevea brasiliensis* were smuggled out of the basin, and used for establishing plantations in Asia. When these began to come into full production, about 1911, the Amazonian boom collapsed; people left the basin by the thousands and the production of wild rubber fell off sharply. The concern over the situation, felt by North American rubber interests, led to, among other things, the organization of the Rubber Mission of 1923–24, mentioned above by Haskins, and led by Dr. William Lytle Schurz (see Chapter II). In part as a result of that mission's work, the Ford Motor Company established its rubber plantations on the Tapajoz River, while the Firestone Tire and Rubber Company opened its plantations in Liberia. But those two plantations were not enough to assure the United States a safe supply of that important industrial raw material, in the event that anything happened to the Asian plantations.

With the onset of World War II, something did happen. The Japanese overran Asia's rubber-producing countries and cut the

United States off from their products. The United States was then forced to turn again to the Amazon basin for its rubber. Millions of dollars were spent; air strips were cut in the jungles; thousands of men were rushed into the basin to tap rubber; the organizers were often hard-put to find food for them; U.S. planes photographed and surveyed thousands of square miles of Amazonian country; dozens of American specialists, geographers, naturalists, men who knew the country, made separate, regional surveys, persuading Indians to tap rubber for the war effort, studying the navigability of various rivers, possibilities for the production of food, and, of course, the availability of accessible rubber trees in many parts of the basin.

That almighty effort amounted in effect to one of the greatest coordinated exploratory programs ever carried out. Carefully studied, the reports of the many men concerned may some day add immensely to the world's detailed knowledge of the Amazon basin. But they have never been studied. At the time of the present writing, those field reports fill many feet of shelf space in Washington's National Archives, where a research worker must have a security clearance before he can go near them.

The only part of that great effort which has left a coherent account of its activities was the Cassiquiare River Expedition, sent out by the U.S. Army Engineers, and in its first few weeks accompanied by this editor as advisor, to study the Canal route (see Chapter XVII) for wartime purposes. As the Amazonian rubber program began to produce, ships were loaded with rubber on the Amazon River and sent to sea. But German submarines waited for them on the Atlantic, and sank a number of them as they left the Amazon's mouths. As the ships went down, much of their rubber bobbed to the surface and floated ashore, where it was picked up and resold to the United States Government. Some of that rubber undoubtedly made the rounds three or four times, and was bought as often.

In view of that disagreeable situation, some of the Washington planners decided to see if it was possible to send the rubber up the Río Negro, through the Cassiquiare "Canal," down the Orinoco, and then into the Atlantic behind well-fortified Trinidad, where the Germans could not get at it so easily. Similarly, it was thought well if fuel oil could be shipped into the basin by a reverse of the same route. In Washington, this editor was approached on the idea and didn't think much of it. During the dry season, in certain places, the Cassiquiare is 18 inches deep, which is fine for canoe travel but hardly sufficient for supporting a war effort. The Río Negro's rapids at São Gabriel, and the Orinoco's far worse rapids at Atures-Maipure, offer formidable obstacles. However, when it became evident that the Army Engineers were determined to go on with the project, this editor agreed to go along as advisor.

(Incidentally, two hours after landing at Puerto Ayacucho on the Orinoco, where I established the "secret" expedition's main base, I listened to shortwave radio broadcasts from Europe in the cluttered general store of my old friend Juan Maniglia. Clear as a bell, a message came from Berlin, welcoming the United States Army Engineers to the Orinoco, and wishing us luck with the Cassiquiare. It was of course possible that friend Maniglia, being an Italian, was also a patriotic one, and that his shortwave radio worked both ways.)

A massive, four-volume report was prepared after the expedition's return, on the work and recommendations of the venture, which had the engaging wartime code name of "Cash and Carry." One section of it carries the diaries of the engineers who comprised the expedition; they say much—not all of it complimentary—about the expedition's leader and advisor, but little about the Orinoco River. On the whole, the report is technical in nature, carrying its statements and recommendations into far greater accuracy than the quality of the field observations warranted. The entire matter resembled the not unknown procedure of observing the sun or certain stars for latitude and longitude, by methods which permit an accuracy no greater than to the nearest full minute of arc, and then—inaccurately—calculating the astronomical coordinates to the nearest hundredth of a second.

Since World War II, a number of expeditions have penetrated several Amazonian regions. Among the most entertaining accounts resulting from such ventures is the book *Journey to the Far Amazon,* by Alain Gheerbrand, published in New York by Simon and Schuster in 1954. Gheerbrand was one of a group of literate Frenchmen who were the first Europeans to cross the difficult, mountainous terrain between the upper Ventuari River and the headwaters of Brazil's Río Branco. The principal obstacle to such a voyage had always been the dangerous hostility of the Guaharibo Indians. Gheerbrand and his companions tamed them beautifully by playing a Mozart symphony to them on their portable record player, thereby bringing out again the fact observed by many, including this editor, that the Amazonian Indians are remarkably musical and equally sophisticated in their musical tastes.

Today, in one degree or another, all six of the nations which share the Amazon basin—Brazil, Peru, Bolivia, Ecuador, Colombia, and Venezuela—are promoting programs for improving the region's accessibility, finding good soils and other natural wealth, and settling it, in part to relieve South America's population pressures, in part to aid the continent's efforts at industrialization and modernization. Together, the soil experts, agronomists, prospectors, river travelers, surveyors, Indian tamers, and the like, who spearhead such programs, are carrying out a mighty program of exploration. So important is their work, not only to South America, but to the entire world as well, that it should not be long before one of our numerous foundations endows a permanent Institute for Amazonian Studies.

Meanwhile, graduate students of geography in some of our American universities, notably Syracuse and the University of Florida, are discovering the Amazon basin, making detailed studies there, and using the results as the raw materials for fashioning doctoral dissertations. During the past ten years, the present editor has had the pleasure of going to Gainesville every year to examine such dissertations written by students at the University of Florida, and to participate in the students' oral examinations. In a real sense of the word, those dissertations are exploration literature, and Dr. Raymond Crist, who heads the program and does considerable fieldwork himself, is to be congratulated on the manner in which he is aiding in the large task of making the interior of South America known to the world, its scientists, technicians, planners, and politicians.

What it all means is that the exploration of South America is not only far from completed, but also that it can *never* be "completed."

INDEX